Math in Focus®

Singapore Math
by Marshall Cavendish

Authors
Shin-Tze Yap
How-Kian Yow

U.S. Consultants
Dr. Richard Bisk
Andy Clark

Marshall Cavendish
Education

U.S. Distributor

Houghton
Mifflin
Harcourt

COMMON
CORE

© 2013 Marshall Cavendish International (Singapore) Private Limited

Published by Marshall Cavendish Education
An imprint of Marshall Cavendish International (Singapore) Private Limited
Times Centre, 1 New Industrial Road, Singapore 536196
Customer Service Hotline: (65) 6213 9444
E-mail: tmesales@sg.marshallcavendish.com
Website: www.marshallcavendish.com/education

Distributed by
Houghton Mifflin Harcourt
222 Berkeley Street
Boston, MA 02116
Tel: 617-351-5000
Website: www.hmheducation.com/mathinfocus

Cover: © Mike Hill/Getty Images

First published 2013

Math in Focus® Course 3 Student Book A
ISBN 978-0-547-56011-3

Printed in United States of America

8 9 10   1401   18 17 16 15 14
4500457784   B C D E

Course 3A Contents

In Student Book A and Student Book B, look for

Practice and Problem Solving	Assessment Opportunities
• **Practice** in every lesson • Real-world and mathematical problems in every chapter • Brain @ Work in every chapter • *Math Journal* exercises	• **Quick Check** at the beginning of every chapter to assess chapter readiness • **Guided Practice** after every Example to assess readiness to continue lesson • **Chapter Review/Test** in every chapter to review or test chapter material • **Cumulative Reviews** five times during the year

CHAPTER

2 Scientific Notation

Big Idea Scientific notation is a way of writing numbers that makes it easier to work with very big or very small numbers.

    • Understand the Need for Scientific Notation • Write Numbers in Scientific
    Notation • Write Numbers in Standard Form • Compare Numbers in Scientific
    Notation

    • Add and Subtract Numbers in Scientific Notation with the Same Power of 10
    • Add and Subtract Numbers in Scientific Notation with Different Powers of 10
    • Introduce the Prefix System

    • Multiply and Divide Numbers in Scientific Notation

CHAPTER

3 Algebraic Linear Equations

CHAPTER

4

Lines and Linear Equations

Big Idea The graph of a linear equation in two variables is a line, and you can write the equation of the line in slope-intercept form.

 • Define the Slope of a Line and Relate Unit Rate to Slope • Find Slopes of Slanted Lines • Find Slopes of Horizontal and Vertical Lines • Understand the Slope Formula

Hands-On Activities • Use Triangles to Find the Slope of a Line • Use Points to Find the Slope of a Line

 • Explore the Relationship Between the Lines $y = mx$ and $y = mx + b$

Technology Activity Explore the Relationship Between $y = mx$ and $y = mx + b$

 • Write an Equation of a Line in Slope-Intercept Form • Identify and Write Equations of Parallel Lines • Write an Equation of a Line Given Its Slope and a Point on the Line • Write an Equation of a Line Given a Point on the Line and the Equation of a Parallel Line • Write an Equation of a Line Given Two Points

5 Systems of Linear Equations

Welcome to

Math in Focus®
Singapore Math
by Marshall Cavendish

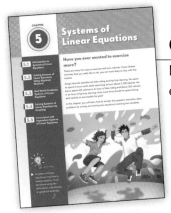

What makes
Math in Focus® different?

This world-class math program comes to you from the country of Singapore. We are sure that you will enjoy learning math with the interesting lessons you will find in these books.

▶ **Two books** The textbook is divided into 2 semesters. Chapters 1–6 are in Book A. Chapters 7–11 are in Book B.

▶ **Longer lessons** More concepts are presented in a lesson. Some lessons may last more than a day to give you time to understand the math.

▶ **Multiple representations** will help you make sense of new concepts and solve real-world and mathematical problems with ease.

About the book Here are the main features in this book.

Chapter Opener

Introduces chapter concepts and big ideas through a story or example. There is also a chapter table of contents.

Recall Prior Knowledge

Assesses previously learned concepts, definitions, vocabulary, and models relevant to the chapter.

Quick Check assesses readiness for the chapter.

Look for these features in each lesson.

Instructions make use of multiple representations to help you become familiar with new ideas.

Model mathematics.

Solve Systems of Linear Equations Using the

You have learned to solve systems of linear equations Look again at the system of linear equations below an them.

$x + y = 8$

$x + 2y = 10$

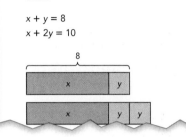

Examples and **Guided Practice** provide step-by-step guidance through solutions.

Example 8 Solve systems of linear equations

Solve the following system of equations by graphin axes to represent 1 unit for the x interval from −1

$2x + y = 7$

$y - 3x = -3$

Solution

STEP 1 Make a table of values for each

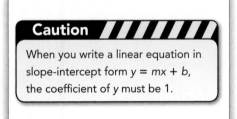

Guided Practice

Solve using the graphical method. Copy and complete the tables of values. Graph the system of linear equations on the same coordinate plane. Use 1 grid square on both axes to represent 1 unit for the x interval from −1 to 3 and the y interval from −1 to 5.

1 $2x + y = 5$

$x - y = -2$

Cautions alert you to common mistakes and misconceptions related to the topics.

Structure, reasoning, and precision.

Caution ////////

When you write a linear equation in slope-intercept form $y = mx + b$, the coefficient of y must be 1.

Math Notes are helpful hints and reminders.

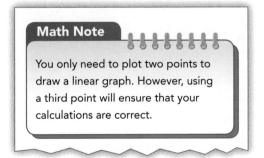

Math Note

You only need to plot two points to draw a linear graph. However, using a third point will ensure that your calculations are correct.

Think Math

What other segment length can be found using the Pythagorean Theorem? What is the length of that segment?

Think Math questions help you reason and explain mathematical situations.

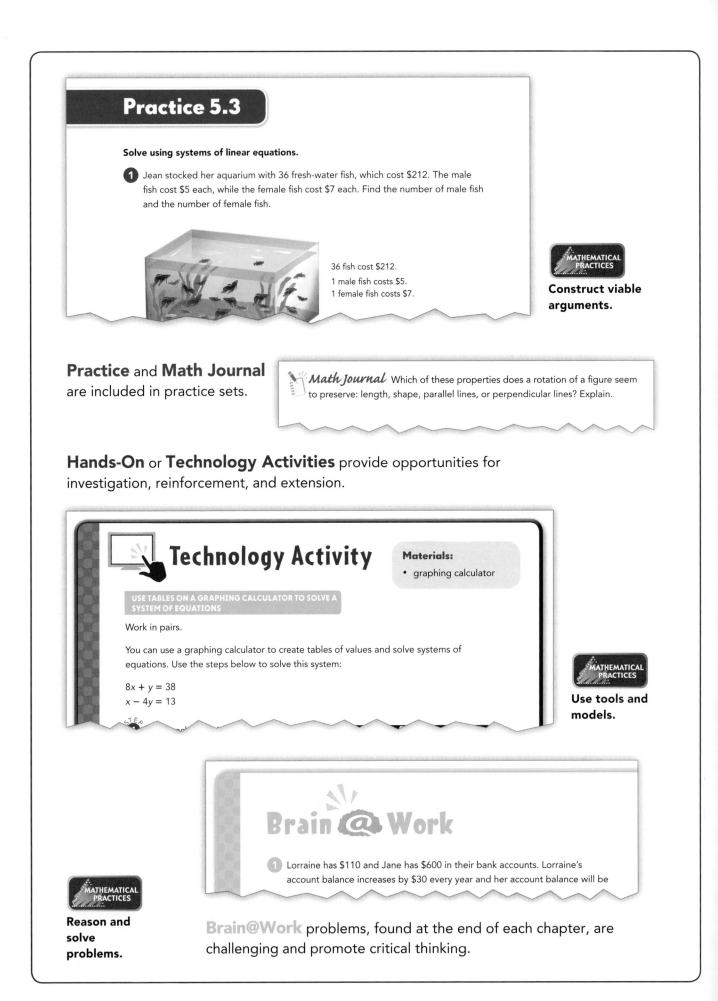

Practice 5.3

Solve using systems of linear equations.

1 Jean stocked her aquarium with 36 fresh-water fish, which cost $212. The male fish cost $5 each, while the female fish cost $7 each. Find the number of male fish and the number of female fish.

36 fish cost $212.
1 male fish costs $5.
1 female fish costs $7.

MATHEMATICAL PRACTICES

Construct viable arguments.

Practice and **Math Journal** are included in practice sets.

Math Journal Which of these properties does a rotation of a figure seem to preserve: length, shape, parallel lines, or perpendicular lines? Explain.

Hands-On or **Technology Activities** provide opportunities for investigation, reinforcement, and extension.

Technology Activity

Materials:
• graphing calculator

USE TABLES ON A GRAPHING CALCULATOR TO SOLVE A SYSTEM OF EQUATIONS

Work in pairs.

You can use a graphing calculator to create tables of values and solve systems of equations. Use the steps below to solve this system:

$8x + y = 38$
$x - 4y = 13$

MATHEMATICAL PRACTICES

Use tools and models.

Brain @ Work

1 Lorraine has $110 and Jane has $600 in their bank accounts. Lorraine's account balance increases by $30 every year and her account balance will be

MATHEMATICAL PRACTICES

Reason and solve problems.

Brain@Work problems, found at the end of each chapter, are challenging and promote critical thinking.

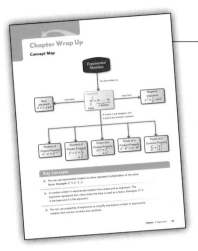

Chapter Wrap Up

Key concepts, definitions, and formulas are summarized for easy review.

The Chapter Wrap Up summaries contain concept maps like the one shown below.

The lines and arrows show how all the concepts in the chapter are related to one another and to the big ideas.

There may be more than one way to draw a concept map. With practice, you should be able to draw your own.

The red center boxes contain the big idea.

Other boxes represent key concepts of the chapter.

Structure, reasoning, and precision.

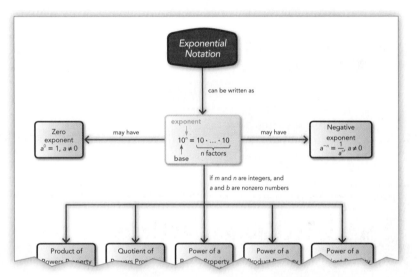

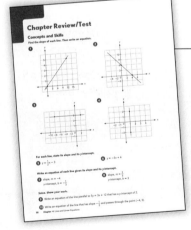

Chapter Review/Test

A practice test is found at the end of each chapter.

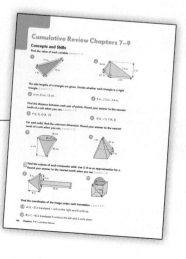

Cumulative Review

Cumulative review exercises can be found after Chapters 2, 4, 6, 9, and 11.

Exponents

BIG IDEA

▶ You can use exponential notation to represent repeated multiplication of the same factor.

How loud is loud?

The human ear can hear a range of noises, from a soft whisper to the enormous blast of a rocket being launched into space. The intensity of sound is measured using a scale that involves powers of 10. A general rule of thumb says that if a noise sounds ten times as loud to your ears as another noise, the intensity is 10 decibels greater for the louder noise. In this chapter, you will learn how to use exponents to compare quantities such as the intensities of different noises.

Recall Prior Knowledge

Interpreting the real number system

A real number may be rational or irrational, and it may be positive, negative, or zero.

A rational number can be expressed as a ratio of two integers. When written as a decimal, it either terminates or repeats. An irrational number cannot be written as a ratio of two integers. When written as a decimal, it does not terminate or repeat.

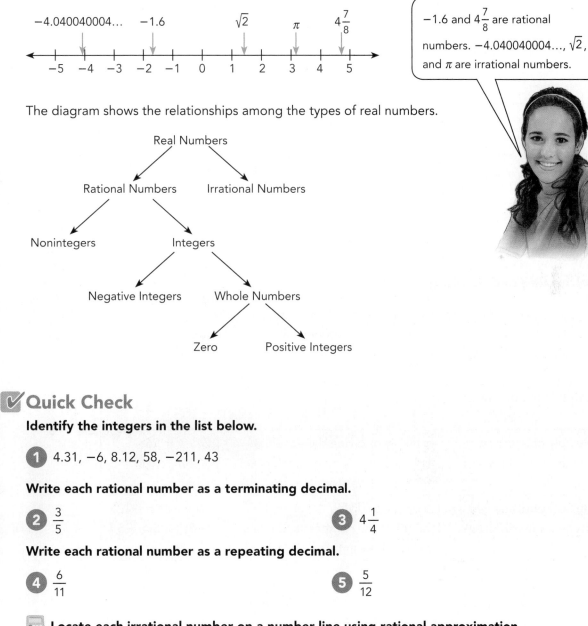

-1.6 and $4\frac{7}{8}$ are rational numbers. $-4.040040004...$, $\sqrt{2}$, and π are irrational numbers.

The diagram shows the relationships among the types of real numbers.

Real Numbers

Rational Numbers   Irrational Numbers

Nonintegers   Integers

Negative Integers   Whole Numbers

Zero   Positive Integers

✓ Quick Check

Identify the integers in the list below.

1 4.31, −6, 8.12, 58, −211, 43

Write each rational number as a terminating decimal.

2 $\frac{3}{5}$

3 $4\frac{1}{4}$

Write each rational number as a repeating decimal.

4 $\frac{6}{11}$

5 $\frac{5}{12}$

🖩 **Locate each irrational number on a number line using rational approximation.**

6 $\sqrt[3]{-47}$

7 $\sqrt{19}$

Adding and subtracting integers

You can use a number line to add and subtract integers. When you add a positive integer, move to the right on the number line. When you add a negative integer, move to the left. You can also use these rules.

Adding or Subtracting Integers	Rule	Expression
Add integers with the **same sign**.	Add the absolute values and keep the **same sign**.	$3 + 5 = 8$
Add integers with **different signs**.	Subtract the absolute values and use the **sign of the number with the greater absolute value**.	$-5 + 8 = 3$
Subtract two integers.	Add the opposite of the number being subtracted.	$8 - 3$ $= 8 + (-3)$ $= 5$

✔ Quick Check

Evaluate each expression.

8 $-3 + (-4)$

9 $-4 - (-2)$

Multiplying and dividing integers

You multiply or divide integers just as you do whole numbers, except you must keep track of the signs. To multiply or divide integers, always multiply or divide the absolute values and use these rules to determine the sign of the result.

Multiplying or Dividing Integers	Rule	Expression
Multiply or divide two integers with the **same sign**.	Multiply or divide the absolute values of the numbers and make the result **positive**.	$24 \cdot 4 = 96$ $(-24) \div (-4) = 6$
Multiply or divide two integers with **different signs**.	Multiply or divide the absolute values of the numbers and make the result **negative**.	$25 \cdot (-5) = -125$ $(-25) \div 5 = -5$

✔ Quick Check

Evaluate each expression.

10 $(-7) \cdot (-3)$

11 $(-12) \div 3$

1.1 Exponential Notation

Lesson Objectives

- Understand and use exponential notation.
- Use exponents to write the prime factorization of a number.

Understand Exponential Notation.

On the decibel scale, the smallest audible sound (near total silence) has an intensity of 0 decibels (dB). A lawnmower is 90 dB, or 1,000,000,000 times louder than near total silence. You can use exponential notation to describe this increase in sound intensity.

$$1{,}000{,}000{,}000 = \underbrace{10 \cdot 10 \cdot 10 \cdot 10 \cdot 10 \cdot 10 \cdot 10 \cdot 10 \cdot 10}_{9 \text{ times}}$$

$$= 10^9 \leftarrow \text{exponent}$$
$$\uparrow$$
$$\text{base}$$

> **Math Note**
>
> In the expression 10^9, the number 10 is said to be "raised to the 9th **power**."

The expression 10^9 is written in exponential notation to show repeated multiplication of the factor 10. 10 is called the **base**, and 9 is called the **exponent**. The exponent represents how many times the base is used as a factor.

Example 1 — Identify the base and exponent.

Identify the base and exponent in each expression.

a) 1.2^6

Solution

The base is 1.2 and the exponent is 6.

b) $(-4)^5$

> In the expression $(-4)^5$, the base is −4 because −4 is inside the parentheses.

Solution

The base is −4 and the exponent is 5.

Guided Practice

Identify the base and exponent in each expression.

1 2^3

2 $(-5)^4$

Example 2 **Write in exponential notation.**

Tell whether each statement is correct. If it is incorrect, state the reason.

a) $2 \cdot 2 \cdot 2 = 6^2$

Solution

Incorrect. The base is 2, not 6, and the exponent is 3, not 2. So, $2 \cdot 2 \cdot 2 = 2^3$.

b) $23^4 = 23 \cdot 23 \cdot 23 \cdot 23$

Solution

Correct.

Guided Practice

Tell whether each statement is correct. If it is incorrect, state the reason.

3 $6^3 = 6 \cdot 6 \cdot 6$

4 $5 \cdot 5 = 2^5$

Example 3 **Write repeated multiplication using exponential notation.**

Write in exponential notation.

a) $5 \cdot 5 \cdot 5 \cdot 5$

Solution

$5 \cdot 5 \cdot 5 \cdot 5 = 5^4$ The base is 5 and the exponent is 4.

b) $(-3) \cdot (-3) \cdot (-3) \cdot (-3) \cdot (-3)$

Solution

$(-3) \cdot (-3) \cdot (-3) \cdot (-3) \cdot (-3) = (-3)^5$ The base is -3 and the exponent is 5.

c) $\left(\dfrac{1}{2}x\right) \cdot \left(\dfrac{1}{2}x\right) \cdot \left(\dfrac{1}{2}x\right)$

Solution

$\left(\dfrac{1}{2}x\right) \cdot \left(\dfrac{1}{2}x\right) \cdot \left(\dfrac{1}{2}x\right) = \left(\dfrac{1}{2}x\right)^3$ The base is $\dfrac{1}{2}x$ and the exponent is 3.

Guided Practice

Write in exponential notation.

5 $2 \cdot 2 \cdot 2 \cdot 2 \cdot 2 \cdot 2$

$2 \cdot 2 \cdot 2 \cdot 2 \cdot 2 \cdot 2 = \underline{\ ?\ }$ The base is $\underline{\ ?\ }$ and the exponent is $\underline{\ ?\ }$.

6 $(-4) \cdot (-4) \cdot (-4)$

$(-4) \cdot (-4) \cdot (-4) = \underline{\ ?\ }$ The base is $\underline{\ ?\ }$ and the exponent is $\underline{\ ?\ }$.

7 $\left(\frac{2}{3}y\right)\left(\frac{2}{3}y\right)\left(\frac{2}{3}y\right)\left(\frac{2}{3}y\right)$

$\left(\frac{2}{3}y\right)\left(\frac{2}{3}y\right)\left(\frac{2}{3}y\right)\left(\frac{2}{3}y\right) = \underline{\ ?\ }$ The base is $\underline{\ ?\ }$ and the exponent is $\underline{\ ?\ }$.

Example 4 **Expand and evaluate expressions in exponential notation.**

Expand and evaluate each expression.

a) 2.5^3

Solution

$$2.5^3 = 2.5 \cdot 2.5 \cdot 2.5$$
$$= 15.625$$

b) $(-4)^2$

Solution

$$(-4)^2 = (-4) \cdot (-4)$$
$$= 16$$

c) $\left(\frac{2}{3}\right)^5$

Solution

$$\left(\frac{2}{3}\right)^5 = \frac{2}{3} \cdot \frac{2}{3} \cdot \frac{2}{3} \cdot \frac{2}{3} \cdot \frac{2}{3}$$
$$= \frac{32}{243}$$

> **Caution** ////////
>
> $(-4)^2 \neq -4^2$
> In $(-4)^2$, the parentheses tell you to raise (-4) to the second power. So, $(-4)^2 = (-4) \cdot (-4)$.
> In -4^2, you are finding the opposite of 4 after raising it to the second power. So, $-4^2 = (-1) \cdot 4 \cdot 4$.

> **Think Math**
>
> Can you write $(-4)^2$ as 4^2? Why or why not?

Guided Practice

Expand and evaluate each expression.

8 3^4

$3^4 = \underline{\ ?\ } \cdot \underline{\ ?\ } \cdot \underline{\ ?\ } \cdot \underline{\ ?\ }$ The base $\underline{\ ?\ }$ is used as a factor four times.

$\quad = \underline{\ ?\ }$ Evaluate.

9 $(-5)^3$

$(-5)^3 = \underline{\ ?\ } \cdot \underline{\ ?\ } \cdot \underline{\ ?\ }$ The base -5 is used as a factor $\underline{\ ?\ }$ times.

$\quad = \underline{\ ?\ }$ Evaluate.

10 $\left(\dfrac{3}{4}\right)^3$

$\left(\dfrac{3}{4}\right)^3 = \underline{\ ?\ } \cdot \underline{\ ?\ } \cdot \underline{\ ?\ }$ The base $\underline{\ ?\ }$ is used as a factor three times.

$\quad = \underline{\ ?\ }$ Evaluate.

Use Exponents to Write the Prime Factorization of a Number.

Any composite number can be written as a product of prime factors. This prime factorization of a number can be expressed using exponents. You may want to use the following divisibility rules to help you to find the prime factors.

Divisibility Rules

A number is divisible by	if ...
2	the last digit is even (0, 2, 4, 6, or 8).
3	the sum of the digits is divisible by 3.
5	the last digit is 0 or 5.
7	the last digit, when doubled, and then subtracted from the number formed by the remaining digits, gives a result of 0 or a number divisible by 7.

Think Math

If the last digit of the number is 0, do you divide the number by 2 or 5 first?

Example 5 Write the prime factorization of a number using exponential notation.

Write the prime factorization of each number in exponential notation.

a) 81

Solution

$$81 = 3 \cdot 27$$ 81 is divisible by 3.

$$\quad = 3 \cdot 3 \cdot 9$$ 27 is divisible by 3.

$$\quad = 3 \cdot 3 \cdot 3 \cdot 3$$ 9 is divisible by 3.

$$\quad = 3^4$$ Simplify.

3	81
3	27
3	9
3	3
	1

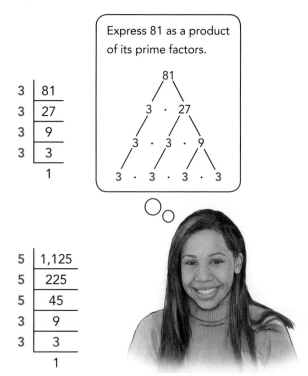

Express 81 as a product of its prime factors.

b) 1,125

Solution

$$1{,}125 = 5 \cdot 225$$ The last digit is 5.

$$\quad = 5 \cdot 5 \cdot 45$$ The last digit is 5.

$$\quad = 5 \cdot 5 \cdot 5 \cdot 9$$ The last digit is 5.

$$\quad = 5 \cdot 5 \cdot 5 \cdot 3 \cdot 3$$ 9 is divisible by 3.

$$\quad = 3^2 \cdot 5^3$$ Simplify.

5	1,125
5	225
5	45
3	9
3	3
	1

c) 1,470

Solution

$$1{,}470 = 5 \cdot 294$$ The last digit is 0.

$$\quad = 5 \cdot 2 \cdot 147$$ The last digit is even.

$$\quad = 5 \cdot 2 \cdot 3 \cdot 49$$ 147 is divisible by 3.

$$\quad = 5 \cdot 2 \cdot 3 \cdot 7 \cdot 7$$ 49 is divisible by 7.

$$\quad = 2 \cdot 3 \cdot 5 \cdot 7^2$$ Simplify.

5	1,470
2	294
3	147
7	49
7	7
	1

Check to see which, if any, of the divisibility rules you can apply.
1,470 ⟶ 1 + 4 + 7 + 0 = 12, which is divisible by 3.

Guided Practice

Write the prime factorization of each number in exponential notation.

11 625

$625 = \underline{\ ?\ } \cdot \underline{\ ?\ }$ The last digit is $\underline{\ ?\ }$.

$= \underline{\ ?\ } \cdot \underline{\ ?\ } \cdot \underline{\ ?\ }$ The last digit is $\underline{\ ?\ }$.

$= \underline{\ ?\ } \cdot \underline{\ ?\ } \cdot \underline{\ ?\ } \cdot \underline{\ ?\ }$ The last digit is $\underline{\ ?\ }$.

$= \underline{\ ?\ }$ Simplify.

?	625
?	?
?	?
?	?
	1

12 630

$630 = \underline{\ ?\ } \cdot \underline{\ ?\ }$ The last digit is $\underline{\ ?\ }$.

$= \underline{\ ?\ } \cdot \underline{\ ?\ } \cdot \underline{\ ?\ }$ The last digit is $\underline{\ ?\ }$.

$= \underline{\ ?\ } \cdot \underline{\ ?\ } \cdot \underline{\ ?\ } \cdot \underline{\ ?\ }$ $\underline{\ ?\ }$ is divisible by $\underline{\ ?\ }$.

$= \underline{\ ?\ } \cdot \underline{\ ?\ } \cdot \underline{\ ?\ } \cdot \underline{\ ?\ } \cdot \underline{\ ?\ }$ $\underline{\ ?\ }$ is divisible by $\underline{\ ?\ }$.

$= \underline{\ ?\ } \cdot \underline{\ ?\ } \cdot \underline{\ ?\ } \cdot \underline{\ ?\ }$ Simplify.

?	630
?	?
?	?
?	?
?	?
	1

Example 6 **Solve a real-world problem using exponential notation.**

a)   There are 20 bacteria in a given sample in a laboratory. During the early phase of culture growth, the number of bacteria keeps doubling every hour. How many bacteria are there after 3 hours? Write your answer in exponential notation.

Solution

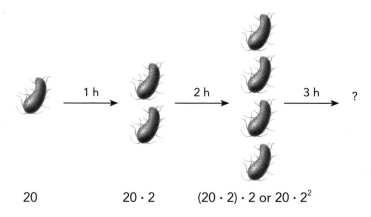

20   20 · 2   (20 · 2) · 2 or 20 · 2^2

Number of bacteria after 3 h

$= $ Initial number of bacteria · Rate of growth over 3 h

$= 20 \cdot 2 \cdot 2 \cdot 2$ Substitute values.

$= 5 \cdot 4 \cdot 2 \cdot 2 \cdot 2$ The last digit of 20 is 0.

$= 5 \cdot 2 \cdot 2 \cdot 2 \cdot 2 \cdot 2$ 4 is even.

$= 2^5 \cdot 5$ Simplify.

There are $2^5 \cdot 5$ bacteria after 3 hours.

b) 🖩 Shana deposits $100 in a bank account that earns 5% interest, compounded yearly. How much will be in her account at the end of 5 years?

Solution

When interest is compounded yearly, a year's interest is deposited in the account at the end of the year. During the next year, interest is earned on this larger balance. Because Shana's deposit increases to 105% of its value each year, she can use the formula $A = P(1 + r)^n$ to find out how much money she has in her account after n years when she invests a principal of P dollars at an interest rate of r%.

$A = P(1 + r)^n$
$\quad = \$100(1 + 0.05)^5$ Substitute 100 for P, 5 for n, and 0.05 for r.
$\quad = \$100(1.05)^5$ Add within the parentheses.
$\quad \approx \$127.63$ Round to the nearest hundredth.

Shana's $100 will be worth $127.63.

Guided Practice

Solve. Show your work.

13 Karen ate at a restaurant. One day later, Karen told three friends about the restaurant. The day after that, each of the friends Karen had told about the restaurant told three more friends about the restaurant. If this pattern continued, how many friends were told about the restaurant five days after Karen ate there?

Number of friends who were told about the restaurant five days after Karen ate there
= Initial number of people who knew about the restaurant · Rate of word-of-mouth referrals over 5 days
$= 1 \cdot \underline{\quad?\quad} \cdot \underline{\quad?\quad} \cdot \underline{\quad?\quad} \cdot \underline{\quad?\quad} \cdot \underline{\quad?\quad}$ Substitute values.
$= \underline{\quad?\quad}$ Simplify.

$\underline{\quad?\quad}$ people were told about the restaurant 5 days after Karen ate there.

14 Dewin, at age 25, invests $2,000 in his retirement account. It will earn 6% interest, compounded yearly. How much will be in his account when he retires at age 65?

Number of years invested $= \underline{\quad?\quad} - \underline{\quad?\quad}$ Substitute values.
$\qquad\qquad\qquad\qquad = \underline{\quad?\quad}$ Simplify.
$A = P(1 + r)^n$
$\quad = \$\underline{\,?\,}(\underline{\,?\,} + \underline{\,?\,})^{\underline{?}}$ Substitute $\underline{\,?\,}$ for P, $\underline{\,?\,}$ for n, and $\underline{\,?\,}$ for r.
$\quad = \$\underline{\,?\,}(\underline{\,?\,})^{\underline{?}}$ Add within the parentheses.
$\quad = \$\underline{\,?\,}$ Round to the nearest hundredth.

Dewin will have $\underline{\,?\,}$ in his account.

Identify the base and exponent in each expression.

1 10^5

2 $(-7)^5$

3 $(0.2)^4$

4 -6^5

5 1^9

6 $\left(\dfrac{4}{5}\right)^5$

Tell whether each statement is correct. If it is incorrect, state the reason.

7 $24^3 = 2 \cdot 4 \cdot 4 \cdot 4$

8 $(-2)^4 = -2 \cdot 2 \cdot 2 \cdot 2$

Write in exponential notation.

9 $\dfrac{1}{3} \cdot \dfrac{1}{3}$

10 $5 \cdot 5 \cdot 5 \cdot 5$

11 $(-2) \cdot (-2) \cdot (-2)$

12 $0.12 \cdot 0.12 \cdot 0.12 \cdot 0.12 \cdot 0.12$

13 $a \cdot a \cdot a$

14 $mn \cdot mn \cdot mn \cdot mn \cdot mn$

Expand and evaluate each expression.

15 2^3

16 $\left(\dfrac{3}{8}\right)^4$

17 10^4

18 🖩 -3.4^4

Write the prime factorization of each number in exponential notation.

19 125

20 4,802

21 91,125

Order the following expressions from least to greatest.

22 -5^2, $(-5)^2$, and -2^5

23 -4^3, -3^4, and $(-3)^4$

Solve. Show your work.

24 Barnard's Star is approximately 10,000,000,000,000,000 meters from the Sun. Epsilon Eridani is at a distance of about 100,000,000,000,000,000 meters from the Sun. Write each distance as 10 raised to a power.

25 🖩 Use the formula $A = P(1 + r)^n$ to find out how much $500 would be worth in 20 years if it increases by 8% each year.

26 Jen cut a piece of paper in half and threw away one half. She cut the remaining paper in half and threw away one half. She continued doing this until she had a piece of paper whose area was $\dfrac{1}{32}$ as great as the area of the original piece of paper. How many cuts did she make?

The Product and the Quotient of Powers

Lesson Objectives

- Understand the product of powers property.
- Understand the quotient of powers property.
- Multiply and divide expressions in exponential notation.

Understand the Product of Powers Property.

You have learned that

$$10^6 = 10 \cdot 10 \cdot 10 \cdot 10 \cdot 10 \cdot 10$$

and that $10^9 = 10 \cdot 10 \cdot 10 \cdot 10 \cdot 10 \cdot 10 \cdot 10 \cdot 10 \cdot 10$.

To see how the exponent in each of these numbers is related to the exponent of their product, you can write the following:

$$10^6 \cdot 10^9 = \underbrace{(10 \cdot 10 \cdot 10 \cdot 10 \cdot 10 \cdot 10)}_{6 \text{ factors}} \cdot \underbrace{(10 \cdot 10 \cdot 10 \cdot 10 \cdot 10 \cdot 10 \cdot 10 \cdot 10 \cdot 10)}_{9 \text{ factors}}$$

$$= \underbrace{10 \cdot 10 \cdot 10 \cdot 10 \cdot 10 \cdot 10 \cdot 10 \cdot 10 \cdot 10 \cdot 10 \cdot 10 \cdot 10 \cdot 10 \cdot 10 \cdot 10}_{15 \text{ factors}}$$

$$= 10^{15}$$

So, you can see that $10^6 \cdot 10^9 = 10^{6+9}$

$$= 10^{15}.$$

Notice that 10^6 and 10^9 have the same base. You can apply the same reasoning you used to find their product to find the product of any powers that have the same base.

$$a^4 \cdot a^3 = \underbrace{(a \cdot a \cdot a \cdot a)}_{4 \text{ factors}} \cdot \underbrace{(a \cdot a \cdot a)}_{3 \text{ factors}}$$

$$= \underbrace{a \cdot a \cdot a \cdot a \cdot a \cdot a \cdot a}_{7 \text{ factors}}$$

$$= a^7$$

So, $a^4 \cdot a^3 = a^{4+3}$

$$= a^7.$$

> When you find the product of two algebraic expressions with the same base, You can add their exponents and use this exponent with the same base.
>
> $$a^m \cdot a^n = a^{m+n}$$
>
> The variable a can represent any number. You can use this property to simplify numerical and algebraic expressions that involve exponents with a common base.

Example 7 **Use the product of powers property to simplify numerical expressions.**

Simplify each expression. Write your answer in exponential notation.

a) $3^6 \cdot 3$

Solution

$3^6 \cdot 3 = 3^{6+1}$ Use the product of powers property.
      $= 3^7$ Simplify.

> When a number or variable does not have an exponent, it means the number or variable is raised to the first power.
> $3 = 3^1$
> $a = a^1$

b) $(-4)^2 \cdot (-4)^4$

Solution

$(-4)^2 \cdot (-4)^4 = (-4)^{2+4}$ Use the product of powers property.
              $= (-4)^6$ Simplify the exponent.
              $= 4^6$ Simplify.

Think Math

$2^4 \cdot 3^4 \neq (2 \cdot 3)^8$

Explain why.

c) $1.2^3 \cdot 1.2^4$

Solution

$1.2^3 \cdot 1.2^4 = 1.2^{3+4}$ Use the product of powers property.
        $= 1.2^7$ Simplify.

Guided Practice

Simplify each expression. Write your answer in exponential notation.

1 $6^4 \cdot 6^3$

$6^4 \cdot 6^3 = \underline{\ \ ?\ \ }$ Use the $\underline{\ ?\ }$ of powers property.
     $= \underline{\ \ ?\ \ }$ Simplify.

2 $(-5) \cdot (-5)^5$

$(-5) \cdot (-5)^5 = \underline{\ \ ?\ \ }$ Use the $\underline{\ ?\ }$ of powers property.
          $= \underline{\ \ ?\ \ }$ Simplify the exponent.
          $= \underline{\ \ ?\ \ }$ Simplify.

3 $\left(\dfrac{1}{5}\right)^3 \cdot \left(\dfrac{1}{5}\right)^4$

$\left(\dfrac{1}{5}\right)^3 \cdot \left(\dfrac{1}{5}\right)^4 = \underline{\ \ ?\ \ }$ Use the $\underline{\ ?\ }$ of powers property.

           $= \underline{\ \ ?\ \ }$ Simplify.

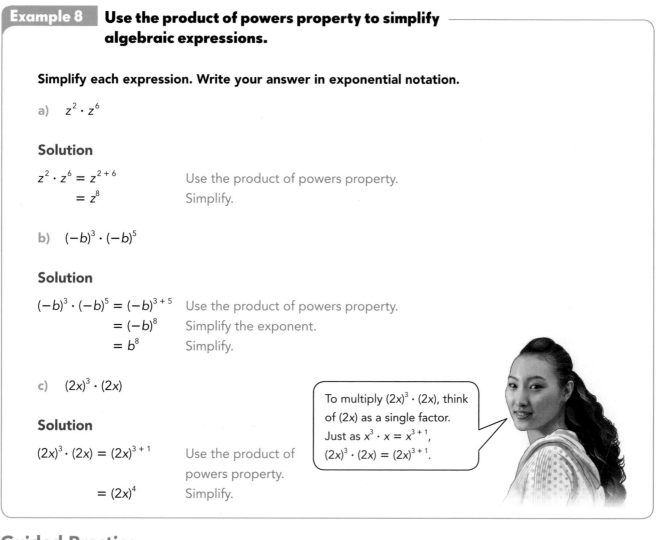

Example 8 **Use the product of powers property to simplify algebraic expressions.**

Simplify each expression. Write your answer in exponential notation.

a) $z^2 \cdot z^6$

Solution

$$z^2 \cdot z^6 = z^{2+6}$$ Use the product of powers property.
$$= z^8$$ Simplify.

b) $(-b)^3 \cdot (-b)^5$

Solution

$$(-b)^3 \cdot (-b)^5 = (-b)^{3+5}$$ Use the product of powers property.
$$= (-b)^8$$ Simplify the exponent.
$$= b^8$$ Simplify.

c) $(2x)^3 \cdot (2x)$

Solution

$$(2x)^3 \cdot (2x) = (2x)^{3+1}$$ Use the product of powers property.

$$= (2x)^4$$ Simplify.

> To multiply $(2x)^3 \cdot (2x)$, think of $(2x)$ as a single factor. Just as $x^3 \cdot x = x^{3+1}$, $(2x)^3 \cdot (2x) = (2x)^{3+1}$.

Guided Practice

Simplify each expression. Write your answer in exponential notation.

4 $p^3 \cdot p^6$

$$p^3 \cdot p^6 = \underline{\quad ? \quad}$$ Use the __?__ of powers property.
$$= \underline{\quad ? \quad}$$ Simplify.

5 $(-c)^4 \cdot (-c)^2$

6 $(3s)^5 \cdot (3s)$

Use the Product of Powers Property with Algebraic Expressions.

You can use the product of powers property to simplify algebraic expressions. Remember that you can use the property only when you multiply powers with the same base.

Example 9 **Use the product of powers property to simplify algebraic expressions.**

Simplify each expression. Write your answer in exponential notation.

a) $b^2 c^3 \cdot b^5 c^5$

> You can rewrite $b^2 c^3$ as $b^2 \cdot c^3$ and $b^5 c^5$ as $b^5 \cdot c^5$. Then use the commutative property of multiplication to regroup factors.

Solution

$$
\begin{aligned}
b^2 c^3 \cdot b^5 c^5 &= b^2 \cdot c^3 \cdot b^5 \cdot c^5 && \text{Rewrite the product.} \\
&= b^2 \cdot b^5 \cdot c^3 \cdot c^5 && \text{Regroup factors with the same base.} \\
&= b^{2+5} \cdot c^{3+5} && \text{Add the exponents of the factors with the same base.} \\
&= b^7 c^8 && \text{Simplify.}
\end{aligned}
$$

b) $2x^4 y^2 \cdot 3x^2 y^6$

Solution

$$
\begin{aligned}
2x^4 y^2 \cdot 3x^2 y^6 &= 2 \cdot x^4 \cdot y^2 \cdot 3 \cdot x^2 \cdot y^6 && \text{Rewrite the product.} \\
&= 2 \cdot 3 \cdot x^4 \cdot x^2 \cdot y^2 \cdot y^6 && \text{Regroup numbers, and regroup factors with the same bases.} \\
&= 6 \cdot x^{4+2} \cdot y^{2+6} && \text{Add the exponents of the factors with the same base.} \\
&= 6x^6 y^8 && \text{Simplify.}
\end{aligned}
$$

Guided Practice

Simplify each expression. Write your answer in exponential notation.

7 $pq^3 \cdot p^5 q^2$

$$
\begin{aligned}
& pq^3 \cdot p^5 q^2 \\
&= \underline{\ ?\ } \cdot \underline{\ ?\ } \cdot \underline{\ ?\ } \cdot \underline{\ ?\ } && \underline{\ ?\ } \text{ the product.} \\
&= \underline{\ ?\ } \cdot \underline{\ ?\ } \cdot \underline{\ ?\ } \cdot \underline{\ ?\ } && \text{Regroup factors with the } \underline{\ ?\ } \text{ base.} \\
&= \underline{\ ?\ } \cdot \underline{\ ?\ } && \underline{\ ?\ } \text{ the exponents of the factors with the same base.} \\
&= \underline{\ ?\ } && \text{Simplify.}
\end{aligned}
$$

8 $4s^4 t^3 \cdot 5s^4 t^6$

$$
\begin{aligned}
& 4s^4 t^3 \cdot 5s^4 t^6 \\
&= \underline{\ ?\ } \cdot \underline{\ ?\ } \cdot \underline{\ ?\ } \cdot \underline{\ ?\ } \cdot \underline{\ ?\ } \cdot \underline{\ ?\ } && \underline{\ ?\ } \text{ the product.} \\
&= \underline{\ ?\ } \cdot \underline{\ ?\ } \cdot \underline{\ ?\ } \cdot \underline{\ ?\ } \cdot \underline{\ ?\ } \cdot \underline{\ ?\ } && \text{Regroup } \underline{\ ?\ }, \text{ and regroup factors with the } \underline{\ ?\ } \text{ bases.} \\
&= \underline{\ ?\ } \cdot \underline{\ ?\ } \cdot \underline{\ ?\ } && \underline{\ ?\ } \text{ the exponents of factors with the same base.} \\
&= \underline{\ ?\ } && \text{Simplify.}
\end{aligned}
$$

Understand the Quotient of Powers Property.

To see how the exponents in 5^5 and 5^2 are related to the exponent of their quotient, you can write the following:

$5^5 \div 5^2 = (5 \cdot 5 \cdot 5 \cdot 5 \cdot 5) \div (5 \cdot 5)$

$$= \frac{\overbrace{5 \cdot 5 \cdot 5 \cdot 5 \cdot 5}^{5 \text{ factors}}}{\underbrace{5 \cdot 5}_{2 \text{ factors}}}$$

$$= \underbrace{5 \cdot 5 \cdot 5}_{3 \text{ factors}}$$

$$= 5^3$$

Notice that $5^3 = 5^{5-2}$. You can find the exponent of the quotient by subtracting the exponent of the divisor from the exponent of the dividend.

So, you can see that $5^5 \div 5^2 = 5^{5-2}$
$$= 5^3.$$

$y^7 \div y^4 = (y \cdot y \cdot y \cdot y \cdot y \cdot y \cdot y) \div (y \cdot y \cdot y \cdot y)$

$$= \frac{\overbrace{y \cdot y \cdot y \cdot y \cdot y \cdot y \cdot y}^{7 \text{ factors}}}{\underbrace{y \cdot y \cdot y \cdot y}_{4 \text{ factors}}}$$

$$= \underbrace{y \cdot y \cdot y}_{3 \text{ factors}}$$

$$= y^3$$

So, $y^7 \div y^4 = y^{7-4}$
$$= y^3.$$

> The variable y can represent any number except 0. Because y is the base in both the dividend and the divisor, you can use the same method.

When you find the quotient of two algebraic expressions with the same base, you can subtract the exponent of the divisor from the exponent of the dividend, and use it with the common base.

$$a^m \div a^n = \frac{a^m}{a^n} = a^{m-n}, \, a \neq 0$$

Example 10 **Use the quotient of powers property to simplify numerical expressions.**

Simplify each expression. Write your answer in exponential notation.

a) $2^9 \div 2^6$

Solution

$2^9 \div 2^6$

$= 2^{9-6}$ Use the quotient of powers property.

$= 2^3$ Simplify.

b) $(-7)^5 \div (-7)$

Solution

$(-7)^5 \div (-7)$

$= (-7)^{5-1}$ Use the quotient of powers property.

$= (-7)^4$ Simplify the exponent.

$= 7^4$ Simplify.

c) $3.5^8 \div 3.5^6$

Solution

$3.5^8 \div 3.5^6$

$= 3.5^{8-6}$ Use the quotient of powers property.

$= 3.5^2$ Simplify.

Think Math

Can you use the quotient of powers property to simplify $5^4 \div 3^{20}$? Explain why.

Guided Practice

Simplify each expression. Write your answer in exponential notation.

9 $10^8 \div 10^5$

$10^8 \div 10^5 = \underline{\ ?\ }$ Use the $\underline{\ ?\ }$ of powers property.

$= \underline{\ ?\ }$ Simplify.

10 $2.7^9 \div 2.7^6$

$2.7^9 \div 2.7^6 = \underline{\ ?\ }$ Use the $\underline{\ ?\ }$ of powers property.

$= \underline{\ ?\ }$ Simplify.

11 $\left(\dfrac{5}{8}\right)^6 \div \left(\dfrac{5}{8}\right)$

$\left(\dfrac{5}{8}\right)^6 \div \left(\dfrac{5}{8}\right) = \underline{\quad?\quad}$ Use the __?__ of powers property.

$= \underline{\quad?\quad}$ Simplify.

Example 11 **Use the quotient of powers property to divide algebraic expressions.**

Simplify each expression. Write your answer in exponential notation.

a) $y^8 \div y^3$

Solution

$y^8 \div y^3$

$= y^{8-3}$ Use the quotient of powers property.

$= y^5$ Simplify.

> When dividing by a variable, remember that the variable can never have a value of 0.

b) $(-x)^6 \div (-x)^2$

Solution

$(-x)^6 \div (-x)^2$

$= (-x)^{6-2}$ Use the quotient of powers property.

$= (-x)^4$ Simplify the exponent.

$= x^4$ Simplify.

Guided Practice

Simplify each expression. Write your answer in exponential notation.

12 $q^7 \div q^2$

$q^7 \div q^2 = \underline{\quad?\quad}$ Use the quotient of powers property.

$= \underline{\quad?\quad}$ Simplify.

13 $(-p)^5 \div (-p)^3$

Use the Quotient of Powers Property with Algebraic Expressions.

You can use the quotient of powers property to simplify algebraic expressions. Remember that you can use the property only when you divide factors with the same base.

Example 12 **Use the quotient of powers property to simplify algebraic expressions.**

Simplify each expression. Write your answer in exponential notation.

a) $h^6k^2 \div h^5k$

Solution

$h^6k^2 \div h^5k$

$= \dfrac{h^6k^2}{h^5k}$ Write the quotient as a fraction.

$= \dfrac{h^6}{h^5} \cdot \dfrac{k^2}{k}$ Rewrite the fraction as a product of two fractions.

$= h^{6-5} \cdot k^{2-1}$ Use the quotient of powers property.

$= hk$ Simplify.

b) $28m^7n^4 \div 7m^3n^2$

Solution

$28m^7n^4 \div 7m^3n^2$

$= \dfrac{28m^7n^4}{7m^3n^2}$ Write the quotient as a fraction.

$= \dfrac{28}{7} \cdot \dfrac{m^7}{m^3} \cdot \dfrac{n^4}{n^2}$ Rewrite the fraction as a product of three fractions.

$= 4 \cdot m^{7-3} \cdot n^{4-2}$ Use the quotient of powers property.

$= 4m^4n^2$ Simplify.

Guided Practice

Simplify each expression. Write your answer in exponential notation.

14 $r^8s^6 \div r^5s^4$

$r^8s^6 \div r^5s^4 = \dfrac{?}{?}$ Write the quotient as a __?__.

$\qquad = \dfrac{?}{?} \cdot \dfrac{?}{?}$ Rewrite the fraction as a __?__ of two fractions.

$\qquad = \underline{\quad?\quad} \cdot \underline{\quad?\quad}$ Use the __?__ of powers property.

$\qquad = \underline{\quad?\quad}$ Simplify.

15 $63x^9y^7 \div 9x^3y^4$

$63x^9y^7 \div 9x^3y^4 = \dfrac{?}{?}$ Write the quotient as a __?__.

$\qquad = \dfrac{?}{?} \cdot \dfrac{?}{?} \cdot \dfrac{?}{?}$ Rewrite the fraction as a __?__ of three fractions.

$\qquad = \underline{\quad?\quad} \cdot \underline{\quad?\quad} \cdot \underline{\quad?\quad}$ Use the __?__ of powers property.

$\qquad = \underline{\quad?\quad}$ Simplify.

Multiply and Divide Expressions in Exponential Notation.

You may have to use both the product of powers and quotient of powers properties together to simplify some numerical and algebraic expressions.

Example 13 **Use exponent properties to simplify numerical and algebraic expressions.**

Simplify each expression. Write your answer in exponential notation.

a) $\dfrac{4^2 \cdot 4^7 \cdot 4}{4^3 \cdot 4 \cdot 4^4}$

Solution

$\dfrac{4^2 \cdot 4^7 \cdot 4}{4^3 \cdot 4 \cdot 4^4} = \dfrac{4^{2+7+1}}{4^{3+1+4}}$ Use the product of powers property.

$\qquad\qquad = \dfrac{4^{10}}{4^8}$ Simplify.

$\qquad\qquad = 4^{10-8}$ Use the quotient of powers property.

$\qquad\qquad = 4^2$ Simplify.

b) $\dfrac{\left(\frac{1}{4}\right)^3 \cdot \left(\frac{1}{4}\right) \cdot \left(\frac{1}{4}\right)^2}{\left(\frac{1}{4}\right) \cdot \left(\frac{1}{4}\right) \cdot \left(\frac{1}{4}\right)}$

Solution

$\dfrac{\left(\frac{1}{4}\right)^3 \cdot \left(\frac{1}{4}\right) \cdot \left(\frac{1}{4}\right)^2}{\left(\frac{1}{4}\right) \cdot \left(\frac{1}{4}\right) \cdot \left(\frac{1}{4}\right)} = \dfrac{\left(\frac{1}{4}\right)^{3+1+2}}{\left(\frac{1}{4}\right)^{1+1+1}}$ Use the product of powers property.

$\qquad\qquad = \dfrac{\left(\frac{1}{4}\right)^6}{\left(\frac{1}{4}\right)^3}$ Simplify.

$\qquad\qquad = \left(\frac{1}{4}\right)^{6-3}$ Use the quotient of powers property.

$\qquad\qquad = \left(\frac{1}{4}\right)^3$ Simplify.

All the numbers in the numerator and denominator have the same base. You can use the product of powers property first and then use the quotient of powers property.

Continue on next page

c) $\dfrac{3x^4 \cdot 5y^5 \cdot 6x^6}{2y \cdot 3x^2 \cdot 5y^3}$

Solution

$$\dfrac{3x^4 \cdot 5y^5 \cdot 6x^6}{2y \cdot 3x^2 \cdot 5y^3} = \dfrac{3 \cdot 5 \cdot 6 \cdot x^4 \cdot x^6 \cdot y^5}{2 \cdot 3 \cdot 5 \cdot x^2 \cdot y \cdot y^3}$$

Regroup the numbers, and regroup the factors with the same bases.

$$= \dfrac{90x^{4+6}y^5}{30x^2 y^{1+3}}$$

Use the product of powers property.

$$= \dfrac{3x^{10}y^5}{x^2 y^4}$$

Simplify.

$$= 3(x^{10-2})(y^{5-4})$$

Use the quotient of powers property.

$$= 3x^8 y$$

Simplify.

Guided Practice

Simplify each expression. Write your answer in exponential notation.

16 $\dfrac{6^7 \cdot 6^3 \cdot 6^2}{6 \cdot 6^4 \cdot 6^5}$

$$\dfrac{6^7 \cdot 6^3 \cdot 6^2}{6 \cdot 6^4 \cdot 6^5} = \dfrac{?}{?}$$

Use the ___?___ of powers property.

$$= \dfrac{?}{?}$$

Simplify.

$$= \underline{}?\underline{}$$

Use the ___?___ of powers property.

$$= \underline{}?\underline{}$$

Simplify.

17 $\dfrac{7.5^5 \cdot 7.5^3 \cdot 7.5}{7.5^2 \cdot 7.5 \cdot 7.5^4}$

$$\dfrac{7.5^5 \cdot 7.5^3 \cdot 7.5}{7.5^2 \cdot 7.5 \cdot 7.5^4} = \dfrac{?}{?}$$

Use the ___?___ of powers property.

$$= \dfrac{?}{?}$$

Simplify.

$$= \underline{}?\underline{}$$

Use the ___?___ of powers property.

$$= \underline{}?\underline{}$$

Simplify.

18 $\dfrac{b^5 \cdot 4a^4 \cdot 9a^3}{2a^2 \cdot b^2 \cdot 6a^2}$

$$\dfrac{b^5 \cdot 4a^4 \cdot 9a^3}{2a^2 \cdot b^2 \cdot 6a^2} = \dfrac{?}{?}$$

Regroup the numbers, and regroup the factors with the same bases.

$$= \dfrac{?}{?}$$

Use the ___?___ of powers property.

$$= \dfrac{?}{?}$$

Simplify.

$$= \underline{}?\underline{}$$

Use the ___?___ of powers property

$$= \underline{}?\underline{}$$

Simplify.

Example 14 **Solve a real-world problem in exponential notation.**

There are approximately 10^{25} water molecules in a liter of water. Patrick has 100 liters of water. How many molecules are there in all? Write your answer in exponential notation.

Solution

Number of molecules in 100 liters of water

= Number of molecules in a liter of water · Number of liters of water

$= 10^{25} \cdot 100$ Substitute values.

$= 10^{25} \cdot 10^{2}$ Rewrite 100 as 10^2.

$= 10^{25 + 2}$ Use the product of powers property.

$= 10^{27}$ Simplify.

There are 10^{27} molecules in 100 liters of water.

Guided Practice

Solve. Show your work.

19 Jupiter is approximately 10^8 kilometers from the Sun. The dwarf planet Eris is about 10^{10} kilometers from the Sun. How many times as far as Jupiter is Eris from the Sun?

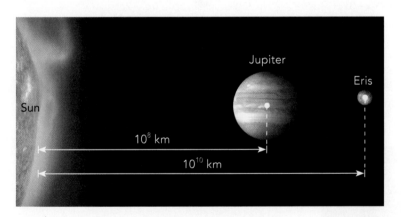

Number of times Eris' distance is as far as Jupiter's distance from the Sun

$= \dfrac{\text{Distance of Eris from the Sun}}{\text{Distance of Jupiter from the Sun}}$

$= \dfrac{?}{?}$ Substitute values.

$= \underline{\ ?\ }$ Use the quotient of powers property.

$= \underline{\ ?\ }$ Simplify.

Eris is $\underline{\ ?\ }$ times as far as Jupiter from the Sun.

Practice 1.2

Simplify each expression. Write your answer in exponential notation.

1 $(-2)^6 \cdot (-2)^2$

2 $7.2^3 \cdot 7.2^4$

3 $10^5 \cdot 10^4$

4 $\left(\dfrac{2}{3}\right) \cdot \left(\dfrac{2}{3}\right)^5$

5 $p \cdot p^8$

6 $q^8 \div q$

7 $xy^2 \cdot x^4y^3$

8 $2x^2y^4 \cdot 5x^5y$

9 $2.5x^3y^6 \cdot 3x^2y^4$

10 $(-3)^4 \div (-3)^2$

11 $2^{10} \div 2^5$

12 $\left(-\dfrac{1}{6}\right)^5 \div \left(-\dfrac{1}{6}\right)^2$

13 $63y^3z^5 \div 9$

14 $h^2k^5 \div hk^4$

15 $64a^8b^5 \div 4a^3b^2$

16 $\dfrac{5^9 \cdot 5^7 \cdot 5^8}{5^3 \cdot 5^2 \cdot 5}$

17 $\dfrac{\left(\frac{4}{9}\right)^6 \cdot \left(\frac{4}{9}\right)^5 \cdot \left(\frac{4}{9}\right)^4}{\left(\frac{4}{9}\right)^3 \cdot \left(\frac{4}{9}\right)^3 \cdot \left(\frac{4}{9}\right)^4}$

18 $\dfrac{a^9 \cdot a^2 \cdot a^3}{a^6 \cdot a^3 \cdot a^4}$

19 $\dfrac{b^4 \cdot b^6 \cdot b}{b^3 \cdot b^3 \cdot b^3}$

20 $\dfrac{3x^3 \cdot z^4 \cdot 4x^3}{2x \cdot x \cdot 3z}$

21 $\dfrac{4c^6 \cdot 3b^4 \cdot 9c^5}{b^3 \cdot 6c^3 \cdot 2c^3}$

Solve. Show your work.

22 Pluto has a diameter of about 10^3 kilometers. The diameter of Saturn is approximately 10^5 kilometers. How many times as great as Pluto's diameter is Saturn's diameter?

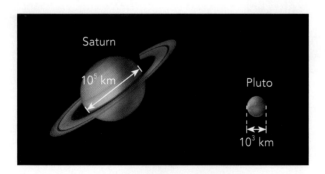

23 Use the rectangular prism shown.

a) Express the volume of the rectangular prism using exponential notation.

b) Another prism has dimensions that are twice the dimensions of the prism shown. Express the volume of that prism using exponential notation.

c) How many times greater is the volume of the larger prism than the volume of the smaller prism?

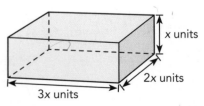

1.3 The Power of a Power

Lesson Objectives

- Understand raising a power to a power.
- Use properties of exponents to simplify expressions.

Understand Raising a Power to a Power.

You can use the order of operations to evaluate the expression $(2^4)^3$. First evaluate the expression inside the parentheses. Then use 16 as a factor 3 times.

$$
\begin{aligned}
(2^4)^3 &= (2 \cdot 2 \cdot 2 \cdot 2)^3 \\
&= (16)^3 \\
&= 16 \cdot 16 \cdot 16 \\
&= 4{,}096
\end{aligned}
$$

You can also evaluate the expression $(2^4)^3$ by using 2 as a factor 12 times.

$$
\begin{aligned}
(2^4)^3 &= (2 \cdot 2 \cdot 2 \cdot 2)^3 \\
&= \underbrace{(2 \cdot 2 \cdot 2 \cdot 2) \cdot (2 \cdot 2 \cdot 2 \cdot 2) \cdot (2 \cdot 2 \cdot 2 \cdot 2)}_{\text{3 groups of 4 factors}} \\
&= \underbrace{2^{4 \cdot 3}}_{4 \cdot 3 = 12 \text{ factors of 2}} \\
&= 2^{12} \\
&= 4{,}096
\end{aligned}
$$

You can use the same method to evaluate $(n^2)^5$.

$$
\begin{aligned}
(n^2)^5 &= (n \cdot n)^5 \\
&= \underbrace{(n \cdot n) \cdot (n \cdot n) \cdot (n \cdot n) \cdot (n \cdot n) \cdot (n \cdot n)}_{\text{5 groups of 2 factors}} \\
&= \underbrace{n^{2 \cdot 5}}_{2 \cdot 5 = 10 \text{ factors of } n} \qquad \text{Use the power of a power property.} \\
&= n^{10} \qquad \text{Simplify.}
\end{aligned}
$$

When you raise a power to a power, keep the base and multiply the exponents.

$$(a^m)^n = a^{m \cdot n} = a^{mn}$$

Hands-On Activity

EXPLORE THE POWER OF A POWER PROPERTY

Work in pairs.

In this activity, you and your partner will play a game in which you write and evaluate expressions in the form $(a^m)^n$. You will get a point for each expression you write, and the person with the greater score wins.

STEP 1 Shuffle each stack of number cards and place them in a pile. Each player randomly draws three cards, one from each pile.

STEP 2 Use your three cards to write an expression in the form $(a^m)^n$. For instance, if you draw 2, 4, and 5, you could write $(2^4)^5$, $(4^2)^5$, or another expression. Write as many expressions as you can. You may want to use a calculator to evaluate your expression. For instance, to evaluate $(2^4)^5$, you can use these keystrokes:

Press (2 ^ 4) ^ 5 ENTER.

STEP 3 Record your expressions and their values. Your partner should also record his or her expressions and their values. Check your partner's work.

STEP 4 Continue the game by replacing the cards you used and shuffling the piles.

Repeat **STEP 1** to **STEP 3** several more times. When you are finished, find each player's score by counting the number of correct expressions that each player has written. The player with the greater score wins.

Math Journal Is it correct to assume that using the greatest number drawn as the base will give the expression with the greatest possible value? Explain or give an example.

Example 15 **Simplify expressions using the power of a power property.**

Simplify each expression. Write your answer in exponential notation.

a) $(3^4)^2$

Solution

$(3^4)^2 = 3^{4 \cdot 2}$ Use the power of a power property.

      $= 3^8$ Simplify.

b) $\left[\left(\dfrac{2}{7}\right)^6\right]^4$

Solution

$\left[\left(\dfrac{2}{7}\right)^6\right]^4 = \left(\dfrac{2}{7}\right)^{6 \cdot 4}$ Use the power of a power property.

      $= \left(\dfrac{2}{7}\right)^{24}$ Simplify.

c) $[(2a)^5]^3$

Solution

$[(2a)^5]^3 = (2a)^{5 \cdot 3}$ Use the power of a power property.

      $= (2a)^{15}$ Simplify.

$(2a)^{15}$ means "Use the expression $2a$ as a factor 15 times."

d) $[(-x)^4]^3$

Solution

$[(-x)^4]^3 = (-x)^{4 \cdot 3}$ Use the power of a power property.

      $= (-x)^{12}$ Simplify the exponent.

      $= x^{12}$ Simplify.

Guided Practice

Simplify each expression. Write your answer in exponential notation.

1 $(5^3)^4$

$(5^3)^4 =$ ___?___   Use the ___?___ of a power property.

$=$ ___?___   Simplify.

2 $(2.3^4)^2$

$(2.3^4)^2 =$ ___?___   Use the ___?___ of a power property.

$=$ ___?___   Simplify.

3 $[(3p)^5]^4$

4 $[(-y)^4]^7$

Use Properties of Exponents to Simplify Expressions.

You may need to use more than one property of exponents to simplify some expressions.

Example 16 **Simplify expressions using properties of exponents.**

Simplify each expression. Write your answer in exponential notation.

a) $[(-4)^2 \cdot (-4)^3]^6$

Solution

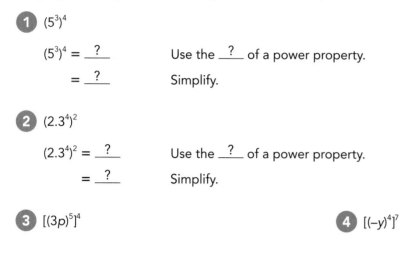

> Follow the order of operations. First multiply within the brackets. Then use the power of a power property.

$\begin{aligned}[(-4)^2 \cdot (-4)^3]^6 &= [(-4)^{2+3}]^6 &&\text{Use the product of powers property.}\\ &= [(-4)^5]^6 &&\text{Simplify.}\\ &= (-4)^{5 \cdot 6} &&\text{Use the power of a power property.}\\ &= (-4)^{30} &&\text{Simplify the exponent.}\\ &= 4^{30} &&\text{Simplify.}\end{aligned}$

Think Math

Is $(-4)^5$ a positive or a negative number? Is $(-4)^{30}$ a positive or negative number? How do you know?

b) $(m^5 \cdot m)^3$

Solution

$(m^5 \cdot m)^3 = (m^{5 + 1})^3$ Use the product of powers property.

$= (m^6)^3$ Simplify.

$= m^{6 \cdot 3}$ Use the power of a power property.

$= m^{18}$ Simplify.

> You can write a variable without an apparent exponent, such as m, as m^1.

c) $\dfrac{(6^4 \cdot 6^3)^4}{(6^2)^5}$

Solution

$\dfrac{(6^4 \cdot 6^3)^4}{(6^2)^5} = \dfrac{(6^{4 + 3})^4}{6^{2 \cdot 5}}$ Use the product of powers and power of a power properties.

$= \dfrac{(6^7)^4}{6^{10}}$ Simplify.

$= \dfrac{6^{7 \cdot 4}}{6^{10}}$ Use the power of a power property.

$= \dfrac{6^{28}}{6^{10}}$ Simplify.

$= 6^{28 - 10}$ Use the quotient of powers property.

$= 6^{18}$ Simplify.

d) $(a^4 \cdot a^2)^4 \div 2a^8$

Solution

$(a^4 \cdot a^2)^4 \div 2a^8 = (a^{4 + 2})^4 \div 2a^8$ Use the product of powers property.

$= (a^6)^4 \div 2a^8$ Simplify.

$= a^{6 \cdot 4} \div 2a^8$ Use the power of a power property.

$= a^{24} \div 2a^8$ Simplify.

$= \dfrac{a^{24 - 8}}{2}$ Use the quotient of powers property.

$= \dfrac{a^{16}}{2}$ Simplify.

Think Math

Suppose a can be any integer in the expression $\dfrac{a^{16}}{2}$. Will the value of the expression be positive or negative? How do you know?

Guided Practice

Simplify each expression. Write your answer in exponential notation.

5 $[(-3) \cdot (-3)^6]^2$

$[(-3) \cdot (-3)^6]^2 = \underline{\ \ ?\ \ }$ Use the $\underline{\ \ ?\ \ }$ of powers property.

$= \underline{\ \ ?\ \ }$ Simplify.

$= \underline{\ \ ?\ \ }$ Use the $\underline{\ \ ?\ \ }$ of a power property.

$= \underline{\ \ ?\ \ }$ Simplify the exponent. $(-3)^{14}$

$= \underline{\ \ ?\ \ }$ Simplify.

6 $(p^4 \cdot p^2)^5$

$(p^4 \cdot p^2)^5 = \underline{\ \ ?\ \ }$ Use the $\underline{\ \ ?\ \ }$ of powers property.

$= \underline{\ \ ?\ \ }$ Simplify.

$= \underline{\ \ ?\ \ }$ Use the $\underline{\ \ ?\ \ }$ of a power property.

$= \underline{\ \ ?\ \ }$ Simplify.

7 $(6^3 \cdot 6^3)^7 \div 6^{10}$

$(6^3 \cdot 6^3)^7 \div 6^{10} = \underline{\ \ ?\ \ } \div \underline{\ \ ?\ \ }$ Use the $\underline{\ \ ?\ \ }$ of powers property.

$= \underline{\ \ ?\ \ } \div \underline{\ \ ?\ \ }$ Simplify.

$= \underline{\ \ ?\ \ } \div \underline{\ \ ?\ \ }$ Use the $\underline{\ \ ?\ \ }$ of a power property.

$= \underline{\ \ ?\ \ } \div \underline{\ \ ?\ \ }$ Simplify.

$= \underline{\ \ ?\ \ }$ Use the $\underline{\ \ ?\ \ }$ of powers property.

$= \underline{\ \ ?\ \ }$ Simplify.

8 $\dfrac{(x^8 \cdot x^4)^2}{(x^3)^6}$

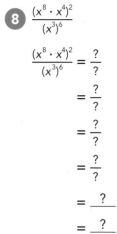

$\dfrac{(x^8 \cdot x^4)^2}{(x^3)^6} = \dfrac{?}{?}$ Use the $\underline{\ \ ?\ \ }$ of powers and $\underline{\ \ ?\ \ }$ of a power properties.

$= \dfrac{?}{?}$ Simplify.

$= \dfrac{?}{?}$ Use the $\underline{\ \ ?\ \ }$ of a power property.

$= \dfrac{?}{?}$ Simplify.

$= \underline{\ \ ?\ \ }$ Use the $\underline{\ \ ?\ \ }$ of powers property.

$= \underline{\ \ ?\ \ }$ Simplify.

Practice 1.3

Simplify each expression. Write your answer in exponential notation.

1 $(2^6)^2$

2 $(3^4)^3$

3 $(10^5)^4$

4 $(10^7)^2$

5 $(25^3)^3$

6 $(x^6)^3$

7 $\left[\left(\dfrac{1}{8}\right)^3\right]^6$

8 $\left[\left(\dfrac{4}{5}\right)^2\right]^4$

9 $[(2y)^3]^8$

10 $[(57p)^4]^4$

11 $[(-6)^4]^3$

12 $[(-p)^2]^{11}$

13  *Math Journal* Michael thinks that $(a^3)^2 = a^5$. Is he correct? Why?

$$(a^3)^2 = a^{3+2}$$
$$= a^5$$

Simplify each expression. Write your answer in exponential notation.

14 $(5^5 \cdot 5^6)^2$

15 $(p^4 \cdot p^2)^6$

16 $\left[\left(\dfrac{1}{2}\right) \cdot \left(\dfrac{1}{2}\right)^3\right]^5$

17 $\left[\left(-\dfrac{4}{9}\right)^2 \cdot \left(-\dfrac{4}{9}\right)^3\right]^2$

18 $(2^2 \cdot 2^4)^3 \div 2^8$

19 $(7 \cdot 7^2)^5 \div 7^3$

20 $(s^6 \cdot s)^2 \div s^4$

21 $(t^4 \cdot t^4)^4 \div t^4$

22 $\dfrac{(8^8 \cdot 8^3)^2}{(8^5)^4}$

23 $\dfrac{(3^4 \cdot 3^2)^4}{(3^5)^2}$

24 $\dfrac{(b \cdot b^3)^5}{(b^2)^4}$

25 $\dfrac{(h^6 \cdot h^4)^2}{(h^3)^5}$

26 $(q^5 \cdot q^2)^3 \div 5q^5$

27 $(c^7 \cdot c^3)^4 \div 6c^2$

28 $\dfrac{\left(\dfrac{2}{3}\right)^2 \cdot \left(\dfrac{2}{3}\right)^6}{\left(\dfrac{2}{3^2}\right)^3}$

29 $\dfrac{\left(\dfrac{x}{2}\right)^3 \cdot \left(\dfrac{x}{2}\right)^4}{\left(\dfrac{x^3}{2}\right)^2}$

1.4 The Power of a Product and the Power of a Quotient

Lesson Objectives

- Understand the power of a product property.
- Understand the power of a quotient property.
- Use properties of exponents to simplify expressions.

Understand the Power of a Product Property.

You can use the order of operations to evaluate the expression $(4 \cdot 5)^3$. First evaluate the expression inside the parentheses. Then use 20 as a factor 3 times.

$$(4 \cdot 5)^3 = (20)^3$$
$$= 20 \cdot 20 \cdot 20$$
$$= 8,000$$

You can also evaluate the expression $(4 \cdot 5)^3$ by using $(4 \cdot 5)$ as a factor 3 times.

$$(4 \cdot 5)^3 = (4 \cdot 5) \cdot (4 \cdot 5) \cdot (4 \cdot 5)$$
$$= \underbrace{(4 \cdot 4 \cdot 4)}_{\text{3 factors of } 4} \cdot \underbrace{(5 \cdot 5 \cdot 5)}_{\text{3 factors of } 5}$$
$$= 4^3 \cdot 5^3$$
$$= 64 \cdot 125$$
$$= 8,000$$

You can use the same method to evaluate $(h \cdot k)^4$.

$$(h \cdot k)^4 = (h \cdot k) \cdot (h \cdot k) \cdot (h \cdot k) \cdot (h \cdot k)$$
$$= \underbrace{(h \cdot h \cdot h \cdot h)}_{\text{4 factors of } h} \cdot \underbrace{(k \cdot k \cdot k \cdot k)}_{\text{4 factors of } k}$$
$$= h^4 \cdot k^4$$

For expressions with the same exponent, you can distribute the exponent to each base.
$$(a \cdot b)^m = a^m \cdot b^m$$

Similarly, to find the product of two algebraic expressions with the same exponent, you can multiply their bases.
$$a^m \cdot b^m = (a \cdot b)^m$$

Example 17 **Use the power of a product property to simplify numerical expressions.**

Simplify each expression. Write your answer in exponential notation.

a) $3^4 \cdot 7^4$

Solution

$3^4 \cdot 7^4 = (3 \cdot 7)^4$ Use the power of a product property.

$= 21^4$ Simplify.

b) $\left(-\dfrac{1}{3}\right)^5 \cdot \left(-\dfrac{2}{5}\right)^5$

Solution

$\left(-\dfrac{1}{3}\right)^5 \cdot \left(-\dfrac{2}{5}\right)^5 = \left[\left(-\dfrac{1}{3}\right) \cdot \left(-\dfrac{2}{5}\right)\right]^5$ Use the power of a product property.

$= \left(\dfrac{2}{15}\right)^5$ Simplify.

> You could also factor out -1 first
> to get $\left[(-1)\left(\dfrac{1}{3}\right)\right]^5 \cdot \left[(-1)\left(\dfrac{2}{5}\right)\right]^5$
> $= \left[(-1) \cdot (-1) \cdot \left(\dfrac{1}{3}\right) \cdot \left(\dfrac{2}{5}\right)\right]^5$
> $= \left[1 \cdot \left(\dfrac{2}{15}\right)\right]^5$
> $= \left(\dfrac{2}{15}\right)^5$

c) $(-2.4)^3 \cdot (0.5)^3$

Solution

$(-2.4)^3 \cdot (0.5)^3 = [(-2.4) \cdot (0.5)]^3$ Use the power of a product property.

$= (-1.2)^3$ Simplify.

$= -1.2^3$ The product of three negative numbers is a negative number.

Guided Practice

Simplify each expression. Write your answer in exponential notation.

1 $6^3 \cdot 7^3$

$6^3 \cdot 7^3 = \underline{\ ?\ }$ Use the power of a $\underline{\ ?\ }$ property.

$= \underline{\ ?\ }$ Simplify.

2 $\left(-\dfrac{5}{6}\right)^4 \cdot \left(-\dfrac{1}{4}\right)^4$

$\left(-\dfrac{5}{6}\right)^4 \cdot \left(-\dfrac{1}{4}\right)^4 = \underline{\ ?\ }$ Use the power of a $\underline{\ ?\ }$ property.

$= \underline{\ ?\ }$ Simplify.

3 $(1.8)^2 \cdot (0.75)^2$

$(1.8)^2 \cdot (0.75)^2 = \underline{\ ?\ }$ Use the power of a $\underline{\ ?\ }$ property.

$= \underline{\ ?\ }$ Simplify.

Example 18 **Use the power of a product property to multiply algebraic expressions.**

Simplify each expression. Write your answer in exponential notation.

a) $a^4 \cdot b^4$

Solution

$a^4 \cdot b^4 = (a \cdot b)^4$ Use the power of a product property.
      $= (ab)^4$ Simplify.

b) $(2r)^5 \cdot (7s)^5$

Solution

$(2r)^5 \cdot (7s)^5 = (2r \cdot 7s)^5$ Use the power of a product property.
              $= (14rs)^5$ Simplify.

c) $\left(\dfrac{1}{4x}\right)^7 (-20x^2)^7$

Solution

$$\left(\frac{1}{4x}\right)^7(-20x^2)^7 = \left[\left(\frac{1}{4x}\right)(-20x^2)\right]^7$$ Use the power of a product property.

$$= \left[\left(\frac{1}{4}\right)\cdot(-20)\cdot\left(\frac{1}{x}\right)\cdot(x^2)\right]^7$$ Regroup the numerals and unknowns.

$$= \left[\left(\frac{1}{4}\right)\cdot(-20)\cdot\left(\frac{x^2}{x}\right)\right]^7$$ Multiply $\dfrac{1}{x} \cdot x^2$ to get $\dfrac{x^2}{x}$.

$$= [(-5)\cdot(x^{2-1})]^7$$ Use the quotient of powers property.

$$= (-5x)^7$$ Simplify the base.

$$= -(5x)^7$$ Simplify.

Guided Practice

Simplify each expression. Write your answer in exponential notation.

4 $p^6 \cdot q^6$

$p^6 \cdot q^6 = \underline{\ ?\ }$ Use the power of a $\underline{\ ?\ }$ property.
     $= \underline{\ ?\ }$ Simplify.

5 $(3a)^4 \cdot (4b)^4$

$(3a)^4 \cdot (4b)^4 = \underline{\ ?\ }$ Use the power of a $\underline{\ ?\ }$ property.
        $= \underline{\ ?\ }$ Simplify.

6 $(-3y^2)^3 \cdot \left(\dfrac{1}{12y}\right)^3$

Understand the Power of a Quotient Property.

You can evaluate the expression $\left(\frac{2}{3}\right)^5$ by using $\frac{2}{3}$ as a factor 5 times.

$$\left(\frac{2}{3}\right)^5 = \frac{2}{3} \cdot \frac{2}{3} \cdot \frac{2}{3} \cdot \frac{2}{3} \cdot \frac{2}{3}$$

$$= \frac{\overbrace{2 \cdot 2 \cdot 2 \cdot 2 \cdot 2}^{\text{5 factors of } 2}}{\underbrace{3 \cdot 3 \cdot 3 \cdot 3 \cdot 3}_{\text{5 factors of } 3}}$$

$$= \frac{2^5}{3^5}$$

$$= \frac{32}{243}$$

You can use the same method to evaluate $\left(\frac{s}{t}\right)^4$.

$$\left(\frac{s}{t}\right)^4 = \frac{s}{t} \cdot \frac{s}{t} \cdot \frac{s}{t} \cdot \frac{s}{t}$$

$$= \frac{\overbrace{s \cdot s \cdot s \cdot s}^{\text{4 factors of } s}}{\underbrace{t \cdot t \cdot t \cdot t}_{\text{4 factors of } t}}$$

$$= \frac{s^4}{t^4}$$

> For expression with the same exponent, you can distribute the exponent to each base.
>
> $$\left(\frac{a}{b}\right)^m = \frac{a^m}{b^m}, \, b \neq 0$$
>
> Similarly, when you find the quotient of two algebraic expressions with the same exponent, you can divide their bases.
>
> $$\frac{a^m}{b^m} = \left(\frac{a}{b}\right)^m, \, b \neq 0$$

You can use this property to simplify algebraic expressions like the one shown below.

$$\left(\frac{2m}{6n}\right)^3 = \frac{(2m)^3}{(6n)^3}$$

$$= \frac{8m^3}{216n^3}$$

$$= \frac{m^3}{27n^3}$$

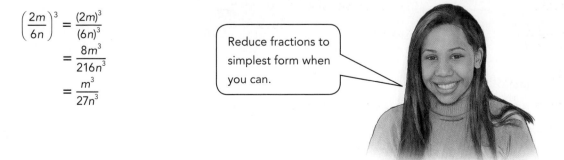

Reduce fractions to simplest form when you can.

Example 19 Use the power of a quotient property to simplify numerical expressions.

Simplify each expression. Write your answer in exponential notation.

a) $2^4 \div 6^4$

Solution

$$2^4 \div 6^4 = \left(\frac{2}{6}\right)^4 \qquad \text{Use the power of a quotient property.}$$

$$= \left(\frac{1}{3}\right)^4 \qquad \text{Simplify.}$$

b) $(-8)^5 \div (-2)^5$

Solution

$$(-8)^5 \div (-2)^5 = \left(\frac{-8}{-2}\right)^5 \qquad \text{Use the power of a quotient property.}$$

$$= 4^5 \qquad \text{Simplify.}$$

Guided Practice

Simplify each expression. Write your answer in exponential notation.

7 $2^5 \div 4^5$

$$2^5 \div 4^5 = \frac{?}{?}$$

$$= \underline{\quad ? \quad}$$

8 $(-9)^3 \div (-3)^3$

$$(-9)^3 \div (-3)^3 = \frac{?}{?}$$

$$= \underline{\quad ? \quad}$$

Example 20 Use the power of a quotient property to divide algebraic expressions.

Simplify each expression. Write your answer in exponential notation.

a) $p^6 \div q^6$

Solution

$$p^6 \div q^6 = \left(\frac{p}{q}\right)^6 \qquad \text{Use the power of a quotient property.}$$

b) $(5x)^9 \div (4y)^9$

Solution

$$(5x)^9 \div (4y)^9 = \left(\frac{5x}{4y}\right)^9 \qquad \text{Use the power of a quotient property.}$$

Guided Practice

Simplify each expression. Write your answer in exponential notation.

9 $x^4 \div y^4$

$x^4 \div y^4 = \dfrac{?}{?}$ Use the power of a __?__ property.

10 $(8p)^5 \div (3q)^5$

Use Properties of Exponents to Simplify Expressions.

You can use both the power of a product and quotient properties together to simplify some numerical and algebraic expressions.

Example 21   **Use exponent properties to simplify expressions.**

Simplify each expression. Write your answer in exponential notation.

a) $\dfrac{4^5 \cdot 4^3}{2^2 \cdot 2^6}$

Solution

$\dfrac{4^5 \cdot 4^3}{2^2 \cdot 2^6} = \dfrac{4^{5+3}}{2^{2+6}}$ Use the product of powers property.

$\phantom{\dfrac{4^5 \cdot 4^3}{2^2 \cdot 2^6}} = \dfrac{4^8}{2^8}$ Simplify.

$\phantom{\dfrac{4^5 \cdot 4^3}{2^2 \cdot 2^6}} = \left(\dfrac{4}{2}\right)^8$ Use the power of a quotient property.

$\phantom{\dfrac{4^5 \cdot 4^3}{2^2 \cdot 2^6}} = 2^8$ Simplify.

b) $\dfrac{5^5 \cdot 2^9 \cdot 5^4}{10^3}$

Solution

$\dfrac{5^5 \cdot 2^9 \cdot 5^4}{10^3} = \dfrac{5^{5+4} \cdot 2^9}{10^3}$ Use the product of powers property.

$\phantom{\dfrac{5^5 \cdot 2^9 \cdot 5^4}{10^3}} = \dfrac{5^9 \cdot 2^9}{10^3}$ Simplify.

$\phantom{\dfrac{5^5 \cdot 2^9 \cdot 5^4}{10^3}} = \dfrac{(5 \cdot 2)^9}{10^3}$ Use the power of a product property.

$\phantom{\dfrac{5^5 \cdot 2^9 \cdot 5^4}{10^3}} = \dfrac{10^9}{10^3}$ Simplify.

$\phantom{\dfrac{5^5 \cdot 2^9 \cdot 5^4}{10^3}} = 10^{9-3}$ Use the product of quotient property.

$\phantom{\dfrac{5^5 \cdot 2^9 \cdot 5^4}{10^3}} = 10^6$ Simplify.

Continue on next page

c) $\dfrac{(7^2)^3 \cdot 4^6}{2^6}$

Solution

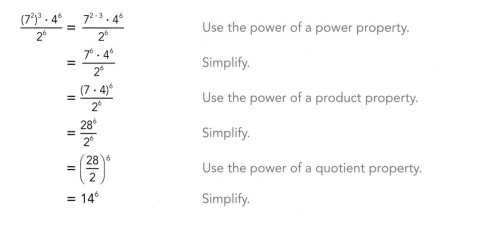

$\dfrac{(7^2)^3 \cdot 4^6}{2^6} = \dfrac{7^{2 \cdot 3} \cdot 4^6}{2^6}$ Use the power of a power property.

$= \dfrac{7^6 \cdot 4^6}{2^6}$ Simplify.

$= \dfrac{(7 \cdot 4)^6}{2^6}$ Use the power of a product property.

$= \dfrac{28^6}{2^6}$ Simplify.

$= \left(\dfrac{28}{2}\right)^6$ Use the power of a quotient property.

$= 14^6$ Simplify.

Guided Practice

Simplify each expression. Write your answer in exponential notation.

11 $\dfrac{6^4 \cdot 6^3}{3^2 \cdot 3^5}$

$\dfrac{6^4 \cdot 6^3}{3^2 \cdot 3^5} = \dfrac{?}{?}$ Use the __?__ of powers property.

$= \dfrac{?}{?}$ Simplify.

$= \dfrac{?}{?}$ Use the power of a __?__ property.

$= \underline{\ ?\ }$ Simplify.

12 $\dfrac{4^6 \cdot 3^8 \cdot 4^2}{12^5}$

$\dfrac{4^6 \cdot 3^8 \cdot 4^2}{12^5} = \dfrac{?}{?}$

$= \dfrac{?}{?}$

$= \dfrac{?}{?}$

$= \dfrac{?}{?}$

$= \underline{\ ?\ }$

$= \underline{\ ?\ }$

13 $\dfrac{(9^4)^2 \cdot 2^8}{3^8}$

$\dfrac{(9^4)^2 \cdot 2^8}{3^8} = \dfrac{?}{?}$

$= \dfrac{?}{?}$

$= \dfrac{?}{?}$

$= \underline{\ ?\ }$

$= \underline{\ ?\ }$

14 $\dfrac{2^5 \cdot 3^{12} \cdot 2^7}{6^7}$

15 $\dfrac{(25^3)^2 \cdot 7^6}{5^6}$

Practice 1.4

Simplify each expression. Write your answer in exponential notation.

1 $5^4 \cdot 6^4$

2 $5.4^3 \cdot 4.5^3$

3 $2^5 \cdot 10^5$

4 $a^3 \cdot b^3$

5 $(2x)^5 \cdot (3y)^5$

6 $(2.5a)^6 \cdot (1.6b)^6$

7 $\left(-\dfrac{1}{3}\right)^4 \cdot \left(-\dfrac{2}{5}\right)^4$

8 $9^2 \div 3^2$

9 $10^6 \div 5^6$

10 $2.8^7 \div 0.7^7$

11 $15^2 \div 25^2$

12 $7.2^9 \div 2.4^9$

13 $(3.3x)^9 \div (1.1y)^9$

14 $(-6)^8 \div (-2)^8$

15 $s^5 \div r^5$

16 $(3a)^6 \div (2b)^6$

17 $(h^2 k^5)^4$

18 $\left(\dfrac{32m^6}{4n^4}\right)^2$

19 $\dfrac{9^2 \cdot 9^7}{3^5 \cdot 3^4}$

20 $\dfrac{6^5 \cdot 2^3 \cdot 6^4}{12^3}$

21 $\dfrac{(5^4)^2 \cdot 6^8}{10^8}$

22 $\dfrac{(6^3)^3 \cdot 4^9}{8^9}$

23 $\dfrac{24^9}{4^3 \cdot 6^2 \cdot 4^6}$

24 $\dfrac{9^{12}}{(3^3)^3 \cdot 3^3}$

25 *Math Journal* Charles thinks that $a^3 \cdot b^3 = ab^6$. Is he correct? Why?

Solve. Show your work.

26 At the beginning of January, Mr. Howard gives his niece $1 to start a savings account. For each month that she can triple the amount in the account, Mr. Howard will double the amount in the account at the end of each month. How much does Mr. Howard's niece have in her account at the beginning of May?

Lesson Objectives

- Understand zero and negative exponents.
- Simplify expressions involving zero and negative exponents.

Hands-On Activity

Materials:
- graphing calculator

UNDERSTAND THE ZERO EXPONENT

Work individually.

STEP 1 Use the power of a quotient property to simplify each expression. Write the quotient as an exponent.

Expression	Exponent
$\dfrac{3^5}{3^2}$	3^3
$\dfrac{3^5}{3^3}$	?
$\dfrac{3^5}{3^4}$	?
$\dfrac{3^5}{3^5}$	?

What expression did you write for $\dfrac{3^5}{3^5}$? What exponent did you use?

STEP 2 In factored form, the quotient $\dfrac{3^5}{3^5}$ is $\dfrac{3 \cdot 3 \cdot 3 \cdot 3 \cdot 3}{3 \cdot 3 \cdot 3 \cdot 3 \cdot 3}$. If you divide out all the common factors in the numerator and denominator, what is the value of $\dfrac{3^5}{3^5}$?

STEP 3 Based on your findings, what can you conclude about the value of 3^0?

STEP 4 Make a prediction about the value of any nonzero number raised to the zero power. Then, use a calculator to check your prediction for several numbers. For example, to raise the number -2 to the zero power, you can enter these keystrokes:

Press (− 2) ^ 0 ENTER .

Does your prediction hold true?

Understand the Zero Exponent.

You have seen that when a number such as 4 is raised to the zero power, its value is 1.
In fact, any number except 0 raised to the zero power is equal to 1.

A nonzero number raised to the zero power is equal to 1.
$$a^0 = 1, a \neq 0$$

Think Math

Explain why the statement $a^0 = 1$ cannot be true when $a = 0$.

Example 22 Simplify expressions involving numbers raised to the zero power.

Simplify each expression and evaluate where applicable.

a) $7^3 \cdot 7^0$

Solution

$7^3 \cdot 7^0 = 7^3 \cdot 1$ Raise to the zero power.
$ = 7^3$ Simplify.
$ = 343$ Evaluate.

You could also use the product of powers property to solve.

$7^3 \cdot 7^0$
$= 7^{3+0}$ Apply the product of powers property.
$= 7^3$ Simplify.
$= 343$ Evaluate.

b) $1 \cdot 10^2 + 2 \cdot 10^1 + 3 \cdot 10^0$

Solution

$1 \cdot 10^2 + 2 \cdot 10^1 + 3 \cdot 10^0 = 1 \cdot 100 + 2 \cdot 10 + 3 \cdot 1$
$ = 123$

Math Note

Because $10^0 = 1$, every place in a place value table can be written as a power of 10.
$1,000 = 10^3$
$100 = 10^2$
$10 = 10^1$
$1 = 10^0$

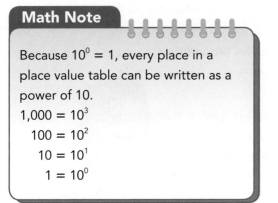

Continue on next page

c) $\dfrac{4^2 \cdot 4^6}{4^8}$

Solution

$\dfrac{4^2 \cdot 4^6}{4^8} = \dfrac{4^{2+6}}{4^8}$ Use the product of powers property.

$= \dfrac{4^8}{4^8}$ Simplify.

$= 4^{8-8}$ Use the quotient of powers property.

$= 4^0$ Simplify.

$= 1$ Evaluate.

d) $(a^4 \div a^0) \cdot a^3$

Solution

$(a^4 \div a^0) \cdot a^3 = a^4 \div 1 \cdot a^3$ Raise to the zero power.

$= a^4 \cdot a^3$ Simplify.

$= a^{4+3}$ Use the product of powers property.

$= a^7$ Simplify.

Guided Practice

Simplify each expression and evaluate where applicable.

1 $1.6^0 \div 0.4^2$

$1.6^0 \div 0.4^2 = \underline{\ ?\ } \div \underline{\ ?\ }$ Raise to the $\underline{\ ?\ }$ power.

$= \dfrac{?}{?}$ Simplify.

$= \underline{\ ?\ }$ Evaluate.

2 $\dfrac{3 \cdot 3^9}{3^{10}}$

$\dfrac{3 \cdot 3^9}{3^{10}} = \dfrac{?}{?}$ Use the $\underline{\ ?\ }$ of powers property.

$= \dfrac{?}{?}$ Simplify.

$= \underline{\ ?\ }$ Use the $\underline{\ ?\ }$ of powers property.

$= \underline{\ ?\ }$ Simplify.

$= \underline{\ ?\ }$ Evaluate.

3 $\dfrac{t^0 \cdot t^7}{t^5}$

Alternatively, you can also apply the product of powers property to the expression $t^0 \cdot t^7$ to get $t^{0+7} = t^7$.

Understand Negative Exponents.

You can use the quotient of powers property to understand the meaning of a number raised to a negative exponent.

 # Hands-On Activity

UNDERSTAND NEGATIVE EXPONENTS

Work individually.

STEP 1 Use the quotient of powers property to simplify each expression. Write the quotient in exponential notation.

Expression	Power
$\dfrac{4^5}{4^3}$	4^2
$\dfrac{4^5}{4^4}$	?
$\dfrac{4^5}{4^5}$	?
$\dfrac{4^5}{4^6}$	?
$\dfrac{4^5}{4^7}$	?

What expression did you write for $\dfrac{4^5}{4^6}$? What exponent did you use?

STEP 2 In factored form, the quotient $\dfrac{4^5}{4^6}$ is $\dfrac{4 \cdot 4 \cdot 4 \cdot 4 \cdot 4}{4 \cdot 4 \cdot 4 \cdot 4 \cdot 4 \cdot 4}$. If you divide out all the common factors in the numerator and denominator, what is the value of $\dfrac{4^5}{4^6}$?

STEP 3 Repeat **STEP 2** for $\dfrac{4^5}{4^7}$. What is the value of $\dfrac{4^5}{4^7}$?

Math Journal Suppose a represents any nonzero number. How would you write a^{-3} using a positive exponent?

For any nonzero real number a and any integer n,

$$a^{-n} = \frac{1}{a^n}, \ a \neq 0$$

Example 23 Write using a positive exponent.

Simplify each expression. Write your answer using a positive exponent.

a) $13^{-4} \cdot 13^7$

Solution

Method 1

$13^{-4} \cdot 13^7$

$= \dfrac{1}{13^4} \cdot 13^7$ Write using a positive exponent.

$= \dfrac{13^7}{13^4}$ Simplify.

$= 13^{7-4}$ Use the quotient of powers property.

$= 13^3$ Simplify.

Method 2

$13^{-4} \cdot 13^7$

$= 13^{-4+7}$ Use the product of powers property.

$= 13^3$ Simplify.

b) $\dfrac{x^{-7}}{x^4}$

Solution

$\dfrac{x^{-7}}{x^4} = \dfrac{1}{x^7} \cdot \dfrac{1}{x^4}$ Write using a positive exponent.

$= \dfrac{1}{x^{11}}$ Simplify.

c) $9m \div 3m^{-2}$

Solution

$9m \div 3m^{-2}$

$= \dfrac{9m}{3m^{-2}}$ Write the division as a fraction.

$= \dfrac{9}{3} \cdot \dfrac{m}{m^{-2}}$ Rewrite the fraction as the product of two fractions.

$= 3 \cdot m^{1-(-2)}$ Use the quotient of powers property.

$= 3m^3$ Simplify.

Math Note

For $3m^{-2}$, only m is raised to the power of -2. For $(3m)^{-2}$, both 3 and m are raised to the power of -2.

Guided Practice

Simplify each expression and evaluate where applicable.

4 $2.5^{-7} \div 2.5^{-4}$

$2.5^{-7} \div 2.5^{-4} = \underline{\quad?\quad}$ Use the $\underline{\quad?\quad}$ of powers property.

$= \underline{\quad?\quad}$ Simplify.

$= \dfrac{?}{?}$ Write using a $\underline{\quad?\quad}$ exponent.

$= \underline{\quad?\quad}$ Evaluate.

5 $\dfrac{(-6)^3}{(-6)^4}$

$\dfrac{(-6)^3}{(-6)^4} = \underline{\quad?\quad}$ Use the $\underline{\quad?\quad}$ of powers property.

$= \underline{\quad?\quad}$ Simplify.

$= \dfrac{?}{?}$ Write using a $\underline{\quad?\quad}$ exponent.

$= \dfrac{?}{?}$ Simplify.

Simplify each expression. Write your answer using a positive exponent.

6 $14a^{-5} \div (7a \cdot 2a^{-4})$

$14a^{-5} \div (7a \cdot 2a^{-4}) = \dfrac{?}{?}$ Write the expression as a $\underline{\quad?\quad}$.

$= \dfrac{?}{?} \cdot \dfrac{?}{?}$ Rewrite the fraction as the product of two fractions.

$= \underline{\quad?\quad} \cdot \underline{\quad?\quad}$ Use the $\underline{\quad?\quad}$ of powers property to the denominator.

$= \underline{\quad?\quad} \cdot \underline{\quad?\quad}$ Use the quotient of powers property to the resulting new fraction.

$= \underline{\quad?\quad}$ Simplify.

$= \underline{\quad?\quad}$ Write using a $\underline{\quad?\quad}$ exponent.

> Usually you should write your answer using a positive exponent unless asked to use a negative exponent.

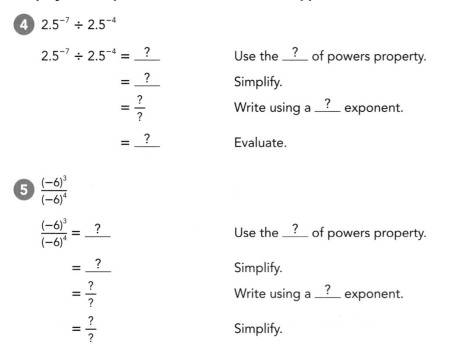

Simplify each expression and evaluate.

1 $8^3 \cdot 8^0$

2 $5^4 \cdot (-5)^0$

3 $\left(\dfrac{1}{3}\right)^4 \cdot \left(\dfrac{1}{3}\right)^0$

4 $7 \cdot 10^3 + 4^2 \cdot 10^2 + 5 \cdot 10^0$

5 $(2.3) \cdot 10^2 + 5 \cdot 10^1 + 1 \cdot 10^0$

6 $\dfrac{7^4 \cdot 7^5}{7^9}$

7 $(9^{-3})^0 \cdot 5^2$

8 $\dfrac{(6^{-3})^{-2} \cdot 8^6}{48^6}$

Simplify each expression. Write your answer using a negative exponent.

9 $7^3 \cdot 7^{-4}$

10 $\dfrac{(-5)^{-2}}{(-5)^3}$

11 $\left(\dfrac{3}{4}\right) \div \left[\left(\dfrac{3}{4}\right)^0 \cdot \left(\dfrac{3}{4}\right)^2\right]$

12 $\left(\dfrac{2}{5}\right)^{-4} \cdot \left(\dfrac{2}{5}\right)^{-1} \div \left(\dfrac{2}{5}\right)^{-3}$

13 $\dfrac{x^0}{x^2 \cdot x^3}$

14 $\dfrac{4h^{-5} \cdot 6h^{-2}}{3h^{-3}}$

Simplify each expression. Write your answer using a positive exponent.

15 $1.2^0 \div 1.8^2$

16 $5.2^{-3} \div 2.6^{-3}$

17 $\dfrac{(-3)^{-4}}{(-3)^2}$

18 $\left(\dfrac{5}{6}\right)^{-4} \cdot \left(\dfrac{5}{6}\right)^{-2} \div \left(\dfrac{5}{6}\right)^{-3}$

19 $\dfrac{9k^{-1} \cdot 2k^{-3}}{27k^{-6}}$

20 $\dfrac{c^{-4} \cdot c^{12}}{c^{-7}}$

Evaluate each numeric expression.

21 $\dfrac{7^{-2} \cdot 7^0}{8^3 \cdot 8^{-5}}$

22 $\dfrac{(7^{-2})^2 \cdot 9^{-4}}{21^{-4}}$

23 $\dfrac{10^0}{2^{-2} \cdot (5^{-1})^2}$

24 $\dfrac{(3^6)^{-2}}{6^{-9}(-2^{10})}$

Simplify each algebraic expression.

25 $\left(\dfrac{7m^3}{-49n^0}\right)^{-1}$

26 $\dfrac{8r^2s}{4s^{-3}r^4}$

1.6 Real-World Problems: Squares and Cubes

Lesson Objectives

- Evaluate square roots and cube roots of positive real numbers.
- Solve real-world problems that use equations involving variables that are squared or cubed.

Evaluate Square Roots of Positive Real Numbers.

When you multiply a number by itself, you are squaring that number, or raising it to the second power. For example, $3^2 = 9$ and $(-3)^2 = 9$.

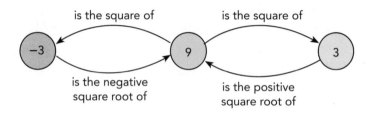

You can use $\sqrt{9} = 3$ to indicate the positive square root of 9, and $-\sqrt{9} = -3$ to indicate the negative square root of 9.

Not every number has a square root. For example, -9 has no square root, because there are no two identical factors of -9. Both $(-3)^2$ and 3^2 are equal to 9.

Example 24 **Find the square roots of a number.**

Find the two square roots of 49.

Solution

$\sqrt{49} = 7$ 7 is the positive square root of 49 since $7 \cdot 7 = 49$.

and

$-\sqrt{49} = -7$ -7 is the negative square root of 49 since $(-7) \cdot (-7) = 49$.

> **Caution** ////////
> Because $\sqrt{49}$ is the positive square root of 49, $\sqrt{49} \neq -7$

Guided Practice

Solve. Show your work.

1 Find the two square roots of 169.

$\sqrt{169} =$ __?__   __?__ is the positive square root of 169 since __?__ · __?__ = 169.

and

$-\sqrt{169} =$ __?__   __?__ is the negative square root of 169 since __?__ · __?__ = 169.

Evaluate Cube Roots of Positive Real Numbers.

When you use a number as a factor three times, you are cubing that number, or raising it to the third power. For example, $4^3 = 64$.

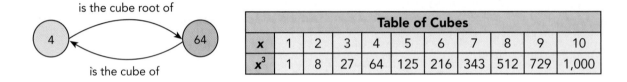

is the cube root of

4   64

is the cube of

Table of Cubes									
x	1	2	3	4	5	6	7	8	9	10
x^3	1	8	27	64	125	216	343	512	729	1,000

For example, $\sqrt[3]{64} = 4$, because $4 \cdot 4 \cdot 4 = 64$. So, 4 is the cube root of 64.

Notice that -4 is not a cube root of 64, because $(-4)^3 = -64$. It is a cube root of -64. So every number, positive, negative, or 0, has exactly one cube root.

Example 25   **Find the cube root.**

Find the cube root of 343.

Solution

$\sqrt[3]{343} = \sqrt[3]{7^3}$ 7 is a cube root since $7 \cdot 7 \cdot 7 = 343$.

$\quad\quad\quad = 7$ Simplify.

Guided Practice

Solve. Show your work.

2 Find the cube root of $\frac{1}{729}$.

$\sqrt[3]{\dfrac{1}{729}} =$ __?__   __?__ is the cube root since __?__ · __?__ · __?__ = $\dfrac{1}{729}$.

$\quad\quad\quad = $ __?__   Simplify.

Solve Equations Involving Squares and Cubes of Variables.

To solve equations like $x^2 = 25$ and $y^3 = 125$, you need to find the value or values of the variable that make each equation a true statement. You can do that by finding the square root or the cube root of both sides of the equation.

Example 26 **Solve an equation involving a variable that is squared or cubed.**

Solve each equation.

a) $x^2 = 4.41$

Solution

> Since $4 = 2^2$, use a guess-and-check strategy to find the square root of 4.41, starting with 2.1, 2.2, and so on.

$x^2 = 4.41$
$x^2 = 2.1^2$ or $(-2.1)^2$ $4.41 = 2.1 \cdot 2.1$ and $4.41 = (-2.1) \cdot (-2.1)$.
 $x = 2.1$ or -2.1 Show both the positive and negative square roots.

b) $x^3 = 1,000$

Solution

$x^3 = 1,000$
$x^3 = 10^3$
$\sqrt[3]{x^3} = \sqrt[3]{10^3}$ Solve for x by taking the cube root of both sides.
 $x = 10$ Show the cube root.

Guided Practice

Solve. Show your work.

3 $x^2 = 2.25$

$x^2 = 2.25$

$x^2 = \underline{}$ or $\underline{}$ $2.25 = \underline{} \cdot \underline{}$ or $(\underline{}) \cdot (\underline{})$

 $x = \underline{}$ or $\underline{}$ Show both the $\underline{}$ and $\underline{}$ roots.

Solve. Show your work.

4 🖩 $x^3 = \dfrac{1}{8}$

$x^3 = \dfrac{1}{8}$

$x^3 = \dfrac{?}{}$

$\dfrac{?}{} = \dfrac{?}{}$ Solve for x by taking the $\underline{}$ root of both sides.

$x = \underline{}$ Show the $\underline{}$ root.

Solve Real-World Problems Involving Squares and Cubes.

You can use equations that involve squares and cubes to solve real-world problems. Sometimes, only one of the square root solutions makes sense for the problem.

For example, suppose an artist makes a cube-shaped sculpture. The area of one face of the sculpture is 144 square inches, and the volume of the sculpture is 1,728 cubic inches. To find the length of an edge of the sculpture, you can write and solve either of the following equations.

Area = 144 in²

$x^2 = 144$ $x^3 = 1{,}728$

The first equation has a positive and a negative solution, but because lengths are always positive, only the positive solution makes sense.

Volume = 1,728 in³

Example 27 **Solve a real-world problem involving squares of unknowns.**

🖩 Theresa wants to put a piece of carpet on the floor of her living room. The floor is a square with an area of 182.25 square feet. How long should the piece of carpet be on each side?

Solution

Let the length of each side of the carpet be x feet.

$x^2 = 182.25$ Translate into an equation.

$\sqrt{x^2} = \sqrt{182.25}$ Solve for x by taking the positive square root of both sides.

$x = 13.5$ Use a calculator to find the square root.

Think Math

Why does the negative square root of 182.25 not make sense for this scenario? Explain.

The length of each side of the carpet is 13.5 feet.

Guided Practice

Solve. Show your work.

5 A square field has an area of 98.01 square meters. Find the length of each side of the field.

Let the length of each side be x meters.

$x^2 =$ __?__   Translate into an equation.

__?__ = __?__   Solve for x by taking the positive __?__ root of both sides.

$x =$ __?__ m   Use a calculator to find the square root.

The length of each side is __?__ meters.

Example 28 **Solve a real-world problem involving cubes of variables.**

 A fully inflated beach ball contains 288π cubic inches of air. What is the radius of the beach ball?

> A beach ball is a sphere, so you can use the formula for the volume of a sphere.
>
> $V = \dfrac{4}{3}\pi r^3$
>
> By substituting 288π for V, you can solve for r.

Solution

Let the radius of the beach ball be r inches.

$\dfrac{4}{3}\pi r^3 = 288\pi$ Substitute values.

$\dfrac{3}{4} \cdot \dfrac{4}{3}\pi r^3 = \dfrac{3}{4} \cdot 288\pi$ Multiply both sides by $\dfrac{3}{4}$.

$\pi r^3 = 216\pi$ Simplify.

$\dfrac{\pi r^3}{\pi} = \dfrac{216\pi}{\pi}$ Divide both sides by π.

$r^3 = 216$ Simplify.

$\sqrt[3]{r^3} = \sqrt[3]{216}$ Solve for x by taking the cube root of both sides.

$r = \sqrt[3]{216}$ Simplify.

$r = 6$ in.   Use a calculator to find the cube root.

The radius of the beach ball is 6 inches.

Think Math

288π cubic inches is an exact volume. What is an approximate volume of the beach ball? Explain.

Guided Practice

Solve. Show your work.

6 Robin bought a crystal globe that has a volume of $1{,}774\frac{2}{3}\pi$ cubic centimeters. Find the radius of the crystal globe.

Math Note

Remember that you can express areas and volumes of circles and spheres in terms of π to simplify calculations.

Let the radius of the crystal globe be r centimeters.

$\frac{4}{3}\pi r^3 = \underline{\ ?\ }$ ⟶ Substitute values.

$\underline{\ ?\ } \cdot \underline{\ ?\ } = \underline{\ ?\ } \cdot \underline{\ ?\ }$ ⟶ Multiply both sides by $\underline{\ ?\ }$.

$\underline{\ ?\ } = \underline{\ ?\ }$ ⟶ Simplify.

$\frac{?}{?} = \frac{?}{?}$ ⟶ Divide both sides by $\underline{\ ?\ }$.

$\underline{\ ?\ } = \underline{\ ?\ }$ ⟶ Simplify.

$\underline{\ ?\ } = \underline{\ ?\ }$ ⟶ Solve for x by taking the $\underline{\ ?\ }$ root of both sides.

$\underline{\ ?\ } = \underline{\ ?\ }$ ⟶ Simplify.

$r = \underline{\ ?\ }$ cm ⟶ Use a calculator to find the cube root.

The radius of the crystal globe is $\underline{\ ?\ }$ centimeters.

7 A spherical watermelon has a volume of 562.5π cubic centimeters. What is the diameter of the watermelon?

Volume
$= 562.5\pi$ cm^3

diameter

Let the radius of the watermelon be r centimeters.

$\frac{4}{3}\pi r^3 = \underline{\ ?\ }$ ⟶ Substitute values.

$\underline{\ ?\ } \cdot \underline{\ ?\ } = \underline{\ ?\ } \cdot \underline{\ ?\ }$ ⟶ Multiply both sides by $\underline{\ ?\ }$.

$\underline{\ ?\ } = \underline{\ ?\ }$ ⟶ Simplify.

$\frac{?}{?} = \frac{?}{?}$ ⟶ Divide both sides by $\underline{\ ?\ }$.

$\underline{\ ?\ } = \underline{\ ?\ }$ ⟶ Simplify.

$\underline{\ ?\ } = \underline{\ ?\ }$ ⟶ Solve for x by taking the $\underline{\ ?\ }$ root of both sides.

$\underline{\ ?\ } = \underline{\ ?\ }$ ⟶ Simplify.

$r = \underline{\ ?\ }$ cm ⟶ Use a calculator to find the cube root.

Diameter $= 2 \cdot r$

$ = 2 \cdot \underline{\ ?\ }$ ⟶ Substitute values.

$ = \underline{\ ?\ }$ cm ⟶ Evaluate.

The diameter of the watermelon is $\underline{\ ?\ }$ centimeters.

Practice 1.6

Find the two square roots of each number. Round your answer to the nearest tenth when you can.

1 25

2 64

3 🖩 80

4 🖩 120

Find the cube root of each number. Round your answer to the nearest tenth when you can.

5 512

6 1,000

7 🖩 999

8 $\frac{64}{343}$

🖩 **Solve each equation involving a variable that is squared. Round your answer to the nearest tenth when you can.**

9 $a^2 = 46.24$

10 $b^2 = \frac{25}{49}$

11 $m^2 = 196$

12 $n^2 = 350$

🖩 **Solve each equation involving a variable that is cubed. Write fractions in simplest form, and round decimal answers to the nearest tenth.**

13 $x^3 = 74.088$

14 $x^3 = \frac{216}{729}$

15 $x^3 = 1,728$

16 $x^3 = 2,500$

🖩 **Solve. Show your work. Round to the nearest tenth.**

17 The volume of a spherical tank is 790.272π cubic feet. What is the diameter of the container?

Volume = 790.272π ft^3

18 An orchard planted on a square plot of land has 3,136 apple trees. If each tree requires an area of 4 square meters to grow, find the length of each side of the plot of land.

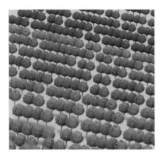

19 Mr. Berman deposited $2,500 in a savings account. Three years later there was $2,812.16 in the savings account. Use the formula $A = P(1 + r)^n$ to find the rate of interest, r percent, that he was paid. A represents the final amount of the investment, P is the original principal, and n is the number of years it was invested.

Brain @ Work

1 Evaluate $\dfrac{4^3 \cdot 10^4}{5^2}$ without using a calculator.

2 Find the values of x and y that make the equation $\dfrac{81x^4 \cdot 16y^4}{[(2y)^2]^2} = 1{,}296$ true.

3 Use each of the numbers 1 to 9 exactly once to fill in the blanks.

$$\dfrac{3^{?-?} \cdot (? + ?)^{?-?}}{\sqrt{? + ?}} = 3^{\frac{?}{?}}$$

4 Jeremy wants to measure the radius of a marble. He uses a tank and filled the tank with 360 identical marbles shown below. If the volume of the tank is 9,720 cubic inches, find the radius of each marble.

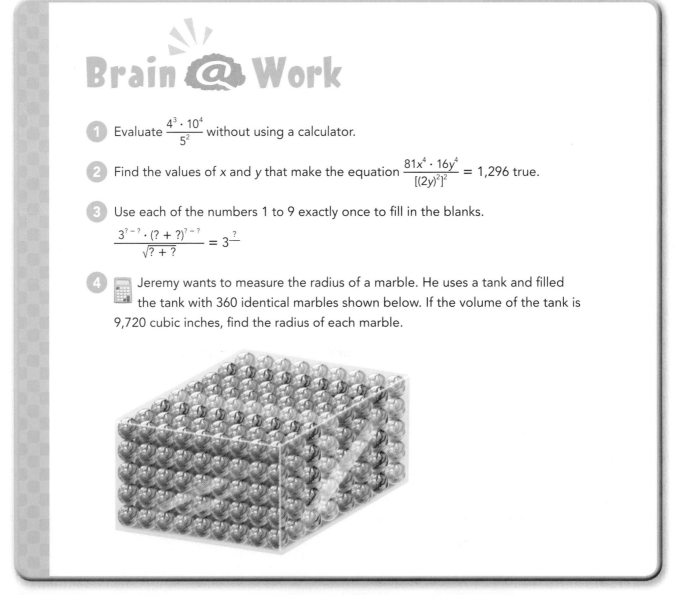

Chapter Wrap Up

Concept Map

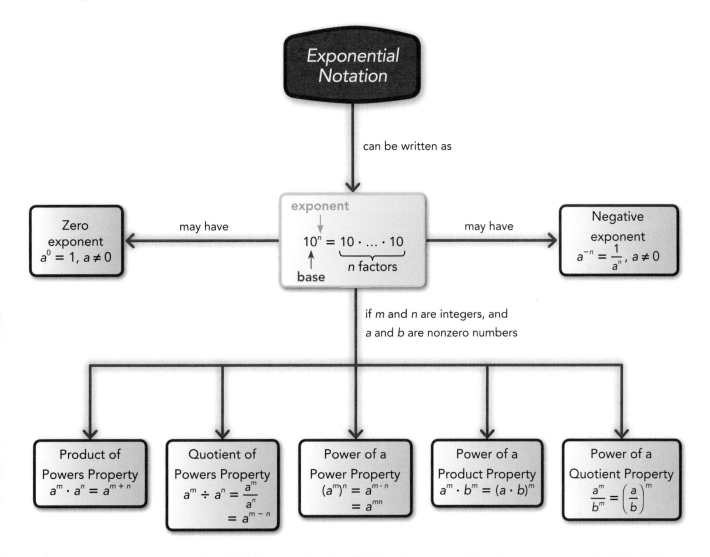

Key Concepts

▶ You can use exponential notation to show repeated multiplication of the same factor. **Example:** $2^3 = 2 \cdot 2 \cdot 2$

▶ A number written in exponential notation has a base and an exponent. The exponent represents how many times the base is used as a factor. **Example:** 9^5, 9 is the base and 5 is the exponent.

▶ You can use properties of exponents to simplify expressions written in exponential notation that involve numbers and variables.

Chapter Review/Test

Concepts and Skills

Identify the base and exponent in each expression.

1 $\left(-\dfrac{1}{5}\right)^{-3}$

2 -0.92^4

Tell whether each statement is correct. If it is incorrect, state the reason.

3 $-0.7^3 = -0.7 \cdot 0.7 \cdot 0.7$

4 $5^{-4} = (-5) \cdot (-5) \cdot (-5) \cdot (-5)$

Write in exponential notation.

5 $2 \cdot 2 \cdot 2 \cdot 2$

6 $4.8 \cdot 4.8$

7 $\dfrac{1}{2} \cdot \dfrac{1}{2} \cdot \dfrac{1}{2}$

8 $c \cdot c \cdot c \cdot c \cdot c \cdot c$

9 $\dfrac{3}{4}k \cdot \dfrac{3}{4}k \cdot \dfrac{3}{4}k \cdot \dfrac{3}{4}k$

10 $(-1.2)(-1.2)(-1.2)(-1.2)$

Write the prime factorization of each number in exponential notation.

11 3,780

12 27,720

Expand and evaluate each expressions.

13 $(-6)^2$

14 1.1^2

15 10^5

16 $\left(\dfrac{2}{3}\right)^3$

Simplify each expression. Write your answer using a positive exponent.

17 $(-3)^{-1} \cdot (-3)^0$

18 $\left(\dfrac{5}{6}\right)^4 \cdot \left(\dfrac{5}{6}\right)^3$

19 $5m^3n^4 \cdot 4m^5n^2$

20 $\left(\dfrac{7}{8}\right) \div \left(\dfrac{7}{8}\right)^3$

21 $(-h)^9 \div (-h)^{15}$

22 $x^8z^5 \div x^3z^9$

23 $25p^6q^9 \div 45p^8q^4$

24 $\left[\left(\dfrac{2}{3}\right)^2 \cdot \left(\dfrac{2}{3}\right)^{-1}\right]^3$

25 $40c^5d^3 \div 10c^9d^2$

26 $\left(\dfrac{72b^{-1}}{32c^{-1}}\right)^{-2}$

27 $\dfrac{(9^{-2})^{-2} \cdot 2^2}{9^2}$

28 $\dfrac{6^8 \cdot 56^{-3}}{6^5 \cdot 7^{-3}}$

29 $\dfrac{42^{-1}}{(2^0)^{12} \cdot 21^{-1}}$

30 $\dfrac{(3^5 \cdot 3^4)^2}{(3^3)^6}$

Solve each equation involving a variable that is squared.

31 $r^2 = 256$

32 $c^2 = \dfrac{121}{169}$

🔲 **Solve each equation involving a variable that is cubed.**

33 $x^3 = 32.768$

34 $t^3 = -\dfrac{27}{343}$

35 The expanded form of a number is $5 \cdot 10^1 + 8 \cdot 10^0 + 1 \cdot 10^{-1} + 9 \cdot 10^{-2}$. What is this number in standard form?

36 The pattern of triangles shown is called the Sierpinski's gasket.

a) Find a pattern in the number of shaded triangles.

b) How many shaded triangles will be in the fifth diagram of this pattern? Write an exponential expression for this number.

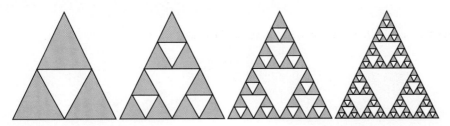

Problem Solving

Solve. Show your work. Round your answer to the nearest tenth.

37 🔲 The Reina Sofia Museum in Spain has a glass elevator. The floor of the elevator shaft is a square with an area of about 42.25 square feet. Find the length of a side of the floor.

38 🔲 Earth's volume is approximately 1,083,210,000,000 cubic kilometers. What is the diameter of the Earth in kilometers?

39 🔲 Koch's snowflake is a pattern that starts with an equilateral triangle. Then, in successive images, each line segment is replaced by 4 line segments, as shown below. How many line segments make up the seventh image of this pattern? Write this number in exponential form and evaluate.

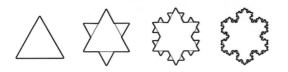

Scientific Notation

How far away are the stars?

When you look at the stars through a telescope, you are seeing light that has traveled an enormous distance. Proxima Centauri, the star that is closest to Earth after the Sun, is about 39,900,000,000,000 kilometers from Earth. Numbers like this one are so large that scientists have invented a method called scientific notation to write them. In this chapter, you will use scientific notation to describe and compare very large and very small numbers.

BIG IDEA

▶ Scientific notation is a way of writing numbers that makes it easier to work with very large or very small numbers.

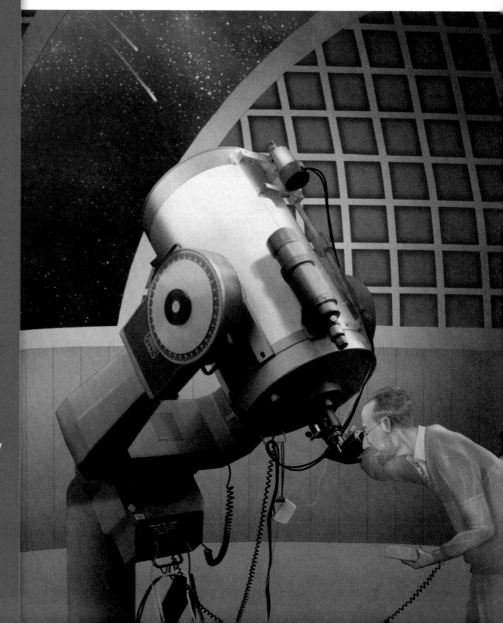

Recall Prior Knowledge

Multiplying and dividing decimals by positive powers of 10

When you multiply a decimal by a positive power of 10, the decimal point moves to the right. For example,

$1.47 \cdot 10 = 14.7$ Multiply by 10^1.

$1.47 \cdot 100 = 147$ Multiply by 10^2.

$-1.47 \cdot 100 = -147$ Multiply by 10^2.

When you divide a decimal by a positive power of 10, the decimal point moves to the left. For example,

$1.2 \div 10 = 0.12$ Divide by 10^1.

$1.2 \div 100 = 0.012$ Divide by 10^2.

$-1.2 \div 100 = -0.012$ Divide by 10^2.

This method works for negative and positive decimals.

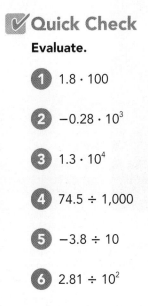

☑ Quick Check

Evaluate.

1 $1.8 \cdot 100$

2 $-0.28 \cdot 10^3$

3 $1.3 \cdot 10^4$

4 $74.5 \div 1{,}000$

5 $-3.8 \div 10$

6 $2.81 \div 10^2$

Understanding Scientific Notation

Lesson Objectives

- Understand the need for scientific notation.
- Write numbers in scientific notation or in standard form.
- Compare numbers in scientific notation.

Vocabulary

scientific notation

coefficient

standard form

Understand the Need for Scientific Notation.

Astronomers have to work with some very large and very small numbers. For instance, the average distance from Earth to the moon is approximately 380,000,000 meters. Light from the moon travels to Earth at a speed of approximately 300,000,000 meters per second. Light moves so fast through space that it travels 1 meter in about $\dfrac{1}{300,000,000}$ of a second. When written as a decimal, that is 0.00000000333… second.

380,000,000 m

It is not easy to keep track of all the zeros in such large and small numbers. For this reason, scientists use scientific notation to represent and compare very large and very small numbers such as these.

Think Math

Describe some real-world quantities that can be expressed in scientific notation.

Write Numbers in Scientific Notation.

You can write a very large number or a very small number in standard form as the product of a number between 1 and 10, inclusive of 1, and an integer power of ten:

$$300,000,000 = 3 \cdot 100,000,000$$
$$= 3 \cdot 10^8$$

$$0.00000000333 = 3.33 \cdot \frac{1}{1,000,000,000}$$
$$= 3.33 \cdot 10^{-9}$$

Math Note

For numbers greater than or equal to 10, use a positive exponent.

For positive numbers less than 1, use a negative exponent.

Numbers written this way are said to be in scientific notation.

Any number can be written in scientific notation by expressing it in two parts: a **coefficient** A where $1 \leq A < 10$, and a power of 10 where the exponent n is an integer.

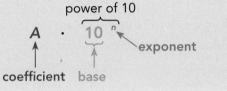

Example 1   **Write numbers in scientific notation.**

Tell whether each number is written correctly in scientific notation. If it is incorrectly written, state the reason.

a)   A horse-chestnut has a diameter of about $2 \cdot 10^0$ centimeters.

b)   Neptune is about $4.488 \cdot 10^9$ kilometers from the Sun.

c)   The approximate wavelength of infrared light is $0.01 \cdot 10^{-5}$ meter.

d)   A football field (excluding end zones) is $10 \cdot 10^1$ yards long.

Solution

a)   Yes

b)   Yes

c)   No. The coefficient is less than 1. It needs to be greater than or equal to 1.

d)   No. The coefficient is 10. It needs to be less than 10.

Guided Practice

Tell whether each number is written correctly in scientific notation. If it is incorrectly written, state the reason.

1 A Brazilian gold frog is about $9.6 \cdot 10^{0}$ millimeters long.

2 The wavelength of green light is about $4.15 \cdot 10^{-7}$ meter.

3 Mars is approximately $0.2244 \cdot 10^{7}$ kilometers from the Sun.

Example 2 **Write numbers in scientific notation.**

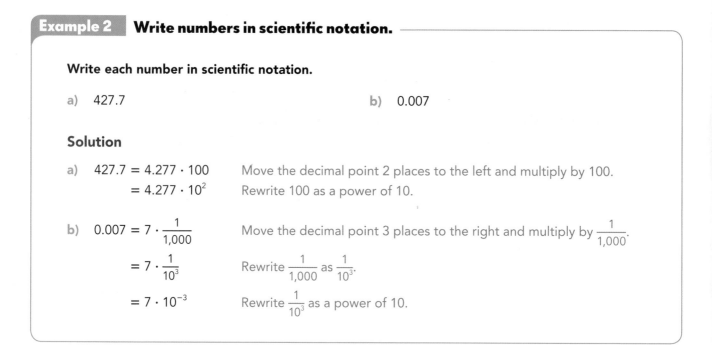

Write each number in scientific notation.

a) 427.7   b) 0.007

Solution

a) $427.7 = 4.277 \cdot 100$ Move the decimal point 2 places to the left and multiply by 100.
    $\quad\quad = 4.277 \cdot 10^{2}$ Rewrite 100 as a power of 10.

b) $0.007 = 7 \cdot \dfrac{1}{1{,}000}$ Move the decimal point 3 places to the right and multiply by $\dfrac{1}{1{,}000}$.

    $\quad\quad = 7 \cdot \dfrac{1}{10^{3}}$ Rewrite $\dfrac{1}{1{,}000}$ as $\dfrac{1}{10^{3}}$.

    $\quad\quad = 7 \cdot 10^{-3}$ Rewrite $\dfrac{1}{10^{3}}$ as a power of 10.

Guided Practice

Write each number in scientific notation.

4 856.2

$856.2 = \underline{\ ?\ } \cdot \underline{\ ?\ }$ Move the decimal point $\underline{\ ?\ }$ places to the left and multiply by $\underline{\ ?\ }$.

$\quad\quad = \underline{\ ?\ } \cdot \underline{\ ?\ }$ Rewrite as a power of 10.

5 0.06

Write Numbers in Standard Form.

You can use what you know about numbers written in scientific notation to represent them in standard form.

Example 3 **Write numbers in standard form.**

Write each number in standard form.

a) $7.1 \cdot 10^3$

Solution

$7.1 \cdot 10^3 = 7.1 \cdot 1,000$ Evaluate the power.

$\qquad\qquad = 7,100$ Multiply by 1,000.

b) $8.12 \cdot 10^{-3}$

Solution

$8.12 \cdot 10^{-3} = 8.12 \cdot \dfrac{1}{1,000}$ Evaluate the power.

$\qquad\qquad = 0.00812$ Divide by 1,000.

10^{-3} has a negative exponent. You have learned that 10^{-3} can be written with a positive exponent as $\dfrac{1}{1,000}$.

Guided Practice

Write each number in standard form.

6 $9 \cdot 10^4$

$9 \cdot 10^4 = \underline{\ ?\ } \cdot \underline{\ ?\ }$ Evaluate the power.

$\qquad = \underline{\ ?\ }$ Multiply by $\underline{\ ?\ }$.

7 $2.5 \cdot 10^{-2}$

$2.5 \cdot 10^{-2} = \underline{\ ?\ } \cdot \underline{\ ?\ }$ Evaluate the power.

$\qquad = \underline{\ ?\ }$ Divide by $\underline{\ ?\ }$.

Compare Numbers in Scientific Notation.

You can compare numbers easily by writing them in scientific notation. Compare the powers of 10 to determine which number is greater. If the powers are equal, compare coefficients.

Example 4 **Compare numbers in scientific notation.**

Identify the greater number in each pair of numbers. Justify your reasoning.

a) $5.6 \cdot 10^2$ and $2.1 \cdot 10^3$

b) $3.4 \cdot 10^{-1}$ and $1.1 \cdot 10^{-1}$

Solution

a) $10^3 > 10^2$ Compare the exponents.
$2.1 \cdot 10^3 > 5.6 \cdot 10^2$. So, $2.1 \cdot 10^3$ is the greater number.

b) Because the exponents are the same, compare the coefficients.
$3.4 > 1.1$ Compare the coefficients.
$3.4 \cdot 10^{-1} > 1.1 \cdot 10^{-1}$. So, $3.4 \cdot 10^{-1}$ is the greater number.

Guided Practice

Identify the lesser number in each pair of numbers. Justify your reasoning.

8 $4.2 \cdot 10^2$ and $6.5 \cdot 10^1$

$\underline{\ ?\ } < \underline{\ ?\ }$ Compare the $\underline{\ ?\ }$.

$\underline{\ ?\ } < \underline{\ ?\ }$. So, $\underline{\ ?\ }$ is the lesser number.

9 $3.6 \cdot 10^{-3}$ and $8.4 \cdot 10^{-3}$

The $\underline{\ ?\ }$ are the same.

$\underline{\ ?\ } < \underline{\ ?\ }$ Compare the $\underline{\ ?\ }$.

$\underline{\ ?\ } < \underline{\ ?\ }$. So, $\underline{\ ?\ }$ is the lesser number.

Example 5 **Compare a number in standard form with a number in scientific notation.**

In 2000, Americans consumed an average of 47.2 pounds of potatoes and $5.936 \cdot 10^2$ pounds of dairy products per person. Did Americans consume more potatoes or dairy products?

Solution

Method 1

$5.936 \cdot 10^2 = 593.6$ lb

$593.6 > 47.2$

So, they consumed more dairy products.

Write the amount of potatoes and dairy products consumed in standard form. Then compare the two numbers.

Method 2

$47.2 = 4.72 \cdot 10^1$

Compare $5.936 \cdot 10^2$ and $4.72 \cdot 10^1$.

$10^2 > 10^1$ Compare the exponents.

So, they consumed more dairy products.

Write the amount of potatoes and dairy products consumed in scientific notation. Then compare the two numbers.

Guided Practice

Complete.

10 An actor has 75,126 fans on a social network. A musician has $8.58 \cdot 10^4$ fans. Who has more fans on the social network?

Write both numbers in either standard form or standard notation. Then compare the two numbers.

Method 1

$8.58 \cdot 10^4 = \underline{\ ?\ }$

$\underline{\ ?\ } > \underline{\ ?\ }$

So, the $\underline{\ ?\ }$ has more fans on the social network.

Method 2

$75,126 = \underline{\ ?\ } \cdot \underline{\ ?\ }$

Compare $\underline{\ ?\ }$ and $\underline{\ ?\ }$.

The $\underline{\ ?\ }$ are the same.

$\underline{\ ?\ } > \underline{\ ?\ }$ Compare the coefficients.

So, the $\underline{\ ?\ }$ has more fans on the social network.

11 The average diameter of a type of round shaped bacteria is 0.0000037 meter. The spacing between two of these bacteria is $2.1 \cdot 10^{-9}$ meter. Which length is shorter?

12 There are $5.816 \cdot 10^4$ spectators in a stadium watching a football game. In a theater, 1,150 people attend an opera. Which venue has more people?

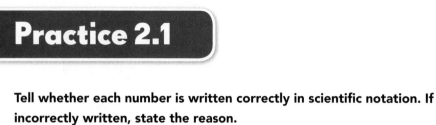

Practice 2.1

Tell whether each number is written correctly in scientific notation. If incorrectly written, state the reason.

1 $71 \cdot 10^{22}$

2 $8 \cdot 10^{-2}$

3 $0.99 \cdot 10^{-3}$

4 $1.2 \cdot 10^{4}$

Write each number in scientific notation.

5 533,000

6 327.8

7 0.0034

8 0.00000728

Write each number in standard form.

9 $7.36 \cdot 10^{3}$

10 $2.431 \cdot 10^{4}$

11 $5.27 \cdot 10^{-2}$

12 $4.01 \cdot 10^{-4}$

Identify the lesser number in each pair of numbers. Justify your reasoning.

13 $8.7 \cdot 10^{6}$ and $5.9 \cdot 10^{3}$

14 $4.8 \cdot 10^{3}$ and $9.6 \cdot 10^{7}$

15 $3.1 \cdot 10^{-5}$ and $7.5 \cdot 10^{-5}$

16 $6.9 \cdot 10^{-3}$ and $4.3 \cdot 10^{-3}$

Solve. Show your work.

17 The table shows population data for some countries. Write each population in scientific notation.

Country	Population
Brazil	190,000,000
Singapore	5,100,000
Monaco	35,000
Fiji	861,000

18 Human blood contains red blood cells, white blood cells, and platelets. The table shows the approximate diameters of each of these cells in fractions of a meter. Write each diameter in scientific notation.

Type of Cell	Diameter (m)
Red blood cell	0.000007
White blood cell	0.00000233
Platelet	0.0000025

19 A praying mantis is approximately 15 centimeters long. A caterpillar is about 76 millimeters long.

a) Write both lengths in millimeters in scientific notation.

b) Write both lengths in centimeters in scientific notation.

How does writing the numbers using the same units help you compare them?

20 A technician reads and records the air pressure from several pressure gauges. The table shows each air pressure reading in pascals (Pa). A pascal is a unit used to measure the amount of force applied on a given area by air or other gases.

Pressure Gauge	Air Pressure (Pa)
A	210,000
B	$5.2 \cdot 10^5$
C	170,000

a) Which pressure gauge has the greatest reading?

b) Which pressure gauge has the lowest reading?

c) The atmospheric pressure when these readings were made was $1.1 \cdot 10^5$ pascals. Which gauge(s) showed a reading greater than the atmospheric pressure?

21 *Math Journal* The table shows some numbers written in standard form and in the equivalent scientific notation. Describe the relationship between the pair of variables described in **a)** and **b)**.

Standard Form	Scientific Notation
0.0007	$7 \cdot 10^{-4}$
0.00182	$1.82 \cdot 10^{-3}$
1.28	$1.28 \cdot 10^9$
7,100	$7.1 \cdot 10^3$
427.7	$4.277 \cdot 10^2$

a) The value of the positive number in standard form and the sign of the exponent when expressed in scientific notation.

b) The sign of the exponent when expressed in scientific notation and the direction the decimal point moves to express the number in standard form.

22 *Math Journal* When visible light passes through a prism, the light waves refract, or bend, and the colors that make up the light can be seen. Each color has a different wavelength, as shown in the diagram, which is refracted to a different degree.

a) Shorter wavelengths refract more than longer wavelengths. Which color of light wave shows the most refraction? Which color of light wave shows the least refraction?

b) The frequency of a light wave is the number of waves that travel a given distance in a given amount of time. The shorter the wavelength, the greater the frequency. Order the wavelengths, in order of their frequencies, from least to greatest.

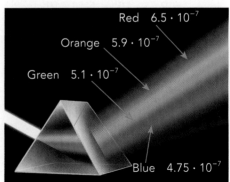

Red $6.5 \cdot 10^{-7}$
Orange $5.9 \cdot 10^{-7}$
Green $5.1 \cdot 10^{-7}$
Blue $4.75 \cdot 10^{-7}$

2.2 Adding and Subtracting in Scientific Notation

Lesson Objectives

- Add and subtract numbers in scientific notation.
- Introduce the prefix system.

Add and Subtract Numbers in Scientific Notation with the Same Power of 10.

A popular social networking site has the most members between the ages of 15 and 28. Within this age group, there are $5.11 \cdot 10^7$ student members and $9.55 \cdot 10^7$ nonstudent members. What is the total number of members in this age group?

Student members + Nonstudent members

$= 5.11 \cdot 10^7 + 9.55 \cdot 10^7$	Substitute.
$= (5.11 + 9.55) \cdot 10^7$	Factor 10^7 from each term.
$= 14.66 \cdot 10^7$	Add within parentheses.
$= 1.466 \cdot 10^1 \cdot 10^7$	Write 14.66 in scientific notation.
$= 1.466 \cdot 10^{1+7}$	Use the product of powers property.
$= 1.466 \cdot 10^8$	Write in scientific notation.

So, the total number of members in this age group is $1.466 \cdot 10^8$.

Suppose you want to find how many more nonstudent members than student members. To answer this question, you can subtract.

Nonstudent members − Student members

$= 9.55 \cdot 10^7 - 5.11 \cdot 10^7$	Substitute.
$= (9.55 - 5.11) \cdot 10^7$	Factor 10^7 from each term.
$= 4.44 \cdot 10^7$	Add within parentheses.

So, there are $4.44 \cdot 10^7$ more nonstudent members than student members.

> To add or subtract numbers in scientific notation, the powers of 10 must be the same.

> When the powers of 10 are the same, then the distributive property can be applied to the sum or difference.

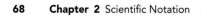

Example 6

Add and subtract very large numbers in scientific notation with the same power of 10.

As of the 2010 census, the population of Wyoming was approximately $5.63 \cdot 10^5$. The population of Vermont was approximately $6.25 \cdot 10^5$.

Population: $5.63 \cdot 10^5$ Population: $6.25 \cdot 10^5$

a) Find the total population of the two states.

Solution

Total population of the two states

= Population of Wyoming + Population of Vermont

$= 5.63 \cdot 10^5 + 6.25 \cdot 10^5$	Substitute.
$= (5.63 + 6.25) \cdot 10^5$	Factor 10^5 from each term.
$= 11.88 \cdot 10^5$	Add within parentheses.
$= 1.188 \cdot 10^1 \cdot 10^5$	Write 11.88 in scientific notation.
$= 1.188 \cdot 10^{1+5}$	Use the product of powers property.
$= 1.188 \cdot 10^6$	Write in scientific notation.

The total population of the two states is $1.188 \cdot 10^6$.

Once you add two numbers in scientific notation, make sure the answer is also written in scientific notation.

b) Find the difference in the population of the two states.

Solution

Difference in the population of the two states

= Population of Vermont − Population of Wyoming

$= 6.25 \cdot 10^5 - 5.63 \cdot 10^5$	Substitute.
$= (6.25 - 5.63) \cdot 10^5$	Factor 10^5 from each term.
$= 0.62 \cdot 10^5$	Subtract within parentheses.
$= 6.2 \cdot 10^{-1} \cdot 10^5$	Write 0.62 in scientific notation.
$= 6.2 \cdot 10^{-1+5}$	Use the product of powers property.
$= 6.2 \cdot 10^4$	Write in scientific notation.

The difference in the population of the two states is $6.2 \cdot 10^4$.

Guided Practice

Complete.

 The population of Washington, D.C., is about $5.9 \cdot 10^5$. South Dakota has a population of approximately $8 \cdot 10^5$.

Population: $5.9 \cdot 10^5$ Population: $8 \cdot 10^5$

a) Find the sum of the populations.

Sum of populations

= Population of Washington, D.C. + Population of South Dakota

= $5.9 \cdot 10^5 + 8 \cdot 10^5$ Substitute.

= (? + ?) · ?   Factor ? from each term.

= ? · ?   ? within parentheses.

= ? · ? · ?   Write ? in scientific notation.

= ? · ?   Use the product of powers property.

= ? · ?   Write in scientific notation.

The sum of the populations is about ? .

b) Find the difference in the populations.

Difference in the populations

= Population of South Dakota − Population of Washington, D.C.

= ? · ? − ? · ?   Substitute.

= (? − ?) · ?   Factor ? from each term.

= ? · ?   ? within parentheses.

The difference in the populations is about ? .

Example 7

Add and subtract very small numbers in scientific notation with the same power of 10.

The approximate thickness of a standard CD is $1.2 \cdot 10^{-3}$ meter. A slim jewel case is about $5.3 \cdot 10^{-3}$ meter thick.

a) The CD is placed on top of the jewel case. What is the total thickness of the CD and jewel case?

Solution

Approximate thickness of the CD and jewel case
= Thickness of CD + Thickness of jewel case
$= 1.2 \cdot 10^{-3} + 5.3 \cdot 10^{-3}$　　　Substitute.
$= (1.2 + 5.3) \cdot 10^{-3}$　　　Factor 10^{-3} from each term.
$= 6.5 \cdot 10^{-3}$ m　　　Add within parentheses.

The total thickness of the CD and jewel case is about $6.5 \cdot 10^{-3}$ meter.

Only when the exponents are the same can you add or subtract numbers in scientific notation.

b) How much thicker is the jewel case than the CD?

Solution

Difference in thickness between the jewel case and CD
= Thickness of jewel case − Thickness of CD
$= 5.3 \cdot 10^{-3} - 1.2 \cdot 10^{-3}$　　　Substitute.
$= (5.3 - 1.2) \cdot 10^{-3}$　　　Factor 10^{-3} from each term.
$= 4.1 \cdot 10^{-3}$ m　　　Subtract within parentheses.

The jewel case is about $4.1 \cdot 10^{-3}$ meter thicker than the CD.

Guided Practice

Complete.

2 The approximate length of the smallest salamander is $1.7 \cdot 10^{-2}$ meter. The smallest lizard is about $1.6 \cdot 10^{-2}$ meter long.

Lizard

Salamander

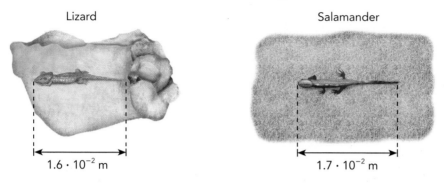

$1.6 \cdot 10^{-2}$ m

$1.7 \cdot 10^{-2}$ m

a) What is the sum of the lengths of the salamander and the lizard?

Sum of the lengths of the salamander and the lizard

= Length of salamander + Length of lizard

= $1.7 \cdot 10^{-2} + 1.6 \cdot 10^{-2}$ Substitute.

= (? + ?) · ?   Factor ? from each term.

= ? · ? m   ? within parentheses.

The sum of the lengths is about ? meter.

b) What is the difference in the length of the reptiles?

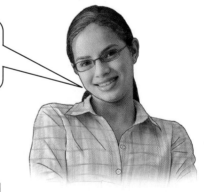

First compare the lengths of the two reptiles to find which one is longer. Then subtract the length of the shorter reptile from the length of the longer one.

Difference in length between the salamander and lizard

= Length of salamander − Length of lizard

= ? · ? − ? · ?   Substitute.

= (? − ?) · ?   Factor ? from each term.

= ? · ?   ? within parentheses.

= ? · ? · ?   Write ? in scientific notation.

= ? · ?   Use the product of powers property.

= ? · ? m   Write in scientific notation.

The salamander is about ? meter longer than the lizard.

Add and Subtract Numbers in Scientific Notation with Different Powers of 10.

When you add or subtract numbers written in scientific notation, first check to make sure the numbers have the same power of 10. If they do not, you can rewrite one or more numbers so that all the numbers have the same power of 10.

Suppose, at the end of one winter, there are about $1.5 \cdot 10^7$ square kilometers of ice in the Arctic Ocean. By the end of summer, much of the ice has melted, and there are only about $7 \cdot 10^6$ square kilometers of ice. How much ice melted?

> Rewrite one number so the two numbers have the same power of 10 as a factor. Then factor out the common factor.

Area of ice melted
= Area of ice at end of winter − Area of ice at end of summer

$= 1.5 \cdot 10^7 - 7 \cdot 10^6$	Substitute.
$= 15 \cdot 10^6 - 7 \cdot 10^6$	Rewrite $1.5 \cdot 10^7$ as $15 \cdot 10^6$.
$= (15 - 7) \cdot 10^6$	Factor 10^6 from each term.
$= 8 \cdot 10^6 \text{ km}^2$	Write in scientific notation.

About $8 \cdot 10^6$ square kilometers of ice melted.

> You can check that you have factored the terms correctly by multiplying again. You get $15 \cdot 10^6 - 7 \cdot 10^6$ when you multiply $(15 - 7) \cdot 10^6$.

Think Math

Can you get the same answer by rewriting $7 \cdot 10^6$ so that it has the same power of 10 as $1.5 \cdot 10^7$? Justify your answer.

Example 8 **Add and subtract very large numbers in scientific notation with different powers of 10.**

The approximate area of the Pacific Ocean is $6.4 \cdot 10^7$ square miles. The area of the Arctic Ocean is about $5.4 \cdot 10^6$ square miles.

a) Find the approximate sum of the areas of the two oceans.

Solution

Approximate sum of the areas of the two oceans
= Area of Pacific Ocean + Area of Arctic Ocean

$= 6.4 \cdot 10^7 + 5.4 \cdot 10^6$	Substitute.
$= 64 \cdot 10^6 + 5.4 \cdot 10^6$	Rewrite $6.4 \cdot 10^7$ as $64 \cdot 10^6$.
$= (64 + 5.4) \cdot 10^6$	Factor 10^6 from each term.
$= \mathbf{69.4 \cdot 10^6}$	Add within parentheses.
$= 6.94 \cdot 10^1 \cdot 10^6$	Write 69.4 in scientific notation.
$= 6.94 \cdot 10^{1+6}$	Use the product of powers property.
$= 6.94 \cdot 10^7 \text{ mi}^2$	Write in scientific notation.

> Choose one of the areas and rewrite it so that it has the same power of 10 as the other area. The larger area is chosen here.

The sum of the areas of the two oceans is about $6.94 \cdot 10^7$ square miles.

> You can also choose to rewrite the smaller area to have the same power of 10 as the larger area.
>
> Sum of the areas of the two oceans
> = Area of Pacific Ocean + Area of Arctic Ocean
>
> $= 6.4 \cdot 10^7 + 5.4 \cdot 10^6$ Substitute.
> $= 6.4 \cdot 10^7 + 0.54 \cdot 10^7$ Rewrite $5.4 \cdot 10^6$ as $0.54 \cdot 10^7$.

b) About how much larger is the area of the Pacific Ocean than the area of the Arctic Ocean?

Solution

Difference in the areas of the two oceans
= Area of Pacific Ocean − Area of Arctic Ocean

$= 6.4 \cdot 10^7 - 5.4 \cdot 10^6$	Substitute.
$= 64 \cdot 10^6 - 5.4 \cdot 10^6$	Rewrite $6.4 \cdot 10^7$ as $64 \cdot 10^6$.
$= (64 - 5.4) \cdot 10^6$	Factor 10^6 from each term.
$= \mathbf{58.6 \cdot 10^6}$	Subtract within parentheses.
$= 5.86 \cdot 10^1 \cdot 10^6$	Write 58.6 in scientific notation.
$= 5.86 \cdot 10^{1+6}$	Use the product of powers property.
$= 5.86 \cdot 10^7 \text{ mi}^2$	Write in scientific notation.

The area of the Pacific Ocean is about $5.86 \cdot 10^7$ square miles larger than the area of the Arctic Ocean.

Guided Practice

Complete.

3 The approximate area of the continent of Australia is $9 \cdot 10^6$ square kilometers. The area of the continent of Antarctica is about $1.37 \cdot 10^7$ square kilometers.

a) Find the approximate sum of the land areas of the two continents.

Choose one of the land areas and rewrite it so that it has the same power of 10 as the other land area. Choose the larger land area.

Approximate sum of the land areas of the two continents

= Area of Australia + Area of Antarctica

$= 9 \cdot 10^6 + 1.37 \cdot 10^7$ Substitute.

$= \underline{} \cdot \underline{} + \underline{} \cdot \underline{}$ Rewrite $\underline{} \cdot \underline{}$ as $\underline{} \cdot \underline{}$.

$= (\underline{} + \underline{}) \cdot \underline{}$ Factor $\underline{}$ from each term.

$= \underline{} \cdot \underline{}$ $\underline{}$ within parentheses.

$= \underline{} \cdot \underline{} \cdot \underline{}$ Write $\underline{}$ in scientific notation.

$= \underline{} \cdot \underline{}$ Use the product of powers property.

$= \underline{} \cdot \underline{} \text{ km}^2$ Write in scientific notation.

The sum of the land areas is about $\underline{}$ square kilometers.

> **Caution** ////////
>
> To find the greater of two numbers written in scientific notation, compare the powers of 10 first, not the coefficients.

To find the difference of the land areas, subtract the smaller area from the larger area. Since $10^7 > 10^6$, the land area of Antarctica is greater.

b) What is the difference in the areas of the two continents?

Difference in the land areas

= Area of Antarctica − Area of Australia

$= \underline{} \cdot \underline{} - \underline{} \cdot \underline{}$ Substitute.

$= \underline{} \cdot \underline{} - \underline{} \cdot \underline{}$ Rewrite $\underline{} \cdot \underline{}$ as $\underline{} \cdot \underline{}$.

$= (\underline{} - \underline{}) \cdot \underline{}$ Factor $\underline{}$ from each term.

$= \underline{} \cdot \underline{} \text{ km}^2$ $\underline{}$ within parentheses.

The land area of Antarctica is about $\underline{}$ square kilometers larger than the land area of Australia.

Example 9 **Add and subtract very small numbers in scientific notation with different powers of 10.**

A standard CD is about $1.2 \cdot 10^{-3}$ meter thick. A thin coating on the CD is approximately $7.0 \cdot 10^{-8}$ meter thick.

a) How thick is the CD with the coating added?

Solution

Choose one of the thickness measures and rewrite it so that it has the same power of 10 as the other thickness measure. In this example, the thickness of the coating is rewritten to have a power of 10^{-3}.

Approximate thickness of the CD and coating
= Thickness of CD + Thickness of coating

$= 1.2 \cdot 10^{-3} + 7.0 \cdot 10^{-8}$ Substitute.

$= 1.2 \cdot 10^{-3} + 0.00007 \cdot 10^{-3}$ Rewrite $7.0 \cdot 10^{-8}$ as $0.00007 \cdot 10^{-3}$.

$= (1.2 + 0.00007) \cdot 10^{-3}$ Factor 10^{-3} from each term.

$= 1.20007 \cdot 10^{-3}$ m   Add within parentheses.

The total thickness of the CD and coating is about $1.20007 \cdot 10^{-3}$ meter.

b) How much thicker is the CD than the coating?

Solution

Difference in thickness between the CD and coating
= Thickness of CD − Thickness of coating

$= 1.2 \cdot 10^{-3} - 7.0 \cdot 10^{-8}$ Substitute.

$= 1.2 \cdot 10^{-3} - 0.00007 \cdot 10^{-3}$ Rewrite $7.0 \cdot 10^{-8}$ as $0.00007 \cdot 10^{-3}$.

$= (1.2 - 0.00007) \cdot 10^{-3}$ Factor 10^{-3} from each term.

$= 1.19993 \cdot 10^{-3}$ m   Add within parentheses.

The CD is about $1.19993 \cdot 10^{-3}$ meter thicker than the coating.

Guided Practice

Solve. Write your answers in scientific notation.

4 A custom-made invitation using a 10-pt card stock is about $2.54 \cdot 10^{-4}$ meter thick. It is placed inside a tissue paper insert that is approximately $6.0 \cdot 10^{-6}$ meter thick.

a) How thick is the invitation when placed in the tissue paper insert?

b) How much thicker is the invitation than the tissue paper insert?

Introduce the Prefix System.

The approximate width of a human hair can be expressed as $1.76 \cdot 10^{-4}$ meter. Using the prefixes shown in the table, you can also express this measure as:
$1.76 \cdot 10^{-7}$ kilometer,
$1.76 \cdot 10^{-1}$ millimeter,
$1.76 \cdot 10^{2}$ micrometer,
and so on.

Prefix	Symbol	10^n	Standard Form	Term
Tera	T	10^{12}	1,000,000,000,000	Trillion
Giga	G	10^{9}	1,000,000,000	Billion
Mega	M	10^{6}	1,000,000	Million
kilo	k	10^{3}	1,000	Thousand
–	–	10^{0}	1	One
milli	m	10^{-3}	0.001	Thousandth
micro	μ	10^{-6}	0.000001	Millionth
nano	n	10^{-9}	0.000000001	Billionth
pico	p	10^{-12}	0.000000000001	Trillionth

Example 10 **Add and subtract numbers in different forms.**

A blue whale has a mass of about 190,000,000 grams. The mass of a whale shark is approximately $2.6 \cdot 10^{4}$ kilograms.

a) What is the approximate sum of the masses of the blue whale and whale shark?

Solution

Mass of blue whale:

190,000,000 g = 190,000 kg   Write in kilograms.

$\qquad\qquad\quad = 1.9 \cdot 10^{5}$ kg   Write in scientific notation.

First rewrite the masses of the two animals using the same units. Then you can write the masses in scientific notation.

Approximate sum of the masses of the blue whale and whale shark
= Mass of blue whale + Mass of whale shark

$= 1.9 \cdot 10^{5} + 2.6 \cdot 10^{4}$ Substitute.

$= 19 \cdot 10^{4} + 2.6 \cdot 10^{4}$ Rewrite $1.9 \cdot 10^{5}$ as $19 \cdot 10^{4}$.

$= (19 + 2.6) \cdot 10^{4}$ Factor 10^{4} from each term.

$= 21.6 \cdot 10^{4}$ Add within parentheses.

$= 2.16 \cdot 10^{1} \cdot 10^{4}$ Write 21.6 in scientific notation.

$= 2.16 \cdot 10^{1+4}$ Use the product of powers property.

$= 2.16 \cdot 10^{5}$ kg   Write in scientific notation.

The sum of the masses of the blue whale and whale shark is about $2.16 \cdot 10^{5}$ kilograms.

Continue on next page

b) Given that the mass of white rhinoceros is about 4,850 kilograms, find the combined mass of the three animals.

Solution

Mass of the white rhinoceros:

$4{,}850 = 4.85 \cdot 10^3$ kg   Write in scientific notation.

Combined masses of the three animals
= Approximate mass of blue whale and whale shark + Mass of white rhinoceros

$= 2.16 \cdot 10^5 + 4.85 \cdot 10^3$	Substitute.
$= 216 \cdot 10^3 + 4.85 \cdot 10^3$	Rewrite $2.16 \cdot 10^5$ as $216 \cdot 10^3$.
$= (216 + 4.85) \cdot 10^3$	Factor 10^3 from each term.
$= 220.85 \cdot 10^3$	Add within parentheses.
$= 2.2085 \cdot 10^2 \cdot 10^3$	Write 220.85 in scientific notation.
$= 2.2085 \cdot 10^{2+3}$	Use the product of powers property.
$= 2.2085 \cdot 10^5$ kg	Write in scientific notation.

The combined mass of the three animals is about $2.2085 \cdot 10^5$ kilograms.

Guided Practice

Complete.

5 On average, Pluto orbits the Sun at a distance of approximately 4,802 gigameters. Uranus's average distance from the Sun is about $2.992 \cdot 10^9$ kilometers. Which planet is farther from the Sun? How much farther?

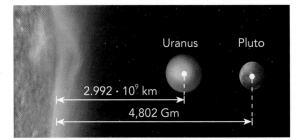

Uranus   Pluto

$2.992 \cdot 10^9$ km

4,802 Gm

Distance of Pluto from the Sun:

$\underline{\ ?\ }$ Gm = $\underline{\ ?\ } \cdot \underline{\ ?\ }$ km   Write in scientific notation.

Difference in distance of Pluto and Uranus from the Sun

= Distance of $\underline{\ ?\ }$ from the Sun − Distance of $\underline{\ ?\ }$ from the Sun

$= \underline{\ ?\ } \cdot \underline{\ ?\ } - \underline{\ ?\ } \cdot \underline{\ ?\ }$ Substitute.

$= (\underline{\ ?\ } - \underline{\ ?\ }) \cdot \underline{\ ?\ }$ Factor $\underline{\ ?\ }$ from each term.

$= \underline{\ ?\ } \cdot \underline{\ ?\ }$ km $\underline{\ ?\ }$ within parentheses.

So, $\underline{\ ?\ }$ is $\underline{\ ?\ }$ kilometers farther from the Sun.

Practice 2.2

Solve. Show your work. Round the coefficient to the nearest tenth.

1 $6.3 \cdot 10^{-2} + 4.9 \cdot 10^{-2}$

2 $7.2 \cdot 10^2 - 3.5 \cdot 10^2$

3 $3.8 \cdot 10^3 + 5.2 \cdot 10^4$

4 $8.1 \cdot 10^5 - 2.8 \cdot 10^4$

Use the table to answer questions 5 to 9.

The table shows the amounts of energy, in Calories, contained in various foods.

Food (per 100 g)	Energy (Cal)
Chicken breast	$1.71 \cdot 10^5$
Raw potato	$7.7 \cdot 10$
Cabbage	$2.5 \cdot 10^4$
Salmon	$1.67 \cdot 10^5$

5 Find the total energy in each food combination. Write your answer in scientific notation. Round coefficients to the nearest tenth.

   a) Chicken breast and cabbage

   b) Cabbage and raw potato

6 How many more Calories are in chicken breast than in salmon?

7 How many more Calories are in salmon than in cabbage?

Solve. Show your work.

8 A flight from Singapore to New York includes a stopover at Hawaii. The distance between Singapore and Hawaii is about $6.7 \cdot 10^3$ miles. The distance between New York and Hawaii is about $4.9 \cdot 10^3$ miles. Write each sum or difference in scientific notation.

   a) Find the total distance from Singapore to New York.

   b) Find the difference in the length of the two flights.

9 Angora wool, obtained from rabbits, has fibers with a diameter of about $1 \cdot 10^{-6}$ meter. Cashmere, obtained from goats, has fibers with a diameter of about $1.45 \cdot 10^{-5}$ meter. Write your answers in the appropriate unit in prefix form.

   a) Find the sum of the diameters of the two types of fiber.

   b) How much wider is the cashmere fiber than the angora fiber?

The average distances of three planets from the Sun are shown in the diagram. Use this information for questions 10 to 13. Express your answers in kilometers.

10 What is the closest Mercury comes to Earth when both are at an average distance from the Sun?

11 What is the closest Saturn comes to Mercury when both are at an average distance from the Sun?

12 What is the closest Saturn comes to Earth when both are at an average distance from the Sun?

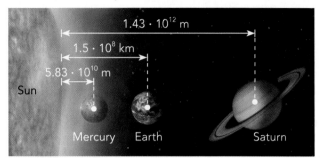

13 Is the distance you found in **12** greater or less than the average distance from Earth to the Sun? Explain.

Solve. Show your work.

14 Factories A and B produce potato chips. They use the same basic ingredients: potatoes, oil, and salt. Last year, each factory used different amounts of these ingredients, as shown in the table.

Ingredient	Factory A Amount Used (lb)	Factory B Amount Used (lb)
Potato	$4.87 \cdot 10^6$	3,309,000
Oil	356,000	$5.61 \cdot 10^5$
Salt	$2.87 \cdot 10^5$	193,500

a) Which factory used more potatoes last year? How many more potatoes did it use?

b) Which factory used more oil last year? How much more oil did it use than the other factory?

c) Find the total weight of the ingredients used by each factory. Write your answer in scientific notation.

15 *Math Journal* The approximate population of the following countries in North America in 2011 are shown in the table. Explain how to use scientific notation to find the total population of the countries.

Country	Population
Mexico	110,000,000
Haiti	9,700,000
Costa Rica	4,600,000
United States	310,000,000

2.3 Multiplying and Dividing in Scientific Notation

Lesson Objectives

- Multiply and divide numbers in scientific notation.
- Solve real-world problems involving the calculation of numbers in different forms.
- Use calculators to operate with numbers written in scientific notation.

Multiply and Divide Numbers in Scientific Notation.

You have learned how to apply the product of powers property and the quotient of powers property to multiply and divide integers with exponents. To multiply 7^5 by 7^2, you add the exponents. To divide 7^5 by 7^2, subtract the second exponent from the first.

$$7^5 \cdot 7^2 = 7^{5+2} \qquad\qquad 7^5 \div 7^2 = 7^{5-2}$$
$$= 7^7 \qquad\qquad\qquad\qquad\quad = 7^3$$

In this lesson, you will learn how to apply these properties when you multiply and divide numbers in scientific notation.

Example 11 Multiply numbers in scientific notation.

a) An Olympic-size swimming pool is about $5 \cdot 10^1$ meters long and $2.5 \cdot 10^1$ meters wide. Find the approximate area of the water's surface.

> Multiplication and addition of numbers is commutative.

Solution

$$
\begin{aligned}
\text{Approximate area of water's surface} &= \text{Length} \cdot \text{Width} \\
&= 5 \cdot 10^1 \cdot 2.5 \cdot 10^1 && \text{Substitute.} \\
&= 5 \cdot 2.5 \cdot 10^1 \cdot 10^1 && \text{Use the commutative property.} \\
&= 12.5 \cdot 10^1 \cdot 10^1 && \text{Multiply the coefficients.} \\
&= 1.25 \cdot 10^1 \cdot 10^1 \cdot 10^1 && \text{Write 12.5 in scientific notation.} \\
&= 1.25 \cdot 10^{1+1+1} && \text{Use the product of powers property.} \\
&= 1.25 \cdot 10^3 \text{ m}^2 && \text{Write in scientific notation.}
\end{aligned}
$$

The area of the water's surface is about $1.25 \cdot 10^3$ square meters.

Continue on next page

b) The length of the Aztec Stadium in Mexico is about $1.05 \cdot 10^2$ meters long and $6.8 \cdot 10^1$ meters wide. Find its approximate area.

Solution

Approximate area of stadium = Length · Width

$$
\begin{aligned}
&= 1.05 \cdot 10^2 \cdot 6.8 \cdot 10^1 && \text{Substitute.}\\
&= 1.05 \cdot 6.8 \cdot 10^2 \cdot 10^1 && \text{Use the commutative property.}\\
&= 7.14 \cdot 10^2 \cdot 10^1 && \text{Multiply the coefficients.}\\
&= 7.14 \cdot 10^{2+1} && \text{Use the product of powers property.}\\
&= 7.14 \cdot 10^3 \text{ m}^2 && \text{Write in scientific notation.}
\end{aligned}
$$

Its area is approximately $7.14 \cdot 10^3$ square meters.

Guided Practice

Complete.

1 In the 19th century, the Law Courts of Brussels was the largest building ever built. Its base area measures about $1.6 \cdot 10^2$ meters by $1.5 \cdot 10^2$ meters. Find the approximate base area of the building.

Approximate base area

= Length · Width

$$
\begin{aligned}
&= \underline{\ ?\ } \cdot \underline{\ ?\ } \cdot \underline{\ ?\ } \cdot \underline{\ ?\ } && \text{Substitute.}\\
&= \underline{\ ?\ } \cdot \underline{\ ?\ } \cdot \underline{\ ?\ } \cdot \underline{\ ?\ } && \text{Use the commutative property.}\\
&= \underline{\ ?\ } \cdot \underline{\ ?\ } \cdot \underline{\ ?\ } && \underline{\ ?\ } \text{ the coefficients.}\\
&= \underline{\ ?\ } \cdot \underline{\ ?\ } && \text{Use the product of powers property.}\\
&= \underline{\ ?\ } \cdot \underline{\ ?\ } \text{ m}^2 && \text{Write in scientific notation.}
\end{aligned}
$$

The base area of the building is about $\underline{\ ?\ }$ square meters.

2 The outer wall of Angkor Wat, a World Heritage site in Cambodia, encloses an area of about $1.02 \cdot 10^3$ meters by $8.02 \cdot 10^2$ meters. Find the approximate area enclosed by the outer wall.

> **Math Note**
>
> You can use the EE function or **2ND** ⬛ on a calculator to multiply numbers in scientific notation.

Approximate area enclosed by outer wall

= Length · Width

$$
\begin{aligned}
&= \underline{\ ?\ } \cdot \underline{\ ?\ } \cdot \underline{\ ?\ } \cdot \underline{\ ?\ } && \text{Substitute.}\\
&= \underline{\ ?\ } \cdot \underline{\ ?\ } \cdot \underline{\ ?\ } \cdot \underline{\ ?\ } && \text{Use the commutative property.}\\
&= \underline{\ ?\ } \cdot \underline{\ ?\ } \cdot \underline{\ ?\ } && \underline{\ ?\ } \text{ the coefficients.}\\
&= \underline{\ ?\ } \cdot \underline{\ ?\ } && \text{Use the product of powers property.}\\
&= \underline{\ ?\ } \cdot \underline{\ ?\ } \text{ m}^2 && \text{Write in scientific notation.}
\end{aligned}
$$

The area enclosed by the outer wall is approximately $\underline{\ ?\ }$ square meters.

Example 12 **Divide numbers in scientific notation.**

Some of the smaller planets in the solar system are Mercury and Mars.

a) The planet Mercury has an approximate mass of $3.3 \cdot 10^{23}$ kilograms. Mars has a mass of about $6.4 \cdot 10^{23}$ kilograms. How many times as great as the mass of Mercury is the mass of Mars? Round the coefficient to the nearest tenth.

You may use the EE function on a graphing calculator to enter numbers in scientific notation. You can do so for b).

Solution

$$\frac{\text{Mass of Mars}}{\text{Mass of Mercury}}$$

$$= \frac{6.4 \cdot 10^{23}}{3.3 \cdot 10^{23}} \qquad \text{Substitute.}$$

$$= \frac{6.4}{3.3} \cdot \frac{10^{23}}{10^{23}} \qquad \text{Divide the coefficients, and divide the powers of 10.}$$

$$\approx 1.9 \cdot 10^{23-23} \qquad \text{Round off the coefficient and use the quotient of powers property.}$$

$$= 1.9 \cdot 10^{0}$$

$$= 1.9 \qquad \text{Simplify. Write in standard form.}$$

Mars has a mass that is approximately 1.9 times as great as the mass of Mercury.

b) Sun's diameter is about $1.4 \cdot 10^{6}$ kilometers. Moon's diameter is approximately $3.5 \cdot 10^{3}$ kilometers. How many times as great as the diameter of the moon is the diameter of the Sun?

Solution

$$\frac{\text{Diameter of the Sun}}{\text{Diameter of the moon}}$$

$$= \frac{1.4 \cdot 10^{6}}{3.5 \cdot 10^{3}} \qquad \text{Substitute.}$$

$$= \frac{1.4}{3.5} \cdot \frac{10^{6}}{10^{3}} \qquad \text{Divide the coefficients, and divide the powers of 10.}$$

$$= 0.4 \cdot 10^{6-3} \qquad \text{Use the quotient of powers property.}$$

$$= 0.4 \cdot 10^{3} \qquad \text{Simplify.}$$

$$= 400 \qquad \text{Write in standard form.}$$

The diameter of the Sun is approximately 400 times as great as the diameter of the moon.

Guided Practice

Complete. Round each coefficient answer to the nearest tenth.

3 The Jean-Luc Lagardere plant in France is the second largest building in the world. It has an approximate volume of $5.6 \cdot 10^6$ cubic meters. The NASA vehicle assembly building in Florida has a volume of about $3.7 \cdot 10^6$ cubic meters. How many times as great as the volume of the NASA vehicle assembly building is the volume of the Jean-Luc Lagardere plant?

$\dfrac{\text{Volume of Jean-Luc Lagardere plant}}{\text{Volume of NASA vehicles assembly building}}$

$= \dfrac{\underline{?} \cdot \underline{?}}{\underline{?} \cdot \underline{?}}$ Substitute.

$= \dfrac{\underline{?}}{\underline{?}} \cdot \dfrac{\underline{?}}{\underline{?}}$ __?__ the coefficients, and __?__ the powers of 10.

$\approx \underline{?} \cdot \underline{?}$ Use the quotient of powers property.

$= \underline{?} \cdot \underline{?}$ Simplify.

$= \underline{?}$ Write in standard form.

The volume of the Jean-Luc Lagardere plant is about __?__ times as great as the volume of the NASA vehicle assembly building.

4 The Abraj Al-Bait towers in Saudi Arabia has a floor area of about $1.5 \cdot 10^6$ square meters. The Palazzo in Las Vegas has an approximate floor area of $6.5 \cdot 10^5$ square meters. How many times as great as the floor area of the Palazzo is the floor area of the Abraj Al-Bait towers?

Abraj Al-Bait
Floor area: $1.5 \cdot 10^6 \text{ m}^2$

Palazzo
Floor area: $6.5 \cdot 10^5 \text{ m}^2$

$\dfrac{\text{Floor area of Abraj Al-Bait towers}}{\text{Floor area of Palazzo}}$

$= \dfrac{\underline{?} \cdot \underline{?}}{\underline{?} \cdot \underline{?}}$ Substitute.

$= \dfrac{\underline{?}}{\underline{?}} \cdot \dfrac{\underline{?}}{\underline{?}}$ __?__ the coefficients, and __?__ the powers of 10.

$\approx \underline{?} \cdot \underline{?}$ Use the quotient of powers property.

$= \underline{?} \cdot \underline{?}$ Simplify.

$= \underline{?} \cdot \underline{?} \cdot \underline{?}$ Write __?__ in scientific notation.

$= \underline{?} \cdot \underline{?}$ Use the product of powers property.

$= \underline{?} \cdot \underline{?}$ Simplify.

$= \underline{?}$ Write in standard form.

The floor area of the Abraj Al-Bait towers is approximately __?__ times greater than the floor area of the Palazzo.

Evaluate each expression in scientific notation, and round the coefficient to the nearest tenth.

1 $7.45 \cdot 10^6 \cdot 5.4 \cdot 10^{-6}$

2 $6.84 \cdot 10^{-5} \cdot 4.7 \cdot 10^{10}$

3 $5.75 \cdot 10^{-5} \div (7.15 \cdot 10^7)$

4 $8.45 \cdot 10^{11} \div (1.69 \cdot 10^{-8})$

The table shows the approximate volumes of some planets. Use the information to answer questions 5 to 7. Round your answers to the nearest tenth.

Planets	Volume (km³)
Venus	$9.4 \cdot 10^{11}$
Earth	$1.1 \cdot 10^{12}$
Mars	$1.6 \cdot 10^{11}$

5 About how many times as great as the volume of Mars is the volume of Venus?

6 About how many times as great as the volume of Mars is the volume of Earth?

7 About how many times as great as the volume of Venus is the volume of Earth?

Solve. Show your work.

8 Suzanne's digital camera has a resolution of $2560 \cdot 1920$ pixels. Douglas' digital camera has a resolution of $3264 \cdot 2448$ pixels.

   a) Express the resolution of the digital cameras in prefix form to the nearest whole unit. Use the most appropriate unit.

   b) Whose camera has a higher resolution?

9 Bobby downloaded pictures of a cruise ship and a ski run from the internet. The file size of the cruise ship is about 794 kilobytes while the file size of the ski run is about 2.6 megabytes.

   a) What is the total file size, in megabytes and in kilobytes, of a file containing the two pictures?

   b) Calculate the difference in file size, in megabytes and in kilobytes, between the two pictures.

   c) To the nearest tenth, about how many times as great as the file size of the ski run picture is the file size of the ship picture?

   d) Bobby saved the two pictures on a thumb drive with a capacity of 256 megabytes. Find the remaining free capacity of the thumb drive to the nearest tenth megabyte after Bobby saved the two pictures in it.

10 The Georgia Aquarium in Atlanta is about $2.63 \cdot 10^3$ inches long, $1.26 \cdot 10^2$ inches wide, and $3 \cdot 10^1$ inches deep at its largest point. Find its approximate volume.

11 The square base of the Great Pyramid of Khufu has a length of approximately $1.476 \cdot 10^3$ feet. Its height is about $2.17 \cdot 10^2$ feet. Find the approximate volume of the pyramid. Write your answer in scientific notation. Round the coefficient to the nearest tenth.

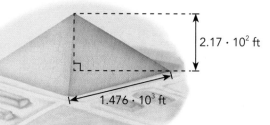

$2.17 \cdot 10^2$ ft

$1.476 \cdot 10^3$ ft

12 The Tropical Islands Resort is housed inside a former airplane hangar approximately $1.18 \cdot 10^3$ feet long, $6.89 \cdot 10^2$ feet wide, and $3.51 \cdot 10^2$ feet high. Use the formula for the volume of a rectangular prism to approximate the volume enclosed by the resort. Round the coefficient to the nearest tenth.

13 The time light takes to travel one meter in a vacuum is about 3.3 nanoseconds. To travel one mile it takes about 5.4 microseconds.

a) Find the difference, in microseconds, between the times taken by light to travel one meter and one mile in a vacuum.

b) How many times longer, to the nearest tenth, does it take light to travel one mile than one meter?

14 A spherical particle was found to have a radius of $3.5 \cdot 10^{-10}$ meter.

a) Express the diameter in the prefix form using picometers.

b) Use your answer in **a)**, express the circumference in the prefix form using nanometers. Use 3.14 as an approximation for π.

Brain @ Work

1 Find the cube root of $2.7 \cdot 10^{10}$.

2 Given that $a = 3 \cdot 10^3$ and $b = 4 \cdot 10^2$, find each value.

a) $2a + b$

b) $\dfrac{2a}{b}$

3 Solve each of the following. Write your answer in scientific notation using the basic unit.

a) 80 micrograms + 200 nanograms

b) 3 gigabytes − 700 megabytes

Chapter Wrap Up

Concept Map

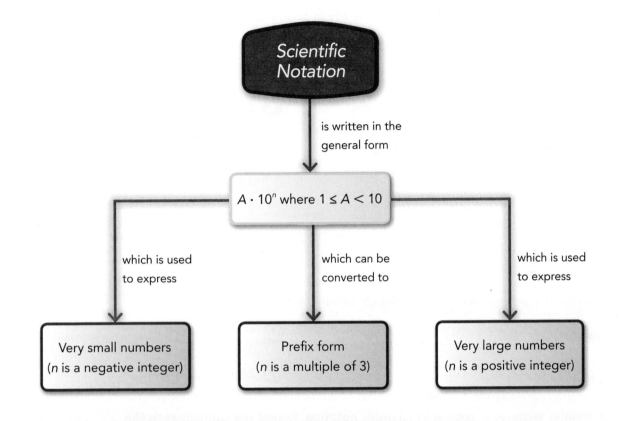

Key Concepts

▶ Scientific notation is a convenient way of writing very large or very small numbers.

▶ The general form of a number in scientific notation is $A \cdot 10^n$, where the coefficient A is at least 1 but less than 10, and the exponent n is any integer.

▶ To compare two numbers in scientific notation, first compare the powers of 10. If they are the same, then compare the coefficients.

▶ To add or subtract numbers in scientific notation, the numbers must be expressed using the same power of 10. Then apply the distributive property.

▶ To multiply or divide numbers in a scientific notation, multiply or divide the coefficients. Then multiply or divide the powers of 10 using properties of exponents.

▶ A prefix that precedes a basic unit of measure indicates a fraction or multiple of the unit. Each prefix has a unique symbol that is placed in front of the unit symbol.

Chapter Review/Test

Concepts and Skills

Tell whether each number is written correctly in scientific notation. If incorrectly written, state the reason.

1 $10 \cdot 10^2$

2 $0.99 \cdot 10^{12}$

3 $1.4 \cdot 10^2$

4 $0.4 \cdot 10^{25}$

Write each number in scientific notation.

5 714,000

6 0.00087

Write each number in standard form.

7 $3.46 \cdot 10^2$

8 $5.4 \cdot 10^4$

Identify the greater number in each pair of numbers.

9 $7.8 \cdot 10^{-5}$ and $5.4 \cdot 10^{-7}$

10 $1.4 \cdot 10^{-5}$ and $6 \cdot 10^{-4}$

11 $6.5 \cdot 10^{-15}$ and $9.3 \cdot 10^{-12}$

12 $3.5 \cdot 10^{-2}$ and $4 \cdot 10^{-3}$

Evaluate. Write your answer in scientific notation. Round the coefficient to the nearest tenth.

13 $2.44 \cdot 10^3 + 1.9 \cdot 10^5$

14 $3.12 \cdot 10^{-3} - 3 \cdot 10^{-3}$

15 $2.4 \cdot 10^{-2} \cdot 5 \cdot 10^{-1}$

16 $3.2 \cdot 10^8 \div (1.6 \cdot 10^4)$

Express each of the following in prefix form. Choose the most appropriate unit.

17 $2.8 \cdot 10^3$ meters

18 $1.5 \cdot 10^{-6}$ meter

19 $6.4 \cdot 10^9$ bytes

20 $4.8 \cdot 10^{-9}$ gram

Problem Solving

The table shows the length of two organisms. Use the table to answer questions **21** to **23**.

Organism	Length
Eriophyid mite	250 µm
Patiriella parvivipara (smallest starfish)	5 mm

21 Which organism is longer?

22 Express the length of the eriophyid mite in millimeters.

23 Write each length in scientific notation using the basic unit.

The top five materials used in the automotive industry in the United States in 2000 are as shown in the table. Use the table to answer questions 24 to 26. Write your answers in scientific notation. Round coefficients to the nearest tenth.

Material	Total Consumption (T)
Plastic	46,240
Aluminium	11,320
Steel	$9.894 \cdot 10^7$
Glass	5,417,000
Rubber	$2.86 \cdot 10^6$

24 How much more plastic was used than aluminium?

25 How much more steel was used than glass?

26 Find the total consumption of these materials used by the automotive industry in 2000.

27 The table shows the weights of some animals. Round your answers to the nearest tenth.

Animal	Weight (lb)
African bush elephant	$2.706 \cdot 10^4$
Hippopotamus	$9.9 \cdot 10^3$
Walrus	$4.4 \cdot 10^3$

a) About how many times greater than the weight of a walrus is the weight of a hippopotamus?

b) About how many times greater than the weight of a hippopotamus is the weight of an African bush elephant?

28 The floor of the Palace of the Parliament in Romania measures $8.9 \cdot 10^2$ feet by $7.9 \cdot 10^2$ feet. The building reaches $2.82 \cdot 10^2$ feet above ground, and $3.02 \cdot 10^2$ feet below ground. Use the formula for the volume of a rectangular prism to estimate the volume inside the palace.

29 The Stockholm Globe Arena in Sweden resembles a hemisphere. It has an inner diameter of about $1.1 \cdot 10^2$ meters. Find the approximate volume of the building. Use 3.14 as an approximation for π.

Cumulative Review Chapters 1–2

Concepts and Skills

Write the prime factorization of each number in exponential notation. (Lesson 1.1)

1 16,807

2 25,920

Simplify each expression. Write your answer in exponential notation. (Lessons 1.2, 1.3)

3 $\dfrac{\left[\left(\dfrac{3}{5}\right) \cdot \left(\dfrac{3}{5}\right)^3\right]^4}{\left[\left(\dfrac{3}{5}\right)^2\right]^2}$

4 $(a^6 \cdot a^7)^3 \div (4a^3)^2$

Simplify each expression. Write your answer using a positive exponent.

(Lessons 1.2, 1.3, 1.4, 1.5)

5 $\dfrac{6^3 \cdot 15^3}{(7^0)^3}$

6 $\dfrac{2^8 \cdot (-3)^8 \cdot 3^0}{5^{-8}}$

7 $[12^2 \cdot 3^2]^3 \div 3^6$

8 $(16^7 \div 16^4) \cdot \dfrac{(5^0)^3}{2^3 \cdot 4^3}$

9 $8^{-2} \cdot \dfrac{3^0 \cdot 8^{-3}}{4^{-5}}$

10 $6^{-4} \cdot (5^0)^{-4} \cdot \left(\dfrac{1}{3}\right)^{-4} \div 3^{-4}$

Evaluate the square roots of each number. Round your answer to the nearest tenth when you can. (Lesson 1.6)

11 576

12 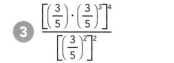 1,003.4

Evaluate the cube root of each number. Round your answer to the nearest tenth when you can. (Lesson 1.6)

13 $\dfrac{27}{216}$

14 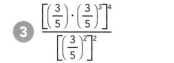 −629.5

Evaluate each expression and write your answer in scientific notation. Identify the greater number. (Lessons 2.1, 2.2, 2.3)

15 $3.27 \cdot 10^{11} + 3.13 \cdot 10^{11}$ and $9.28 \cdot 10^{11} - 4.15 \cdot 10^{11}$

16 $9.1 \cdot 10^{-5} - 8.2 \cdot 10^{-6}$ and $1.2 \cdot 10^{-6} - 5.5 \cdot 10^{-7}$

17 $8.4 \cdot 10^5 \cdot 2 \cdot 10^5$ and $3.2 \cdot 10^{-7} \cdot 2 \cdot 10^{-5}$

18 $9.1 \cdot 10^3 \div (7 \cdot 10^5)$ and $7.2 \cdot 10^{-4} \div (1.2 \cdot 10^{-4})$

Write each measurement in the appropriate unit in prefix form. (Lesson 2.2)

19 0.000020 meter

20 0.070 gram

21 35,000,000 bytes

22 42,000 volts

Problem Solving

Solve. Show your work.

23 The total surface area of a cube is 4,704 square inches. What is the length of each side? (Chapter 1)

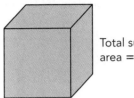

Total surface area = 4,704 in²

24 The volume of a spherical balloon is 12.348π cubic feet. (Chapter 1)

a) Find its radius. Round to the nearest tenth.

b) Air is pumped into the balloon, so that its radius doubles every 10 seconds. Using 3.14 as an approximation for π, find its surface area after 30 seconds. Round to the nearest tenth.

25 An oxygen atom has a total of 8 protons. If the mass of one proton is $1.67 \cdot 10^{-24}$ gram, find the total mass of the protons in the oxygen atom. Write your answer in scientific notation. Round the coefficient to 3 significant digits. (Chapters 1, 2)

26 The table lists the energy in Calories contained in 100 grams of fruits. (Chapter 2)

Fruits (per 100 g)	Energy (Cal)
Apple	$4.9 \cdot 10^4$
Orange	$6.2 \cdot 10^4$
Pear	$3.5 \cdot 10^4$

a) Calculate the total energy of the three fruits. Write your answer in scientific notation.

b) Find the difference in energy contained between 100 grams of apple and 100 grams of pear.

c) How many times more energy does 100 grams of orange have compared to 100 grams of apple? Round to the nearest tenth.

27 Jim deposits $2,000 in a bank, which gives 6% interest, compounded yearly. Use the formula $A = P(1 + r)^n$ to find the amount of money in his account after 15 years. A represents the final amount of investment, P is the original principal, r is the interest rate, and n is the number of years it was invested. (Chapter 1)

CHAPTER

3

Algebraic Linear Equations

Who wants to go bowling?

You and three friends want to go bowling. The bowling alley charges $3.25 for each pair of shoes you rent and $1.75 per game. All three of you need to rent shoes, and you aren't sure yet how many games you'll play. What will be your group's total cost?

In this situation, there are two quantities that can vary: the number of games your group plays and the group's total cost. In this chapter, you will learn how to write linear equations to represent situations in which there are two variables.

BIG IDEA

▶ Linear equations can be used to solve mathematical and real-world problems. A linear equation with one variable can have one solution, no solution, or infinitely many solutions.

Recall Prior Knowledge

Understanding equivalent equations

Equivalent equations are equations that have the same solution. Performing the same operation on both sides of an equation produces an equivalent equation.

For example, $x = 8$ and $x - 2 = 6$ are equivalent equations. If you subtract 2 from both sides of $x = 8$, you get $x - 2 = 6$. The solution to both equations is 8.

✔ Quick Check

Explain why each pair of equations is equivalent or not equivalent.

1 $x + 4 = 10$ and $x - 1 = 3$

2 $\frac{1}{5}x = 4$ and $x = 20$

3 $0.5x + 1 = 1.5x$ and $2x = 2$

4 $2(x + 9) = 14$ and $2(x - 7) = -18$

Expressing the relationship between two quantities with a linear equation

A wall has width w feet and length $2w$ feet. The perimeter P of the wall is $2w + 2w + w + w = 6w$ feet.

You can express the relationship between the perimeter and the width of the wall with a linear equation $P = 6w$. In the equation, w is the independent variable and P is the dependent variable because the value of P depends on the value of w.

✔ Quick Check

Write a linear equation for each situation. State the independent and dependent variables for each equation.

5 A manufacturer produces beverages in small and large bottles. Each small bottle contains s liters of beverages. Each large bottle contains t liters, which is 1 more liter than the quantity in the small bottle. Express t in terms of s.

6 Hazel is 4 years younger than Alphonso. Express Alphonso's age, a, in terms of Hazel's age, h.

7 A bouquet of lavender costs $12. Find the cost, C, of n bouquets of lavender.

8 The distance, d miles, traveled by a bus is 40 times the time, t hours, used for the journey. Find d in terms of t.

Solving algebraic equations

To solve an equation, you isolate the variable on one side of the equation. To isolate the variable on one side, you can add, subtract, multiply, or divide both sides of the equation by the same nonzero number.

Remember to keep an equation balanced by performing the same operation on both sides.

When an equation has variables on both sides, you isolate the variables on the same side of the equation.

$$
\begin{aligned}
4x + 7 &= 3x + 14 \\
4x - 3x + 7 &= 3x - 3x + 14 && \text{Subtract 3x from both sides.} \\
x + 7 &= 14 && \text{Simplify.} \\
x + 7 - 7 &= 14 - 7 && \text{Subtract 7 from both sides.} \\
x &= 7 && \text{Simplify.}
\end{aligned}
$$

To solve the equation $5x + 3(x - 2) = 50$, which includes an expression with parentheses, you need to use the distributive property.

$$
\begin{aligned}
5x + 3(x - 2) &= 50 \\
5x + 3x - 6 &= 50 && \text{Use the distributive property.} \\
8x - 6 &= 50 && \text{Combine like terms.} \\
8x - 6 + 6 &= 50 + 6 && \text{Add 6 to both sides.} \\
8x &= 56 && \text{Simplify.} \\
\frac{8x}{8} &= \frac{56}{8} && \text{Divide both sides by 8.} \\
x &= 7 && \text{Simplify.}
\end{aligned}
$$

✓ Quick Check

Solve each equation.

9 $4x = 14 + 2x$

10 $\frac{1}{3}v = 2 - \frac{2}{9}v$

11 $c + 2(1 - c) = 10 - 3c$

12 $3(2 + 3x) = 13(x + 2)$

Representing fractions as repeating decimals

A repeating decimal has a group of one or more digits that repeat endlessly.
Use bar notation to show the digits that repeat.

Write the decimal form of each fraction.

a) $\dfrac{5}{12}$

b) $\dfrac{40}{33}$

....

a)
```
        0.4166
   12 ) 5.0000
        4 8
        ───
          20
          12
        ────
            80
            72
          ────
            80
            72
          ────
             8
```
Divide until the remainders start repeating.

So, $\dfrac{5}{12} = 0.4166... = 0.41\overline{6}$.

b)
```
         1.2121
   33 ) 40.0000
        33
        ──
         7 0
         6 6
        ────
           40
           33
          ───
            70
            66
          ────
             40
             33
           ────
              7
```

So, $\dfrac{40}{33} = 1.2121... = 1.\overline{21}$.

☑ Quick Check

Write the decimal for each fraction. Use bar notation.

13 $\dfrac{3}{18}$

14 $\dfrac{16}{99}$

15 $\dfrac{13}{12}$

16 $\dfrac{5}{27}$

3.1 Solving Linear Equations with One Variable

Lesson Objectives

- Solve linear equations with one variable.
- Solve real-world problems involving linear equations with one variable.

Solve Linear Equations with One Variable.

You have learned how to solve linear equations with one variable. For example, you can solve the equation $x + \frac{x}{10} = 44$ using the steps shown below.

$$x + \frac{x}{10} = 44$$

$$\frac{10x}{10} + \frac{x}{10} = 44 \qquad \text{Write terms with a common denominator.}$$

$$\frac{11x}{10} = 44 \qquad \text{Combine into a single fraction in } x.$$

$$\frac{^1 \cancel{11}x}{_1 \cancel{10}} \cdot \frac{\cancel{10}^1}{\cancel{11}_1} = {}^4\cancel{44} \cdot \frac{10}{\cancel{11}_1} \qquad \text{Multiply both sides by } \frac{10}{11}.$$

$$x = 40 \qquad \text{Simplify.}$$

> You can factor $x + \frac{x}{10}$ to get $x\left(1 + \frac{1}{10}\right)$, which is $\frac{11x}{10}$.

Math Note

The coefficients and constants in linear equations may involve integers, fractions, and decimals. When solving equations, you use the same number properties and properties of equality as you do when working with numbers.

Example 1 **Solve linear equations involving the distributive property.**

Solve the equation $\dfrac{3x}{4} - \dfrac{2x + 1}{4} = -1.5$.

Solution

$$\dfrac{3x}{4} - \dfrac{2x + 1}{4} = -1.5$$

$$\dfrac{3x - (2x + 1)}{4} = -1.5 \qquad \text{Rewrite the left side as a single fraction. Use the distributive property.}$$

$$\dfrac{3x - 2x - 1}{4} = -1.5$$

$$\dfrac{x - 1}{4} = -1.5 \qquad \text{Simplify the numerator.}$$

$$\dfrac{x - 1}{4} \cdot 4 = -1.5 \cdot 4 \qquad \text{Multiply both sides by 4.}$$

$$x - 1 = -6 \qquad \text{Simplify.}$$

$$x - 1 + 1 = -6 + 1 \qquad \text{Add 1 to both sides.}$$

$$x = -5 \qquad \text{Simplify.}$$

> **Math Note**
>
> Notice that $2x + 1$ is placed in parentheses, because the fraction bar acts as a grouping symbol. So, $-\dfrac{2x + 1}{4}$ can be written as $\dfrac{-(2x + 1)}{4}$.

> The first three steps involve simplifying the expression on the left side of the equation.

Guided Practice

Solve each linear equation.

1 $\dfrac{2x}{3} - \dfrac{2 + x}{3} = -4$

$$\dfrac{2x}{3} - \dfrac{2 + x}{3} = -4$$

$$\dfrac{?}{3} = -4 \qquad \text{Rewrite the left side as a single fraction.}$$

$$\dfrac{?}{3} = -4 \qquad \text{Use the distributive property.}$$

$$\dfrac{?}{3} = -4 \qquad \text{Simplify the numerator.}$$

$$\dfrac{?}{3} \cdot \underline{\ ?\ } = -4 \cdot \underline{\ ?\ } \qquad \text{Multiply both sides by } \underline{\ ?\ }.$$

$$\underline{\ ?\ } = \underline{\ ?\ } \qquad \text{Simplify.}$$

$$\underline{\ ?\ } + \underline{\ ?\ } = \underline{\ ?\ } + \underline{\ ?\ } \qquad \text{Add } \underline{\ ?\ } \text{ to both sides.}$$

$$x = \underline{\ ?\ } \qquad \text{Simplify.}$$

2 $0.6(1 - x) + 0.2(x - 5) = 10$

3 $\dfrac{3x}{5} + \dfrac{x - 1}{3} = \dfrac{2}{15}$

Write the decimal $0.1\overline{6}$ as a fraction.

Solution

STEP 1 Assign a variable to the repeating decimal.

Let $x = 0.1\overline{6}$.

$x = 0.166666...$ $10x = 1.6666666...$

Notice that if you multiply both sides of this equation by 10, the infinite number of repeating digits does not change. So you can subtract one equation from the other to eliminate the infinite string of digits.

STEP 2 Subtract x from $10x$ to get a terminating decimal.

$$10x - x = 1.\overline{6} - 0.1\overline{6} \quad\text{or}\quad$$

$$9x = 1.5$$

$$\begin{array}{r} 10x = 1.6666666... \\ -\quad x = -0.1666666... \\ \hline 9x = 1.50000 \end{array}$$

STEP 3 Solve for x.

$$\frac{9x}{9} = \frac{1.5}{9} \qquad \text{Divide both sides by 9.}$$

$$x = \frac{1}{6} \qquad \text{Simplify.}$$

$$\boxed{\frac{1.5}{9} = \frac{3}{18} = \frac{1}{6}}$$

So, $0.1\overline{6} = \frac{1}{6}$.

Think Math

If a decimal, x, has two digits that repeat instead of one, what number do you multiply x by before subtracting? Explain.

Guided Practice

Write each repeating decimal as a fraction. Show your work.

 $0.\overline{09}$

5 $0.\overline{8}$

 $0.0\overline{6}$

Solve Real-World Problems Involving Linear Equations with One Variable.

You have learned that to solve real-world problems algebraically, you represent unknown quantities with variables and model the problems with algebraic equations.

A belt costs $30 less than a pair of jeans. The ratio of the cost of the jeans to the cost of a shirt is 2 : 1. If the total cost of the three items is $75, find the cost of the jeans.

You represent the costs using bar models as shown below.

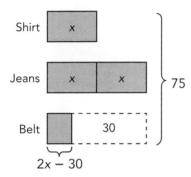

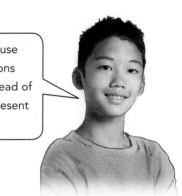

After this, you will use algebraic expressions and equations instead of bar models to represent relationships.

Let the cost of the shirt be x dollars. Then the pair of jeans costs $2x$ dollars and the belt costs $(2x - 30)$ dollars. So, the total cost of the three items is $(x + 2x + 2x - 30)$ dollars.

Because they cost $75 altogether,

$x + 2x + 2x - 30 = 75$	Write an equation.
$5x - 30 = 75$	Add the like terms.
$5x - 30 + 30 = 75 + 30$	Add 30 to both sides.
$5x = 105$	Simplify.
$\dfrac{5x}{5} = \dfrac{105}{5}$	Divide both sides by 5.
$x = 21$	Simplify.

Cost of the jeans: $\$21 \cdot 2 = \$42$

The jeans cost $42.

You can check the reasonableness of the solution by using mental estimation. The shirt costs about $20, so the jeans cost about $40 and the belt costs about $10. The three items cost about $70 in total, which is close to $75.

Example 3 **Solve real-world problems involving linear equations with one variable.**

Mr. Gates' bathroom walls are $91\frac{1}{4}$ inches tall. He wants to mount a mirror with a height of $28\frac{1}{4}$ inches on the wall. The distance from the top of the mirror to the ceiling should be $\frac{1}{2}$ the distance from the bottom of the mirror to the floor. Find the distance of the mirror from the floor.

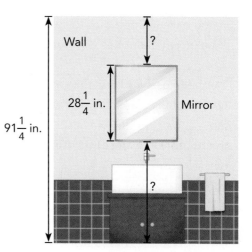

Solution

Let the distance of the mirror from the floor be x inches.

So, the distance of the mirror from the ceiling is $\frac{1}{2}x$ inches.

$$x + 28\frac{1}{4} + \frac{1}{2}x = 91\frac{1}{4}$$ Write an equation.

$$\frac{3}{2}x + 28\frac{1}{4} = 91\frac{1}{4}$$ Add like terms.

$$\frac{3}{2}x + 28\frac{1}{4} - 28\frac{1}{4} = 91\frac{1}{4} - 28\frac{1}{4}$$ Subtract $28\frac{1}{4}$ from both sides.

$$\frac{3}{2}x = 63$$ Simplify.

$$\frac{3}{2}x \cdot \frac{2}{3} = 63 \cdot \frac{2}{3}$$ Multiply both sides by $\frac{2}{3}$.

$$x = 42$$ Simplify.

The distance of the mirror from the floor is 42 inches.

The wall's height is about 90 inches, and the mirror's height is about 30 inches. So, the total distance above and below the mirror is about 60 inches.

$\frac{2}{3}$ of 60 inches is 40 inches. So, the answer is reasonable.

Guided Practice

Write an equation and solve. Show your work.

7 Mr. Johnson wants to add a circular pond to his backyard. The backyard is $20\frac{1}{2}$ yards long, and the pond will be $6\frac{1}{4}$ yards across. He wants the pond set back from the house, so that the distance from the pond to the back fence is half the distance from the pond to the back of the house. How far should the pond be from the back of the house?

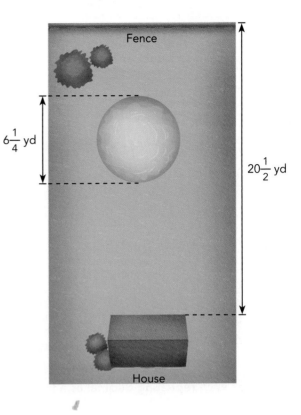

Fence

$6\frac{1}{4}$ yd

$20\frac{1}{2}$ yd

House

Let the distance from the pond to the house be x yards.

So, the distance from the pond to the fence is $\frac{1}{2}$x yards.

$\underline{\quad?\quad} = 20\frac{1}{2}$ Write an equation.

$\underline{\quad?\quad} = 20\frac{1}{2}$ Add like terms.

$\underline{\quad?\quad} = 20\frac{1}{2} - \underline{\;?\;}$ Subtract $\underline{\;?\;}$ from both sides.

$\underline{\quad?\quad} = \underline{\;?\;}$ Simplify.

$\underline{\;?\;} \cdot \underline{\;?\;} = \underline{\;?\;} \cdot \underline{\;?\;}$ Multiply both sides by $\underline{\;?\;}$.

$x = \underline{\;?\;}$ Simplify.

The distance from the pond to the house is $\underline{\;?\;}$ yards.

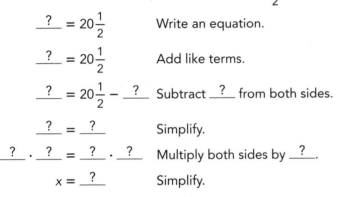

The length of the backyard is about $\underline{\;?\;}$ yards and the width of the pond is about $\underline{\;?\;}$ yards. So the total distance of the pond to the house and of the pond to the gate is around $\underline{\;?\;}$ yards.

$\underline{\;?\;}$ of $\underline{\;?\;}$ yards is about $\underline{\;?\;}$ yards. So, the answer is reasonable.

8 A packager of tea leaves blends 3.5 pounds of Tea Leaf A with 1.5 pounds of Tea Leaf B to make a special blend. One pound of Tea Leaf B costs $2 less than one pound of Tea Leaf A. The packager finds that the cost of making the blend is $3 per pound. Find the cost of one pound of Tea Leaf B.

Solve each linear equation. Show your work.

1 $4x - (10 - x) = \dfrac{15}{2}$

2 $0.5(x + 1) - 1 = 0.2$

3 $2(x - 1) - 6 = 10(1 - x) + 6$

4 $8(x - 3) - (x - 3) = 0.7$

5 $2(x - 4) + 0.5(2 + 8x) = 0$

6 $5 - 3(x - 7) = 2(2 - x) - 8$

7 $3x - 0.4(5 - 2x) = 5.6$

8 $6 + \dfrac{1}{3}(x - 9) = \dfrac{1}{2}(2 - x)$

9 $\dfrac{3x - 2}{8} + \dfrac{2 - x}{4} = -\dfrac{1}{2}$

10 $-\dfrac{x + 1}{6} - \dfrac{5 - 3x}{4} = \dfrac{1}{3}$

11 $\dfrac{5(x + 2)}{3} - \dfrac{x - 1}{3} = 1$

12 $\dfrac{4(2x + 3)}{5} - \dfrac{x + 1}{4} = \dfrac{31}{5}$

Express each repeating decimal as a fraction. Show your work.

13 $0.8\overline{3}$

14 $0.0\overline{8}$

15 $0.\overline{1}$

16 $0.08\overline{3}$

17 $0.0\overline{5}$

18 $0.0\overline{45}$

Solve each problem algebraically. Show your work.

19 Logan saves $5.50 in dimes and quarters over a week. He has 20 more dimes than quarters. Find the number of dimes and quarters he saves.

20 Maggie makes some fruit punch. She mixes $2\dfrac{1}{2}$ quarts of grape juice with $1\dfrac{1}{2}$ quarts of orange juice. One quart of grape juice costs $1 less than one quart of orange juice. She finds that the total cost of making the fruit punch is $12.50. Calculate the cost of each quart of grape juice and each quart of orange juice.

21 Ms. Handler walks to work at an average speed of 5 kilometers per hour. If she increases her speed to 6 kilometers per hour, she will save 10 minutes.

a) Complete the table.

Speed (km/h)	Distance (km)	Time (h)	Time (min)
5	d	?	?
6	d	?	?

b) Find the distance she walks.

22 Jane is x years old today. Her brother Kenny is 4 years older. After seven years, their total combined age will be 24 years.

    a)   Write a linear equation for their total combined age after 7 years.

    b)   Find Jane's age today.

23 Casper bought some pencils at 50¢ each. He had $3 left after the purchase. If he wanted to buy the same number of note pads at 80¢ each, he would be short $1.50. Write a linear equation for the number of pencils he purchased. Then solve it.

24 Alexis earns $2\frac{1}{2}$ times as much as Gary in a day. James earns $18 more than Gary in a day. If the total daily salary of all three people is $306, find Alexis's salary.

25 A store has y shirts. It sold most of them for $16 each, and the last dozen were sold on sale for $14 each. If it sold all the shirts for $616, find the number of shirts sold.

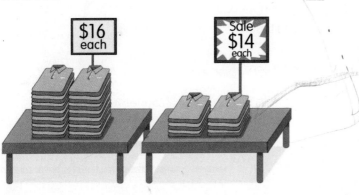

26 There are 40 questions on a class test. Six points are given for each correct answer and three points are deducted for each wrong or missing answer. Find the number of correct answers for a test score of 105.

27 🖊️📓 *Math Journal* Georgina was given that the length of a rectangle was 2.5 inches longer than its width, and that the perimeter of the rectangle was 75.4 inches. She found the length and width algebraically. How could she use estimation to check if her answers were reasonable?

28 🖊️📓 *Math Journal* Consider the decimal $0.\overline{9}$.

    a)   Find the fraction equivalent of $0.\overline{9}$.

    b)   The decimal $0.\overline{9}$ can be thought of as being equal to the following sum, in which the pattern shown continues forever.

       0.9 + 0.09 + 0.009 + 0.0009 + ...

    How can thinking about this sum help you explain the result you saw in **a)**?

3.2 Identifying the Number of Solutions to a Linear Equation

Lesson Objectives

- Understand and identify linear equations with no solution.
- Understand and identify linear equations with infinitely many solutions.

Vocabulary

inconsistent equation

consistent equation

identity

Understand and Identify Linear Equations with No Solution.

So far, the linear equations you have encountered have had one solution. For example, $x + 4 = 9$ has one solution, because you get an equivalent equation of the form $x = a$, where a is a numerical value. In this case, the solution is 5. However, not all linear equations have one solution.

Try solving the equation $x + 4 = x$.

$$x + 4 \overset{?}{=} x$$

$$x + 4 - x \overset{?}{=} x - x \qquad \text{Subtract } x \text{ from both sides.}$$
$$4 \neq 0 \qquad\qquad \text{Simplify. False statement.}$$

The variable x has disappeared. 4 is not equal to 0. Because the solving ends with a false statement, the equation has no solution.

Math Note

$x + 4 = x$ cannot have a solution because no number is equal to 4 added to the number.

An **inconsistent equation** is an equation with no solution.

Example 4 **Identify a linear equation with no solution.**

Tell whether each equation is inconsistent. Justify your answer.

a) $5(x + 3) = 5x + 3$

Solution

$$5(x + 3) \overset{?}{=} 5x + 3$$

$$5x + 15 \overset{?}{=} 5x + 3 \qquad \text{Use the distributive property.}$$

$$5x + 15 - 5x \overset{?}{=} 5x + 3 - 5x \qquad \text{Subtract } 5x \text{ from both sides.}$$
$$15 \neq 3 \qquad\qquad\qquad \text{Simplify.}$$

Because $15 \neq 3$, the equation has no solution. So, the equation is inconsistent.

b) $3(x - 4) = 2(x - 1)$

Solution

$$3(x - 4) \stackrel{?}{=} 2(x - 1)$$

$3x - 12 \stackrel{?}{=} 2x - 2$	Use the distributive property.
$3x - 12 - 2x \stackrel{?}{=} 2x - 2 - 2x$	Subtract 2x from both sides.
$x - 12 \stackrel{?}{=} -2$	Simplify.
$x - 12 + 12 \stackrel{?}{=} -2 + 12$	Add 12 to both sides.
$x = 10$	Simplify.

Because the equation has one solution, it is **consistent**.

Guided Practice

Tell whether each equation is consistent or inconsistent. Justify your answer by simplifying each equation. Write +, −, ×, or ÷ for each ❓ .

1 $7(x - 3) - 7x - 21 = 0$

$$7(x - 3) - 7x - 21 \stackrel{?}{=} 0$$

$\underline{\quad?\quad}\; \boxed{?} \;\underline{\quad?\quad} - 7x - 21 \stackrel{?}{=} 0$	Use the distributive property.
$\underline{\quad?\quad} \neq 0$	Simplify.

Because $\underline{\;?\;} \neq 0$, the equation has $\underline{\;?\;}$ solution. The equation is $\underline{\;?\;}$.

2 $5\left(x + \dfrac{1}{5}\right) = 5x + 3$

3 $x + \dfrac{1}{4} = -\dfrac{1}{4}(4x - 1)$

Understand and Identify Linear Equations with Infinitely Many Solutions.

Consider the equation $3x + 5 = x + 2x + 5$. If you try solving the equation, see what happens.

$3x + 5 \stackrel{?}{=} x + 2x + 5$	
$3x + 5 \stackrel{?}{=} 3x + 5$	Combine like terms.
$3x + 5 - 3x \stackrel{?}{=} 3x + 5 - 3x$	Subtract 3x from both sides.
$5 = 5$	Simplify.

> **Caution** ///////
>
> 5 = 5 does not mean that x = 5.

Once again, the variable x has disappeared. $5 = 5$ is always true, no matter what the value of x is. Because the solving ends with a true statement, the equation has infinitely many solutions.

> An **identity** is an equation that is true for all values of the variable.

Example 5 **Identify a linear equation with infinitely many solutions.**

Tell whether each equation is an identity. Justify your answer.

a) $7x - 10 = 3(x - 2) + 4(x - 1)$

Solution

$7x - 10 \stackrel{?}{=} 3(x - 2) + 4(x - 1)$

$7x - 10 \stackrel{?}{=} 3x - 6 + 4x - 4$ Use the distributive property.

$7x - 10 \stackrel{?}{=} 7x - 10$ Combine like terms.

$7x - 10 - 7x \stackrel{?}{=} 7x - 10 - 7x$ Subtract 7x from both sides.

$-10 = -10$ Simplify.

Because $-10 = -10$ is always true, the linear equation is true for any value of x.
So, this equation has infinitely many solutions, and it is an identity.

b) $\dfrac{x}{3} + \dfrac{2(2x + 1)}{5} = \dfrac{1}{3}$

Solution

$\dfrac{x}{3} + \dfrac{2(2x + 1)}{5} \stackrel{?}{=} \dfrac{1}{3}$

$\dfrac{5x}{15} + \dfrac{3 \cdot 2(2x + 1)}{15} \stackrel{?}{=} \dfrac{1}{3}$ Write equivalent fractions using the LCD, 15.

$\dfrac{5x + 6(2x + 1)}{15} \stackrel{?}{=} \dfrac{1}{3}$ Write the left side as a single fraction.

$\dfrac{5x + 12x + 6}{15} \stackrel{?}{=} \dfrac{1}{3}$ Use the distributive property.

$\dfrac{17x + 6}{15} \stackrel{?}{=} \dfrac{1}{3}$ Combine like terms.

$15 \cdot \dfrac{17x + 6}{15} \stackrel{?}{=} 15 \cdot \dfrac{1}{3}$ Multiply both sides by 15.

$17x + 6 \stackrel{?}{=} 5$ Simplify.

$17x + 6 - 6 \stackrel{?}{=} 5 - 6$ Subtract 6 from both sides.

$17x \stackrel{?}{=} -1$ Simplify.

$\dfrac{17x}{17} \stackrel{?}{=} \dfrac{-1}{17}$ Divide both sides by 17.

$x = -\dfrac{1}{17}$ Simplify.

Because the equation has one solution, $-\dfrac{1}{17}$, it is not an identity.

It is a consistent equation.

Guided Practice

Tell whether each equation is an identity. Justify your answer by simplifying each equation. Write +, −, ×, or ÷ for each ⬤? . Write = or ≠ for each ⬛? .

4 $2(x - 1) + 3 = 2x + 1$

$$2(x - 1) + 3 \stackrel{?}{=} 2x + 1$$

$\underline{\quad?\quad} \; \text{⬤?} \; \underline{\quad?\quad} + 3 \stackrel{?}{=} 2x + 1$ Use the distributive property.

$\underline{\quad?\quad} \stackrel{?}{=} 2x + 1$ Combine like terms.

$\underline{\quad?\quad} \stackrel{?}{=} 2x + 1 - \underline{\quad?\quad}$ Subtract $\underline{\quad?\quad}$ from both sides.

$\underline{\quad?\quad} = \underline{\quad?\quad}$ Simplify.

Because $\underline{\quad?\quad} = \underline{\quad?\quad}$, the equation has $\underline{\quad?\quad}$ solution(s). The equation is a(n) $\underline{\quad?\quad}$.

5 $6(x + 5) - 10 = 3(2x - 3)$

$$6(x + 5) - 10 \stackrel{?}{=} 3(2x - 3)$$

$\underline{\quad?\quad} \; \text{⬤?} \; \underline{\quad?\quad} - 10 \stackrel{?}{=} \underline{\quad?\quad} \; \text{⬤?} \; \underline{\quad?\quad}$ Use the distributive property.

$\underline{\quad?\quad} \stackrel{?}{=} \underline{\quad?\quad}$ Combine like terms.

$\underline{\quad?\quad} \stackrel{?}{=} \underline{\quad?\quad}$ Subtract $\underline{\quad?\quad}$ from both sides.

$\underline{\quad?\quad} \; \text{⬛?} \; \underline{\quad?\quad}$ Simplify.

Because $\underline{\quad?\quad} \; \text{⬛?} \; \underline{\quad?\quad}$, the equation has $\underline{\quad?\quad}$ solution(s). The equation is a(n) $\underline{\quad?\quad}$.

> Try substituting some values of x into the equation. If you find that the left side is always equal to the right side, the equation is an identity.

Tell whether each equation has one solution, no solution, or an infinite number of solutions. Justify your answer.

1 $2x - 3 = -2\left(\dfrac{3}{2} - x\right)$

2 $2x + 5 = -4\left(\dfrac{3}{2} - x\right)$

3 $3x + 5 = 2x - 7$

4 $5y + (86 - y) = 86 + 4y$

5 $0.5(6x - 3) = 3(1 + x)$

6 $4(18a - 7) + 40 = 3(4 + 24a)$

7 $\dfrac{1}{7}(7x - 21) = 8x + 7x - 24$

8 $\dfrac{1}{6}(12x - 18) = 2\left(x - \dfrac{3}{2}\right)$

9 $7 - 0.75x = -7\left(\dfrac{3}{28}x + 1\right)$

10 $6 + 0.5y = -2\left(3 - \dfrac{1}{4}y\right)$

11 $\dfrac{x - 3}{4} = 0.25x - 0.75$

12 $\dfrac{1}{3}x + 5 = \dfrac{1}{6}\left(2x - 5\right)$

Solve. Show your work.

13 Cabinet A is 5 inches taller than Cabinet B. Cabinet C is 3 inches taller than Cabinet B whose height is x inches.

a) Write algebraic expressions for the heights of cabinets A and C.

b) If the total height of the three cabinets is (3x + 8) inches, can you solve for the height of Cabinet B? Explain.

14 A room's floor is y meters long. Its width is 5 meters shorter. If the perimeter of the floor is (4y + 1) meters, can you solve for its length? Explain.

15 *Math Journal* Grace gave her sister a riddle: I have a number x. I add 15 to twice x to get result A. I subtract 4 from x to get result B. I multiply result B by 3 to get result C. Result A is equal to result C. Grace's sister said the riddle cannot be solved, but Grace thought otherwise. Who is right? Explain.

16 *Math Journal* Look at this "proof" that 2 = 0.

> When $a = 1$ and $b = 1$, then
> $(a - b)(a + b) = 0$
> $a + b = 0$ Divide both sides by $a - b$.
> $1 + 1 = 0$ Substitute for a and b.
> $2 = 0$ Simplify.

What is wrong with this proof? How can a true statement lead to an inconsistent equation?

3.3 Understanding Linear Equations with Two Variables

Lesson Objectives

- Represent a relationship between two variables using a linear equation.
- Represent a linear relationship using a table of values.

Represent a Relationship Between Two Variables Using a Linear Equation.

You have worked with linear equations with one variable. Linear equations can also have two variables.

Consider the following situation: Dorothy has a younger brother, Benjamin. The table shows their ages over five years.

	2008	2009	2010	2011	2012
Benjamin's Age	1	2	3	4	5
Dorothy's Age	4	5	6	7	8

Notice that Dorothy's age is always 3 years more than Benjamin's age. You can represent the relationship between their ages using a linear equation with two variables.

If Benjamin is x years old and Dorothy is y years old, the variables x and y are related by the linear equation $y = x + 3$.

Look for a pattern between the values for Benjamin's age and the values for Dorothy's age.

Think Math

What expression can you write to express Benjamin's age in terms of Dorothy's age? What equation can you write using this expression? Is the equation equivalent to $y = x + 3$? Explain.

Example 6 **Express a linear relationship between two variables.**

Solve. Show your work.

a) Write a linear equation for the relationship between hours, h, and minutes, m.

Solution

An hour has 60 minutes. So a linear equation for m in terms of h is $m = 60h$.

You could also write the equation $h = \frac{m}{60}$ to represent the relationship between h and m. The equations $m = 60h$ and $h = \frac{m}{60}$ are equivalent.

b) Ms. Ford heated a liquid and measured its temperature. She recorded the results in the following table. Write a linear equation for the relationship between the time, t, and the liquid's temperature, T.

Time (*t* minutes)	0	1	2	3	4
Temperature (*T* °C)	25	30	35	40	45

Solution

The initial temperature is 25°C. After that, the temperature rises by 5°C for every minute. You can make a table of values of t and T as follows.

t	*T*
0	$25 = 25 + 0 = 25 + 5 \cdot 0$
1	$30 = 25 + 5 = 25 + 5 \cdot 1$
2	$35 = 25 + 10 = 25 + 5 \cdot 2$
3	$40 = 25 + 15 = 25 + 5 \cdot 3$
4	$45 = 25 + 20 = 25 + 5 \cdot 4$

Observe that the expressions for T follow a pattern. They also contain a varying number that has the same value as t. You can replace the varying number by t to get the general expression $25 + 5t$ for T.

A linear equation for T in terms of t is $T = 25 + 5t$.

Guided Practice

Complete.

1 Write a linear equation for the relationship between days, d, and weeks, w.

A week has __?__ days. So a linear equation for d in terms of w is __?__.

2 George rented a car from a company for a week. The table shows the rental charges.

Distance (d miles)	0	1	2	3	4
Rental Charge (C dollars)	100	100.10	100.20	100.30	100.40

The company charged a $__?__ flat fee plus $__?__ for every mile of travel.

d	C
0	100 $= 100 + \underline{\ ?\ } = 100 + \underline{\ ?\ } \cdot \underline{\ ?\ }$
1	$100.10 = 100 + \underline{\ ?\ } = 100 + \underline{\ ?\ } \cdot \underline{\ ?\ }$
2	$100.20 = 100 + \underline{\ ?\ } = 100 + \underline{\ ?\ } \cdot \underline{\ ?\ }$
3	$100.30 = 100 + \underline{\ ?\ } = 100 + \underline{\ ?\ } \cdot \underline{\ ?\ }$
4	$100.40 = 100 + \underline{\ ?\ } = 100 + \underline{\ ?\ } \cdot \underline{\ ?\ }$

A linear equation for C in terms of d is __?__.

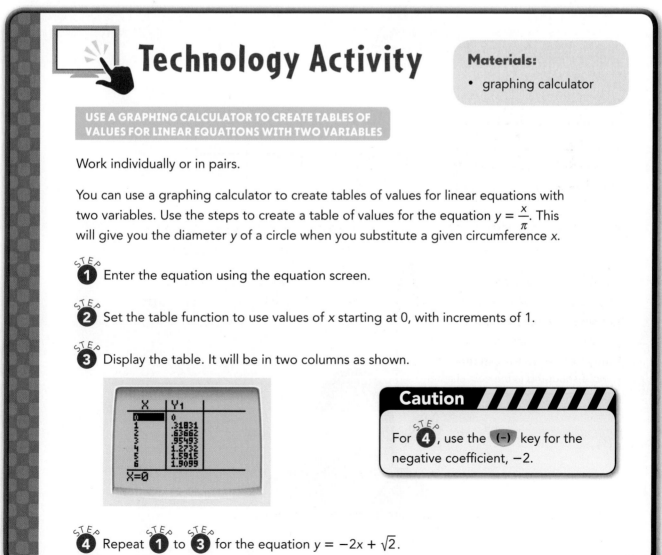

Technology Activity

Materials:
• graphing calculator

USE A GRAPHING CALCULATOR TO CREATE TABLES OF VALUES FOR LINEAR EQUATIONS WITH TWO VARIABLES

Work individually or in pairs.

You can use a graphing calculator to create tables of values for linear equations with two variables. Use the steps to create a table of values for the equation $y = \dfrac{x}{\pi}$. This will give you the diameter y of a circle when you substitute a given circumference x.

STEP 1 Enter the equation using the equation screen.

STEP 2 Set the table function to use values of x starting at 0, with increments of 1.

STEP 3 Display the table. It will be in two columns as shown.

X	Y1
0	0
1	.31831
2	.63662
3	.95493
4	1.2732
5	1.5915
6	1.9099

X=0

Caution ///////

For **STEP 4**, use the (−) key for the negative coefficient, −2.

STEP 4 Repeat **STEP 1** to **STEP 3** for the equation $y = -2x + \sqrt{2}$.

Represent a Linear Relationship Using a Table of Values.

You have learned to write a linear equation to represent a relationship between two variables. The relationship can also be represented by a table of values.

You know that the sum of the angle measures of a triangle is 180°. You can use this fact to find the sum of the angle measures of a polygon with any number of sides. The polygons shown are divided into triangles. The sum, S, of the angle measures of the triangles equals the sum of measures of the angles in the polygon. Because there are 2 fewer triangles than the number of sides, n, of a polygon, the relationship can be represented by the equation $180(n - 2) = S$.

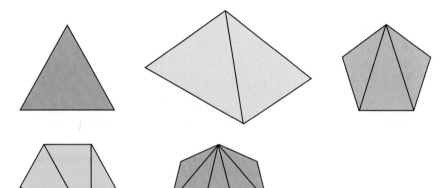

Number of Sides of Polygon (n)	3	4	5	6	7
Sum of Angle Measures ($S°$)	180	360	540	720	900

So, you can create a table of values for a linear relationship between two variables by substituting values for one variable into the linear equation. Then calculate the corresponding values for the other variable.

A table of values for a linear relationship is useful for drawing the graph of the relationship. You will learn more about this in the next chapter.

Example 7 **Evaluate linear equations with two variables.**

Find the value of y when $x = 7$ in each of the equations.

a) $y = \dfrac{x - 5}{2}$

Solution

$y = \dfrac{7 - 5}{2}$ Substitute 7 for x.

$y = \dfrac{2}{2}$ Subtract.

$y = 1$ Simplify.

b) $3y + 4 = 2x$

Solution

$3y + 4 = 2(7)$ Substitute 7 for x.

$3y + 4 - 4 = 14 - 4$ Subtract 4 from both sides.

$3y = 10$ Simplify.

$\dfrac{3y}{3} = \dfrac{10}{3}$ Divide both sides by 3.

$y = 3\dfrac{1}{3}$ Simplify.

> **Math Note**
>
> Observe that in a), y is already expressed in terms of x. You just have to substitute for x to evaluate y. In b) and c), when you substitute a value for x, you get an equation with one variable y. You have to solve this one-variable equation to find the value of y.

c) $x = \dfrac{9}{2}y - 15.5$

Solution

$7 = \dfrac{9}{2}y - 15.5$ Substitute 7 for x.

$7 + 15.5 = \dfrac{9}{2}y - 15.5 + 15.5$ Add 15.5 to both sides.

$22.5 = \dfrac{9}{2}y$ Simplify.

$22.5 \cdot 2 = \dfrac{9}{2}y \cdot 2$ Multiply both sides by 2.

$45 = 9y$ Simplify.

$45 \div 9 = 9y \div 9$ Divide both sides by 9.

$5 = y$ Simplify.

> In b) and c), another way to find the value of y is to express y in terms of x before substituting the value of x into the expression for y. You will learn how to do this in the next lesson.

Guided Practice

Find the value of y when $x = -4$.

3 $y = 7 + 3x$

4 $\dfrac{1}{3}y = 2\left(x - \dfrac{1}{6}\right)$

5 $-6x - y = 17.75$

Solve. Show your work.

a) Create a table of x- and y-values for the equation $\frac{y}{2} = \frac{3}{2}x + 2$. Use integer values of x from -1 to 1.

Solution

Substitute -1 for x into the equation:

$$\frac{y}{2} = \frac{3}{2}(-1) + 2$$

$$\frac{y}{2} = \frac{1}{2} \qquad \text{Simplify.}$$

$$\frac{y}{2} \cdot 2 = \frac{1}{2} \cdot 2 \qquad \text{Multiply both sides by 2.}$$

$$y = 1 \qquad \text{Simplify.}$$

Substitute 0 for x into the equation:

$$\frac{y}{2} = \frac{3}{2}(0) + 2$$

$$\frac{y}{2} = 2 \qquad \text{Simplify.}$$

$$\frac{y}{2} \cdot 2 = 2 \cdot 2 \qquad \text{Multiply both sides by 2.}$$

$$y = 4 \qquad \text{Simplify.}$$

> **Math Note**
>
> Remember to substitute 0 as one of the integers.

Substitute 1 for x into the equation:

$$\frac{y}{2} = \frac{3}{2}(1) + 2$$

$$\frac{y}{2} = \frac{7}{2} \qquad \text{Simplify.}$$

$$\frac{y}{2} \cdot 2 = \frac{7}{2} \cdot 2 \qquad \text{Multiply both sides by 2.}$$

$$y = 7 \qquad \text{Simplify.}$$

So the table of values is:

x	−1	0	1
y	1	4	7

> When solving a linear equation in two variables, you know that each x-value has a corresponding y-value. So every equation has an infinite number of solutions. One way to represent some of these solutions is with a table of values.

b) Complete the table of values for the equation $8y = 5(x - 4)$.

x	2	?	6
y	?	0	?

Solution

Substitute 2 for x into the equation:

$8y = 5(2 - 4)$

$8y = -10$ Simplify.

$8y \div 8 = -10 \div 8$ Divide both sides by 8.

$y = -1.25$ Simplify.

Substitute 0 for y into the equation:

$0 = 5(x - 4)$

$0 \div 5 = 5(x - 4) \div 5$ Divide both sides by 5.

$0 = x - 4$ Simplify.

$0 + 4 = x - 4 + 4$ Add 4 to both sides.

$4 = x$ Simplify.

To solve the equation $0 = 5(x - 4)$, you should be able to recognize that $x - 4$ is 0 because any number multiplied by 0 equals 0.

Substitute 6 for x into the equation:

$8y = 5(6 - 4)$

$8y = 10$ Simplify.

$8y \div 8 = 10 \div 8$ Divide both sides by 8.

$y = 1.25$ Simplify.

So the table of values is:

x	2	4	6
y	−1.25	0	1.25

Guided Practice

Create a table of x- and y-values for each equation. Use integer values of x from 1 to 3.

6 $2y = 1.2x + 1$

7 $4y - 11x = 6$

Complete the table of x- and y-values for each equation.

8 $\dfrac{y - 2}{3} = x$

x	?	0	1
y	−1	?	?

9 $3(x + 1) - 2y = 0$

x	?	?	?
y	9	$16\frac{1}{2}$	24

Practice 3.3

Write a linear equation for the relationship between the given quantities.

1 meters, m, and centimeters, c

2 hours, h, and seconds, s

3 feet, f, and inches, i

4 dollars, d, and cents, c

Find the value of y when $x = 2$.

5 $2x - 1 = y + 4$

6 $y = \frac{1}{7}(x + 5)$

7 $3x - 11 = 2(y - 4)$

8 $4y = 5(x - 1)$

Find the value of x when $y = -7$.

9 $2(3x - 7) = 9y$

10 $\frac{2x - 1}{5} = 2(y + 7)$

11 $2x + y = 0.1(y + 3)$

12 $2y - 5x = 26$

Create a table of x- and y-values for each equation. Use integer values of x from 1 to 3.

13 $y = \frac{1}{4}(8 - x)$

14 $x + 7 = \frac{1}{2}(y - 5)$

15 $-4y = 2x + 5$

16 $\frac{1}{2}(x + 4) = \frac{1}{3}(y + 1)$

Complete the table of x- and y-values for each equation.

17 $y = 5(x + 3)$

x	0	1	2
y	?	?	?

18 $\frac{x}{4} + y = 1$

x	2	?	?
y	?	0	-0.5

19 $3x - 4y = \frac{5}{3}$

x	?	-2	-1
y	$-2\frac{2}{3}$	?	?

20 $5(y + 4) = 8x$

x	?	?	?
y	-4	12	28

Solve. Show your work.

21 A research student recorded the distance traveled by a car for every gallon of gasoline used. She recorded the results in the following table. Write a linear equation for the distance traveled, d miles, in terms of the amount of gasoline used, g gallons.

Amount of Gasoline Used (g gallons)	1	2	3	4
Distance Traveled (d miles)	40.5	81	121.5	162

22 Mr. Taransky sells blood pressure monitors. He earns a monthly salary that includes a basic amount of $750 and $5 for each monitor sold.

a) Write a linear equation for his monthly salary, M dollars, in terms of the number of monitors sold, n.

b) Use the equation to complete the table of values below.

n	0	?	?	150
M	?	1,000	1,250	?

c) Calculate his salary when he sold 300 monitors in a month.

d) His salary was $1,450 in January. How many monitors did he sell that month?

23 Bernadette's cell phone plan costs a basic charge of $20 a month plus 5¢ per minute of calling time after she uses the first 300 minutes of calling time in a month.

a) Write a linear equation for the total cost, C dollars, in terms of the total number of minutes of calling time, t minutes.

b) Create a table of t- and C-values for the linear equation. Use $t = 300, 400,$ and 500.

c) Find the total number of minutes of calling time Bernardette uses in a month when her bill is $32.

24 A parking lot charges $1.50 for the first hour or part of an hour. After the first hour, parking costs 70¢ for each half hour, or part of a half hour. Mr. Fischer parked his car in the parking lot for t hours.

a) Write a linear equation for the total cost of parking, y dollars, in terms of t.

b) Find the amount Mr. Fischer had to pay if he parked his car for 40 minutes.

c) What was the total cost if he parked for 1 hour and 40 minutes?

PARKING	
First hour or part of hour	$1.50
Every half hour or part of half hour after first hour	$0.70

3.4 Solving for a Variable in a Two-Variable Linear Equation

Lesson Objective

• Solve for a variable in a two-variable linear equation.

Solve for a Variable in a Two-Variable Linear Equation.

Consider the formula for the perimeter, P units, of a square with a side length of ℓ units, $P = 4\ell$.

You can use this formula to find the value of ℓ when you know the value of P.

For example, if $P = 18$, you can find the value of ℓ by substituting the value of P into the equation and solving for ℓ.

$$P = 4\ell$$
$$18 = 4\ell \qquad \text{Substitute 18 for } P.$$
$$\frac{18}{4} = \frac{4\ell}{4} \qquad \text{Divide both sides by 4.}$$
$$4.5 = \ell \qquad \text{Simplify.}$$

Suppose you are given many values of P and asked to find the corresponding values of ℓ. You may find it convenient to solve the equation for ℓ. That is, you can express ℓ in terms of P before substituting values of P.

To solve the equation for ℓ, you can carry out the following steps.

$$P = 4\ell$$
$$\frac{P}{4} = \frac{4\ell}{4} \qquad \text{Divide both sides by 4.}$$
$$\frac{P}{4} = \ell \qquad \text{Simplify.}$$

> Using either method, you get the same value for ℓ.

Evaluate ℓ when $P = 18$ again.

$$\ell = \frac{P}{4}$$
$$\ell = \frac{18}{4} \qquad \text{Substitute 18 for } P.$$
$$\ell = 4.5 \qquad \text{Simplify.}$$

Example 9 **Solve for a variable in a linear equation with parentheses.**

The formula for converting a temperature in degrees Fahrenheit, $F°F$, to a temperature in degrees Celsius, $C°C$, is $C = \dfrac{5}{9}(F - 32)$.

a) Express F in terms of C.

Solution

$$C = \frac{5}{9}(F - 32)$$

To solve the equation for F, you have to isolate F on one side of the equation.

$$C \cdot \frac{9}{5} = \frac{5}{9}(F - 32) \cdot \frac{9}{5} \qquad \text{Multiply both sides by } \frac{9}{5}.$$

$$\frac{9}{5}C = F - 32 \qquad \text{Simplify.}$$

$$\frac{9}{5}C + 32 = F - 32 + 32 \qquad \text{Add 32 to both sides.}$$

$$\frac{9}{5}C + 32 = F \qquad \text{Simplify.}$$

> **Math Note**
>
> Notice that the equation of F in terms of C and the equation of C in terms of F are both linear. If an equation with two variables is linear, expressing either variable in terms of the other produces an equivalent linear equation.

b) Create a table of C- and F-values for $C = 10, 20, 30,$ and 40.

Solution

Substitute 10, 20, 30, and 40 for C into the equation $F = \dfrac{9}{5}C + 32$:

$$F = \frac{9}{5}(10) + 32 \qquad F = \frac{9}{5}(20) + 32 \qquad F = \frac{9}{5}(30) + 32 \qquad F = \frac{9}{5}(40) + 32$$

$$= 50 \qquad\qquad = 68 \qquad\qquad = 86 \qquad\qquad = 104$$

So, the table of values is:

C	10	20	30	40
F	50	68	86	104

> **Think Math**
>
> Do you think it is easier to find the values of F by expressing F in terms of C first? Why?

Guided Practice

Solve. Show your work.

1 Express x in terms of y for the equation $2(x - 3) = 3y - 1$. Find the value of x when $y = 3$.

$$\underline{\ ?\ } = 3y - 1 \qquad \text{Use the distributive property.}$$

$$\underline{\ ?\ } = 3y - 1 + \underline{\ ?\ } \qquad \text{Add } \underline{\ ?\ } \text{ to both sides.}$$

$$\underline{\ ?\ } = \underline{\ ?\ } \qquad \text{Simplify.}$$

$$\underline{\ ?\ } \div \underline{\ ?\ } = \underline{\ ?\ } \div \underline{\ ?\ } \qquad \text{Divide both sides by } \underline{\ ?\ }.$$

$$x = \underline{\ ?\ } \qquad \text{Simplify.}$$

Substitute 3 for y into the equation $x = \underline{\ ?\ }$:

$$x = \underline{\ ?\ } \qquad\qquad\qquad \text{Substitute 3 for } y.$$

$$x = \underline{\ ?\ } \qquad\qquad\qquad \text{Simplify.}$$

2 Express x in terms of y for the equation $y = \dfrac{2x + 3}{2}$. Find the value of x when $y = -13$.

Example 10 **Solve for a variable in a linear equation when parentheses are needed.**

Solve. Show your work.

In a right isosceles triangle, the lengths of the sides can be expressed as s units, s units, and $s\sqrt{2}$ units. So, its perimeter is given by $P = s + s + s\sqrt{2}$.

> **Math Note**
>
> The expression $s\sqrt{2}$ means s times the square root of 2.

a) Express s in terms of P.

Solution

$$P = s + s + s\sqrt{2}$$

$$P = 2s + s\sqrt{2} \qquad \text{Simplify.}$$

$$P = (2 + \sqrt{2})s \qquad \text{Factor the right side.}$$

$$\frac{P}{2 + \sqrt{2}} = \frac{(2 + \sqrt{2})s}{2 + \sqrt{2}} \qquad \text{Divide both sides by } 2 + \sqrt{2}.$$

$$\frac{P}{2 + \sqrt{2}} = s \qquad \text{Simplify.}$$

> $\dfrac{P}{2 + \sqrt{2}} = s$ is a linear equation that is equivalent to $P = s + s + s\sqrt{2}$.

b) Create a table of values for P and s when $P = 4, 6, 8,$ and 10. Round the values of s to 2 decimal places.

Solution

Substitute 4, 6, 8, and 10 for P into the equation $s = \dfrac{P}{2 + \sqrt{2}}$.

$$s = \frac{4}{2 + \sqrt{2}}$$
$$\approx 1.17$$

$$s = \frac{6}{2 + \sqrt{2}}$$
$$\approx 1.76$$

$$s = \frac{8}{2 + \sqrt{2}}$$
$$\approx 2.34$$

$$s = \frac{10}{2 + \sqrt{2}}$$
$$\approx 2.93$$

So, the table of values is:

P	4	6	8	10
s	1.17	1.76	2.34	2.93

Guided Practice

Solve. Show your work.

3 The mean (or average) of three numbers x, $x\sqrt{3}$, and 2 is M.

a) Express x in terms of M.

$M = \underline{\ ?\ }$ Write an equation of M in terms of x.

$3 \cdot M = \underline{\ ?\ }$ Multiply both sides by 3.

$3M = \underline{\ ?\ }$ Simplify.

$3M - \underline{\ ?\ } = \underline{\ ?\ }$ Subtract $\underline{\ ?\ }$ from both sides.

$\underline{\ ?\ } = \underline{\ ?\ }$ Simplify.

$\underline{\ ?\ } = \underline{\ ?\ }$ Factor the right side.

$\dfrac{?}{?} = \dfrac{?}{?}$ Divide both sides by $\underline{\ ?\ }$.

$\underline{\ ?\ } = x$ Simplify.

b) Create a table of values for M and x when $M = 0, 1, 2,$ and 3. Round each x-value to the nearest hundredth.

Substitute 0, 1, 2, and 3 for M into the equation $x = \underline{\ ?\ }$.

M	0	1	2	3
x	$\underline{\ ?\ }$	$\underline{\ ?\ }$	$\underline{\ ?\ }$	$\underline{\ ?\ }$

Express y in terms of x. Find the value of y when x = −1.

1 $5 - y = 3x$

2 $-3(x + 2) = 5y$

3 $6(x - y) = 19$

4 $4x - 3 = 0.4x - 2y$

5 $\frac{1}{6}x + \frac{3}{4}y = 4$

6 $0.5y - 2 = 0.25x$

Express x in terms of y. Find the value of x when y = 5.

7 $5x - y = 3(x + y)$

8 $3(x + 2y) = 2x + 5y$

9 $1.5(x - y) = 1$

10 $2y + 8 = \frac{1}{4}x$

11 $\frac{2(x - 3)}{y} = 5$

12 $\frac{1}{3}(6x - 1) = \frac{6y}{5}$

Solve. Show your work.

13 The perimeter, P inches, of a semicircle of diameter, d inches, is represented by $P = 0.5\pi d + d$.

   a) Express d in terms of P.

   b) Find the diameter if the perimeter is 36 inches. Use $\frac{22}{7}$ as an approximation for π.

14 The horizontal distance, X inches, and vertical distance, Y inches, of each step of a staircase are related by the linear equation $X = \frac{1}{2}(20 + Y)$.

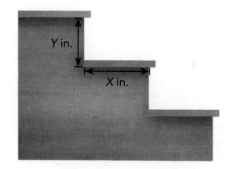

   a) Express Y in terms of X.

   b) Complete the table below.

X	?	16	?	?	19
Y	10	?	14	16	?

   c) Find the value of X and Y if X = Y.

15 Use the isosceles triangle.

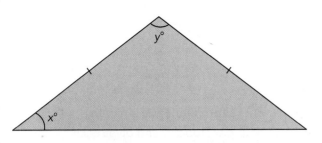

a) Write an equation for y in terms of x.

b) Find the value of y when $x = 24.5$.

16 At a travel agency, the cost of a trip to Mexico is $350 for an adult and $200 for a child. One month, the agency sold 50 trips. Of these trips, y trips were for children. The travel agency collected C dollars from selling all 50 trips.

a) Write a linear equation for C in terms of y.

b) Express y in terms of C.

c) If $15,250 was collected, find the number of children going on the trip.

Adult : $350
Child : $200

17 A trash disposal company charges according to the weight of trash it disposes. The charge, y dollars, for x pounds of trash is represented by the equation

$$y = 2\left(\frac{1}{4}x - 10\right).$$

a) Write an equation for x in terms of y.

b) Create a table of x- and y-values for $y = 60, 80, 100, 120,$ and 140.

18 The mean, or average, of three numbers 17.4, 23.8, and x is M.

a) Write an equation for x in terms of M.

b) Create a table of values for $M = 15, 17, 19, 21,$ and 23.

19 A rectangle has a width of w units and a length of 5 units. Its perimeter is given by $P = 2(w + 5)$. Solve for w in terms of P. Create a table of values for $P = 12, 14, 16,$ and 18.

20 In the number pattern 3, 7, 11, 15, 19, ..., each new number is 4 greater than the previous number. To find the number L in the nth position, use the formula $L = 3 + 4(n - 1)$.

a) What number is in the tenth position?

b) In which position is the number 63?

Brain @ Work

1. Lynnette runs a private tutoring business. She rents a room for $500 a month, which is her only expense. She charges $50 an hour per student, and gives each student two lessons per month. Each lesson lasts 1.5 hours.

   a) Write an equation for her monthly profit, P, in terms of s, the number of students she has.

   b) Find her monthly profit if she has 40 students.

   c) Find the minimum number of students she needs if she wants to make a monthly profit of at least $4,600.

$$x^2 + x - 1 = 0$$

2. Stefanie's train will leave her train station in 24 minutes and she is y miles from the station. To catch the train, she walks at a speed of 4 miles per hour and later runs at a speed of 8 miles per hour.

   a) Write an equation in terms of y for the distance she has to walk, w, to reach the station in 24 minutes.

   b) Solve for y in terms of w. How far is she from the station if she has to walk 1 mile to reach the station on time?

   c) Why do the values of y have to be between 1.6 and 3.2?

3. A polygon has n sides. The sum of the measures of a polygon's interior angles is equal to the sum of the measures of r right angles. A table of r- and n-values is shown below. Explain how you would find a linear equation involving r and n.

n	3	4	5	6
r	2	4	6	8

Chapter Wrap Up

Concept Map

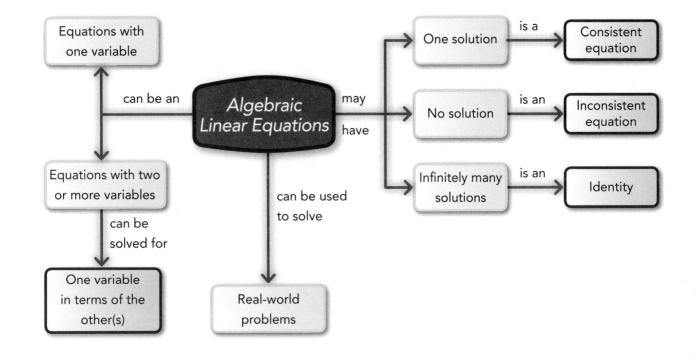

Key Concepts

▶ A linear equation can have one or more variables.

▶ Solving a linear equation involves applying arithmetic and algebraic rules.

▶ A linear equation may have one solution, no solution, or infinitely many solutions.

▶ A consistent equation in one variable is an equation that has one solution.

▶ An inconsistent equation is an equation that has no solution.

▶ An identity is an equation that is true for all values of the variable.

▶ A linear relationship between two variables can be represented with an equation or a table of values.

▶ Solving for a variable in a multi-variable linear equation means expressing the variable in terms of the other variable(s).

▶ Linear equations can be used to represent and solve real-world problems.

Chapter Review/Test

Concepts and Skills

Solve each linear equation. Show your work.

1 $2(x - 5) - 8 = 20$

2 $2x - (5 - x) = \dfrac{5}{2}$

3 $\dfrac{1}{4}(x + 2) - 2 = 0.5$

4 $4x - \dfrac{5 - 2x}{5} = \dfrac{3}{5}$

Write each repeating decimal as a fraction. Show your work.

5 $0.\overline{2}$

6 $0.9\overline{3}$

7 $0.2\overline{6}$

8 $0.3\overline{16}$

Tell whether each equation has one solution, no solution, or an infinite number of solutions. Show your work.

9 $2x + 4 = -2\left(\dfrac{1}{2} - x\right)$

10 $6y + (16 - 2y) = 4(4 + y)$

11 $4x + 5 = 2x - 7$

12 $2x + 5 = -4\left(-\dfrac{5}{4} - \dfrac{1}{2}x\right)$

Find the value of y when x = 4.

13 $4x - 2 = y + 5$

14 $x - 4y = 2$

15 $y - x = \dfrac{1}{3}(x + 14)$

16 $\dfrac{3x - 7}{y} = \dfrac{1}{3}$

17 $\dfrac{1}{7}(3x + y) = x$

18 $\dfrac{3y + 1}{4} = 2x$

Express x in terms of y. Find the value of x when y = −2.

19 $4x + y = 2(x + 3y)$

20 $3(x - 2y) = 4x + 5y$

21 $\dfrac{1}{3}x + \dfrac{5}{6}y = 2$

22 $\dfrac{0.5(x - 3)}{y} = 10$

23 $0.25(x + y) = 15 - x$

24 $\dfrac{y}{2} - \dfrac{2x + y}{5} = 7$

Problem Solving

Solve. Show your work.

25 A circular pizza with a radius of 7 inches is cut into four quadrants. The perimeter Q of each quadrant can be found using the formula $Q = d\left(1 + \dfrac{\pi}{4}\right)$, where d is the diameter of the pizza. Find the perimeter of each quadrant of the pizza. Use $\dfrac{22}{7}$ as an approximation for π.

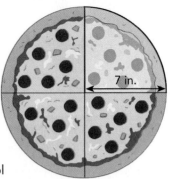

7 in.

26 Some students painted a design on the wall of the cafeteria using the school colors. The middle section of the design is 4.2 feet tall, and is painted white. The top section is red, and the bottom section is blue. The ratio of the height of the blue section to the height of the red section is 1 : 2. The total height of the design is 10.5 feet. Find the height of the red section of the design.

27 In a grocery store, each pound of green beans costs one and a quarter times the price of each pound of potatoes. Mrs. Gomez bought 4 pounds of green beans and 5 pounds of potatoes. Miss Jacobs bought 10 pounds of potatoes. They paid the same amount.

   a) Write a linear equation to find the cost of each pound of potatoes, p dollars.

   b) Tell whether the equation has one solution, is inconsistent, or is an identity. Explain your reasoning.

28 A department store is offering a percent discount on the original price of a watch. The original price of the watch is $80.

   a) Let r represent the percent discount, written as a decimal. Write an equation to find the discounted price, y dollars, of the watch.

   b) The store gave discounts of 5%, 10%, and 15% during this sale in the three previous years. Create a table of r- and y-values for the equation.

29 The company Jake uses for Internet service charges $25 each month plus $0.04 for each minute of usage time.

   a) Write a linear equation for the monthly charge, M dollars, in terms of usage time, t minutes.

   b) Express t in terms of M.

   c) Calculate his usage time in hours if he paid $49 for his Internet bill in November.

Lines and Linear Equations

How steep is that slope?

If you like to snowboard, you probably want to know how steep a mountain is before you try to go down it. You can describe how steep a mountain is by using a ratio to compare the change in elevation between two points to the horizontal distance between the two points. The greater that ratio, the steeper the mountain. In this chapter, you will learn how to find slopes of lines on coordinate planes.

BIG IDEA

▶ The graph of a linear equation in two variables is a line, and you can write the equation of the line in slope-intercept form.

Recall Prior Knowledge

Interpreting direct proportion

If $\frac{y}{x} = k$ or $y = kx$, where k is a constant value, then y is said to be directly proportional to x. The constant value k in a direct proportion is called the constant of proportionality. The graph of a direct proportion is always a line through the origin $(0, 0)$ but does not lie along the horizontal or vertical axis.

The constant of proportionality in a direct proportion often represents a unit rate k. In general, you can use the point $(1, y)$ on a direct proportion graph to find a constant of proportionality. You can then use the unit rate to write a direct proportion equation $y = kx$.

The graph shows that y is directly proportional to x. The line passes through the point $(1, 2)$. The unit rate is 2. So, the equation of the direct proportion is $y = 2x$.

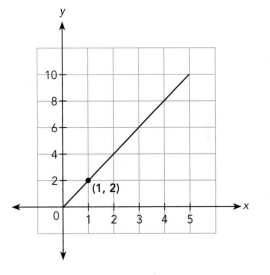

Quick Check

Tell whether each graph represents a direct proportion. If so, find the constant of proportionality. Then write a direct proportion equation.

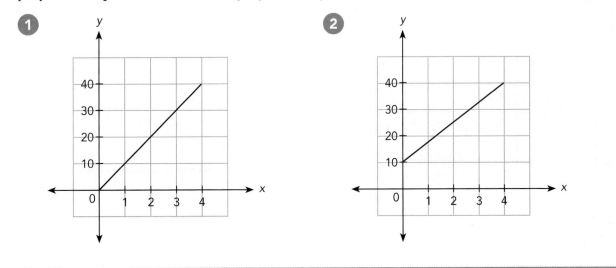

1

2

4.1 Finding and Interpreting Slopes of Lines

Lesson Objective

- Find slopes of lines.

Vocabulary

slope   rise

run

Define the Slope of a Line and Relate Unit Rate to Slope.

If you leave home and walk in a given direction at a steady pace, your distance, d feet, from home is directly proportional to the time, x minutes, you walk. You can use a table and a graph to represent this proportional relationship. From the table, you can see that the constant of proportionality is 250.

Time (x minutes)	1	2	3	4	5
Distance from Home (d feet)	250	500	750	1,000	1,250

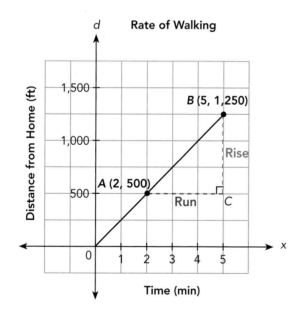

Math Note

The slope of a line graph that does not represent a direct proportion cannot be found by simply choosing a point $(1, y)$ on the line.

You have learned that you can use any point on a direct proportion graph to find the constant of proportionality. You have also learned that the point $(1, y)$ can be used to find the constant of proportionality. A third way to find the constant of proportionality is to find the slope of the line. You can find the slope by choosing two points and comparing the vertical change from the first point to the second to the horizontal change from the first point to the second. The vertical change is called the **rise** and the horizontal change is called the **run**.

Suppose you choose the points A (2, 500) and B (5, 1,250) from the graph.

Run = Horizontal change   Rise = Vertical change

     = 5 − 2   = 1,250 − 500

     = 3   = 750

$$\frac{\text{Rise}}{\text{Run}} = \frac{750}{3}$$

$$= 250$$

As you can see, for this graph of a direct proportion, the slope of the line is 250, which is equal to the constant of proportionality.

🖐 Hands-On Activity

Materials:
- graph paper

USE TRIANGLES TO FIND THE SLOPE OF A LINE

Work in pairs.

You can find the slope of any nonvertical line, not just a line that represents a direct proportion, by finding the ratio of the rise to the run.

STEP 1 Graph the line below on graph paper. The line should pass through the points (0, 1) and (6, 4). Then draw and label three right triangles on the line as shown. The triangles should be the same shape but different sizes. Make sure that each right angle lies on the intersection of two grid lines.

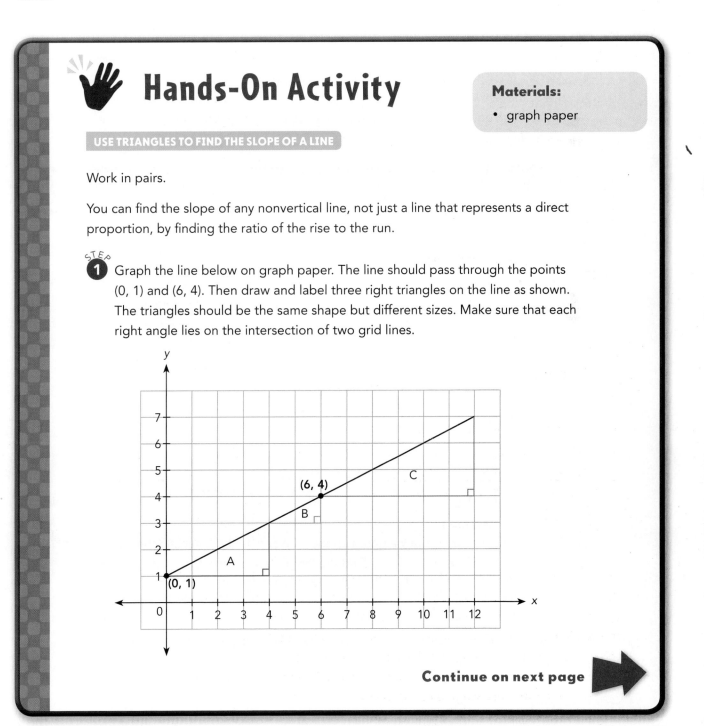

Continue on next page

STEP 2 Copy and complete the table.

Triangle	Length of Vertical Side	Length of Horizontal Side	Length of vertical side / Length of horizontal side
A	2	4	$\frac{2}{4} = \frac{1}{2}$
B	?	?	?
C	?	?	?

STEP 3 What do you observe about the ratios in the last column of the table?

Math Journal As you have learned, the slope of a line is the ratio of the rise to the run. Which side of each triangle has a length equal to the rise? Which has a length equal to the run? For each line you drew, what did you notice about the three ratios you calculated?

Hands-On Activity

Materials:
• graph paper

USE POINTS TO FIND THE SLOPE OF A LINE

Work in pairs.

STEP 1 Graph the line that passes through each pair of points, using 1 grid square to represent 1 unit on both axes for the interval from 0 to 7.

a) Line 1: (0, 1) and (4, 2)

b) Line 2: (0, 1) and (4, 5)

c) Line 3: (0, 1) and (4, 7)

STEP 2 For each line you drew, draw a right triangle. The segment connecting the two points should be the longest side. Find the length of the vertical side, the length of horizontal side, and the ratio $\frac{\text{Length of vertical side}}{\text{Length of horizontal side}}$.

Math Journal Of the three lines drawn in **STEP 1**, which line has the greatest slope? Which line has the least slope? How can you tell by looking at the lines? How can you tell from the ratios you calculated?

Example 1 **Use slopes to compare two unit rates.**

The graphs give information about a penguin's number of heart beats, *b*, over time, *t* minutes, during normal resting and just before diving. When is the penguin's heart rate greater, during normal resting, or just before diving?

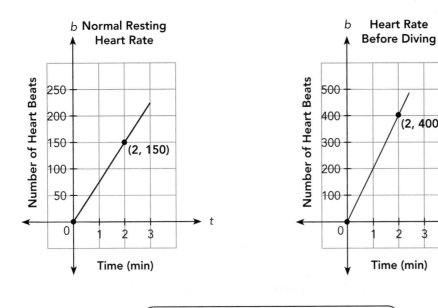

> To find each heart rate, find the unit rate for each graph. To find the unit rate, you can find the slope of the line. To find each slope, find the ratio $\frac{\text{Rise}}{\text{Run}}$ from the point (0, 0) to a convenient point on the graph.

Solution

Normal resting heart rate: Unit rate $= \frac{\text{Rise}}{\text{Run}}$

$$= \frac{150}{2}$$

$$= 75$$

Heart rate before diving: Unit rate $= \frac{\text{Rise}}{\text{Run}}$

$$= \frac{400}{2}$$

$$= 200$$

Math Note

Because the graphs have different scales on their vertical axes, you may not be able to tell just by looking that one line's slope is greater than the other line's. You need to calculate the slopes of the lines to see which is greater.

The slope for the normal resting heart rate graph is 75, so the unit rate is 75 beats per minute. The slope for the heart rate before diving graph is 200, so the unit rate is 200 beats per minute.

A penguin's heart rate before diving is greater than its normal resting heart rate.

Guided Practice

Complete.

1 The graphs give information about the distance, *d* miles, traveled over time, *t* hours, by cars and trucks on a California highway. Which speed is slower?

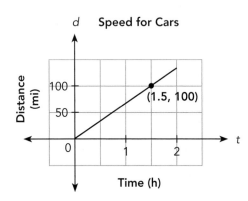

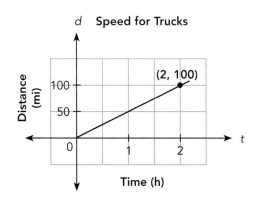

To find each speed, find the unit rate, in miles per hour, for each graph. To find the unit rate, you can find the slope of the line. To find each slope, find the ratio $\frac{\text{Rise}}{\text{Run}}$ from the point (0, 0) to a convenient point on the graph.

Speed for cars:

Unit rate $= \dfrac{\text{Rise}}{\text{Run}}$

$\phantom{\text{Unit rate}} = \dfrac{?}{?}$

$\phantom{\text{Unit rate}} = \underline{?}$ mi/h

Speed for trucks:

Unit rate $= \dfrac{\text{Rise}}{\text{Run}}$

$\phantom{\text{Unit rate}} = \dfrac{?}{?}$

$\phantom{\text{Unit rate}} = \underline{?}$ mi/h

The slope for the car speed graph is __?__ , so the unit rate is __?__ miles per hour.
The slope for the truck speed graph is __?__ , so the unit rate is __?__ miles per hour.

The speed for __?__ is slower than the speed for __?__.

Find Slopes of Slanted Lines.

You notice that some line graphs go up from left to right. Others go down from left to right. The direction a line slopes and how steep the line is are both determined by the value of the line's slope.

Think about a line graph that goes up from left to right.

When the graph goes up from left to right, the run and the rise are both positive.

$$\text{Slope} = \frac{\text{Positive rise}}{\text{Positive run}}$$

So, the slope is positive.

Think about a line graph that goes down from left to right.

When the graph goes down from left to right, the run is positive, but the rise is negative.

$$\text{Slope} = \frac{\text{Negative rise}}{\text{Positive run}}$$

So, the slope is negative.

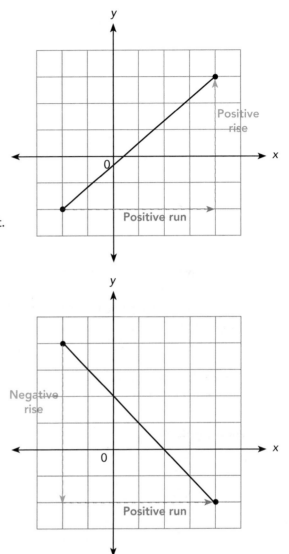

When you divide a negative number by a positive number, you get a negative quotient.

A line graph has a positive slope if it goes up from left to right. It has a negative slope if it goes down from left to right.

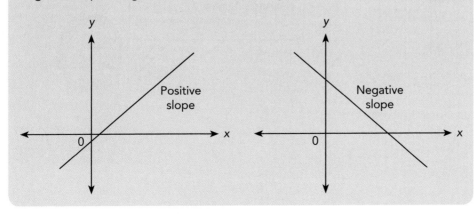

Example 2   Find the slope of a line given the graph.

Find the slope of each line.

a)

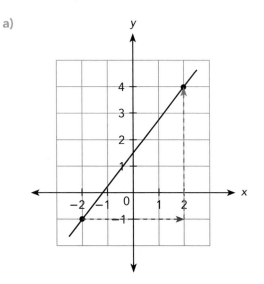

Move from $(-2, -1)$ to $(2, 4)$:

Vertical change $= 4 - (-1)$

$\quad = 5$ units

Horizontal change $= 2 - (-2)$

$\quad = 4$ units

So, the rise is 5 units, and the run is 4 units.

Solution

The graph passes through the points $(-2, -1)$ and $(2, 4)$.

$$\text{Slope} = \frac{\text{Rise}}{\text{Run}}$$

$$= \frac{4 - (-1)}{2 - (-2)}$$

$$= \frac{5}{4}$$

The slope is $\frac{5}{4}$.

Math Note

It is important to remember to subtract the coordinates in the same order in both numerator and denominator.

b)

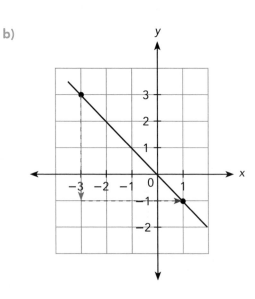

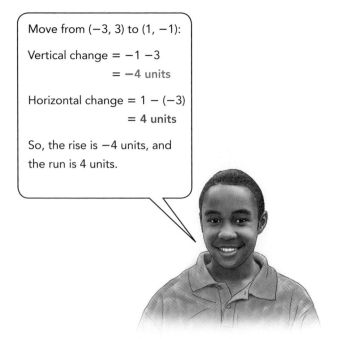

Move from $(-3, 3)$ to $(1, -1)$:

Vertical change $= -1 - 3$

$\quad = -4$ units

Horizontal change $= 1 - (-3)$

$\quad = 4$ units

So, the rise is -4 units, and the run is 4 units.

Solution

The graph passes through the points $(-3, 3)$ and $(1, -1)$.

$$\text{Slope} = \frac{\text{Rise}}{\text{Run}}$$

$$= \frac{-1 - 3}{1 - (-3)}$$

$$= \frac{-4}{4}$$

$$= -1$$

The slope is -1.

Guided Practice

Complete.

2 The graph passes through the points (_?_ , _?_)
and (_?_ , _?_).

$$\text{Slope} = \frac{\text{Rise}}{\text{Run}}$$

$$= \frac{?}{?}$$

$$= \frac{?}{?}$$

$$= \frac{?}{?}$$

The slope is _?_ .

3 The graph passes through the points (_?_ , _?_)
and (_?_ , _?_).

$$\text{Slope} = \frac{\text{Rise}}{\text{Run}}$$

$$= \frac{?}{?}$$

$$= \frac{?}{?}$$

$$= \frac{?}{?}$$

The slope is _?_ .

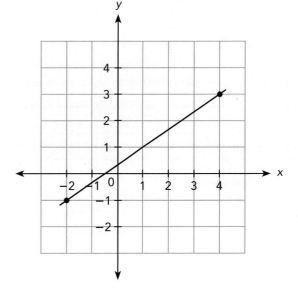

A red car and a blue car leave the same garage at the same time. Each driver drives at a steady rate. The graph represents the distance, *d* miles, traveled by the red car over time, *t* hours. The blue car traveled 140 miles over the same length of time.

a) At what speed is the red car traveling?

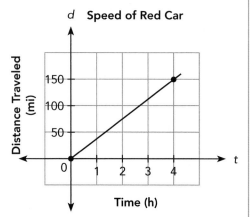

Solution

Find the slope of the graph and use the slope to find the rate, or speed, of the red car.

$$\text{Slope} = \frac{\text{Rise}}{\text{Run}}$$

$$= \frac{150}{4}$$

$$= 37.5 \text{ mi/h}$$

The red car's speed is 37.5 miles per hour.

> The vertical axis shows distance in miles, and the horizontal axis shows time in hours. So, the rate is in miles per hour.

b) At what speed is the blue car traveling?

Solution

You are given that the blue car traveled 140 miles in 4 hours.

$$\text{Speed} = \frac{\text{Distance}}{\text{Time}}$$

$$= \frac{140}{4}$$

$$= 35 \text{ mi/h}$$

c) Suppose you graph a line showing the distance traveled by the blue car after *t* hours on the same coordinate plane as the one showing the distance traveled by the red car after *t* hours. Would the blue car's graph be steeper or gentler than the red car's graph?

Think Math

How are the quantities on the graph related to the formula

$$\text{Speed} = \frac{\text{Distance}}{\text{Time}}?$$

How is the formula for speed related to the slope formula

$$\text{Slope} = \frac{\text{Rise}}{\text{Run}}?$$

Solution

The blue car's speed is 35 miles per hour, which is less than the red car's speed. The slope of its graph will be 35, which is less than the slope of the red car's graph. So, its graph will be less steep.

Guided Practice

Solve. Show your work.

4 The graphs represent the amount of water, *w* gallons, in Pool A over time, *t* hours, and the amount of water, *w* gallons, left in Pool B over time, *t* hours.

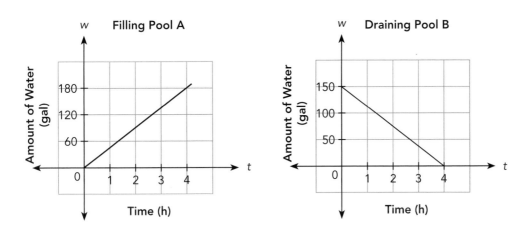

a) Find the slope of the line graph for Pool A. What does it represent?

b) Find the slope of the line graph for Pool B. What does it represent?

Find Slopes of Horizontal and Vertical Lines.

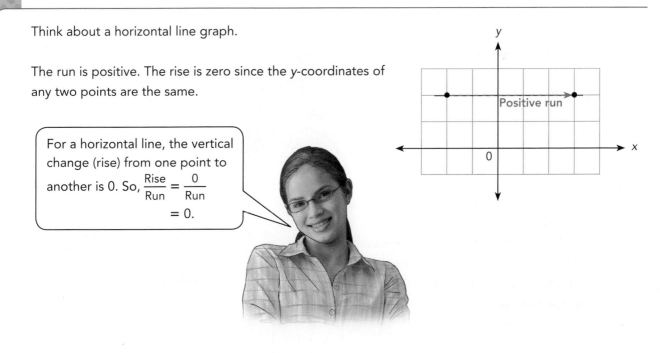

Think about a horizontal line graph.

The run is positive. The rise is zero since the *y*-coordinates of any two points are the same.

For a horizontal line, the vertical change (rise) from one point to another is 0. So, $\dfrac{\text{Rise}}{\text{Run}} = \dfrac{0}{\text{Run}}$
$= 0.$

$$\text{Slope} = \frac{0}{\text{Positive run}}$$

So, the slope is always zero.

Continue on next page

Think about a vertical line graph.

The rise is positive. The run is zero since the *x*-coordinates of any two points are the same.

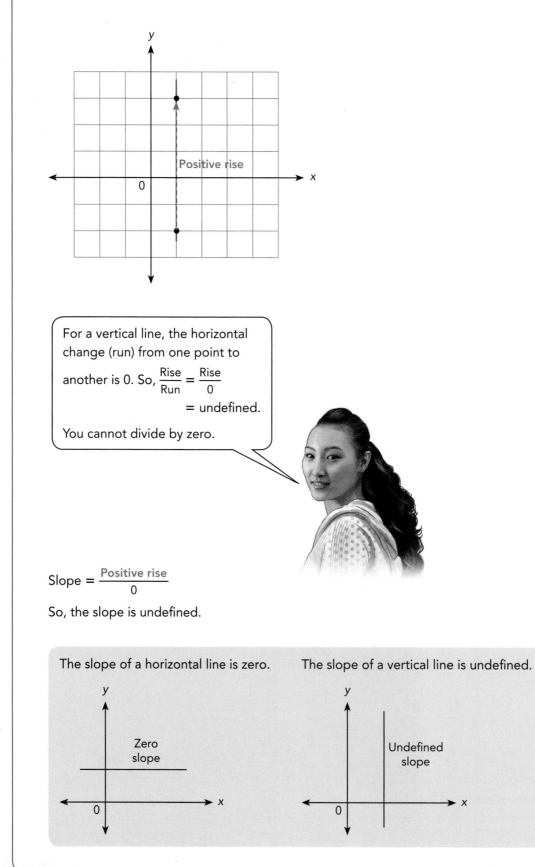

For a vertical line, the horizontal change (run) from one point to another is 0. So, $\dfrac{\text{Rise}}{\text{Run}} = \dfrac{\text{Rise}}{0}$

$= \text{undefined.}$

You cannot divide by zero.

Slope $= \dfrac{\text{Positive rise}}{0}$

So, the slope is undefined.

The slope of a horizontal line is zero.	The slope of a vertical line is undefined.
Zero slope	Undefined slope

Example 4 **Find the slope of horizontal and vertical lines.**

Find the slope of the line.

Solution

Use the points $(-2, 2)$ and $(4, 2)$:

$$\text{Slope} = \frac{\text{Rise}}{\text{Run}}$$

$$= \frac{2 - 2}{4 - (-2)}$$

$$= \frac{0}{6}$$

$$= 0$$

The slope is 0.

Guided Practice

Complete.

5

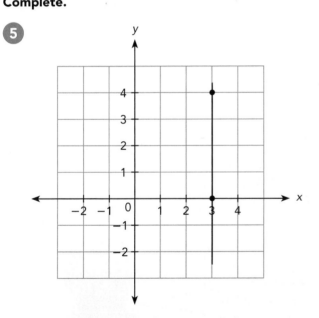

Use the points ($\underline{\ ?\ }$, $\underline{\ ?\ }$) and ($\underline{\ ?\ }$, $\underline{\ ?\ }$):

$$\text{Slope} = \frac{\text{Rise}}{\text{Run}}$$

$$= \frac{?}{?}$$

$$= \frac{?}{?}$$

$$= \underline{\ ?\ }$$

The slope is $\underline{\ ?\ }$.

Understand the Slope Formula.

You do not need to draw a line to find its slope.

Given any two points $A(x_1, y_1)$ and $B(x_2, y_2)$ on a line, you can find the rise and the run by subtracting coordinates.

Rise = $y_2 - y_1$
Run = $x_2 - x_1$

So, slope = $\dfrac{\text{Rise}}{\text{Run}}$

$\quad\quad = \dfrac{y_2 - y_1}{x_2 - x_1}.$

Find the rise from point A to point B by subtracting the y-coordinate of point A from the y-coordinate of point B. Find the run from point A to point B by subtracting the x-coordinate of point A from the x-coordinate of point B.

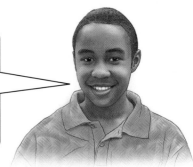

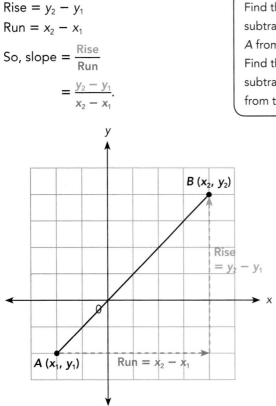

When you find the rise or the run, it does not matter whether you subtract the coordinates of A from the coordinates of B, or the other way around. What does matter is that you use the same order for both rise and run.

Rise = $y_1 - y_2$
Run = $x_1 - x_2$

So, slope = $\dfrac{\text{Rise}}{\text{Run}}$

$\quad\quad = \dfrac{y_1 - y_2}{x_1 - x_2}.$

Find the rise from point B to point A by subtracting the y-coordinate of point B from the y-coordinate of point A. Find the run from point B to point A by subtracting the x-coordinate of point B from the x-coordinate of point A.

So, the slope formula can be stated as follows:
The slope of a line passing through two points (x_1, y_1) and (x_2, y_2) is equal to $\dfrac{y_2 - y_1}{x_2 - x_1}$ or $\dfrac{y_1 - y_2}{x_1 - x_2}$.

Caution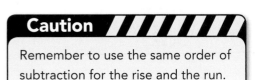

Remember to use the same order of subtraction for the rise and the run.

Example 5 **Find the slope of a line passing through two given points.**

Find the slope of each line.

a) Find the slope of the line passing through the points A (4, 8) and B (1, 4).

Solution

Let A (4, 8) be (x_1, y_1) and B (1, 4) be (x_2, y_2).

Method 1

$$\text{Slope} = \frac{y_1 - y_2}{x_1 - x_2}$$
$$= \frac{8 - 4}{4 - 1}$$
$$= \frac{4}{3}$$

You can find the slope of the line by calculating the rise and the run either from point A to point B or from point B to point A.

Method 2

$$\text{Slope} = \frac{y_2 - y_1}{x_2 - x_1}$$
$$= \frac{4 - 8}{1 - 4}$$
$$= \frac{-4}{-3} = \frac{4}{3}$$

The slope is $\frac{4}{3}$.

b) Find the slope of the line passing through the points P (2, 5) and Q (8, 2).

Solution

Let P (2, 5) be (x_1, y_1) and Q (8, 2) be (x_2, y_2).

Method 1

$$\text{Slope} = \frac{y_1 - y_2}{x_1 - x_2}$$
$$= \frac{5 - 2}{2 - 8}$$
$$= \frac{3}{-6} = -\frac{1}{2}$$

Method 2

$$\text{Slope} = \frac{y_2 - y_1}{x_2 - x_1}$$
$$= \frac{2 - 5}{8 - 2}$$
$$= \frac{-3}{6} = -\frac{1}{2}$$

The slope is $-\frac{1}{2}$.

Guided Practice

Find the slope of the line passing through each pair of points.

 6 $M\,(-2,\,0)$ and $N\,(0,\,4)$

Let $M\,(-2,\,0)$ be $(x_1,\,y_1)$ and $N\,(0,\,4)$ be $(x_2,\,y_2)$.

Method 1

$$\text{Slope} = \frac{y_1 - y_2}{x_1 - x_2}$$

$$= \frac{?}{?}$$

$$= \frac{?}{?}$$

$$= \underline{\quad ? \quad}$$

Method 2

$$\text{Slope} = \frac{y_2 - y_1}{x_2 - x_1}$$

$$= \frac{?}{?}$$

$$= \frac{?}{?}$$

$$= \underline{\quad ? \quad}$$

The slope is $\underline{\quad ? \quad}$.

You can use $\dfrac{y_1 - y_2}{x_1 - x_2}$ or $\dfrac{y_2 - y_1}{x_2 - x_1}$ to evaluate the slope.

 7 $S\,(-5,\,8)$ and $T\,(-2,\,2)$

Let $S\,(-5,\,8)$ be $(x_1,\,y_1)$ and $T\,(-2,\,2)$ be $(x_2,\,y_2)$.

Method 1

$$\text{Slope} = \frac{y_1 - y_2}{x_1 - x_2}$$

$$= \frac{?}{?}$$

$$= \frac{?}{?}$$

$$= \underline{\quad ? \quad}$$

Method 2

$$\text{Slope} = \frac{y_2 - y_1}{x_2 - x_1}$$

$$= \frac{?}{?}$$

$$= \frac{?}{?}$$

$$= \underline{\quad ? \quad}$$

The slope is $\underline{\quad ? \quad}$.

Practice 4.1

Find the slope of each line using the points indicated.

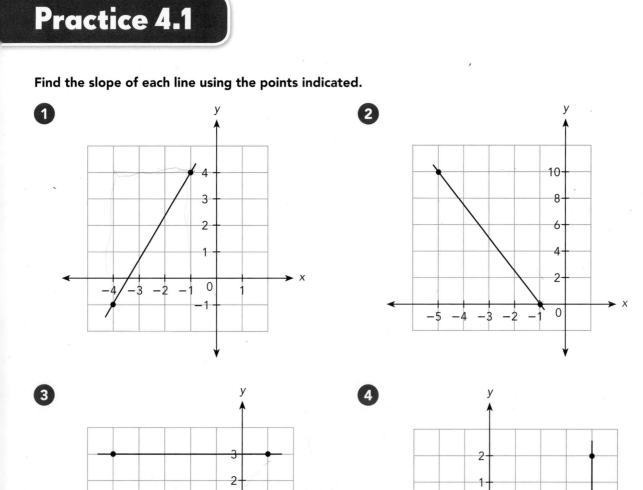

1.

2.

3.

4.

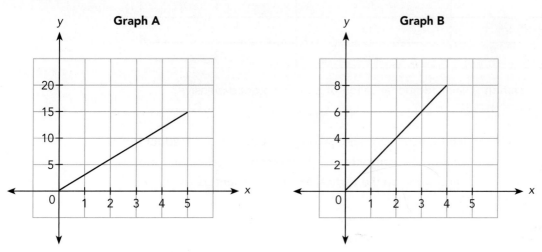

5. ✏️ *Math Journal* Jason says that the line in Graph B has a greater slope than the line in Graph A because it is steeper. What error is Jason making? Justify your answer.

Graph A

Graph B

6 ✏️📓 *Math Journal* Andy graphs a vertical line through the points (5, 2) and (5, 5). He says the slope of the line is $\frac{3}{0}$. What error is he making?

Find the slope of the line passing through each pair of points.

7 $A\ (-10, 3),\ B\ (0, 3)$

8 $S\ (5, -2),\ T\ (2, -5)$

9 $P\ (0, -7),\ Q\ (-3, 5)$

10 $X\ (4, 4),\ Y\ (4, -2)$

11 ✏️📓 *Math Journal* Two points have the same x-coordinates but different y-coordinates. Make a prediction about the slope of a line drawn through the points. Justify your prediction.

12 ✏️📓 *Math Journal* Two points have the same y-coordinates but different x-coordinates. Make a prediction about the slope of a line drawn through the points. Justify your prediction.

Solve. Show your work.

13 In the Fahrenheit system, water freezes at 32°F and boils at 212°F. In the Celsius system, water freezes at 0°C and boils at 100°C.

   a) Translate the verbal description into a pair of points in the form (temperature in °C, temperature in °F).

   b) Find the slope of the line passing through the pair of points in **a)**.

   c) Suppose the temperature in a room goes up by 5°C. By how much does the temperature go up in degrees Fahrenheit? Explain.

14 The table shows how much a certain amount of gasoline costs at two gasoline stations on a particular day.

Amount of Gasoline (x gallons)	Cost at Station A (y dollars)	Cost at Station B (y dollars)
1	3	4
3	11	10
5	19	16

   a) At which station is each additional gallon of gasoline more expensive? Explain.

   b) Graph the relationship between cost and gallons of gasoline purchased for each station. Use 1 unit on the horizontal axis to represent 1 gallon for the x interval from 0 to 5, and 1 unit on the vertical axis to represent $2 for the y interval from 0 to 20.

   c) Which graph is steeper?

Understanding Slope-Intercept Form

Lesson Objective

- Explore the relationship between the lines $y = mx$ and $y = mx + b$.

Explore the Relationship Between the Lines $y = mx$ and $y = mx + b$.

Time (x seconds)	0	1	2	3	4	5	6
Jim's distance from curb (y feet)	0	4	8	12	16	20	24
Sam's distance from curb (y feet)	4	8	12	16	20	24	28

Jim and his brother, Sam, walk from one end of a block to the other. The table shows their record of times, in x seconds, and corresponding distances, in y feet. Jim starts at the curb, and Sam starts 4 feet ahead of him. Both brothers walk at a rate of 4 feet per second. The graph shows each brother's distance from the curb after x seconds.

Jim's graph represents a direct proportion. The rate, 4 feet per second, is also the slope of the red line and the equation of the red line is given by $y = 4x$. Sam is always 4 feet ahead of Jim, but traveling at the same rate of 4 feet per second. So, for Sam's graph, the equation of the blue line is given by $y = 4x + 4$.

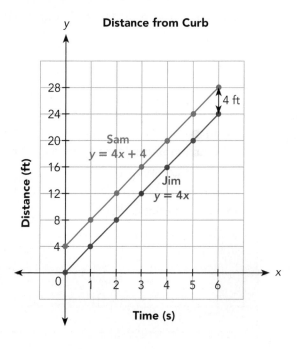

Jim's graph and Sam's graph have the same slope because they walked at the same rate of 4 feet per second. So, their equations involve the same rate of change. Their graphs are different because they cross the y-axis at different points. Jim's graph passes through the point $(0, 0)$. Sam's graph crosses the y-axis at the point $(0, 4)$.

The **y-intercept** of a line is the y-coordinate of the point where the line intersects the y-axis. The y-intercept of Jim's graph is 0, so the equation is given by $y = 4x + 0 = 4x$. The y-intercept of Sam's graph is 4, so the equation is given by $y = 4x + 4$.

Continue on next page

The **x-intercept** of a line is the *x*-coordinate of the point where the line intersects the *x*-axis.

A linear equation written in the form $y = mx + b$ is said to be written in **slope-intercept form**. The constant *m* represents the slope of the line, and the constant *b* represents the *y*-intercept of the line.

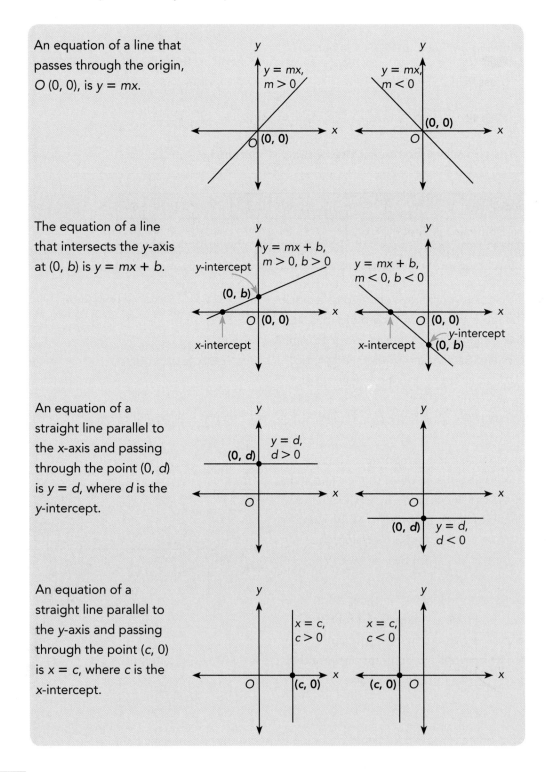

An equation of a line that passes through the origin, O (0, 0), is $y = mx$.

The equation of a line that intersects the *y*-axis at (0, *b*) is $y = mx + b$.

An equation of a straight line parallel to the *x*-axis and passing through the point (0, *d*) is $y = d$, where *d* is the *y*-intercept.

An equation of a straight line parallel to the *y*-axis and passing through the point (*c*, 0) is $x = c$, where *c* is the *x*-intercept.

Technology Activity

Materials:
• graphing calculator

EXPLORE THE RELATIONSHIP BETWEEN $y = mx$ **AND** $y = mx + b$

Work in pairs.

STEP 1 Press ⟨Y=⟩ to display the $Y =$ window. Enter an equation from the table below. Then press ⟨GRAPH⟩ to graph the function.

STEP 2 Press ⟨2ND⟩ ⟨TRACE⟩ to select 6: dy/dx. Then press ⟨ENTER⟩ to find the slope.

STEP 3 Press ⟨2ND⟩ ⟨TRACE⟩ to select 1: Value. Then press ⟨0⟩ to find the y-intercept.

STEP 4 Repeat **STEP 1** to **STEP 3** to the other equations in the table. Record your results.

Equation	$y = 3x + 5$	$y = -2x + 1$	$y = 1.5x + 2$
m	?	?	?
b	?	?	?

✎ *Math Journal* The equation of another line is given by $2y = 5x - 4$. It can also be written as $y = 2.5x - 2$. Predict the y-intercept. Use the graphing calculator to check your prediction. Is your prediction correct?

Example 6 | **Write an equation of a line in the form $y = mx$ or $y = mx + b$.**

Write an equation in the form $y = mx$ or $y = mx + b$ for each line.

a)

Continue on next page

Solution

The line passes through the points $(-3, -2)$ and $(3, 2)$.

$$\text{Slope } m = \frac{2 - (-2)}{3 - (-3)}$$

$$= \frac{4}{6}$$

$$= \frac{2}{3}$$

The line passes through the y-axis at the point $(0, 0)$.

So, the y-intercept, b, is 0.

Slope-intercept form: $y = \frac{2}{3}x + 0$ Substitute the values of m and b.

$$y = \frac{2}{3}x$$ Simplify.

So, an equation of the line is $y = \frac{2}{3}x$.

b)

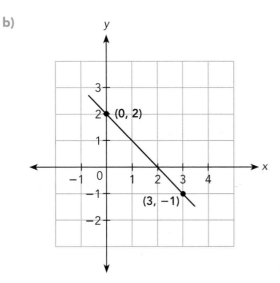

Solution

The line passes through the points $(0, 2)$ and $(3, -1)$.

$$\text{Slope } m = \frac{-1 - 2}{3 - 0}$$

$$= \frac{-3}{3}$$

$$= -1$$

The line intersects the y-axis at the point $(0, 2)$.

So, the y-intercept, b, is 2.

Slope-intercept form: $y = (-1)x + 2$ Substitute the values of m and b.

$$y = -x + 2$$ Simplify.

So, an equation of the line is $y = -x + 2$.

Guided Practice

Write an equation for each line.

1 The line passes through the points (__?__, __?__)

and (__?__, __?__).

Slope $m = \dfrac{?-?}{?-?}$

$= \dfrac{?}{?}$

$= \underline{?}$

The line intersects the y-axis at the

point (__?__, __?__).

So, the y-intercept is __?__.

So, the equation of the line is __?__.

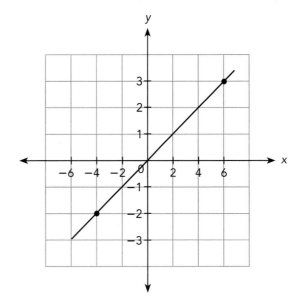

2 The line passes through the points (__?__, __?__)

and (__?__, __?__).

Slope $m = \dfrac{?-?}{?-?}$

$= \dfrac{?}{?}$

$= \underline{?}$

The line intersects the y-axis at the

point (__?__, __?__).

So, the y-intercept is __?__.

So, the equation of the line is __?__.

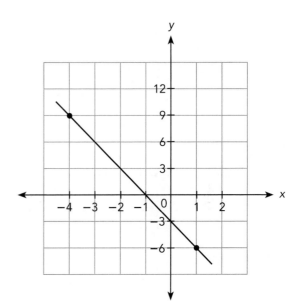

3

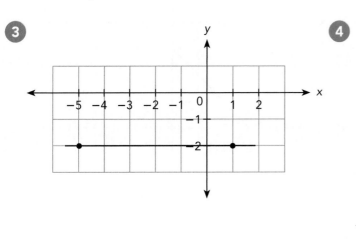

4

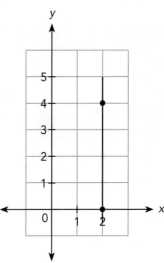

Identify the y-intercept. Then calculate the slope using the points indicated.

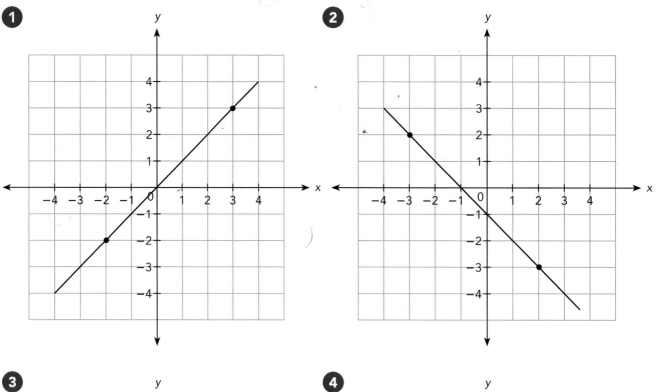

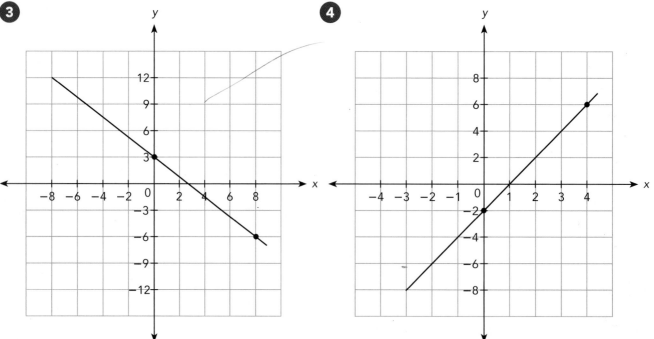

Write an equation in the form $y = mx$ or $y = mx + b$ for each line.

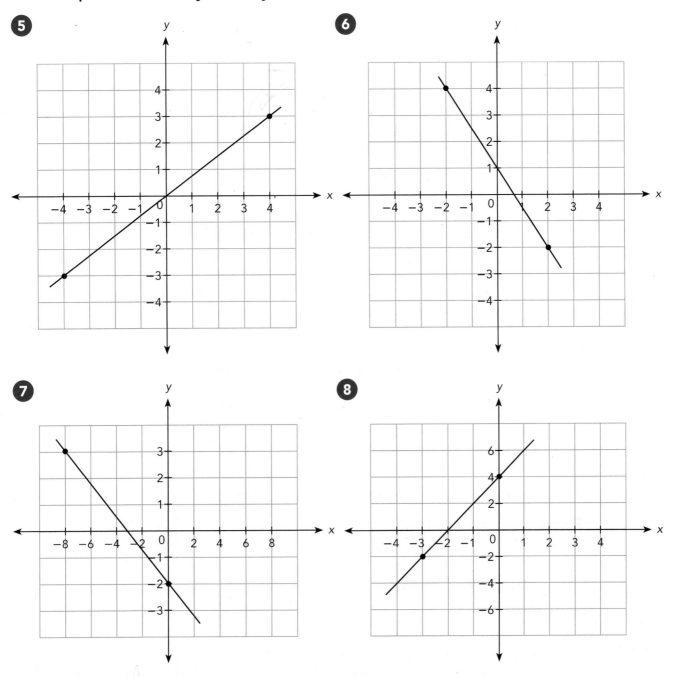

Graph each line using 1 grid square to represent 1 unit on both axes for the interval from −4 to 4. Then write the equation for each line.

9 The line passes through the points (−4, 3) and (−4, −2).

10 The line passes through the points (−3, 4) and (1, 4).

11 *Math Journal* Line A passes through the origin and has a negative slope. Line B has a positive *y*-intercept and a positive slope. Line C has a negative slope and a negative *y*-intercept. Give a possible equation for each line. Justify your answer.

 **Writing Linear Equations**

Lesson Objectives

- Write an equation of a line in slope-intercept form.
- Write an equation of a line parallel to another line.

Write an Equation of a Line in Slope-Intercept Form.

You have learned that the slope-intercept form of an equation of a line is given by $y = mx + b$. Given the slope, m, and y-intercept, b, of a line, you can substitute these values into $y = mx + b$ to write an equation of the line.

When given an equation, you can add, subtract, multiply, or divide both sides of the equation by the same number to write an equivalent equation in slope-intercept form.

Example 7 **Use the slope-intercept form to identify slopes and y-intercepts.**

An equation of a line is given. State the slope and y-intercept of the line.

$y + 2x - 6 = 0$

Solution

First write the equation in slope-intercept form.

$$y + 2x - 6 = 0$$
$$y + 2x - 6 + 6 = 0 + 6 \qquad \text{Add 6 to both sides.}$$
$$y + 2x = 6 \qquad \text{Simplify.}$$
$$y + 2x - 2x = 6 - 2x \qquad \text{Subtract 2x from both sides.}$$
$$y = -2x + 6 \qquad \text{Write in slope-intercept form.}$$

Comparing the equation
$y = -2x + 6$ with $y = mx + b$:
Slope: $m = -2$
y-intercept: $b = 6$

Think Math

Paula notices that the ordered pair $(0, 6)$ is a solution of $y = -2x + 6$. Is this ordered pair also a solution of $y + 2x - 6 = 0$? Is any ordered pair (x, y) that is a solution of $y = -2x + 6$ also a solution of $y + 2x - 6 = 0$? Why or why not?

Guided Practice

For each line, state its slope and its y-intercept.

1 $5x + 4y = 8$

First write the equation in the slope-intercept form.

$5x + 4y = 8$

$5x + 4y - \underline{\ ?\ } = 8 - \underline{\ ?\ }$ Subtract 5x from both sides.

$\underline{\ ?\ } = \underline{\ ?\ }$ Simplify.

$\underline{\ ?\ } = \underline{\ ?\ }$ Divide both sides by $\underline{\ ?\ }$.

$y = \underline{\ ?\ }$ Write in slope-intercept form.

Comparing the equation $y = \underline{\ ?\ }$ with $y = mx + b$:

Slope: $m = \underline{\ ?\ }$

y-intercept: $b = \underline{\ ?\ }$

2 $2x - 3y = 7$

First write the equation in the slope-intercept form.

$2x - 3y = 7$

$2x - 3y + \underline{\ ?\ } = 7 + \underline{\ ?\ }$ Add 3y to both sides.

$\underline{\ ?\ } = \underline{\ ?\ }$ Simplify.

$\underline{\ ?\ } = \underline{\ ?\ }$ Subtract $\underline{\ ?\ }$ from both sides.

$\underline{\ ?\ } = \underline{\ ?\ }$ Simplify.

$\underline{\ ?\ } = \underline{\ ?\ }$ Divide both sides by $\underline{\ ?\ }$.

$y = \underline{\ ?\ }$ Write in slope-intercept form.

Comparing the equation $y = \underline{\ ?\ }$ with $y = mx + b$:

Slope: $m = \underline{\ ?\ }$

y-intercept: $b = \underline{\ ?\ }$

3 $5y - x = 15$

4 $2y - 3x = -4$

5 $6y + 5x = 24$

6 $3y + 4x = 3$

Example 8 **Write an equation of a line given its slope and *y*-intercept.**

Use the given slope and *y*-intercept of a line to write an equation in slope-intercept form.

a) Slope, $m = \dfrac{1}{4}$

y-intercept, $b = 3$

Solution

$y = mx + b$

$y = \dfrac{1}{4}x + 3$ Substitute the given values for *m* and *b*.

b) Slope, $m = -2$
    y-intercept, $b = -5$

Solution

$y = mx + b$
$y = -2x + (-5)$ Substitute the given values for *m* and *b*.
$y = -2x - 5$ Simplify.

Think Math

If you graphed the equations in Example 8, which line would go upward from left to right? Which would go downward from left to right? Which line would be steeper? Explain.

Guided Practice

Use the given slope and *y*-intercept of a line to write an equation in slope-intercept form.

7 Slope, $m = -\dfrac{2}{3}$

y-intercept, $b = 4$

$y = mx + b$

$y = \underline{\ ?\ }$ Substitute the given values for $\underline{\ ?\ }$ and *b*.

8 Slope, $m = 4$
    y-intercept, $b = -7$

Identify and Write Equations of Parallel Lines.

The lines shown at the right are parallel. Lines in the coordinate plane that have the same slope but different y-intercepts are always parallel.

You can use the equations of the lines to predict that the lines are parallel.

$$y = \frac{2}{3}x + 2$$

$$y = \frac{2}{3}x + 5$$

You can use the fact that parallel lines have the same slope but different y-intercepts to write equations for parallel lines.

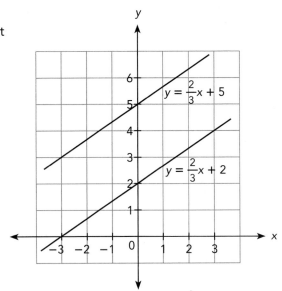

Example 9 **Write an equation of a line, given its y-intercept and the equation of another line parallel to the line.**

Write an equation.

An equation of a line is $2y = 6 - 3x$. Write an equation of a line parallel to this given line that has a y-intercept of 6.

Solution

First write the given equation in slope-intercept form.

$2y = 6 - 3x$

$\dfrac{2y}{2} = \dfrac{6 - 3x}{2}$ Divide both sides by 2.

$y = 3 - \dfrac{3}{2}x$ Simplify.

$y = -\dfrac{3}{2}x + 3$ Write in slope-intercept form.

The given line has slope $m = -\dfrac{3}{2}$ and y-intercept $b = 3$.

Then write an equation for the parallel line with slope $m = -\dfrac{3}{2}$, and y-intercept $b = 6$.

$y = -\dfrac{3}{2}x + 6$ Substitute the values for m and b.

So, an equation of the line with a y-intercept of 6 and parallel to $2y = 6 - 3x$ is $y = -\dfrac{3}{2}x + 6$.

Think Math

Give an example of another equation for a line that is parallel to the two lines in Example 9.

Solve.

 A line has the equation $3y + 6 = 10x$. Write an equation of a line parallel to this given line that has a *y*-intercept of 2.

First write the given equation in slope-intercept form.

$$3y + 6 = 10x$$

$3y + 6 - \underline{} = 10x - \underline{}$ Subtract both sides by 6.

$\underline{} = \underline{}$ Simplify.

$y = \underline{}$ Divide both sides by $\underline{}$.

$y = \underline{}$ Write in slope-intercept form.

The line has slope $m = \underline{}$ and *y*-intercept $b = \underline{}$.

Then write an equation for the parallel line with slope $m = \underline{}$ and *y*-intercept $b = \underline{}$.

$y = \underline{}$.   Substitute the values of *m* and *b*.

So, an equation of the line parallel to $3y = 10x - 6$ is $\underline{}$.

Write an Equation of a Line Given Its Slope and a Point on the Line.

You have learned to find the equation of a line by substituting the values of the given slope and *y*-intercept into $y = mx + b$. But you can also find an equation of a line if you are given the slope and any point on the line.

For example, the line shown has a slope of $\frac{2}{5}$ and passes through the point (2, 3). You know the slope, but you do not know the *y*-intercept.

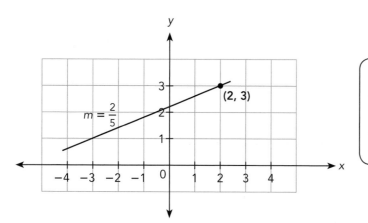

From the graph, you can estimate that the line intersects the *y*-axis somewhere between 2 and 3.

To write an equation in slope-intercept form, you can follow these steps.

STEP 1 Substitute the given slope and the *x*- and *y*-coordinates of the given point into the equation $y = mx + b$.

$y = \dfrac{2}{5}x + b$ Substitute the slope, $\dfrac{2}{5}$, in the equation.

$3 = \dfrac{2}{5}(2) + b$ Substitute 3 for *y* and 2 for *x* in the equation.

$3 = \dfrac{4}{5} + b$ Simplify.

STEP 2 Solve the equation to find the *y*-intercept *b*.

$3 - \dfrac{4}{5} = \dfrac{4}{5} + b - \dfrac{4}{5}$ Subtract $\dfrac{4}{5}$ from both sides.

$\dfrac{11}{5} = b$ Simplify.

STEP 3 Use the given slope and the value for *b* to write an equation for the line.

$y = \dfrac{2}{5}x + \dfrac{11}{5}$ Substitute the values of *m* and *b*.

Example 10 **Write an equation of a line given its slope and a point on the line.**

Write an equation.

A line has slope −5 and passes through the point (1, −8). Write an equation of the line.

> Because (1, −8) lies on the line, $x = 1$ and $y = -8$ are a solution of the equation.

Solution

First use the given slope, −5, and the values $x = 1$ and $y = -8$ to find the *y*-intercept.

$y = mx + b$ Write the slope-intercept form.
$-8 = -5(1) + b$ Substitute the values for *m*, *x*, and *y*.
$-8 = -5 + b$ Simplify.
$-8 + 5 = -5 + b + 5$ Add 5 to both sides.
$-3 = b$ Simplify.

The *y*-intercept is −3.

Then use the given slope, −5, and the *y*-intercept, −3, to write an equation in slope-intercept form.

$y = mx + b$ Write the slope-intercept form.
$y = -5x + (-3)$ Substitute the values for *m* and *b*.
$y = -5x - 3$ Simplify.

So, an equation of the line is $y = -5x - 3$.

Guided Practice

Solve.

10 A line has slope -3 and passes through the point $(-6, 8)$. Write an equation of the line.

11 A line has slope $\frac{1}{3}$ and passes through the point $(0, 1)$. Write an equation of the line.

12 A line has slope 2 and passes through the point $(1, 5)$. Write an equation of the line.

Write an Equation of a Line Given a Point on the Line and the Equation of a Parallel Line.

An equation for the red line shown in the graph is $y = \frac{3}{4}x + 1$. You can use the equation of the red line to find the equation of the blue line.

The blue line is parallel to the red line and passes through the point $(2, 3)$. Because the blue line and the red line are parallel, you know they have the same slope, $\frac{3}{4}$.

So, you know the slope of the blue line and that it passes through the point $(2, 3)$. Then you can use the slope and the given point to write and solve an equation to find b, the y-intercept of the line.

$$y = mx + b \qquad \text{Write in slope-intercept form.}$$

$$y = \frac{3}{4}x + b \qquad \text{Substitute the slope } \frac{3}{4} \text{ in the equation.}$$

$$3 = \frac{3}{4}(2) + b \qquad \text{Substitute 3 for } y \text{ and 2 for } x \text{ in the equation.}$$

$$3 = \frac{3}{2} + b \qquad \text{Multiply.}$$

$$3 - \frac{3}{2} = \frac{3}{2} + b - \frac{3}{2} \qquad \text{Subtract } \frac{3}{2} \text{ from both sides.}$$

$$\frac{3}{2} = b \qquad \text{Simplify.}$$

So, the equation of the blue line is $y = \frac{3}{4}x + \frac{3}{2}$.

From the graph, you can see that the blue line intersects the y-axis at 1.5. So, y-intercept is 1.5.

(2, 3)

$y = \frac{3}{4}x + 1$

Example 11 **Write an equation of a line, given a point on the line and the equation of a parallel line.**

Write an equation.

A line passes through the point $\left(\frac{1}{4}, 8\right)$ and is parallel to the line represented by the equation $y = 2 - 4x$. Write the equation of the line.

Solution

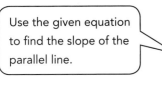

Use the given equation to find the slope of the parallel line.

First write the equation $y = 2 - 4x$ in slope-intercept form.

$y = 2 - 4x$

$y = -4x + 2$ Write in slope-intercept form.

The line has slope $m = -4$.

So, the line parallel to $y = 2 - 4x$ has slope $m = -4$.

Then write the equation of a line that passes through $\left(\frac{1}{4}, 8\right)$ and has slope -4.

$y = mx + b$	Write in slope-intercept form
$8 = -4\left(\frac{1}{4}\right) + b$	Substitute the values for m, x, and y.
$8 = -1 + b$	Multiply.
$8 + 1 = -1 + b + 1$	Add 1 to both sides.
$9 = b$	Simplify.

The y-intercept is 9.

So, the equation of the line is $y = -4x + 9$.

Think Math

If you graph the parallel lines $y = 2 - 4x$ and $y = -4x + 9$ on the same coordinate plane, will the graph of $y = -4x + 9$ lie above or below the graph of $y = 2 - 4x$? Explain.

Guided Practice

Solve.

13 Write an equation of the line that passes through the point (−2, 1) and is parallel to $y = 5 - 3x$.

First write the equation in slope-intercept form.

$y = 5 - 3x$

$y =$ ___?___   Write in slope-intercept form.

The line has slope $m =$ ___?___.

So, the line parallel to $y = 5 - 3x$ has slope $m =$ ___?___.

Then use the slope $m =$ ___?___ and the fact that (−2, 1) lies on the parallel line to find the y-intercept.

$y = mx + b$ Write in slope-intercept form.

___?___ = ___?___   Substitute the values for m, x, and y.

___?___ = ___?___   Simplify.

___?___ = ___?___   Subtract ___?___ from both sides.

___?___ = ___?___   Simplify.

The y-intercept is ___?___.

So, an equation of the line is ___?___.

Write an Equation of a Line Given Two Points.

You can also find an equation of a line if two points on the line are given. You first use the two given points to find the slope. Then use this slope and either one of the given points to find the equation.

You substitute the values of m and the coordinates of either point into the slope-intercept form of an equation to find the y-intercept. Then write the equation.

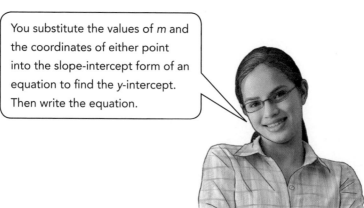

Example 12 **Write an equation of a line given two points on a line.**

Write an equation of the line that passes through the pair of points (1, 3) and (2, −4).

Solution

First use the slope formula to find the slope.

Let (1, 3) be (x_1, y_1) and (2, −4) be (x_2, y_2).

Slope $= \dfrac{y_2 - y_1}{x_2 - x_1}$ \qquad Use the slope formula.

$= \dfrac{(-4) - 3}{2 - 1}$ \qquad Substitute values.

$= \dfrac{-7}{1}$ \qquad Subtract.

$= -7$ \qquad Simplify.

The line has slope $m = -7$.

Method 1

Use the slope $m = -7$ and the point (1, 3) to find the y-intercept.

$y = mx + b$ \qquad Write in slope-intercept form.

$3 = -7(1) + b$ \qquad Substitute the values for m, x, and y.

$3 = -7 + b$ \qquad Multiply.

$3 + 7 = -7 + b + 7$ \qquad Add 7 to both sides.

$10 = b$ \qquad Simplify.

Method 2

Use the slope $m = -7$ and the point (2, −4) to find the y-intercept.

$y = mx + b$ \qquad Write in slope-intercept form.

$-4 = -7(2) + b$ \qquad Substitute the values for m, x, and y.

$-4 = -14 + b$ \qquad Multiply.

$-4 + 14 = -14 + b + 14$ \qquad Add 14 to both sides.

$10 = b$ \qquad Simplify.

The y-intercept is 10.

So, an equation of the line is $y = -7x + 10$.

Guided Practice

Solve.

14 Write an equation of the line that passes through the pair of points (−2, −5) and (2, −1).

Practice 4.3

Find the slope and the *y*-intercept of the graph of each equation.

1 $y = -5x + 7$

2 $y = 2x + 3$

3 $5x + 2y = 6$

4 $2x - 7y = 10$

Use the given slope and *y*-intercept of a line to write an equation in slope-intercept form.

5 Slope, $m = \dfrac{1}{2}$
y-intercept, $b = 3$

6 Slope, $m = -2$
y-intercept, $b = 5$

Solve. Show your work.

7 A line has the equation $4y = 3x - 8$. Find an equation of a line parallel to this line that has a *y*-intercept of 2.

8 A line has the equation $3y = 3 - 2x$. Find an equation of a line parallel to this line that has a *y*-intercept of 5.

9 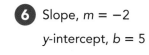 *Math Journal* Ira says that the graphs of the equations $y = -3x + 7$ and $y = 3x - 7$ are parallel lines. Do you agree? Explain.

10 Find an equation of the line that passes through the point (0, 4) and has a slope of $-\dfrac{1}{3}$.

11 A line has slope $-\dfrac{1}{2}$ and passes through the point (−4, −2). Write an equation of the line.

12 Find an equation of the line that passes through the point (−5, 7) and is parallel to $y = 4 - 3x$.

13 Find an equation of the line that passes through the point (0, 2) and is parallel to $6y = 5x - 24$.

14 Find an equation of the line that passes through the pair of points (−5, −1) and (0, 4).

15 Find an equation of the line that passes through the pair of points (−3, 2) and (−2, 5).

16 *Math Journal* Can you write a linear equation in the slope-intercept form using the points (3, 4) and (5, 8)? Explain.

Sketching Graphs of Linear Equations

Lesson Objectives

- Understand graphing linear equations.
- Sketch a linear graph by using m and b.
- Sketch a linear graph by using m and a point on the line.

Understand Graphing Linear Equations.

You have learned that a linear equation $y = mx + b$ has a graph that is a line. A linear equation has an infinite number of solutions, and each of them lies on the graph of the equation. You will learn to draw graphs of linear equations in this lesson.

Graph the equation $y = \frac{1}{2}x + 1$ using the following steps.

STEP 1 Construct a table of values. Choose three values for x and solve to find corresponding values for y.

x	2	4	6
y	2	3	4

STEP 2 Graph the equation using the table of values.

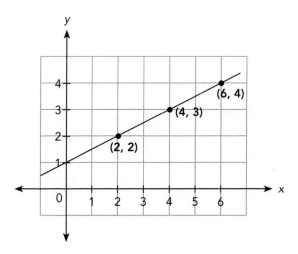

Choose values of x that give integer values of y.

When $x = 2$, $y = \frac{1}{2}(2) + 1 = 2$.

When $x = 4$, $y = \frac{1}{2}(4) + 1 = 3$.

When $x = 6$, $y = \frac{1}{2}(6) + 1 = 4$.

Think Math

Can you draw the graph with just two points? Why is it a good idea to include a third point when you graph an equation?

Example 13 **Graph a linear equation by using two or more points.**

Graph the equation $y = \frac{3}{4}x + 2$. Use 1 grid square on both axes to represent 1 unit for the x interval from -4 to 4, and the y interval from -1 to 5.

Solution

STEP 1   Construct a table of values. Choose three values for x and solve to find corresponding values for y.

x	−4	0	4
y	−1	2	5

> You may evaluate values of x that give integer values of y.

STEP 2   Graph the equation using the table of values.

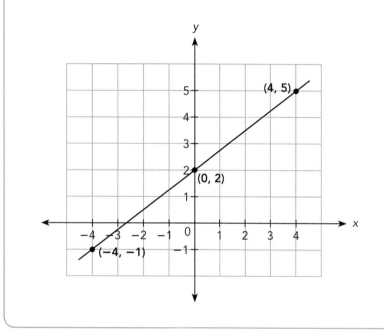

Guided Practice

Use graph paper. Use 1 grid square to represent 1 unit for the x interval from -2 to 2, and the y interval from -2 to 4.

1 Graph the equation $y = \frac{3}{2}x + 1$.

Sketch a Linear Graph by Using m and b.

One way to graph an equation in slope-intercept form is to use the y-intercept to plot a point on the y-axis. Then use the slope of the line to find a second point on the line.

Example 14 **Graph a linear equation by using *m* and *b*.**

Graph each equation.

a) Graph the equation $y = x + 2$. Use 1 grid square on both axes to represent 1 unit for the *x* interval from 0 to 4, and the *y* interval from 2 to 6.

Solution

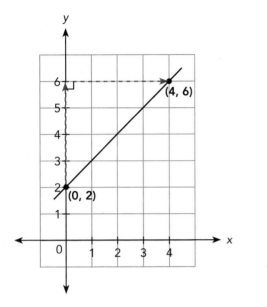

STEP 1 Plot a point on the *y*-axis.

$y = x + 2$ has *y*-intercept $b = 2$. So, it passes through the point (0, 2). Plot the point (0, 2) on the graph.

STEP 2 Use the slope to find another point on the graph.

The slope of the line is 1, so the ratio $\frac{\text{Rise}}{\text{Run}} = 1$.

$$\frac{\text{Rise}}{\text{Run}} = \frac{1}{1} = \frac{2}{2} = \frac{3}{3} = \frac{4}{4} = \ldots$$

Using $\frac{4}{4}$, you can move up 4 units and then over 4 units to the right to plot a point at (4, 6).

You can use convenient points, integer values, for the rise and the run as long as the ratio $\frac{\text{Rise}}{\text{Run}} = 1$. In this case, you use 4 for both the rise and the run.

Math Note

The line graph contains all the points (*x*, *y*) with the values of *x* and *y* that make the equation true. Only some of those points can be seen on this graph. So, you can choose any convenient points of integer values for *x* and *y*.

STEP 3 Use a ruler and draw a line through the points. This line is the graph of the equation $y = x + 2$.

Continue on next page

b) Graph the equation $y = -\frac{1}{2}x - 3$. Use 1 grid square on both axes to represent 1 unit for the x interval from 0 to 4, and the y interval from −5 to 0.

Solution

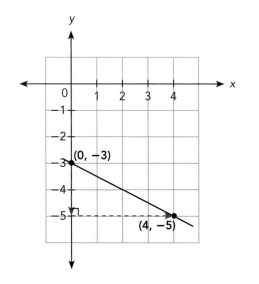

STEP 1 Plot a point on the y-axis.

$y = -\frac{1}{2}x - 3$ has y-intercept $b = -3$. So, it passes through the point $(0, -3)$. Plot the point $(0, -3)$ on the graph.

STEP 2 Use the slope to find another point on the graph.

The slope of the line is $-\frac{1}{2}$, so the ratio $\frac{\text{Rise}}{\text{Run}} = -\frac{1}{2}$.

$\frac{\text{Rise}}{\text{Run}} = \frac{-1}{2} = \frac{1}{-2} = \frac{-2}{4} = \frac{2}{-4} = \ldots$

Using $\frac{-2}{4}$, you can move down 2 units and then over 4 units to the right to plot a point at $(4, -5)$.

> You can use any two integers for the rise and the run as long as the ratio $\frac{\text{Rise}}{\text{Run}} = -\frac{1}{2}$. In this case, you use −1 for the rise and 2 for the run.

STEP 3 Use a ruler and draw a line through the points. This line is the graph of the equation $y = -\frac{1}{2}x - 3$.

Think Math

Suppose that you are given the slope of a line and, instead of the y-intercept, a point on the line. For example, suppose you know a line passes through the point (4, 5) and has slope 3. Explain how you could graph the line.

Guided Practice

Use graph paper. Use 1 grid square to represent 1 unit on both axes for the x interval from 0 to 3, and the y interval from −3 to 7.

2 Graph the equation $y = 2x + 1$.

3 Graph the equation $y = -\frac{1}{3}x - 2$.

Sketch a Linear Graph by Using *m* and a Point.

You can also graph a line using the information from a point on the line and the slope of the line, as shown in the example below.

Example 15 **Graph a linear equation given *m* and a point.**

Graph a line with slope 4 that passes through the point (3, 2). Use 1 grid square on both axes to represent 1 unit for the interval from 0 to 6.

Solution

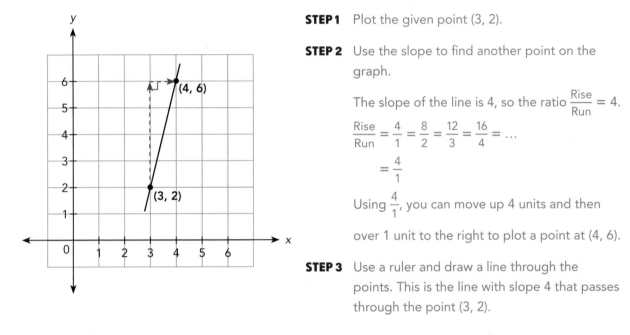

STEP 1 Plot the given point (3, 2).

STEP 2 Use the slope to find another point on the graph.

The slope of the line is 4, so the ratio $\dfrac{\text{Rise}}{\text{Run}} = 4$.

$$\frac{\text{Rise}}{\text{Run}} = \frac{4}{1} = \frac{8}{2} = \frac{12}{3} = \frac{16}{4} = \dots$$

$$= \frac{4}{1}$$

Using $\dfrac{4}{1}$, you can move up 4 units and then over 1 unit to the right to plot a point at (4, 6).

STEP 3 Use a ruler and draw a line through the points. This is the line with slope 4 that passes through the point (3, 2).

Guided Practice

Use graph paper. Use 1 grid square to represent 1 unit on both axes for the *x* interval from −2 to 2, and the *y* interval from 0 to 10.

4 Graph a line with slope −2 that passes through the point (2, 2).

5 Graph a line with slope 2 that passes through the point (−2, 1).

Practice 4.4

For this practice, use 1 grid square to represent 1 unit on both axes for the interval from −6 to 6.

Graph each linear equation.

1 $y = \frac{1}{3}x + 1$

2 $y = \frac{1}{6}x + 3$

3 $y = \frac{1}{2}x + 2$

4 $y = \frac{2}{3}x - 1$

5 $y = -x + 5$

6 $y = 3 - \frac{1}{4}x$

7 $y = 1 - \frac{1}{2}x$

8 $y = -\frac{1}{5}x - 2$

9 *Math Journal* Graph the equation $y = 2 - \frac{2}{3}x$. Explain how to use the graph to find other solutions of the equation.

10 *Math Journal* Martha says that the point $(4, -2)$ lies on the graph of the equation $y = -\frac{1}{4}x - 1$. Explain how you can find out if she is right without actually graphing the equation.

Graph each line with the given slope that passes through the given point.

11 Slope $= \frac{2}{5}$; $(5, 4)$

12 Slope $= \frac{2}{3}$; $(6, 1)$

13 Slope $= -3$; $(1, 0)$

14 Slope $= -2$; $(-1, -2)$

15 *Math Journal* Suppose that Emily shows you some of her homework:

Graph the equation $y = -2x + \frac{1}{2}$.

Describe Emily's mistake. Graph the equation correctly.

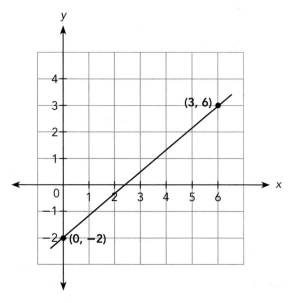

Real-World Problems: Linear Equations

Lesson Objective

• Explain slope and y-intercept in the context of real-world problems.

Vocabulary
linear relationship

Explain Slope and y-intercept in the Context of Real-World Problems.

You have learned previously that a direct proportion relationship is a relationship between two variable quantities x and y, where y is a constant multiple k of x. You can use an equation in the form $y = kx$, where k is a constant value, to represent a direct proportion relationship.

When there is a constant variation between two quantities, the relationship between the two quantities is a **linear relationship**. The relationship can be represented on a coordinate plane as a line. You can use an equation in the form $y = mx + b$, where m is the slope of the line and b is the y-intercept, to graph a linear relationship.

Think about the graph of the linear equation $y = 2x + 1$ and the rate of change $\frac{\text{Change in } y}{\text{Change in } x}$ between any two points on the line.

Find the rate of change for the points (0, 1) and (3, 7).

x	0	3
y	1	7

$$\frac{\text{Change in } y}{\text{Change in } x} = \frac{7 - 1}{3 - 0}$$

$$= \frac{6}{3} = 2$$

Find the rate of change for the points (1, 3) and (2, 5).

x	1	2
y	3	5

$$\frac{\text{Change in } y}{\text{Change in } x} = \frac{5 - 3}{2 - 1}$$

$$= \frac{2}{1} = 2$$

You can see that for any two points on the line, the

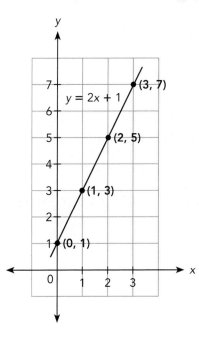

Continue on next page

unit rate of change, change in y per change in x, is the same as the slope of the equation.

Other variables may be used to describe quantities in a linear relationship. For any linear relationship, you can think of the quantity on the horizontal axis of a graph of the relationship as the independent variable. The quantity on the vertical axis of the graph is the dependent variable.

Math Note

The vertical intercept of a line is the value of the dependent variable when the value of the independent variable is 0.

When you graph a real-world linear relationship, the slope of the line is the rate of change in the dependent variable to the change in the independent variable.

Example 16 **Explain the meaning of the slope and y-intercept in real-world problems.**

A swimming pool when full holds a certain amount of water. When the drain is opened, the amount of water in the pool drains out at a constant rate. The graph shows the amount of water, y gallons, in the pool x hours after the drain is opened.

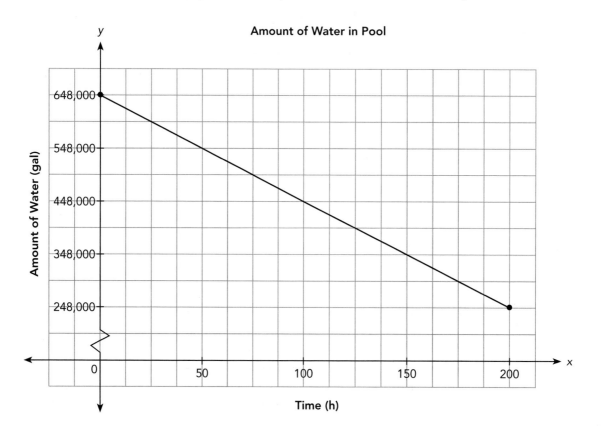

Amount of Water in Pool

In this situation, the amount of water in the pool depends on the number of hours the pool has been draining. So, the amount of water is the dependent variable, and the number of hours is the independent variable.

a) Find the vertical intercept of the graph and explain what information it gives about the situation.

Solution

From the graph, the vertical intercept is 648,000.

This is the number of gallons of water in the pool when it is full.

The vertical intercept, or y-intercept, corresponds to the initial number of gallons of water in the pool before it begins to drain.

b) Find the slope of the graph and explain what information it gives about the situation.

Solution

Let (200, 248,000) be (x_1, y_1) and (0, 648,000) be (x_2, y_2).

$$\text{Slope} = \frac{y_2 - y_1}{x_2 - x_1} \qquad \text{Use the slope formula.}$$

$$= \frac{648,000 - 248,000}{0 - 200} \qquad \text{Substitute values.}$$

$$= \frac{400,000}{-200} \qquad \text{Subtract.}$$

$$= -2,000 \qquad \text{Simplify.}$$

The negative slope means that as time increases, the amount of water decreases.

The line has slope $m = -2,000$.

The slope represents the rate, in gallons per hour, at which water is draining out of the pool. So 2,000 gallons of water drains from the pool every hour.

Think Math

Write an equation of the line.

Guided Practice

Solve. Show your work.

1 Jeanette rents a bike while visiting a city. She pays $7 per hour to rent the bike. She also pays $8 to rent a baby seat for the bike. She pays this amount for the baby seat no matter how many hours she rents the bike. The graph shows her total cost, y dollars, after x hours.

Bike $7 per hour
Child Seat $8

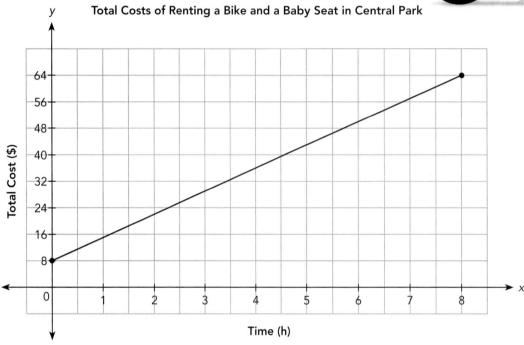

Total Costs of Renting a Bike and a Baby Seat in Central Park

Total Cost ($)

Time (h)

a) Find the vertical intercept of the graph and explain what information it gives about the situation.

From the graph, the vertical intercept is __?__. It represents __?__.

b) Find the slope of the graph and explain what information it gives about the situation.

The graph passes through (__?__, __?__) and (__?__, __?__).

Let (__?__, __?__) be (x_1, y_1) and (__?__, __?__) be (x_2, y_2).

Slope = $\dfrac{y_2 - y_1}{x_2 - x_1}$ Use the slope formula.

     = $\dfrac{?}{?}$ Substitute values.

     = $\dfrac{?}{?}$ Subtract.

     = __?__   Simplify.

The line has slope $m =$ __?__. It represents __?__.

Joanne and Chris are salespeople. Each of them earns a fixed monthly salary. They also earn an additional percent of the amount, in dollars, that they sell that month. So, the total monthly amount, *y* dollars, each salesperson earns depends on how much, in *x* dollars, he or she sells.

Total Earnings in One Month

a) Find the fixed monthly salary for each person.

Solution

From the graph, the vertical intercept for Joanne's graph is 2,500.
So, Joanne's fixed monthly salary is $2,500.

From the graph, the vertical intercept for Chris's graph is 1,500.
So, Chris's fixed monthly salary is $1,500.

b) Both Joanne and Chris earn a percent commission. Who earns a greater commission rate?

Solution

For each dollar a salesperson makes in sales, that person earns a certain amount of money as a commission. The person's commission rate is usually expressed as a percent. The rate is also the slope of the line graph for that person. You can see that Chris's line is steeper, so Chris earns a greater commission rate.

Continue on next page

c) Find each person's rate of commission.

Think Math

Because Joanne's base salary is greater, she assumes that she will earn more than Chris in any given month. Is this true? Explain.

Solution

Find the slope of Joanne's line graph.

Joanne's line graph passes through (0, 2,500) and (5,000, 2,750).

Let (0, 2,500) be (x_1, y_1) and (5,000, 2,750) be (x_2, y_2).

$\text{Slope} = \dfrac{y_2 - y_1}{x_2 - x_1}$ Use the slope formula.

$= \dfrac{2,750 - 2,500}{5,000 - 0}$ Substitute values.

$= \dfrac{250}{5,000}$ Subtract.

$= \dfrac{1}{20}$ Simplify.

$\text{Commission rate} = \dfrac{1}{20} \cdot 100\%$ Express the slope as a percent.

$= \dfrac{100}{20}\%$ Multiply.

$= 5\%$ Simplify.

Joanne's commission rate is 5% of her sales.

Find the slope of Chris's line graph.

Chris's line graph passes through (0, 1,500) and (2,500, 2,000).

Let (0, 1,500) be (x_1, y_1) and (2,500, 2,000) be (x_2, y_2).

$\text{Slope} = \dfrac{y_2 - y_1}{x_2 - x_1}$ Use the slope formula.

$= \dfrac{2,000 - 1,500}{2,500 - 0}$ Substitute values.

$= \dfrac{500}{2,500}$ Subtract.

$= \dfrac{1}{5}$ Simplify.

$\text{Commission rate} = \dfrac{1}{5} \cdot 100\%$ Express the slope as a percent.

$= \dfrac{100}{5}\%$ Multiply.

$= 20\%$ Simplify.

Chris's commission rate is 20% of his sales.

Guided Practice

Solve. Show your work.

2 Both Zack and Joy are salespeople. Each of them earns a fixed weekly salary
and a percent commission based on the total sales he or she makes in a week.
The graphs show the total earnings, *E* dollars, each person can make in one week,
based on the person's total sales, *S* dollars.

a) Find the fixed weekly salary for each person.

b) Both Zack and Joy earn a percent commission. Who earns a greater percent in commission?

c) Find each person's rate of commission.

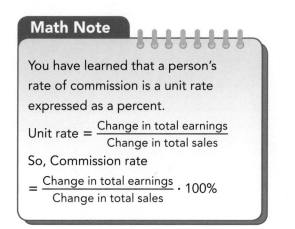

Math Note

You have learned that a person's rate of commission is a unit rate expressed as a percent.

$$\text{Unit rate} = \frac{\text{Change in total earnings}}{\text{Change in total sales}}$$

So, Commission rate

$$= \frac{\text{Change in total earnings}}{\text{Change in total sales}} \cdot 100\%$$

Example 18 **Compare two different linear relationships given one graph and one equation.**

Britney and Scarlet each have a coin bank. Britney starts with a certain amount of money and adds money at regular intervals. Scarlet starts with a different amount of money and takes money out over time. The amount of money, y dollars, in Scarlet's coin bank after x weeks is given by the equation $y = -24x + 120$. The graph shows the amount of money in Britney's coin bank after x weeks.

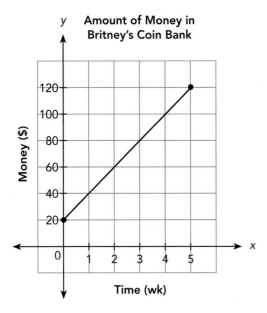

a) Find the vertical intercept of Britney's graph and explain what information it gives about the situation.

Solution

From the graph, the vertical intercept is 20. This is the amount of money, $20, that Britney starts with.

b) Find the slope of Britney's graph and explain what information it gives about the situation.

Solution

The graph passes through (0, 20) and (5, 120).

Let (0, 20) be (x_1, y_1) and (5, 120) be (x_2, y_2).

$$\text{Slope} = \frac{y_2 - y_1}{x_2 - x_1} \qquad \text{Use the slope formula.}$$

$$= \frac{120 - 20}{5 - 0} \qquad \text{Substitute values.}$$

$$= \frac{100}{5} \qquad \text{Subtract.}$$

$$= 20 \qquad \text{Simplify.}$$

The line has slope $m = 20$.

The slope represents the rate at which Britney is adding money. So Britney adds $20 every week.

c)   Is Britney adding money at a faster rate or is Scarlet taking out money at a faster rate? Explain.

Solution

Find the rate at which Scarlet is taking money out of her bank. From the equation $y = -24x + 120$, you can see that each week she takes out $24.

Because $24 > $20, Scarlet is taking out money at a faster rate than Britney is adding money.

Think Math

Suppose you were to graph Scarlet's equation on the same coordinate plane as Britney's graph. What would be the slope and vertical intercept of the graph? What information would they give you about the situation?

Guided Practice

Solve. Show your work.

3 Isaac and George are brothers who live at the same house, but go to different cities for vacation. When their vacation is over, they begin driving back home at the same time, but drive home at different speeds. Isaac's distance D miles from their house x hours after he starts driving is given by the equation $D = -50x + 150$. The graph shows George's distance D miles from their house x hours after he starts driving home.

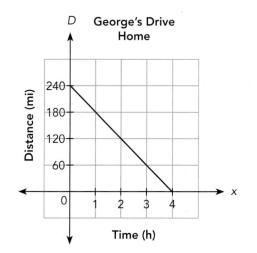

When comparing rates of change in c), you only look at the absolute value of the slope. The sign is not taken into consideration.

a)   Find the vertical intercept of George's graph and explain what information it gives about the situation.

b)   Find the slope of George's graph and explain what information it gives about the situation.

c)   Which brother is driving faster? How do you know?

Solve. Show your work.

1. Joe pays a fixed amount each month to use his cell phone. He also pays for each minute that he makes calls on the phone. The graph shows the amount, *C* dollars, he pays in a given month, based on the airtime, *x* minutes, he uses to make calls.

   a) Find the vertical intercept of the graph and explain what information it gives about the situation.

   b) Find the slope of the graph and explain what information it gives about the situation.

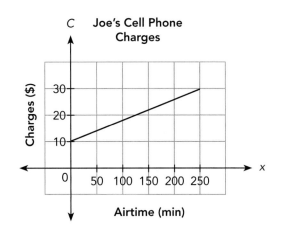

2. Ricky and Aaron are brothers, and each of them has a coin bank. In January, the boys had different amounts of money in their coin banks. Then, for each month after that, each boy added the same amount of money to his coin bank. The graph shows the amount of savings, *S* dollars, in each coin bank after *t* months.

   a) Find the initial amount of money in each coin bank.

   b) Who added a greater amount of money each month into his coin bank?

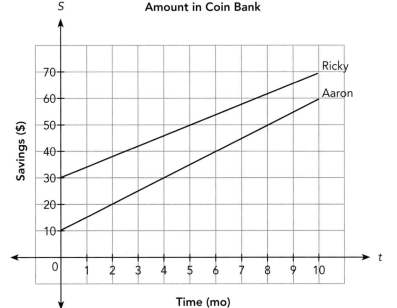

3. Raymond and Randy drive from Town A to Town B in separate cars. The initial amount of gasoline in each car is different. The graphs show the amount of gasoline, *y* gallons, in each person's car after *x* miles.

   a) Find the initial amount of gasoline in each car.

   b) Whose car uses more gasoline?

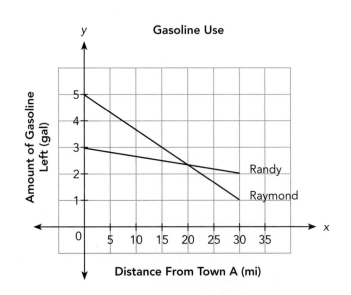

4 Pete and Winnie visit Star Café every day and they pay for the items using a gift card. The amount, y dollars, on Winnie's gift card after x days is given by the equation $y = 100 - 19x$. The graph shows the amount on Pete's gift card over x days.

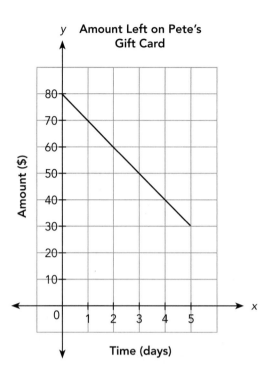

y **Amount Left on Pete's Gift Card**

Amount ($)

Time (days)

a) Write an equation for the amount on Pete's gift card.

b) Using your answer in a), whose gift card had a higher initial amount?

c) Using your answer in a), who spends more each day?

Use graph paper. Solve.

5 A scientist attaches a spring that is 11 inches long to the ceiling and hangs weights from the spring to see how far it will stretch. The scientist records the length of the spring, y inches, for different weights x pounds.

Weight (x pounds)	0	1	2	3	4
Length of Spring (y inches)	11	13	15	17	19

11 in.

a) Graph the relationship between the length of the spring for different weights. Use 1 grid square to represent 1 unit on the horizontal axis for the x interval 0 to 4, and 1 grid square for 2 units on the vertical axis for the y interval 11 to 19.

b) Find the vertical intercept of the graph and explain what information it gives about the situation.

c) Find the slope of the graph and explain what information it gives about the situation.

d) Write an equation relating the spring length and the pounds of weights hung from the spring.

Brain @ Work

1 Conrad and Angeline each receive an allowance. Conrad gets the entire week's allowance on Monday. He spends the same amount every day. Angeline gets a daily allowance starting on Monday. She saves the same amount every day. After four days, both have the same amount of money. The graph shows the amount of money, y dollars, Conrad has after x days during one week.

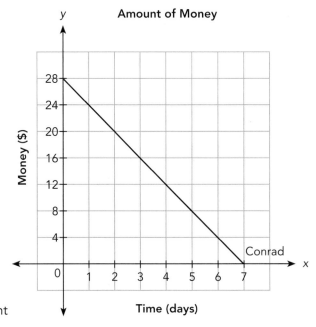

a) Copy the graph. Then draw a line to represent the amount of money Angeline has after x days.

b) Find the slope of Conrad's graph and explain what information it gives about the situation.

c) Write an equation to represent the amount of money each person has during that week.

2 Gordon left Townsville at 12 P.M. and started biking to Kingston 50 miles away. One and a half hours later, Jonathan left Kingston and started biking toward Townsville at a speed of 20 miles per hour. The graph shows Gordon's distance, d miles, from Townsville after t hours.

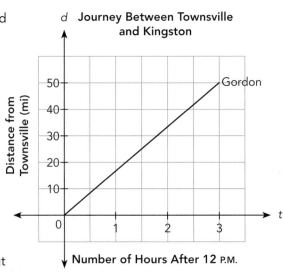

a) Copy the graph. Then draw a line to represent Jonathan's distance from Kingston after t hours.

b) Find the slope of Gordon's graph and explain what information it gives about this situation.

c) Write an equation to represent each person's distance from Townsville after t hours.

Chapter Wrap Up

Concept Map

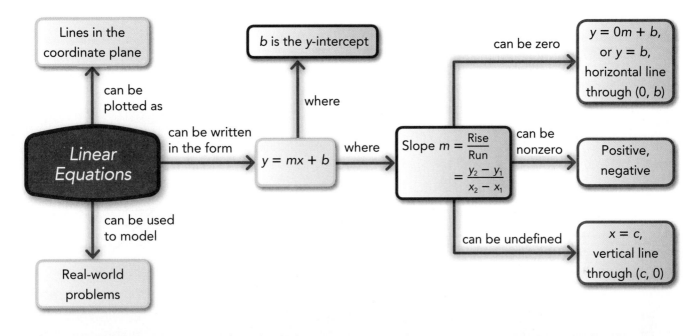

Key Concepts

▶ The slope-intercept form of a linear equation is given by $y = mx + b$, where m represents the slope and b is the y-intercept of the graph of the equation.

▶ The slope of a line passing through two points (x_1, y_1) and (x_2, y_2) is equal to $\frac{y_2 - y_1}{x_2 - x_1}$ or $\frac{y_1 - y_2}{x_1 - x_2}$.

▶ The slope is always the same between any two distinct points on a line and can be positive, negative, zero, or undefined.

▶ The y-intercept, b, is the y-coordinate of the point where a line intersects the y-axis.

▶ The equation of a horizontal line through the point (c, d) is $y = d$. The equation of a vertical line through the point (c, d) is $x = c$.

▶ You can write an equation of a line given the slope m and the y-intercept b, the slope m and a point, or the coordinates of two points.

▶ You can write an equation of a line parallel to a given line if you know the y-intercept of the line you want to draw, or the coordinates of a point on the line you want to draw.

▶ You can use linear equations and graphs to model and solve real-world problems.

Chapter Review/Test

Concepts and Skills

Find the slope of each line using the points indicated. Then write an equation for it.

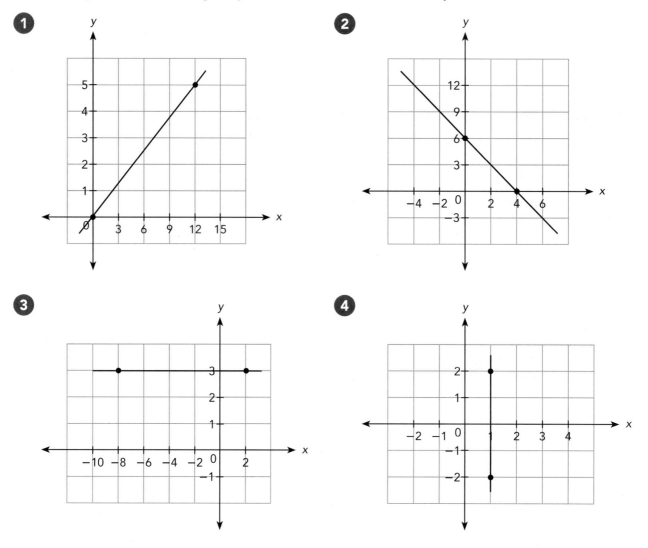

For each line, state its slope and its *y*-intercept.

5 $y = \frac{1}{2}x - 3$

6 $y = -3x + 4$

Write an equation of each line given its slope and its *y*-intercept.

7 Slope, $m = -4$
   y-intercept, $b = -\frac{1}{3}$

8 Slope, $m = \frac{2}{5}$
   y-intercept, $b = 3$

Solve. Show your work.

9 Write an equation of the line parallel to $5y = 3x + 12$ that has a *y*-intercept of 2.

10 Write an equation of the line that has slope $-\frac{1}{2}$ and passes through the point $(-4, 5)$.

11 Write an equation of the line that passes through the point $(-4, -4)$ and is parallel to $2y - x = -6$.

12 Write an equation of the line that passes through the point $(-4, -3)$ and is parallel to $4y - x = -16$.

Write an equation of the line that passes through each pair of points.

13 $(0, 0)$ and $(7, 7)$

14 $(1, 2)$ and $(4, 8)$

Use graph paper. Graph each linear equation. Use 1 grid square on both axes to represent 1 unit for the interval from −5 to 5.

15 $4y = -3x - 8$

16 Slope $= \dfrac{1}{3}$; $(0, -2)$

Problem Solving

Solve. Show your work.

17 Landscaping Company A and Company B each charges a certain amount, C dollars, as consultation fee, plus a fixed hourly charge.

a) Find the amount each landscaping company charges as its consultation fee.

b) Which company charges a greater amount per hour?

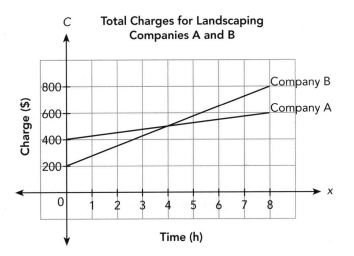

18 The operator of a charter bus service charges a certain amount for a bus, plus per-passenger charge. The graph shows the total charges, C dollars, for carrying x passengers.

a) Find the vertical intercept and explain what information it gives about the situation.

b) Find the slope of the graph and explain what information it gives about the situation.

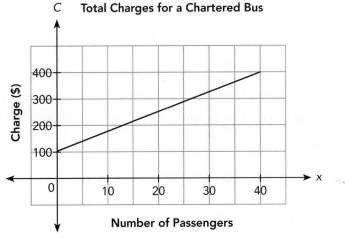

Cumulative Review Chapters 3–4

Concepts and Skills

Solve each equation. Show your work. (Lesson 3.1)

1 $0.2(x + 2) - 2 = 0.4$

2 $2(x - 5) - 3(3 - x) = \frac{1}{2}(x - 2)$

3 $\frac{x}{3} + \frac{3 + x}{6} = 3$

4 $\frac{2(x + 3)}{5} - \frac{x - 1}{2} = 2$

Express each decimal as a fraction, without the use of calculator. (Lesson 3.1)

5 $0.\overline{5}$

6 $0.\overline{8}$

7 $0.2\overline{7}$

8 $0.\overline{09}$

Tell whether each equation has one solution, no solution, or an infinite number of solutions. Show your work. (Lesson 3.2)

9 $3x - 2 = -3\left(\frac{2}{3} - x\right)$

10 $3x + 6 = -2\left(\frac{3}{2} - x\right)$

11 $5(6a - 6) + 40 = 3(10a - 7) + 31$

12 $3x + 7 = -8\left(\frac{3}{4} - x\right)$

13 $\frac{1}{4}(2x - 1) = \frac{1}{2}x + \frac{3}{8}$

14 $\frac{1}{8}x + 6 = \frac{1}{16}(2x - 96)$

Find the value of y when x = 4. (Lesson 3.3)

15 $2x - 1 = \frac{1}{2} + y$

16 $\frac{1}{4}(2y - 1) = 0.6 + \frac{5x}{8}$

Express y in terms of x. Find the value of y when x = 4. (Lesson 3.4)

17 $6(3x + y) = 3$

18 $\frac{2x - 1}{4} = 3y$

Express x in terms of y. Find the value of x when y = −2. (Lesson 3.4)

19 $\left(\frac{2x - y}{5}\right) = 9$

20 $0.75(x + y) = 12$

Find the slope of the line passing through each pair of points. (Lesson 4.1)

21 $A (1, 2), B (4, 8)$

22 $C (1, 4), D (2, 7)$

23 $E (0, 0), F (-7, 7)$

24 $G (-3, 0), F (0, -6)$

Identify the *y*-intercept. Then calculate the slope using the points indicated.
(Lessons 4.1, 4.2)

25

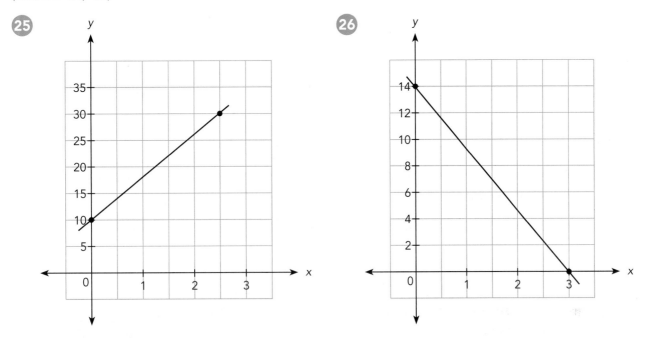

For each equation, find the slope and the *y*-intercept of the graph of the equation.
(Lesson 4.3)

27 $y = 7x + 1$

28 $y = -2x - 5$

29 $2y = 4x + 6$

30 $4y + 3x = 8$

Use the given slope and *y*-intercept of a line to write an equation in slope-intercept form. (Lesson 4.3)

31 Slope, $m = 3$
  y-intercept, $b = 2$

32 Slope, $m = -1$
  y-intercept, $b = 4$

33 Slope, $m = 5$
  y-intercept, $b = -2$

34 Slope, $m = -\dfrac{3}{2}$
  y-intercept, $b = -5$

Solve. Show your work. (Lesson 4.3)

35 Write an equation of the line parallel to $2y = 4x + 3$ that has a *y*-intercept of 4.

36 A line has slope -4 and passes through the point $\left(\dfrac{3}{4}, 3\right)$. Write an equation of the line.

37 Write an equation of the line that passes through the point $(2, 3)$ and is parallel to $3y + 2x = 7$.

Use graph paper. Graph each linear equation. Use 1 grid scale to represent 1 unit on both axes for the interval −5 to 5. (Lesson 4.4)

38 $y = -2x + 8$ **39** $y = -2 - 3x$ **40** $y = \frac{1}{2}x - 3$

Solve. Show your work. (Lesson 4.5)

41 Bobby and Chloe each have a bank account. The balance, y dollars, in each account for x weeks, is shown in the graph.

  a) Who saved money and who withdrew money during the 10 weeks?

  b) Whose balance changed more over 10 weeks?

  c) Explain what information the coordinates of P give about the situation.

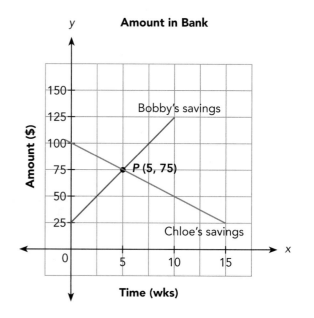

Problem Solving

Solve. Show your work.

42 The diagram shows a sheet of metal of width y inches. It is bent into a U-shaped gutter that is used to channel rain from a roof. The horizontal section of the gutter shown on the right is 10 inches wide and the heights are in the ratio of 2 : 3. (Chapter 3)

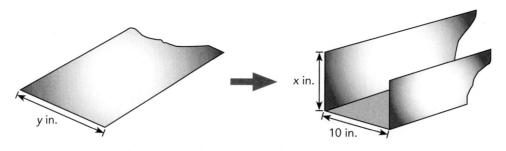

  a) Let x represents the longer height of the gutter, in inches. Write a linear equation for the width of the sheet of metal, y inches, in terms of the longer height of the gutter, x inches.

  b) The width of the sheet of metal is 30 inches. Calculate the longer height of the gutter.

43 In a grocery store, each apple costs $0.50, each orange costs $0.40, and each pear costs $0.30. Mrs. Fortney bought y apples, three times as many oranges as apples, and 7 fewer pears than apples. She spent a total of $19.90 on the fruits. (Chapter 3)

a) Write a linear equation to find the amount spent on each fruit.

b) Find the total cost spent on apples and pears.

44 Jack traveled from his home to Denver at an average speed of x miles per hour. He arrived in $\frac{3}{4}$ hour and took a 15-minute break. From Denver, he traveled at an average speed of $(x + 2)$ miles per hour and reached his grandmother's place in 1.5 hours. (Chapter 3)

a) Write a linear equation for the total distance traveled, D miles, in terms of average speed, x miles per hour.

b) The total distance traveled for the whole journey was 120 miles. Find the average speed for both parts of the journey.

Use graph paper. Solve.

45 Xavier walks into an elevator in the basement of a building. Its control panel displays "0" for the floor number. As Xavier goes up, the numbers increase one by one on the display. The table shows the floor numbers and the distance from ground level. (Chapter 4)

Floor Number (x)	0	1	2	3	4
Distance (y feet)	−10	0	10	20	30

a) Graph the relationship between the distance of the elevator from ground level at different floor numbers. Use 1 grid square to represent 1 unit on the horizontal axis for the x interval 0 to 4, and 1 grid square for 10 units on the vertical axis for the y interval −10 to 30.

b) Find the vertical intercept of the graph and explain what information it gives about the situation.

c) Find the slope of the graph and explain what information it gives about the situation.

d) Write an equation relating the distance of the elevator from ground level and the floor number on the display.

e) What is the distance of the elevator from ground level of the highest floor that is less than 165 feet? Is there a floor number with a distance from ground level of exactly 165 feet?

CHAPTER

5

Systems of Linear Equations

Have you ever wanted to exercise more?

There are many fun ways to exercise and burn calories. If you choose activities that you really like to do, you are more likely to stay with the routine.

Greg's favorite activities are bike riding and hip-hop dancing. He wants to spend 6 hours each week exercising to burn about 2,100 calories. He burns about 425 calories in an hour of bike riding and about 325 calories in an hour of hip-hop dancing. How much time should he spend doing each activity to accomplish his goal?

In this chapter, you will learn how to answer this question and solve other problems by writing and solving two equations involving two variables.

BIG IDEA

▶ A system of linear equations may have a unique solution. It can be solved using the elimination, substitution, or graphical methods.

Recall Prior Knowledge

Graphing linear equations using a table of values

To graph a linear equation, you can first construct a table of x- and y-values.

For example, you substitute 0 for x in the equation $y = 2x + 1$ to get the corresponding value of y.

$y = 2(0) + 1$
$\quad = 1$

x	0	1	2	3
y	1	3	5	7

From the table of values, you plot the pairs of values on a coordinate grid. Then join the points using a straight line to graph the linear equation.

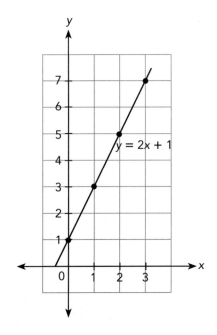

☑ Quick Check

Complete the table of values and graph each linear equation.

1 $y = 5x$

x	0	1	2	3
y	?	?	?	?

2 $y = -x + 2$

x	0	1	2	3
y	?	?	?	?

Solving real-world problems algebraically

Real-world problems can be modeled using algebraic equations. You use algebraic reasoning to translate the problem into algebraic expressions. Then write an algebraic equation and solve it.

For example, Mary has 4 more pencils than Ann. If they have 12 pencils altogether, find the number of pencils Mary has.

> You can use a letter, called a variable, to represent the unknown quantity.

Let the number of pencils that Mary has be x.   Define the variable.

Then the number of pencils that Ann has: $x - 4$
Total number of pencils that the girls have: $x + x - 4 = 12$

Find the number of pencils that Mary has:

$x + x - 4 = 12$	Write an equation.
$2x - 4 = 12$	Add the like terms.
$2x - 4 + 4 = 12 + 4$	Add 4 to both sides.
$2x = 16$	Simplify.
$\dfrac{2x}{2} = \dfrac{16}{2}$	Divide both sides by 2.
$x = 8$	Simplify.

The solution of the equation is $x = 8$. So, Mary has 8 pencils.

✓ Quick Check

Solve. Show your work.

3   Samuel bought 30 books. The hardcover books cost $20 each while the rest, which are paperbacks, cost $8 each. If he spent a total of $480, how many paperbacks did he buy?

5.1 Introduction to Systems of Linear Equations

Lesson Objective

- Understand systems of linear equations.

Vocabulary

system of linear equations

unique solution

Understand Systems of Linear Equations.

You have learned to solve linear equations with one variable. To solve an equation with two variables, you need to use two equations.

Consider the following situation. A farmer, Mr. McDowell, has x goats and y cows. He has 9 goats and cows altogether. How many of each animal does he have?

You can represent the total number of goats and cows using the linear equation $x + y = 9$. The table shows pairs of numbers that satisfy the equation $x + y = 9$.

Number of Goats (x)	0	1	2	3	4	5	6	7	8	9
Number of Cows (y)	9	8	7	6	5	4	3	2	1	0

There are many pairs of possible values of x and y. You need more information to find the number of goats and cows Mr. McDowell has.

Suppose you have additional information: Mr. McDowell has twice as many goats as cows. You can represent the number of goats using the linear equation $x = 2y$. The table below shows some possible pairs of numbers that satisfy the equation $x = 2y$.

x	0	2	4	6	8
y	0	1	2	3	4

Again you have many possible values of x and y.

Note that the values of x and y must satisfy both equations. So, the same pair of x- and y-values must appear in both tables. When you compare the two tables, you see that there is only one such pair of x- and y-values: $x = 6$ and $y = 3$. So, Mr. McDowell has 6 goats and 3 cows.

> A set of linear equations that has more than one variable is called a system of linear equations. The single pair of variables that satisfies both equations is their **unique solution**.

Lionel is x years old and his younger brother is y years old. The difference in their ages is 1 year. The sum of 4 times Lionel's age and his brother's age is 14 years. The related system of linear equations is:

$x - y = 1$
$4x + y = 14$

Solve the system of linear equations by making tables of values. Then find Lionel's age and his brother's age.

Solution

Make a table of values for each equation.

> Since x and y represent ages, both will be positive integers.

$x - y = 1$

x	2	3	4
y	1	2	3

$4x + y = 14$

x	1	2	3
y	10	6	2

Only the pair of values $x = 3$ and $y = 2$ appear in both tables.
So, the solution to the system of equations is $x = 3$, $y = 2$.

Lionel's age is 3 years and his brother's age is 2 years.

Think Math

Why is $x \neq 1$ in the first equation?

Guided Practice

Solve the system of linear equations by copying and completing the tables of values. The values x and y are positive integers.

1. A bottle of water and a taco cost \$3. The cost of 3 bottles of water is \$1 more than the cost of a taco. Let x be the price of a bottle of water and y be the price of a taco in dollars. The related system of equations and tables of values are:

$3x - y = 1$
$x + y = 3$

$3x - y = 1$

x	1	2
y	?	?

$x + y = 3$

x	1	2
y	?	?

> The equation $x + y = 3$ suggests that x and y can only be 1 or 2 since they are positive integers.

Only the pair of values $x = \underline{}$ and $y = \underline{}$ appear in both tables.
So, the solution to the system of equations is $x = \underline{}$, $y = \underline{}$.

The cost of a bottle of water is \$$\underline{}$ and the cost of a taco is \$$\underline{}$.

Solve each system of equations by making tables of values. x and y are positive integers.

2 $x + y = 6$
   $x + 2y = 8$

3 $x + y = 8$
   $x - 3y = -8$

> For each linear equation, list in a table enough values for x and y to obtain a solution. Remember that they must be positive integers.

Technology Activity

Materials:
- graphing calculator

USE TABLES ON A GRAPHING CALCULATOR TO SOLVE A SYSTEM OF EQUATIONS

Work in pairs.

You can use a graphing calculator to create tables of values and solve systems of equations. Use the steps below to solve this system:

$8x + y = 38$
$x - 4y = 13$

STEP 1 Solve each equation for y in terms of x. Input the two resulting expressions for y into the equation screen.

Caution ////////

Use parentheses around fractional coefficients and the (−) key for negative coefficients.

STEP 2 Set the table function to use values of x starting at 0, with increments of 1.

STEP 3 Display the table. It will be in three columns as shown.

X	Y1	Y2
0	38	-3.25
1	30	-3

STEP 4 Find the row where the two y-values are the same. This y-value and the corresponding x-value will be the solution to the equations.

The solution to the system of equations is given by $x =$ __?__ and $y =$ __?__ .

 Math Journal How can you tell from the two columns of y-values that there is only one row where the y-values are the same?

Solve each system of linear equations by making tables of values. Each variable x is a positive integer less than 6.

1 $2x + y = 5$
$x - y = -2$

2 $x + 2y = 4$
$x = 2y$

3 $3x + 2y = 10$
$5x - 2y = 6$

4 $x - 2y = -5$
$x = y$

5 $2y - x = -2$
$x + y = 2$

6 $2x + y = 3$
$x + y = 1$

7 $x + 2y = 1$
$x - 2y = 5$

8 $2x - y = 5$
$2x + y = -1$

9 $2y + x = -1$
$x + y = 1$

Solve by making a table of values. The values x and y are integers.

10 A shop sells a party hat at x dollars and a mask at y dollars. On a particular morning, 10 hats and 20 masks were sold for $30. In the afternoon, 8 hats and 10 masks were sold for $18. The related system of linear equations is:

$10x + 20y = 30$
$8x + 10y = 18$

Solve the system of linear equations. Then find the cost of each hat and each mask.

11 Alicia is x years old and her cousin is y years old. Alicia is 2 times as old as her cousin. Three years later, their combined age will be 27 years. The related system of linear equations is:

$x = 2y$
$x + y = 21$

Solve the system of linear equations. Then find Alicia's age and her cousin's age.

12 Steve and Alex start driving at the same time from Boston to Paterson. The journey is d kilometers. Steve drives at 100 kilometers per hour and takes t hours to complete the journey. Alex, who drives at 80 kilometers per hour, is 60 kilometers away from Paterson when Steve reaches Paterson. The related system of linear equations is:

$100t = d$
$80t = d - 60$

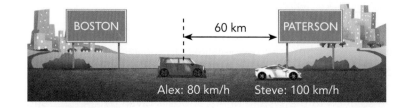

Solve the system of linear equations by making tables of values. Then find the distance between Boston and Paterson.

Solving Systems of Linear Equations Using Algebraic Methods

Lesson Objectives

- Solve systems of linear equations using the elimination method.
- Solve systems of linear equations using the substitution method.

Vocabulary

common term

elimination method

substitution method

Solve Systems of Linear Equations with a Common Term Using the Elimination Method.

You have learned to solve systems of linear equations using tables of values. You may have noticed that it is not always easy to find the solution, so you need to adopt a more systematic approach.

Consider the system of linear equations:

$x + y = 8$ — Equation 1
$x + 2y = 10$ — Equation 2

You can represent these equations using bar models:

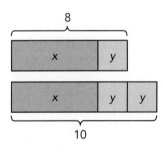

The difference in length of the two bar models is 2 units. The second model is also one y-section longer, so $y = 2$.

From the bar models, $y = 10 - 8 = 2$.
Look again at the bar model representing Equation 1:

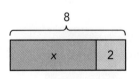

From the bar model, $x + 2 = 8$. You can see that $x = 8 - 2$.

So, $x = 8 - 2$
    $x = 6$

Continue on next page

Algebraically, you can use the same approach.

$x + y = 8$ — Equation 1
$x + 2y = 10$ — Equation 2

Both equations have an x term. If you subtract the two equations, you will have one equation with only one variable y.

Subtract Equation 1 from Equation 2:
$(x + 2y) - (x + y) = 10 - 8$

$x + 2y - x - y = 2$ Use the distributive property.

$x - x + 2y - y = 2$ Group like terms.

$y = 2$ Simplify. x is eliminated.

Left side:	Right side:
$x + 2y$	10
$-x - y$	-8
y	2

So, $y = 2$.

Subtracting two equations is another form of the subtraction property of equality. You have subtracted the same number from both sides of an equation before. Now you are subtracting equal expressions from both sides of the equation.

Substitute 2 for y into Equation 1:
$x + 2 = 8$
$x + 2 - 2 = 8 - 2$
$x = 6$

Caution ///////

When you subtract one equation from another, remember to use parentheses to group the expression after the minus sign.

So, the solution to the system of linear equations is given by $x = 6$, $y = 2$.

By adding or subtracting two equations with a common term, you get an equation with only one variable. This method of solving systems of equations is known as the elimination method.

Example 2  **Solve systems of linear equations with a common term using the elimination method.**

Solve the system of linear equations using the elimination method.

$4x + y = 9$ — Equation 1
$3x - y = 5$ — Equation 2

The common terms of a system of equations are two or more like terms with the same or opposite coefficients such as y and $-y$. To eliminate the y terms, add the two equations.

Solution

Add Equation 1 and Equation 2:
$(4x + y) + (3x - y) = 9 + 5$

$4x + 3x + y - y = 14$ Group like terms.

$7x = 14$ Simplify. y is eliminated.

$\dfrac{7x}{7} = \dfrac{14}{7}$ Divide both sides by 7.

$x = 2$ Simplify.

To find y, substitute 2 for x into Equation 1 or Equation 2:

$4(2) + y = 9$

$\quad 8 + y = 9$ Simplify.

$\quad\quad\quad y = 1$ Subtract 8 from both sides.

So, the solution of the system to linear equations is given by $x = 2$, $y = 1$.

Check: Substitute the solution into Equation 2.

$3 \cdot 2 - 1 = 5$

When $x = 2$ and $y = 1$, the equation $3x - y = 5$ is true. So, $x = 2$ and $y = 1$ gives the solution.

> The value of x was substituted into Equation 1 to solve for y. So use Equation 2 to check the solution.

Guided Practice

Solve each system of linear equations using the elimination method.

1 $2a + 3b = 29$ — Equation 1

     $2a - b = 17$ — Equation 2

Subtract Equation 2 from Equation 1:

$2a + 3b - (2a - b) = 29 - 17$

$\quad\quad\quad \underline{\ ?\ } = \underline{\ ?\ }$ Use the distributive property.

$\quad\quad\quad \underline{\ ?\ } = \underline{\ ?\ }$ Group like terms and simplify. The variable a is eliminated

$\quad\quad\quad \dfrac{?}{?} = \dfrac{?}{?}$ Divide both sides by $\underline{\ ?\ }$.

$\quad\quad\quad b = \underline{\ ?\ }$ Simplify.

Substitute $\underline{\ ?\ }$ for b into Equation 2:

$2a - \underline{\ ?\ } = 17$

$\quad\quad \underline{\ ?\ } = \underline{\ ?\ }$ Add $\underline{\ ?\ }$ to both sides.

$\quad\quad \underline{\ ?\ } = \underline{\ ?\ }$ Simplify.

$\quad\quad \underline{\ ?\ } = \underline{\ ?\ }$ Divide both sides by $\underline{\ ?\ }$.

$\quad\quad\quad a = \underline{\ ?\ }$ Simplify.

The solution to the system of linear equations is $a = \underline{\ ?\ }$, $b = \underline{\ ?\ }$.

2 $2x - y = 2$

     $3x + y = 13$

3 $x + 6y = 1$

     $x + y = 6$

Solve Systems of Linear Equations Without Common Terms Using the Elimination Method.

Consider the following system of linear equations. You cannot immediately use the elimination method, because the equations have no common term. But you can still solve the system using the method.

$2x + 3y = 7$ — Equation 1
$x + 6y = 8$ — Equation 2

You can represent these equations using bar models:

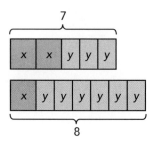

You can redraw the bar models, using two copies of the second bar model.

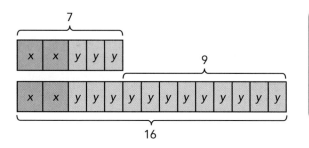

In the redrawn models, x and y still represent the same numbers, because the sections are still the same size. You can see that $9y = 9$, so $y = 1$.

From the bar models, you can see that the solution is $x = 2$, $y = 1$.

You can write the equation that the redrawn second bar model represents by multiplying both sides of Equation 2 by 2:

$2 \cdot (x + 6y) = 2 \cdot 8$
$2x + 12y = 16$ — Equation 3   Use the distributive property and simplify.

Now you have two equations with a common x term. You can use the elimination method to solve this system, and the solution will be the solution to the original system.

$2x + 3y = 7$ — Equation 1
$2x + 12y = 16$ — Equation 3

Multiplying Equation 2 by 2 produces an equivalent equation, that is, one with exactly the same solution as Equation 2. So, the solution to the system does not change.

If the coefficients of x or y are multiples, you can rewrite equations with a common term by multiplying one of the equations.

Example 3 **Solve systems of linear equations without common terms using the elimination method.**

Solve the system of linear equations using the elimination method.

$2x + 5y = 11$ — Equation 1
$9x + 2y = -12$ — Equation 2

Solution

Method 1

Eliminate the x terms first.

If you multiply $2x$ by 9, and $9x$ by 2, you will get $18x$ in each case. So you can multiply both sides of Equation 1 by 9, and both sides of Equation 2 by 2 to eliminate the x terms.

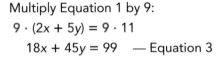

Multiply Equation 1 by 9:
$9 \cdot (2x + 5y) = 9 \cdot 11$
$18x + 45y = 99$ — Equation 3

Multiply Equation 2 by 2:
$2 \cdot (9x + 2y) = 2 \cdot (-12)$
$18x + 4y = -24$ — Equation 4

Subtract Equation 4 from Equation 3:
$(18x + 45y) - (18x + 4y) = 99 - (-24)$

$18x + 45y - 18x - 4y = 123$	Use the distributive property.
$41y = 123$	Simplify. $18x$ is eliminated.
$\dfrac{41y}{41} = \dfrac{123}{41}$	Divide both sides by 41.
$y = 3$	Simplify.

Substitute 3 for y into Equation 1:

$2x + 5(3) = 11$	
$2x + 15 = 11$	
$2x + 15 - 15 = 11 - 15$	Subtract 15 from both sides.
$2x = -4$	Simplify.
$\dfrac{2x}{2} = \dfrac{-4}{2}$	Divide both sides by 2.
$x = -2$	Simplify.

The solution to the system of linear equations is given by $x = -2$, $y = 3$.

Continue on next page

Method 2

Eliminate the y terms first.

Multiply Equation 1 by 2:
$2 \cdot (2x + 5y) = 2 \cdot 11$
$4x + 10y = 22$ — Equation 5

Multiply Equation 2 by 5:
$5 \cdot (9x + 2y) = 5 \cdot (-12)$
$45x + 10y = -60$ — Equation 6

Subtract Equation 6 from Equation 5:
$(4x + 10y) - (45x + 10y) = 22 - (-60)$

$4x + 10y - 45x - 10y = 82$	Use the distributive property.
$-41x = 82$	Simplify.
$x = -2$	Divide both sides by -41.

Either way, the solution to the system is given by $x = -2$ and $y = 3$.

Check: Substitute the solution into Equation 2.

$9(-2) + 2(3) = -12$

When $x = -2$ and $y = 3$, the equation $9x + 2y = -12$ is true.
So, $x = -2$ and $y = 3$ gives the solution.

> **Think Math**
>
> In **Method 2**, does it matter which equation you substitute x into to find the value of y? Explain.

Guided Practice

Solve each system of linear equations using the elimination method.

4 $7m + 2n = -8$
$2m = 3n - 13$

5 $3x - 2y = 24$
$5x + 4y = -4$

6 $2x + 7y = -32$
$4x - 5y = 12$

Solve Systems of Linear Equations Using the Substitution Method.

You have learned to solve systems of linear equations using the elimination method. Look again at the system of linear equations below and the bar models representing them.

$x + y = 8$
$x + 2y = 10$

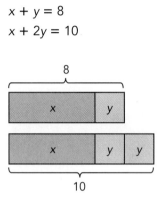

You can redraw the bar representing x as $8 - y$.

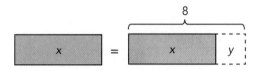

You can redraw the bar model for $x + 2y = 10$ by replacing x with $8 - y$:

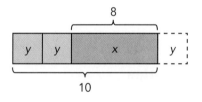

Observe $8 + y = 10$ from the bar model:

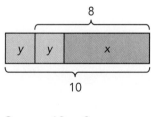

The equation $x + 2y = 10$ becomes $(8 - y) + 2y = 10$.

So, $y = 10 - 8$
    $y = 2$

From the bar model representing Equation 1, $x + 2 = 8$, so $x = 6$.

Continue on next page

You can solve this system of equations using the same approach algebraically.

$x + y = 8$ — Equation 1
$x + 2y = 10$ — Equation 2

Use Equation 1 to express x in terms of y:

$x + y = 8$
$x + y - y = 8 - y$ Subtract y from both sides.
$x = 8 - y$ — Equation 3   Simplify.

Think Math

Could you solve for y in terms of x and then solve the system of equations using the same method? Justify your answer.

Substitute Equation 3 into Equation 2 to get an equation with only one variable:

$(8 - y) + 2y = 10$
$8 + y = 10$ Simplify.
$8 + y - 8 = 10 - 8$ Subtract 8 from both sides.
$y = 2$ Simplify.

Substitute 2 for y into Equation 3 to get $x = 8 - 2 = 6$.

So, the solution to the system of equations is $x = 6$, $y = 2$.

Math Note

The elimination method and the substitution method give the same solution.

This method, called the substitution method, consists of three steps:

STEP 1   Select one equation. Express one variable in terms of the other.
STEP 2   Substitute this new equation into the second equation to find the value of one variable.
STEP 3   Substitute this value in one of the equations to find the value of the other variable.

Example 4   **Solve systems of linear equations using the substitution method.**

Solve each system of linear equations using the substitution method.

a) $3x - y = 18$ — Equation 1
   $y = x - 4$ — Equation 2

Solution

Substitute Equation 2 into Equation 1:

$3x - (x - 4) = 18$
$3x - x + 4 = 18$ Use the distributive property.
$2x + 4 = 18$ Simplify.
$2x + 4 - 4 = 18 - 4$ Subtract 4 from both sides.
$2x = 14$ Simplify.
$2x \div 2 = 14 \div 2$ Divide both sides by 2.
$x = 7$ Simplify.

Substitute 7 for x into Equation 2 to get $y = 7 - 4 = 3$.

So, the solution to the system of linear equations is given by $x = 7$, $y = 3$.

Check: Substitute the solution into Equation 1.

$3(7) - 3 = 18$

When $x = 7$ and $y = 3$, the equation $3x - y = 18$ is true.
So, $x = 7$ and $y = 3$ gives the solution.

b) $3p + 2q = 4$ — Equation 1
    $3p - 5q = \dfrac{1}{2}$ — Equation 2

Solution

Use Equation 1 to express $3p$ in terms of q:

$3p + 2q = 4$

$3p + 2q - 2q = 4 - 2q$ Subtract $2q$ from both sides.

$\qquad\qquad 3p = 4 - 2q$ — Equation 3   Simplify.

Substitute Equation 3 into Equation 2:

$4 - 2q - 5q = \dfrac{1}{2}$

$4 - 7q - 4 = \dfrac{1}{2} - 4$ Subtract 4 from both sides.

$\qquad -7q = -\dfrac{7}{2}$ Simplify.

$\qquad \dfrac{-7q}{-7} = \dfrac{-7}{2(-7)}$ Divide each side by -7.

$\qquad\qquad q = \dfrac{1}{2}$ Simplify.

> **Think Math**
>
> You cannot substitute Equation 3 into Equation 1. Why?

Substitute $\dfrac{1}{2}$ for q into Equation 3:

$\qquad 3p = 4 - 2\left(\dfrac{1}{2}\right)$

$\qquad 3p = 3$

$3p \div 3 = 3 \div 3$

$\qquad p = 1$

> You can also substitute $\dfrac{1}{2}$ for q into Equation 1 or 2 and get $p = 1$. However, you get the value of p more quickly by substituting $\dfrac{1}{2}$ for q into Equation 3.

So, the solution to the system of linear equations is given by $p = 1$, $q = \dfrac{1}{2}$.

Check: Substitute the solution into Equation 2.

$3(1) - 5\left(\dfrac{1}{2}\right) = \dfrac{1}{2}$

When $p = 1$ and $q = \dfrac{1}{2}$, the equation $3p - 5q = \dfrac{1}{2}$ is true.

So, $p = 1$ and $q = \dfrac{1}{2}$ gives the solution.

Guided Practice

Solve each system of linear equations by using the substitution method.

7 $2x + y = 5$ — Equation 1
$y = 4x - 7$ — Equation 2

Substitute Equation 2 into Equation 1:

$$\underline{\quad?\quad} = \underline{\quad?\quad}$$

$$\underline{\quad?\quad} = \underline{\quad?\quad} \qquad \text{Simplify.}$$

$$\underline{\quad?\quad} = \underline{\quad?\quad} \qquad \text{Add } \underline{\;?\;} \text{ to both sides.}$$

$$\underline{\quad?\quad} = \underline{\quad?\quad} \qquad \text{Simplify.}$$

$$\underline{\;?\;} \div \underline{\;?\;} = \underline{\;?\;} \div \underline{\;?\;} \qquad \text{Divide both sides by } \underline{\;?\;}.$$

$$x = \underline{\;?\;} \qquad \text{Simplify.}$$

Substitute $\underline{\;?\;}$ for x into Equation 2:

$$y = 4(\underline{\;?\;}) - 7$$

$$= \underline{\;?\;} - 7 = \underline{\;?\;}$$

The solution to the system of equations is given by $x = \underline{\;?\;}$ and $y = \underline{\;?\;}$.

8 $4x + 3y = 23$ — Equation 1
$5x + y = 15$ — Equation 2

Use Equation 2 to express y in terms of x:

$5x + y = 15$

$$\underline{\quad?\quad} = \underline{\quad?\quad} \qquad \text{Subtract } \underline{\;?\;} \text{ from both sides.}$$

$$\underline{\quad?\quad} = \underline{\quad?\quad} \quad \text{— Equation 3} \quad \text{Simplify.}$$

Substitute Equation 3 into Equation 1:

$$4x + \underline{\;?\;} = 23$$

$$\underline{\quad?\quad} = \underline{\quad?\quad} \qquad \text{Use the distributive property.}$$

$$\underline{\quad?\quad} = \underline{\quad?\quad} \qquad \text{Simplify.}$$

$$\underline{\quad?\quad} = \underline{\quad?\quad} \qquad \text{Subtract } \underline{\;?\;} \text{ from both sides.}$$

$$\underline{\quad?\quad} = \underline{\quad?\quad} \qquad \text{Simplify.}$$

$$\underline{\;?\;} \div \underline{\;?\;} = \underline{\;?\;} \div \underline{\;?\;} \qquad \text{Divide both sides by } \underline{\;?\;}.$$

$$x = \underline{\;?\;} \qquad \text{Simplify.}$$

Substitute $\underline{\;?\;}$ for x into Equation 3:

$$y = \underline{\;?\;}$$

$$= \underline{\;?\;}$$

The solution to the system of equations is given by $x = \underline{\;?\;}$ and $y = \underline{\;?\;}$.

9 $3x - y = 8$
$2x + 3y = 9$

10 $7m + 2n = -8$
$2m = 3n - 13$

Example 5 **Choose a method to solve a system of equations.**

Solve each system of linear equations using the elimination method or the substitution method.

a) $3p + 2q = 1$ — Equation 1
    $2p - 5q = -12$ — Equation 2

> If you use the substitution method, you have to express p in terms of q or q in terms of p. Either way, you get an algebraic fraction that makes the steps complicated. So, you may want to use the elimination method instead.

Solution

Use the elimination method to solve the equations.

Multiply Equation 1 by 2:
  $2 \cdot (3p + 2q) = 1 \cdot 2$
  $2 \cdot 3p + 2 \cdot 2q = 1 \cdot 2$ Use the distributive property.
      $6p + 4q = 2$ — Equation 3   Simplify.

Multiply Equation 2 by 3:
  $3 \cdot (2p - 5q) = -12 \cdot 3$
  $3 \cdot 2p - 3 \cdot 5q = -12 \cdot 3$ Use the distributive property.
      $6p - 15q = -36$ — Equation 4   Simplify.

Subtract Equation 4 from Equation 3:
  $6p + 4q - (6p - 15q) = 2 - (-36)$
    $6p + 4q - 6p + 15q = 2 + 36$ Use the distributive property.
                    $19q = 38$ Simplify.
              $19q \div 19 = 38 \div 19$ Divide both sides by 19.
                      $q = 2$ Simplify.

Substitute 2 for q into Equation 1:
  $3p + 2(2) = 1$
    $3p + 4 = 1$ Simplify.
  $3p + 4 - 4 = 1 - 4$ Subtract 4 from both sides.
        $3p = -3$ Simplify.
      $3p \div 3 = -3 \div 3$ Divide both sides by 3.
          $p = -1$ Simplify.

The solution to the system of linear equations is given by $p = -1$, $q = 2$.

Check: Substitute the solution into Equation 2.

$2(-1) - 5(2) = -12$

When $p = -1$ and $q = 2$, the equation $2p - 5q = -12$ is true.
So $p = -1$ and $q = 2$ gives the solution.

Continue on next page

b) $5a - 2b = 8$ — Equation 1

     $b = 2a - 2$ — Equation 2

Solution

Use the substitution method to solve the equations.

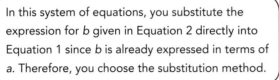

In this system of equations, you substitute the expression for b given in Equation 2 directly into Equation 1 since b is already expressed in terms of a. Therefore, you choose the substitution method.

Substitute Equation 2 into Equation 1:

$5a - 2(2a - 2) = 8$

    $5a - 4a + 4 = 8$ Use the distributive property.

      $a + 4 - 4 = 8 - 4$ Subtract 4 from both sides.

            $a = 4$ Simplify.

Substitute 4 for a into Equation 2:

$b = 2(4) - 2$

  $= 6$ Simplify.

So the solution to the system of linear equations is given by $a = 4$ and $b = 6$.

Check: Substitute the solution into Equation 1.

$5(4) - 2(6) = 8$

When $a = 4$ and $b = 6$, the equation $5a - 2b = 8$ is true.

So, $a = 4$ and $b = 6$ gives the solution.

Guided Practice

Solve each system of linear equations using the elimination method or substitution method. Explain why you choose each method.

11 $2x + 3y = 29$

    $2x - 17 = y$

12 $3a - 2b = 5$

    $2a - 5b = 51$

Solve each system of linear equations using the elimination method.

1 $2j + k = 6$
$j - k = 8$

2 $2j + 3k = 11$
$2j - 5k = 3$

3 $3m + n = 30$
$2m - n = 20$

4 $3x - y = 9$
$2x - y = 7$

5 $5s - t = 12$
$3s + t = 12$

6 $2b + c = 10$
$2b - c = 6$

7 $3m - n = 7$
$21m + 6n = -29$

8 $7a + b = 10$
$2a + 3b = -8$

9 $2p + 5q = 4$
$7p + 15q = 9$

Solve each system of linear equations using the substitution method.

10 $2j + k = 3$
$k = j - 9$

11 $2h + 3k = 13$
$h = 2k - 4$

12 $3m + b = 23$
$m - b = 5$

13 $3h - k = 10$
$h - k = 2$

14 $3s - t = 5$
$s + 2t = 4$

15 $2x + y = 20$
$3x + 4y = 40$

16 $3x + 2y = 0$
$5x - 2y = 32$

17 $5x - y = 20$
$4x + 3y = 16$

18 $3p + 4q = 3$
$\dfrac{1}{2} + q = 3p$

Solve each system of linear equations using the elimination method or substitution method. Explain why you choose each method.

19 $2x + 7y = 32$
$4x - 5y = -12$

20 $3x + 3y = 22$
$3x - 2y = 7$

21 $7m + 2n = 20$
$2m = 3n - 5$

22 $3h - 4k = 35$
$k = 2h - 20$

23 $2h + 7k = 32$
$3h - 2k = -2$

24 $2m + 4 = 3n$
$5m - 3n = -1$

Solve.

25 *Math Journal* Sam solves the following system of linear equations by the elimination method, without using calculator.

$2x + 3y = 1$
$3x - 17y = 23$

He can multiply the first equation by 3 and the second equation by 2 in order to eliminate x. Or he can eliminate y by multiplying the first equation by 17 and the second equation by 3. Which way should Sam choose? Explain.

Real-World Problems: Systems of Linear Equations

Lesson Objective

- Solve real-world problems using systems of linear equations.

Vocabulary
standard form

Solve Real-World Problems Using Systems of Linear Equations.

You have learned to write single equations in two variables. You can use this skill to write two equations in two variables, as the following example shows.

At a carnival, 700 tickets were sold for a total amount of $5,500. An adult ticket cost $10 and a children's ticket cost $5. Find the number of adult tickets and the number of children's tickets sold.

This problem gives you data about the numbers of tickets and the prices of tickets, so the given information can be organized into a table. Let the two variables represent the number of adult tickets sold and the number of children's tickets sold, because this is what you are asked to find.

Let a be the number of adult tickets sold and c be the number of children's tickets sold.

	Number of Tickets	Ticket Sales (dollars)
Adult Tickets	a	$10a$
Children's Tickets	c	$5c$
Total	$a + c$	$10a + 5c$

Then write two algebraic equations using the algebraic expressions. Remember you know the total number of tickets sold (700) and the total sales of these tickets ($5,500).

Relate the sales of the tickets:

$$10a \quad + \quad 5c \quad = \quad 5,500$$

Sales of $10 tickets $\quad$ Sales of $5 tickets $\quad$ Total sales

Relate the number of tickets:

$$a \quad + \quad c \quad = \quad 700$$

Number of adult tickets sold $\quad$ Number of children's tickets sold $\quad$ Total tickets sold

Math Note

The linear equations in a system of equations are usually written in the form $ax + by = c$. This is called the **standard form** of a linear equation. When solving a system of equations by elimination, both equations may be in standard form.

Next solve the system of linear equations.

$10a + 5c = 5,500$ — Equation 1
$a + c = 700$ — Equation 2

You can choose the elimination method or the substitution method to solve a system of equations. The elimination method is used here.

Multiply Equation 2 by 10:
$10 \cdot (a + c) = 10 \cdot 700$
$10a + 10c = 7,000$ — Equation 3   Use the distributive property.

Subtract Equation 1 from Equation 3:
$(10a + 10c) - (10a + 5c) = 7,000 - 5,500$
$10a + 10c - 10a - 5c = 1,500$ Use the distributive property.
$5c = 1,500$ Simplify.
$5c \div 5 = 1,500 \div 5$ Divide both sides by 5.
$c = 300$ Simplify.

Substitute 300 for c into Equation 2:
$a + 300 = 700$
$a + 300 - 300 = 700 - 300$ Subtract 300 from both sides.
$a = 400$ Simplify.

400 adult tickets and 300 children's tickets were sold.

To check real-world problems, remember to substitute the values into the original problem to see if they make sense. That way you can be sure you used the right equations to begin with.

Example 6 **Solve real-world problems using systems of linear equations.**

The difference between the length ℓ and width w of one face of a box is 4 inches. The face has a perimeter of 52 inches. Find the length and width.

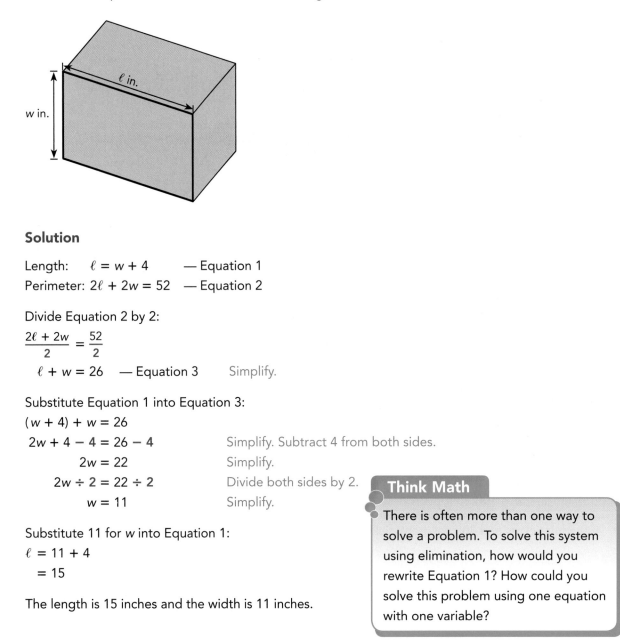

Solution

Length: $\ell = w + 4$ — Equation 1
Perimeter: $2\ell + 2w = 52$ — Equation 2

Divide Equation 2 by 2:

$$\frac{2\ell + 2w}{2} = \frac{52}{2}$$
$\ell + w = 26$ — Equation 3   Simplify.

Substitute Equation 1 into Equation 3:

$(w + 4) + w = 26$
$2w + 4 - 4 = 26 - 4$ Simplify. Subtract 4 from both sides.
$2w = 22$ Simplify.
$2w \div 2 = 22 \div 2$ Divide both sides by 2.
$w = 11$ Simplify.

Substitute 11 for w into Equation 1:

$\ell = 11 + 4$
$\ = 15$

The length is 15 inches and the width is 11 inches.

Think Math

There is often more than one way to solve a problem. To solve this system using elimination, how would you rewrite Equation 1? How could you solve this problem using one equation with one variable?

Guided Practice

Solve using systems of linear equations.

1 Two bowls and one cup have a mass of 800 grams. One bowl and two cups have a mass of 700 grams. Find the mass of a bowl and the mass of a cup.

Let the mass of a bowl be b grams and the mass of a cup be c grams.

Mass of two bowls and one cup: $\underline{\ ?\ } = \underline{\ ?\ }$ — Equation 1

Mass of one bowl and two cups: $\underline{\ ?\ } = \underline{\ ?\ }$ — Equation 2

Use Equation 1 to express c in terms of b:

$$\underline{\ ?\ } - \underline{\ ?\ } = \underline{\ ?\ } - \underline{\ ?\ }$$ Subtract $\underline{\ ?\ }$ from both sides.

$$c = \underline{\ ?\ } \quad \text{— Equation 3}$$ Simplify.

Substitute Equation 3 into Equation 2:

$$\underline{\ ?\ } = \underline{\ ?\ }$$

$$\underline{\ ?\ } = \underline{\ ?\ }$$ Use the distributive property.

$$\underline{\ ?\ } = \underline{\ ?\ }$$ Subtract $\underline{\ ?\ }$ from both sides.

$$\underline{\ ?\ } = \underline{\ ?\ }$$ Simplify.

$$\underline{\ ?\ } \div \underline{\ ?\ } = \underline{\ ?\ } \div \underline{\ ?\ }$$ Divide both sides by $\underline{\ ?\ }$.

$$b = \underline{\ ?\ }$$ Simplify.

Substitute $\underline{\ ?\ }$ for b into Equation 3:

$$c = \underline{\ ?\ }$$

$$= \underline{\ ?\ }$$

The mass of a bowl is $\underline{\ ?\ }$ grams and the mass of a cup is $\underline{\ ?\ }$ grams.

Example 7 **Solve word problems using systems of linear equations.**

Sasha has a riddle: There are two numbers. The sum of the first number and twice the second number is 14. When the second number is subtracted from the first number, the result is 2. What are the two numbers?

Solution

Let the first number be x and the second number be y.

Sum of the first number and twice the second number:
$x + 2y = 14$ — Equation 1

Second number subtracted from first number:
$x - y = 2$ — Equation 2

Subtract Equation 2 from Equation 1:
$x + 2y - (x - y) = 14 - 2$

$\quad x + 2y - x + y = 12$ Use the distributive property.

$\qquad\qquad 3y = 12$ Simplify.

$\qquad 3y \div 3 = 12 \div 3$ Divide both sides by 3.

$\qquad\qquad y = 4$ Simplify.

The elimination method is used here to solve the system of equations. Practice solving by using the substitution method.

Substitute 4 for y into Equation 2:
$\qquad x - 4 = 2$

$x - 4 + 4 = 2 + 4$ Add both sides by 4.

$\qquad\quad x = 6$ Simplify.

The two numbers are 6 and 4.

Guided Practice

Solve using systems of linear equations.

2 Elizabeth is thinking of a two-digit number. When the tens digit is subtracted from the ones digit, the difference is 2. One-fifth of the number is 1 less than the sum of the digits. What is the number?

Let the tens digit be c and the ones digit be d.

Tens digit subtracted from ones digit:

$\underline{\quad?\quad} = \underline{\quad?\quad}$ — Equation 1

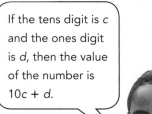

If the tens digit is c and the ones digit is d, then the value of the number is $10c + d$.

One-fifth of the number is 1 less than sum of digits:

$\underline{\quad?\quad} = \underline{\quad?\quad}$ — Equation 2

Use Equation 1 to express d in terms of c:

$\underline{\quad?\quad} = \underline{\quad?\quad}$ Add c to both sides.

$d = \underline{\quad?\quad}$ — Equation 3   Simplify.

Substitute Equation 3 into Equation 2:

$\underline{\quad?\quad} = \underline{\quad?\quad}$

$\underline{\quad?\quad} = \underline{\quad?\quad}$ Subtract 1 from both sides.

$\underline{\quad?\quad} = \underline{\quad?\quad}$ Simplify.

$\underline{\quad?\quad} \cdot \underline{\quad?\quad} = \underline{\quad?\quad} \cdot \underline{\quad?\quad}$ Multiply both sides by $\underline{\quad?\quad}$.

$\underline{\quad?\quad} = \underline{\quad?\quad}$ Simplify.

$\underline{\quad?\quad} = \underline{\quad?\quad}$ Use the distributive property.

$\underline{\quad?\quad} = \underline{\quad?\quad}$ Subtract $10c$ from both sides.

$\underline{\quad?\quad} = \underline{\quad?\quad}$ Simplify.

$\underline{\quad?\quad} = \underline{\quad?\quad}$ Subtract 2 from both sides.

$c = \underline{\quad?\quad}$ Simplify.

Substitute 3 for c into Equation 3:

$d = \underline{\quad?\quad}$

$= \underline{\quad?\quad}$

The number is $\underline{\quad?\quad}$.

3 Christopher is thinking of two positive integers. The sum of the integers is 27. When twice the first integer is added to half of the second integer, the sum is 24. Find the integers.

Solve using systems of linear equations.

1 Jean stocked her aquarium with 36 fresh-water fish, which cost $212. The male fish cost $5 each, while the female fish cost $7 each. Find the number of male fish and the number of female fish.

36 fish cost $212.
1 male fish costs $5.
1 female fish costs $7.

2 Seventy concert tickets were sold for $550. Each adult ticket cost $9 and each children's ticket cost $5. Find the number of adult tickets and the number of children's tickets sold.

3 George paid $2.75 for 4 granola bars and 1 apple. Addison paid $2.25 for 2 granola bars and 3 apples. Find the cost of each granola bar and each apple.

4 4 thumb drives and 1 compact disk have a total capacity of 9 gigabytes. 5 thumb drives have 9 gigabytes more capacity than 1 compact disk. Find the capacity of 1 thumb drive and the capacity of 1 compact disk.

5 A book cover has the length and width (in inches) shown in the diagram.

   a) Find the values of a and b.

   b) Find the perimeter of the book cover.

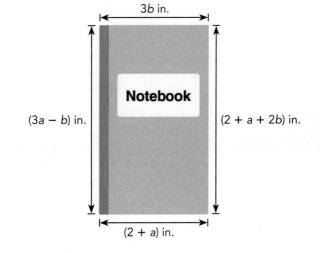

6 Eileen saves dimes and quarters. She has 40 coins, which totaled $6.55, in her bank. How many of each coin does she have?

7 Aiden is a percussionist in his school band. One instrument he plays is in the shape of an equilateral triangle shown below. The side lengths are in inches. Find x and y.

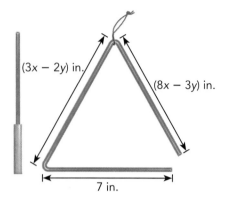

(3x − 2y) in.

(8x − 3y) in.

7 in.

8 Mrs. Green gave three riddles for her class to solve.

a) The sum of the digits of a two-digit number is 11. Twice the tens digit plus 2 equals ten times the ones digit. What is the number?

b) There are two numbers. The first number minus the second number is 15. One-third of the sum of the numbers is one quarter of the first number. What are the two numbers?

c) A two-digit number is 1 more than eight times the sum of the digits. The ones digit is 3 less than the tens digit. What is the number?

9 On Saturday, $585 was collected from the sale of 55 tickets for a performance. The table below shows the information about the sale of the tickets. Find the number of adult tickets and the number of student's tickets sold on that day.

	Number of Tickets	Cost of Each Ticket ($)
Adult Tickets	a	12
Student's Tickets	s	25% discount

10 Eight years ago, Mr. Fontana was six times as old as his son. In twelve years' time, he will be twice as old as his son. How old are they now?

	Mr. Fontana's Age (yr)	His Son's Age (yr)
Eight Years Ago	f − 8	s − 8
In Twelve Years' Time	f + 12	s + 12

11 A restaurant sells four combo meals. Jolly Meal, which cost $12.60, consists of 2 yogurt cups and 1 sandwich. The Special Meal, which is made up of 2 sandwiches and 1 yogurt cup, cost $13.50. Calculate the cost of the following combo meals if the charge for sandwiches and yogurt cups are the same for all combo meals.

a) Children's Meal: 1 sandwich and 1 yogurt cup

b) Family Meal: 2 sandwiches and 3 yogurt cups

12 In a boat race, Jenny's team rowed their boat from point A to point B and back to point A. Points A and B are 30 miles apart. During the race, there was a constant current flowing from A to B. She took 2 hours to travel from A to B and 2.5 hours to travel from B to A.

a) Calculate the speed of the boat from A to B and the speed from B to A.

b) Find the speed of the boat from A to B if there was no current.

c) Find the speed of the current.

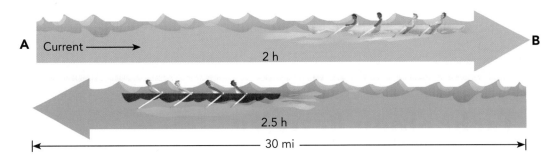

13 Alex deposited $3,500 in two banks. The first bank paid 2% simple interest per year while the second bank paid 3%. At the end of one year, the difference in the interest amounts was $30. Find the amount Alex deposited in each bank.

14 Greg's favorite activities are bike riding and hip-hop dancing. He wants to try to do these activities for 6 hours each week. He would also like to try to burn off about 2,100 calories a week. He finds that biking uses about 425 calories each hour and hip-hop dancing uses about 325 calories each hour. He wants to do bike riding for x hours and hip-hop dancing for y hours each week.

a) Copy and complete the following table.

	Hours	Calories Burned
Bike Riding	x	?
Hip-Hop Dancing	y	?
Total	?	?

b) How much time should he spend doing each activity to accomplish his goal?

15 In an experiment, Matthew was given two saline (salt) solutions, whose concentrations are shown below. He had to prepare 10 fluid ounces of a new saline solution with a 27% concentration from the two solutions. Calculate the volume of each solution used to prepare the new solution.

	Volume of Solution (fl oz)	Concentration of Solution (%)
Saline Solution A	x	30
Saline Solution B	y	18

5.4 Solving Systems of Linear Equations by Graphing

Lesson Objective

- Solve systems of linear equations using the graphical method.

Vocabulary

graphical method

point of intersection

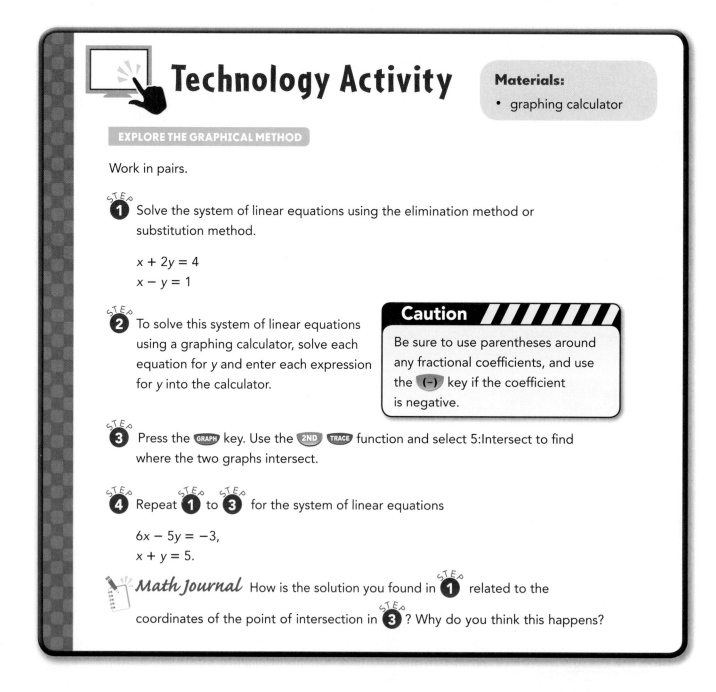

Technology Activity

Materials:
- graphing calculator

EXPLORE THE GRAPHICAL METHOD

Work in pairs.

STEP 1 Solve the system of linear equations using the elimination method or substitution method.

$x + 2y = 4$
$x - y = 1$

STEP 2 To solve this system of linear equations using a graphing calculator, solve each equation for y and enter each expression for y into the calculator.

Caution ///////////

Be sure to use parentheses around any fractional coefficients, and use the (–) key if the coefficient is negative.

STEP 3 Press the GRAPH key. Use the 2ND TRACE function and select 5:Intersect to find where the two graphs intersect.

STEP 4 Repeat **STEP 1** to **STEP 3** for the system of linear equations

$6x - 5y = -3,$
$x + y = 5.$

Math Journal How is the solution you found in **STEP 1** related to the coordinates of the point of intersection in **STEP 3**? Why do you think this happens?

Solve Systems of Linear Equations Using the Graphical Method.

You can solve systems of linear equations using the graphical method.
Consider this system of linear equations.

$y - x = 3$ — Equation 1
$x + y = -1$ — Equation 2

First rewrite the Equation 1 in slope-intercept form as $y = x + 3$. Then graph of the
linear equation $y - x = 3$ on a coordinate plane.

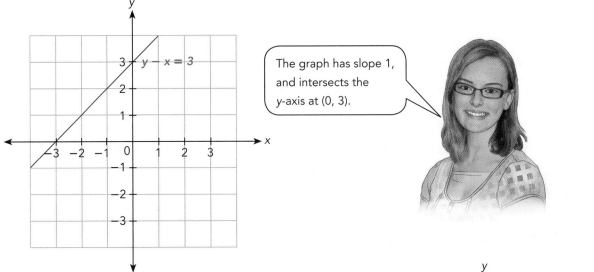

The graph has slope 1,
and intersects the
y-axis at (0, 3).

The point $(-3, 0)$ lies on the graph. It corresponds to
values, $x = -3$ and $y = 0$, which satisfy the equation
$y - x = 3$. All pairs of values of x and y, which satisfy
the equation $y - x = 3$ are represented by the points
on the graph.

Next rewrite Equation 2 in slope-intercept form as
$y = -x - 1$ and graph the linear equation $x + y = -1$
on the same coordinate plane.

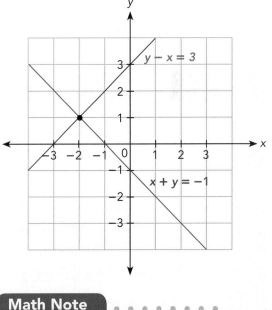

All pairs of values of x and y that satisfy the equation
$x + y = -1$ are represented by the points on its graph.

The two graphs intersect at A $(-2, 1)$. You say that A is
the **point of intersection** of $y - x = 3$ and $x + y = -1$.

A is the only point that lies on both graphs. This means
that the corresponding values, $x = -2$ and $y = 1$, are
the only pair of values that satisfy both equations.

So, the system of linear equations has a unique
solution $x = -2$ and $y = 1$.

Math Note

The solution to a system of equations
can be written as an ordered pair,
such as $(-2, 1)$.

Continue on next page

Check: Substitute the solution into both equations.

For $y - x = 3$, $1 - (-2) = 3$.

For $x + y = -1$, $-2 + 1 = -1$.

When $x = -2$ and $y = 1$, both equations are true.
So, $x = -2$, $y = 1$ gives the solution.

This method of solving systems of linear equations is called the graphical method. The coordinates of the point of intersection may not be integers. In that case, you have to estimate the coordinates, and the solution is approximate.

Example 8 **Solve systems of linear equations by graphing.**

Solve the following system of equations by graphing. Use 1 grid square on both axes to represent 1 unit for the x interval from −1 to 4 and the y interval from 0 to 7.

$2x + y = 7$
$y - 3x = -3$

Solution

STEP 1 Make a table of values for each equation.

$2x + y = 7$

x	1	2	3
y	5	3	1

$y - 3x = -3$

x	1	2	3
y	0	3	6

> **Math Note**
>
> You only need to plot two points to draw a linear graph. However, using a third point will ensure that your calculations are correct.

STEP 2 Plot the points represented by the tables of values. Then draw the graph of each equation.

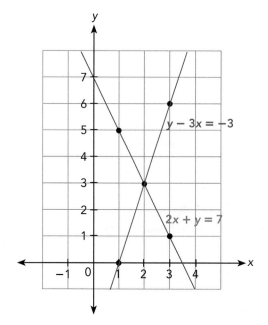

STEP 3 Locate the point of intersection of the graphs.

From the diagram, the coordinates of the point of intersection are (2, 3). These coordinates are the solution to the system of equations. So the solution to the system of equations is $x = 2$, $y = 3$.

Check: Substitute the solution into both equations.

For $2x + y = 7$, $2(2) + 3 = 7$.

For $y - 3x = -3$, $3 - 3(2) = -3$.

When $x = 2$ and $y = 3$, both equations are true.
So $x = 2$ and $y = 3$ gives the solution.

> Two intersecting lines can have only one point of intersection. So a system whose graphs are two intersecting lines has a unique solution.

Guided Practice

Solve using the graphical method. Copy and complete the tables of values. Graph the system of linear equations on the same coordinate plane. Use 1 grid square on both axes to represent 1 unit for the x interval from −1 to 3 and the y interval from −1 to 5.

1. $2x + y = 5$
   $x - y = -2$

$2x + y = 5$

x	0	1	2
y	?	?	?

$x - y = -2$

x	0	1	2
y	?	?	?

From the graph, the slope of $2x + y = 5$ is __?__ and the y-intercept is __?__.
The slope of $x - y = -2$ is __?__ and its y-intercept is __?__.

The point of intersection is (__?__, __?__). Therefore, the solution to the system of equations is $x = $ __?__ and $y = $ __?__.

Solve using the graphical method. Graph each system of linear equations on the same coordinate plane. Use 1 grid square on both axes to represent 1 unit for the interval from −4 to 4.

2. $x + 2y = 5$
   $x + y = 2$

3. $3x + 2y = 8$
   $x - y = 1$

Example 9 **Solve real-world systems of linear equations using the graphical method.**

Two cars are traveling along a highway in the same direction. They take x hours to travel y miles from point A on the highway. Their motions are described by the linear equations

$y = 60x$
$y = 50x + 20$

Solve the system of equations graphically. When will the cars meet?

Solution

Sketch the graphs of the two equations using the slope and y-intercept values.

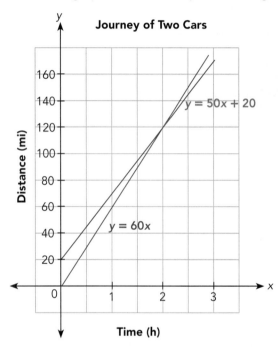

Because Distance = Rate · Time, these two equations tell me many things about the journey of the two cars. For example, the speed of each car, whether they start at the same time, and whether they start at the same place.

The point of intersection of the graphs is (2, 120). So, the solution to the system of equations is given by $x = 2$ and $y = 120$.

The cars will meet 2 hours later.

Guided Practice

Use graph paper. Use 1 grid square on both axis to represent 10 seconds for the t interval from 110 to 150 seconds, and 10°F for the T interval from 300 to 350°F.

4 Two ovens are being heated. Their temperatures are represented by the equations

Oven 1: $T = t + 200$
Oven 2: $T = 2t + 80$

where T is the temperature in °F of the oven and t is the time in seconds. Solve the system of linear equations graphically. When will the temperatures of the ovens be the same?

For this practice, unless otherwise stated, use 1 grid square to represent 1 unit on both axes for the interval from −8 to 8. Solve each system of linear equations using the graphical method.

1 $x + y = 6$
$2x + y = 8$

a) Copy and complete the tables of values for the system of linear equations.

$x + y = 6$

x	0	1	2
y	6	?	?

$2x + y = 8$

x	0	1	2
y	?	6	?

b) Graph $x + y = 6$ and $2x + y = 8$ on the same coordinate plane. Find the point of intersection.

c) Use the graph in **b)** to solve the system of linear equations.

2 $x + y = 5$
$x - y = 2$

a) Copy and complete the tables of values for the system of linear equations.

$x + y = 5$

x	0	1	2
y	5	?	?

$x - y = 2$

x	0	1	2
y	?	−1	?

b) Graph $x + y = 5$ and $x - y = 2$ on the same coordinate plane. Find the point of intersection.

c) Use the graph in **b)** to solve the system of linear equations.

3 $x + 2y = 5$
$2x - 2y = 1$

a) Graph $x + 2y = 5$ and $2x - 2y = 1$ on the same coordinate plane. Find the point of intersection of the graphs.

b) Use the graph in **a)** to solve the system of linear equations.

4 $2x + 3y = -1$
$x - 2y = 3$

a) Graph $2x + 3y = -1$ and $x - 2y = 3$ on the same coordinate plane. Find the point of intersection of the graphs.

b) Use the graph in **a)** to solve the system of linear equations.

Solve each system of equations using the graphical method.

5 $x = 2y$
$y = x + 2$

6 $y = 3$
$y = 2x + 1$

7 $x = 2$
$y = 2x - 8$

8 $3x - 2y = 19$
$3y = 2x - 21$

9 $2x + y = 11$
$x + 3y = 18$

10 $x + 2y = 1$
$4y - x = 17$

Solve. Show your work.

Walter
$2d + 14t = 15$

Marianne
$d = 8t$

11 Marianne jogged from point P to point Q while Walter jogged from point Q to point P. Point P and point Q are 7.5 kilometers apart. Marianne's motion is represented by $d = 8t$ and Walter's motion is represented by $2d + 14t = 15$, where t hours is the time and d kilometers is the distance from point P.

a) Solve the system of linear equations using the graphical method.

b) When did Marianne and Walter meet? How far from point Q did they meet?

$P \kern-0.3em\longleftarrow\kern-8em\longrightarrow Q$
7.5 km

12 *Math Journal* Explain when it is convenient to use each method of solving a system of linear equations: Elimination, substitution, and graphical. Give an example for each method.

13 Two cyclists are traveling along a track in the same direction. Their motions are described by the linear equations $d = 10t$ and $d - 8t = 2$, where t hours is the time and d miles is the distance from point A on the track.

a) Solve the system of linear equations using a graphing calculator.

b) When will the cyclists meet?

14 Dr. Murray is heating a beaker containing Liquid A and a beaker containing Liquid B. The temperature of Liquid A is represented by $T = 2t + 140$ and the temperature of Liquid B is represented by $T = t + 160$, where $T°$F is the temperature of the liquid after t seconds.

a) Solve the system of linear equations using a graphing calculator.

b) When will the temperatures of the liquids be the same?

15 A carpenter is hammering an iron nail and another carpenter is hammering a copper nail. The temperatures of the nails increase during the hammering. The temperature of the iron nail is represented by $T = 2t + 70$ and the temperature of the copper nail is represented by $T = 3t + 65$, where $T°$F is the temperature of the nail after t seconds.

a) Solve the system of linear equations using a graphing calculator.

b) When will the temperatures of the nails be the same?

Inconsistent and Dependent Systems of Linear Equations

Lesson Objectives

- Understand and identify inconsistent systems of linear equations.
- Understand and identify dependent systems of linear equations.

Understand and Identify Inconsistent Systems of Linear Equations.

You have learned to find the unique solution to a system of linear equations, when it exists. However, not every system of linear equations has a unique solution.

Consider this system of linear equations.

$2x + y = 1$ — Equation 1
$4x + 2y = 4$ — Equation 2

Look what happens when you try to solve the system of linear equations using the elimination method.

Multiply Equation 1 by 2:
$2(2x + y) = 2 \cdot 1$
   $4x + 2y = 2$ — Equation 3   Use the distributive property.

Subtract Equation 3 from Equation 2:
$(4x + 2y) - (4x + 2y) = 4 - 2$
   $4x + 2y - 4x - 2y = 2$ Use the distributive property.
            $0 = 2$ Simplify. False statement.

Because $0 \neq 2$, the system of equations has no solution.

A system of equations with no solution is an inconsistent system of equations.

Sometimes when you try to eliminate a variable, you end up eliminating both of them. Then you cannot have a unique solution.

Continue on next page

Look what happens when you try to solve the system of linear equation using the graphical method. Make a table of values for each equation.

$2x + y = 1$

x	0	1	2
y	1	−1	−3

$4x + 2y = 4$

x	0	1	2
y	2	0	−2

Graph the system of equations on the same coordinate plane using the tables of values.

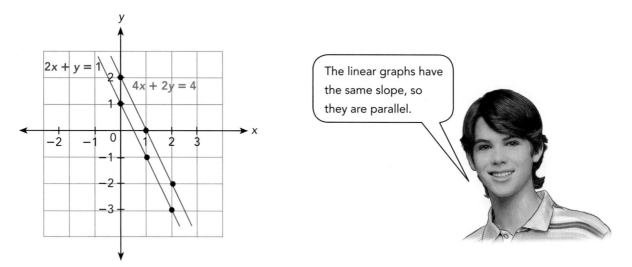

The linear graphs have the same slope, so they are parallel.

The graphs of the equations are parallel lines, so there is no point of intersection. Since there are no points that lie on both graphs, the system of linear equations has no solution.

Write each linear equation in the form $y = mx + b$ to find the slope and y-intercept of its graph.

$$2x + y = 1$$
$$2x + y - 2x = 1 - 2x \qquad \text{Subtract } 2x \text{ from both sides.}$$
$$y = -2x + 1 \qquad \text{Simplify and write in slope-intercept form.}$$

So, the graph of the Equation 1 has slope −2 and y-intercept 1.

$$4x + 2y = 4$$
$$(4x + 2y) \div 2 = 4 \div 2 \qquad \text{Divide both sides by 2.}$$
$$2x + y = 2 \qquad \text{Simplify.}$$
$$2x + y - 2x = 2 - 2x \qquad \text{Subtract } 2x \text{ from both sides.}$$
$$y = -2x + 2 \qquad \text{Simplify and write in slope-intercept form.}$$

So, the graph of the Equation 2 has slope −2 and y-intercept 2.

When two graphs have the same slope and different y-intercepts, they are parallel. This system of linear equations has no solution.

A system of linear equations is inconsistent when the graphs of the equations have the same slope but different y-intercepts.

Consider another system of linear equations.

$-3x + 2y = 2$ — Equation 3
$-6x + 4y = 6$ — Equation 4

Again, graph the system of linear equations on the same coordinate plane using tables of values.

$-3x + 2y = 2$

x	0	1	2
y	1	2.5	4

$-6x + 4y = 6$

x	−1	0	1
y	0	1.5	3

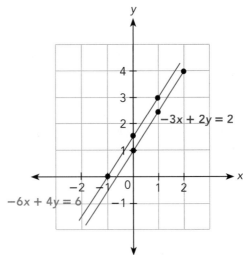

The graphs of the equations are parallel lines. So, this system of linear equations has no solution.

The two systems of linear equations that you have seen in this lesson have no solution and are inconsistent systems of linear equations.

$2x + y = 1$ — Equation 1 $-3x + 2y = 2$ — Equation 3
$4x + 2y = 4$ — Equation 2 $-6x + 4y = 6$ — Equation 4

Compare the coefficients and constants of Equation 2 to Equation 1 in the first system of linear equations.

	Coefficient of x	Coefficient of y	Constant
Equation 1	2	1	1
Equation 2	4	2	4
Ratio	2	2	4

> **Math Note**
>
> The equations must be in the same form before you make the comparison. In this case, the equations are in standard form.

Observe that the coefficients of x and the coefficients of y have the same ratio and the constants have a different ratio. You can make the same observation in the second system of linear equations when you compare the coefficients and constants of Equation 4 to Equation 3.

	Coefficient of x	Coefficient of y	Constant
Equation 3	−3	2	2
Equation 4	−6	4	6
Ratio	2	2	3

> If the coefficients of one equation are multiples of the coefficients of the other equation and the constants are in a different ratio, the system of linear equations is inconsistent.

Example 10 **Identify inconsistent systems of linear equations.**

Identify whether the system of linear equations is inconsistent or has a unique solution. Justify your reasoning.

a) $2x + 2y = 3$ —— Equation 1
   $x + y = 5$ —— Equation 2

Solution

Method 1

Rewrite each linear equation in slope-intercept form, $y = mx + b$.

Equation 1

$$2x + 2y = 3$$
$$2x + 2y - 2x = 3 - 2x \qquad \text{Subtract } 2x \text{ from both sides.}$$
$$2y = 3 - 2x \qquad \text{Simplify.}$$
$$\frac{2y}{2} = \frac{3 - 2x}{2} \qquad \text{Divide both sides by 2.}$$
$$y = \frac{3}{2} - x \qquad \text{Simplify.}$$
$$y = -x + \frac{3}{2} \qquad \text{Write in slope-intercept form.}$$

> **Caution** ///////
>
> When you write a linear equation in slope-intercept form $y = mx + b$, the coefficient of y must be 1.

Equation 2

$$x + y = 5$$
$$x + y - x = 5 - x \qquad \text{Subtract } x \text{ from both sides.}$$
$$y = 5 - x \qquad \text{Simplify.}$$
$$y = -x + 5 \qquad \text{Write in slope-intercept form.}$$

The slope of the graph of the Equation 1 is -1 and the y-intercept is $\frac{3}{2}$.

The slope of the graph of the Equation 2 is -1 and the y-intercept is 5.

Because the graphs of the linear equations have the same slope and different y-intercepts, the system of linear equations is inconsistent.

Method 2

Compare the coefficients and constants of Equation 2 to Equation 1.

	Coefficient of x	Coefficient of y	Constant
Equation 1	2	2	3
Equation 2	1	1	5
Ratio	$\frac{1}{2}$	$\frac{1}{2}$	$\frac{5}{3}$

The coefficients of x and y in Equation 1 are twice those of Equation 2. But the constant term in Equation 1 is not twice the constant term in Equation 2. So, the system of linear equations is inconsistent.

b) $2x - 2y = 3$ — Equation 1
  $x + 4y = 20$ — Equation 2

Solution

Rewrite the linear equations in slope-intercept form $y = mx + b$.

Equation 1

$$2x - 2y = 3$$
$$2x - 2y - 2x = 3 - 2x \qquad \text{Subtract } 2x \text{ from both sides.}$$
$$-2y = 3 - 2x \qquad \text{Simplify.}$$
$$\frac{-2y}{-2} = \frac{3 - 2x}{-2} \qquad \text{Divide both sides by } -2.$$
$$y = x - \frac{3}{2} \qquad \text{Simplify and write in slope-intercept form.}$$

Equation 2

$$x + 4y = 20$$
$$x + 4y - x = 20 - x \qquad \text{Subtract } x \text{ from both sides.}$$
$$4y = 20 - x \qquad \text{Simplify.}$$
$$\frac{4y}{4} = \frac{20 - x}{4} \qquad \text{Divide both sides by 4.}$$
$$y = -\frac{x}{4} + 5 \qquad \text{Simplify and write in slope-intercept form.}$$

The slope of the graph of the Equation 1 is 1 and the y-intercept is $-\dfrac{3}{2}$.

The slope of the graph of the Equation 2 is $-\dfrac{1}{4}$ and the y-intercept is 5.

Because the graphs of the linear equations have different slopes and different y-intercepts, the system of linear equations is not inconsistent.

In this case, the system of linear equations has a unique solution.

> **Think Math**
>
> Can you identify the system of linear equations by observing the coefficients of x and y, and the constants? Explain.

Guided Practice

Identify whether each system of linear equations is inconsistent or has a unique solution. Justify your reasoning.

1 $11x + y = 2$ — Equation 1
$22x + 2y = 3$ — Equation 2

Rewrite each linear equations in slope-intercept form $y = mx + b$.

Equation 1
$11x + y = 2$

$\underline{\quad?\quad} = \underline{\quad?\quad}$ Subtract 11x from both sides.

$y = \underline{\quad?\quad}$ Simplify.

Equation 2
$22x + 2y = 3$

$\underline{\quad?\quad} = \underline{\quad?\quad}$ Subtract 22x from both sides.

$\underline{\quad?\quad} = \underline{\quad?\quad}$ Simplify.

$\underline{\quad?\quad} = \underline{\quad?\quad}$ Divide both sides by 2.

$y = \underline{\quad?\quad}$ Simplify.

The slope of the graph of the Equation 1 is $\underline{\quad?\quad}$ and the y-intercept is $\underline{\quad?\quad}$.

The slope of the graph of the Equation 2 is $\underline{\quad?\quad}$ and the y-intercept is $\underline{\quad?\quad}$.

The graphs of the linear equations have the same $\underline{\quad?\quad}$ and different $\underline{\quad?\quad}$. The system of linear equations is $\underline{\quad?\quad}$, because the system of linear equations has no solution.

2 $13x + y = 23$

$26x + 2y = 21$

3 $\frac{1}{2}x + y = 4$

$3x + 8y = 16$

4 $\frac{1}{3}x + y = 7$

$x + 3y = 6$

Understand and Identify Dependent Systems of Linear Equations.

Consider this system of linear equations.

$x + 2y = 2$ — Equation 1
$2x + 4y = 4$ — Equation 2

Look what happens when you try to solve the system of linear equations using the substitution method.

Use Equation 1 to express x in terms of y:

$x + 2y = 2$

$x + 2y - 2y = 2 - 2y$ Subtract 2y from both sides.

$x = 2 - 2y$ — Equation 3   Simplify.

Substitute Equation 3 into Equation 2:

$2(2 - 2y) + 4y = 4$

$\quad 4 - 4y + 4y = 4$ Use the distributive property.

$\quad\quad\quad\quad 4 = 4$ Simplify.

Since $4 = 4$ is always true, the system of linear equations has an infinite number of solutions.

> A system of linear equations with an infinite number of solutions is a dependent system of equations.

Look what happens when you solve the system of linear equations graphically. Make a table of values for each equation. Graph the system of linear equations on the same coordinate plane using the tables of values.

$x + 2y = 2$

x	−1	0	1
y	1.5	1	0.5

$2x + 4y = 4$

x	−1	0	1
y	1.5	1	0.5

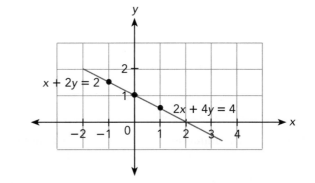

The two graphs form a single line. Since there are an infinite number of common points on the two graphs, the system of linear equations has an infinite number of solutions.

Write each linear equation in the slope-intercept form $y = mx + b$.

Equation 1

$\quad\quad x + 2y = 2$

$x + 2y - x = 2 - x$ Subtract x from both sides.

$\quad\quad\quad 2y = -x + 2$ Simplify.

$\quad\quad\quad \dfrac{2y}{2} = \dfrac{-x + 2}{2}$ Divide both sides by 2.

$\quad\quad\quad\quad y = -0.5x + 1$ Simplify.

> When two linear graphs have the same slope and y-intercept, the graphs are the same. This system of linear equations has an infinite number of solutions.

So the graph of the Equation 1 has a slope of −0.5 and a y-intercept of 1.

Equation 2

$\quad\quad 2x + 4y = 4$

$2x + 4y - 2x = 4 - 2x$ Subtract 2x from both sides.

$\quad\quad\quad 4y = -2x + 4$ Simplify.

$\quad\quad\quad \dfrac{4y}{4} = \dfrac{-2x + 4}{4}$ Divide both sides by 4.

$\quad\quad\quad\quad y = -0.5x + 1$ Simplify.

So, the graph of the Equation 2 also has slope −0.5 and y-intercept 1.

Continue on next page

You may notice that Equation 1 and Equation 2 are equivalent if you multiply Equation 1 by 2.

$$2(x + 2y) = 2 \cdot 2$$
$$2x + 4y = 4$$

Checking to see if one equation is a multiple of the other is another way to check for dependent systems of equations.

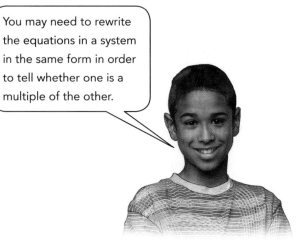

You may need to rewrite the equations in a system in the same form in order to tell whether one is a multiple of the other.

Consider another system of linear equations.

$-3x + 2y = 2$ — Equation 3
$-6x + 4y = 4$ — Equation 4

Make a table of values for each equation.

$-3x + 2y = 2$

x	0	1	2
y	1	2.5	4

$-6x + 4y = 4$

x	0	1	2
y	1	2.5	4

Graph the system of linear equations on the same coordinate plane using the tables of values.

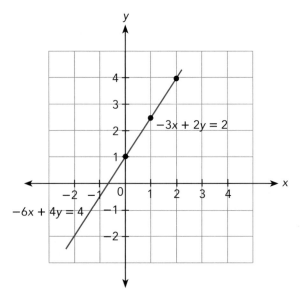

The graphs of the equations are the same. So, this system of linear equations has an infinite number of solutions.

> A system of linear equations is dependent when the graphs of the equations have the same slopes and y-intercepts or if one equation is a multiple of the other.

Example 11 **Identify dependent systems of linear equations.**

Identify whether the following systems of linear equations are dependent. Justify your reasoning.

a) $3x = 3 - 3y$
    $x + y = 1$

Solution

$3x = 3 - 3y$ — Equation 1
$x + y = 1$ — Equation 2

Divide Equation 1 by 3 and write the equation in standard form.

$$\frac{3x}{3} = \frac{3 - 3y}{3}$$

$x = 1 - y$ Simplify.
$x + y = 1 - y + y$ Add y to both sides.
$x + y = 1$ Simplify.

> You can also solve this by writing Equation 1 in standard form, $3x + 3y = 3$, first. This equation is three times Equation 2, so the two equations are equivalent.

Since Equation 1 and Equation 2 are equivalent, they have an infinite number of solutions. Therefore, the system of linear equations is dependent.

b) $4x + y = 2$
    $x + y = 20$

Solution

$4x + y = 2$ — Equation 1
$x + y = 20$ — Equation 2

> There is no number you can multiply Equation 2 by to get Equation 1, so these equations cannot be equivalent.

Solve for y in both Equations 1 and 2:

$4x + y = 2$
$4x + y - 4x = 2 - 4x$ Subtract $4x$ from both sides.
$y = -4x + 2$ Simplify.

$x + y = 20$
$x + y - x = 20 - x$ Subtract x from both sides.
$y = -x + 20$ Simplify.

The slopes and y-intercepts of the graphs of the equations are different. So, the system of linear equations is not dependent.

Guided Practice

Identify whether each system of linear equations is inconsistent, dependent, or has a unique solution. Justify your reasoning.

5 $5x + 2y = 4$
$20x + 8y = 30$

6 $7x + y = 14$
$10x + 4y = 32$

7 $12x + 4y = 16$
$9x + 3y = 12$

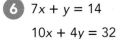
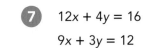

Graph each system of linear equations using a graphing calculator. State whether each system of equations is inconsistent or has a unique solution.

1 $3x + y = 4$
$6x + 2y = 14$

2 $10x + 5y = 15$
$x + y = 3$

3 $x - 2y = 14$
$4y = 5 + 2x$

State whether each system of linear equations is inconsistent, dependent, or has a unique solution. Justify each answer. Solve each system of linear equations if possible.

4 $x + y = 3$
$8x + 8y = 32$

5 $6x + 2y = 12$
$3x + y = 21$

6 $3x - 6y = 12$
$x - 2y = 4$

7 $-15x + 3y = 3$
$-5x + y = 21$

8 $2x + y = 8$
$4x - 2y = 24$

9 $8x + 7y = 9$
$40x + 35y = 45$

10 $x + 3y = 9$
$2x + 6y = 5$

11 $9x + 21y = 27$
$6x + 14y = 18$

12 $5x + 4y = 6$
$15x + 12y = 18$

Solve. Show your work.

13 David says he bought 9 apples and 6 apricots for $8.50 yesterday and bought 3 apples and 2 apricots for $7.40 today.

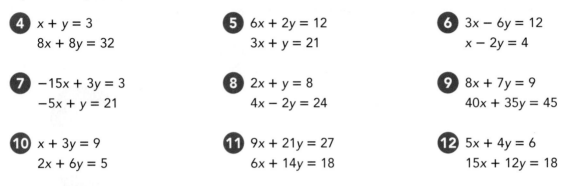

Yesterday
$8.50
9 apples
6 apricots

a)   Write a system of equations to find the cost of an apple and an apricot.

b)   State with reasons whether the system of equations has a unique solution, is inconsistent, or is dependent.

c)   What does this tell you about the cost of apples and apricots on those two days?

Today
$7.40
3 apples
2 apricots

14 Ms. Cohen gave a riddle: A string is 2 meters longer than a rod. Half of the rod is 1 meter shorter than half of the string. Is this true or false?

a)   Write a system of equations to find the length of the string and the length of the rod.

b)   State with reasons whether the system of equations has a unique solution, is inconsistent, or is dependent.

c)   Comment on Ms. Cohen's riddle.

15 *Math Journal* Mr. Braunstein uses a cell phone plan that charges 2¢ per minute for local calls and 3.5¢ per minute for long distance calls. He made x minutes of local calls and y minutes of long distance calls in June. In July, he made $2x$ minutes of local calls and $2y$ minutes of long distance calls. His bill was $12 in June and $24 in July. Can he find how many minutes of each type of call he made each month? Explain.

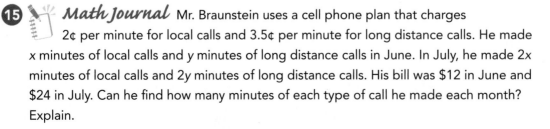

Brain @ Work

1. Lorraine has $110 and Jane has $600 in their bank accounts. Lorraine's account balance increases by $30 every year and her account balance will be C dollars in x years. Jane's account balance reduces by $40 every year and her account balance will also be C dollars in x years.

    a) Write two equations of C in terms of x.

    b) Solve this system of linear equations to find the amount in the girls' account balances when they are equal.

2. The diagram below shows a 1-centimeter block of metals A and B.

    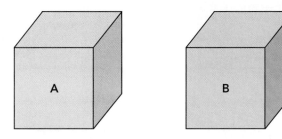

    Five blocks of A and two blocks of B have a total mass of 44 grams. Three blocks of A and five blocks of B have a total mass of 34 grams. An alloy is made by melting and mixing two blocks of metal A and one block of metal B.

    Using the density formula, Density $= \dfrac{\text{Mass}}{\text{Volume}}$, find the density of the alloy.

3. The table shows Joseph's phone usage and the total charges over three months.

	Local Voice Calls (min)	Out-of-State Voice Calls (min)	Total Charges ($)
January	60	30	45
February	80	20	46
March	40	20	34

    Joseph suspects that there are errors in the charges. Use systems of linear equations to check whether the charges are correct.

Chapter Wrap Up

Concept Map

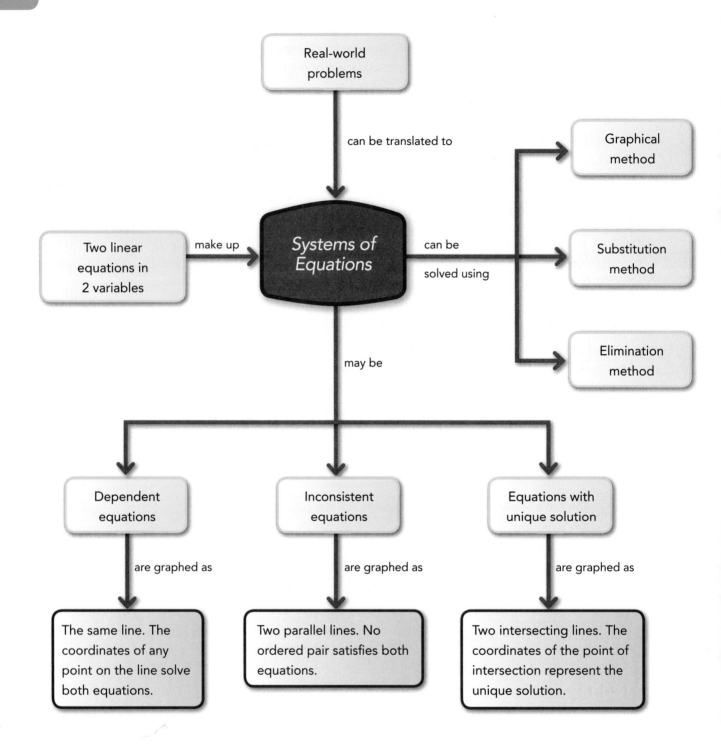

Key Concepts

▶ A set of linear equations with more than one variable is called a system of linear equations.

▶ A system of linear equations can have a unique solution, no solution, or infinitely many solutions.

▶ A system of linear equations can be solved algebraically by using
- the elimination method: eliminate one variable by adding or subtracting two equations with a common term, or
- the substitution method: solve one equation for one variable and substitute the expression into the other equation.

▶ A system of linear equations can be solved geometrically by graphing the equations and finding a point (or points) that both graphs have in common. If the coordinates of the points are not integers, the solution may only be an estimate.

▶ A system of linear equations is
- inconsistent if the graphs of the equations have the same slope and different intercepts. The graphs of the two equations are parallel lines. Since the graphs have no points in common, the system has no solution.
- dependent if the graphs of the equations have the same slope and same y-intercept. The graphs of the two equations coincide, so every point on the line satisfies both equations.
- solvable with a unique solution if the two equations have different slopes. The graphs of the two equations are two intersecting lines, and the coordinates of the point of intersection represent the solution to the system.

▶ When the equations of a linear system are written in standard form, the two equations are
- dependent if one equation is a multiple of the other,
- inconsistent if only the coefficients of x and y in one equation are multiples of the coefficients of the other equation, or
- solvable with a unique solution for all other equations.

▶ Real-world problems can be solved by writing and solving systems of linear equations.

Chapter Review/Test

Concepts and Skills

Solve each system of linear equations using the elimination method.

1 $3x + 2y = 18$

$2x + 3y = 22$

2 $5x + y = 8$

$x + 3y = 10$

3 $\frac{1}{2}a + b = 7$

$a + 3b = 19$

Solve each system of linear equations using the substitution method.

4 $a + 2b = 1$

$2a + b = 8$

5 $2x + 11y = 15$

$x - y = 1$

6 $\frac{1}{2}x + \frac{1}{2}y = 7$

$3x - y = 22$

Solve each system of linear equations using the graphical method. Use 1 grid square to represent 1 unit on both axes for the interval −3 to 8.

7 $2x + 3y = 24$

$2x + y = 12$

8 $2x + 5y = 1$

$3x - y = -7$

9 $x + 0.5y = 6$

$3x - y = 13$

Solve each system of linear equations. Explain your choice of method.

10 $x = 4y - 1$

$2x - 6y = -1$

11 $3x - 14y = -49$

$5x + 2y = 45$

12 $x - \frac{1}{3}y = 6$

$2x + y = 2$

Identify whether each system of equations is inconsistent, dependent, or has a unique solution. Justify your answer. Solve the system of linear equations if it has a unique solution.

13 $3x + 2y = 8$

$6x + 4y = 16$

14 $\frac{x}{3} + y = 8$

$x + 3y = 10$

15 $\frac{1}{2}x + y = 7$

$x + 2y = 14$

16 $2x - \frac{1}{2}y = 10$

$y = 4x + 11$

17 $2x - 5y = -21$

$4x + 3y = 23$

18 $6y - 12x = 60$

$4y - 40 = 8x$

Problem Solving

Solve. Show your work.

19 Andy and Ben both worked a total of 88 hours one week. Ben worked 8 hours more than Andy. Find the number of hours each man had worked.

20 In three years' time, Mr. Sullivan will be 3 times as old as his daughter. Six years ago, he was 6 times as old as she was. How old are they now?

21 Samantha has a riddle for her sister: Find a pair of integers x and y that satisfy $7x + 3y = 64$ and one of the integers is 3 times the other.

22 The shape ABC in the quilt block below is an isosceles triangle. In triangle ABC, $AB = AC$. The perimeter of triangle ABC is 27.3 inches. Find the values of x and y. Then find the length of each side of the triangle in inches.

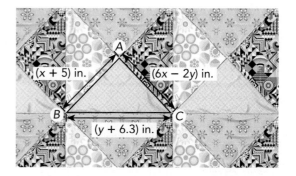

23 A bus company requires 4 buses and 8 vans to take 240 school children to the library. It requires 2 buses and 9 vans to take 170 children to the museum. Calculate the number of children a bus can carry and the number of children a van can carry.

24 At noon, Balloon M is 60 meters above ground, and Balloon N is 50 meters above ground. Balloon M is rising at the rate of 10 meters per second, while Balloon N is rising at the rate of 15 meters per second.

a) Write a system of two linear equations in which each equation gives the height, h meters, of a balloon t seconds after noon. Then solve the system using a graphing calculator.

b) How many seconds after noon will the two balloons be at the same height? How do you know?

25 The water levels in two identical tanks rise at a rate of 4 inches per second. The water level, h inches, in Tank A is 3 inches at $t = 0$. The water level in Tank B is 16 inches at $t = 3$ seconds.

a) Write a system of equations for the water level h in the two tanks in terms of t.

b) Graph the two equations on the same coordinate plane. Use 1 grid square on both axes to represent 1 unit for the interval 0 to 10.

c) When will the two tanks have the same water level? How do you know?

26 Natalie has x bags of onions and y bags of potatoes. There are a total of 8 bags. Each bag weighs 2 pounds. The total weight of the bags is 16 pounds. She wants to find the value of x and y.

a) Write a system of two linear equations.

b) State with reasons whether the system of equations has a unique solution, is inconsistent, or is dependent.

c) Can Natalie find the value of x and y? Why?

Functions

How do you identify people using fingerprints?

Everyone has unique fingerprints. In other words, there is a one-to-one relationship between a person and his or her fingerprints. In mathematics, this type of relationship is called a function.

In this chapter, you will learn how to identify mathematical functions, and also how to represent them using tables, equations, and graphs.

BIG IDEA

▶ A function is a relation between a set of inputs and a set of outputs, in which every input has exactly one output. You can use tables, graphs, and equations to represent many functions.

Recall Prior Knowledge

Writing algebraic expressions to represent unknown quantities

Sue buys 8 ribbons at x dollars each. She then spends another $5. Write an algebraic expression for the total amount of money she spends.

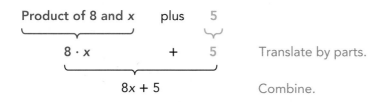

$8 \cdot x \qquad + \quad 5$ Translate by parts.

$8x + 5$ Combine.

She spends (8x + 5) dollars in total.

✔ Quick Check

Write an algebraic expression for each of the following.

1 Benedict has 7 packs of cards. Each pack has x cards. He gives 3 cards to his sister. Write an algebraic expression for the number of cards that he has left.

2 y highlighters are shared equally among 9 students. One of the students, Jessie, then buys another 3 highlighters. Write an algebraic expression for the number of highlighters she has in total.

Evaluating algebraic expressions

Evaluate an algebraic expression by replacing all its variables with their assigned values. Given that $x = -2$ in the expression $3x + 8$, find the value of the expression.

$$3x + 8 = 3 \cdot (-2) + 8$$
$$= -6 + 8$$
$$= 2$$

✔ Quick Check

Evaluate each expression for the given value of the variable.

3 $5x + 7$ when $x = -3$

4 $-4x - 1$ when $x = 3$

5 $3 - \frac{1}{2}x$ when $x = -5$

6 $\frac{3}{4}x - 2$ when $x = 7$

Lesson Objectives

- Understand relations.
- Identify functions.

Vocabulary

relation	input
output	mapping diagram
one-to-one	one-to-many
many-to-one	many-to-many
function	vertical line test

Understand Relations.

Mrs. Hayward plans to bring some of her students to a museum. The admission fee is $7 per adult and $3.50 per student. Suppose that she brings 10 students. She will need to buy tickets for 1 adult and 10 students.

Total admission fee: Ticket cost for 1 adult + Ticket cost for 10 students

$$= \$7 + 10 \cdot (\$3.50)$$
$$= \$7 + \$35$$
$$= \$42$$

When you find the cost for Mrs. Hayward to take a given number of students to the museum, you are pairing two quantities: the number of students and the total admission fee. The pairing of the two quantities as ordered pairs (number of students, total admission fee) is called a **relation**.

For the relation described above, notice that the number of students determines the total admission fee. The number of students is called the independent variable or **input**, while the total admission fee is called the dependent variable or **output**. You know that if Mrs. Hayward brings 10 students with her, she will have to pay a $42 admission fee. So, the input 10 results in an output of 42. You can represent this relation by the ordered pair (10, 42).

(10, 42)

input   output

A relation pairs a set of inputs with a set of outputs.

Often, you decide which quantity should be the input and which should be the output in a relation. If Mrs. Hayward has a certain amount of money to spend on the total admission fee, and she wants to find the number of students she can bring to the museum, the input is the total admission fee while the output is the number of students.

Represent Relations Using Mapping Diagrams.

You can use a mapping diagram like the one below to show the relationship between the inputs and the outputs in a relation. This relation consists of the ordered pairs (0, 0), (0, 1), (0, 2), and (1, 2).

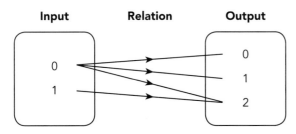

An arrow is used to map each input onto one or more outputs.

There are four different types of relations.
You can use mapping diagrams to represent the different types of relations as follows:

1. **One-to-one** relation
   Each input is mapped onto only one output.

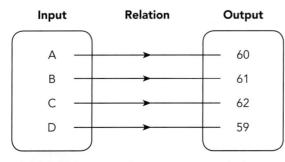

The inputs and outputs in a relation do not have to be numbers. Here the inputs are letters, and the outputs are numbers.

2. **One-to-many** relation
   One input is mapped onto many outputs.

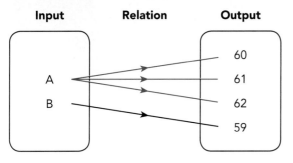

Continue on next page

3. **Many-to-one** relation

Many inputs are mapped onto one output.

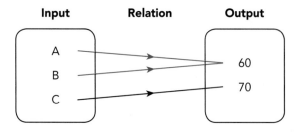

4. **Many-to-many** relation

One input is mapped onto many outputs, and also, one output is related to many inputs.

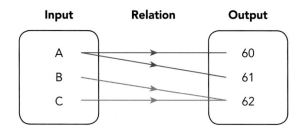

Example 1 **Use a mapping diagram to represent a relation.**

The table shows the test scores of five students.

Name of Student	John	Harry	Sylvia	Karla	Mark
Test Score	60	59	62	60	61

Use a mapping diagram to show the relation between the students and their test scores. Then identify the type of relation between the students and their test scores.

Solution

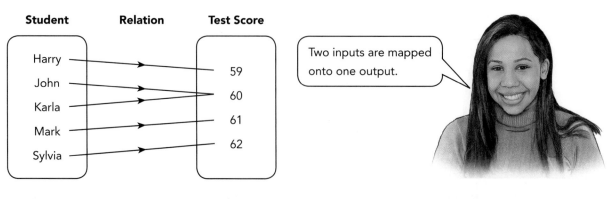

The relation between the students and their test scores is a many-to-one relation.

Guided Practice

Complete.

 1 Describe the relation between the inputs and the outputs.

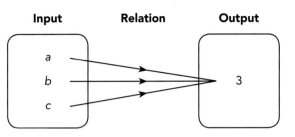

The relation between the inputs and the outputs is a ___?___-to-___?___ relation.

2 Describe the relation between the inputs and the outputs.

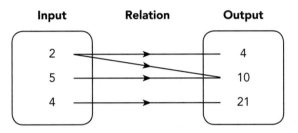

The relation between the inputs and the outputs is a ___?___-to-___?___ relation.

3 The table shows the relation between the heights of five statues and their weights.

Height (in.)	40	35	56	70	47
Weight (lb)	85	84	90	99	86

Copy and complete the mapping diagram to show the relation between the heights of the five statues and their weights. Then identify the type of relation between the heights and the weights.

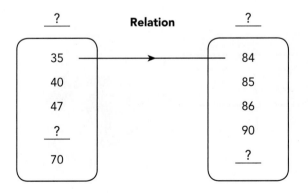

The relation between the heights and the weights is a ___?___-to-___?___ relation.

Understand Functions.

A function is a special type of relation in which each input relates to exactly one output. All functions are either one-to-one relations or many-to-one relations.

> A function is a type of relation that assigns exactly one output to each input.

Functions are common in everyday life.

Examples of real-world situations involving functions

1. The relation between pressing a key on the keyboard and the letter that appears on the monitor screen is a function. Each key you press on the keyboard will result in a specific letter appearing on the monitor screen. You can see a one-to-one relation on the mapping diagram.

Key Pressed   **Relation**   **Letter on Screen**

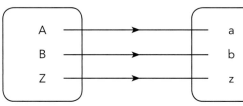

Key Pressed	Letter on Screen
A →	a
B →	b
Z →	z

You can represent the function using a table.

Input	Output
A	a
B	b
Z	z

2. The relation of buying any product in a store that is selling everything in the store for $2 is a function. Every product you buy will result in you having to pay $2. You can see a many-to-one relation on the mapping diagram.

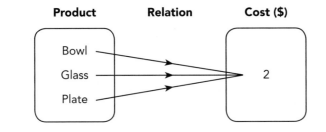

Product   Relation   Cost ($)

Bowl
Glass   →   2
Plate

> Each input, the product you buy, has exactly one output, a price of $2.

3. The relation between a football player and his lineup position is a function. Each player can play only one position at a time. You can see a many-to-one relation on the mapping diagram.

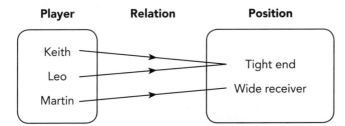

Player   Relation   Position

Keith
Leo   →   Tight end
Martin   Wide receiver

In all the examples above, each input produces exactly one output. Thus the three relations are all functions.

> All functions are relations, but not all relations are functions.

Continue on next page

When at least one input in a relation has more than one output, the relation is *not* a function.

For example, some libraries use the Dewey Decimal System to categorize books. All books about philosophy and psychology, for example, have a number in the 100's. You can think of the numbers in the list below as inputs. The outputs are books that can be matched to those categories. You can see from the mapping diagram, for any given input, a category number, there may be more than one output, a book title.

Dewey Decimal System
000 Computer Science and Information
100 Philosophy and Psychology
200 Religion and Mythology
300 Social Science
400 Language
500 Science and Mathematics
600 Technology
700 Arts and Recreation
800 Literature
900 History and Geography

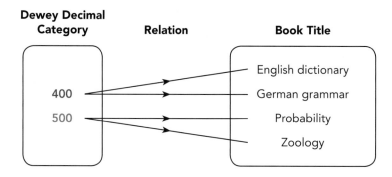

The mapping diagram shows a one-to-many relation. Because the inputs have more than one output, the relation is not a function.

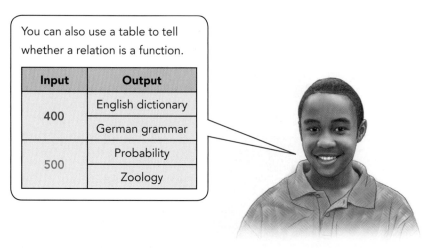

You can also use a table to tell whether a relation is a function.

Input	Output
400	English dictionary
400	German grammar
500	Probability
500	Zoology

Example 2 **Tell whether a relation is a function from a mapping diagram.**

The high jumpers at a track meet are wearing numbers on their uniforms. Each of the five high jumpers on the team made one jump. The height cleared by each athlete is shown in the table.

Athlete Number	1	2	3	4	5
Height Cleared (cm)	145	143	139	151	151

You can also write ordered pairs to show the relation between the athletes (represented by numbers) and the heights they cleared: (1, 145), (2, 143), (3, 139), (4, 151), and (5, 151).

a) Use a mapping diagram to represent the relation between the numbers of the athletes and the heights they cleared.

Solution

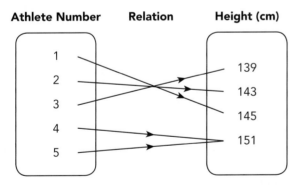

b) Tell whether the relation is a function and explain why.

Solution

The relation between the numbers of the athletes and the heights they cleared is a function because from the mapping diagram, each input is mapped to exactly one output. It is impossible for each high jumper to have two different recorded heights in one jump.

Continue on next page

c) Suppose the inputs are the heights cleared by the athletes, and the outputs are the athletes' numbers. Use a mapping diagram to represent the relation. Is this relation a function?

Solution

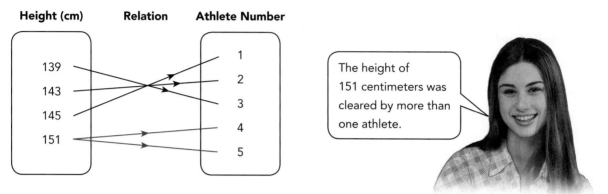

The height of 151 centimeters was cleared by more than one athlete.

The relation is not a function because one of the inputs has more than one output. From the mapping diagram, it is a one-to-many relation.

Guided Practice

Tell whether each relation is a function. Explain.

4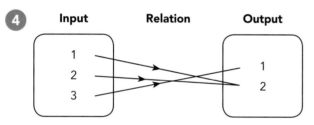

Because the mapping diagram shows a __?__-to-__?__ relation, it __?__ a function.

5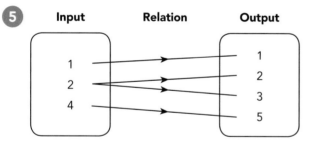

Because the mapping diagram shows a __?__-to-__?__ relation, it __?__ a function.

6

Input	Output
1	2
3	4
5	6
7	8

Because the table shows a __?__-to-__?__ relation, it __?__ a function.

Identify Functions Graphically.

One way to see if a relation is a function is to use a mapping diagram. Another way is to use a graph.

For example, the mapping diagram shows a relation between a set of values of x that are paired with a set of values of y. The relation is a function because each input has exactly one output.

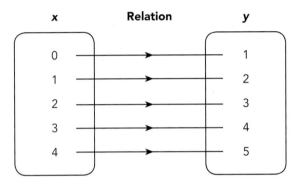

You can also represent this function using a graph by writing and graphing ordered pairs (input x, output y) as points on a coordinate plane. Notice that if you draw a vertical line through each point, each vertical line intersects exactly one point.

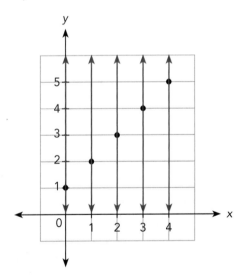

Vertical line test
If a relation is a function, then any vertical line drawn through a graph of the relation will always intersect the graph at exactly one point.

Suppose there is another relation that is represented by the mapping diagram below.

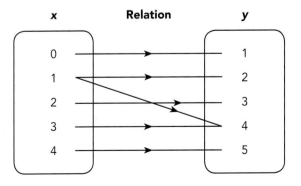

Continue on next page

You can graph the relation by writing and graphing the ordered pairs. From the mapping diagram, the ordered pairs are (0, 1), (1, 2), (1, 4), (2, 3), (3, 4), and (4, 5).

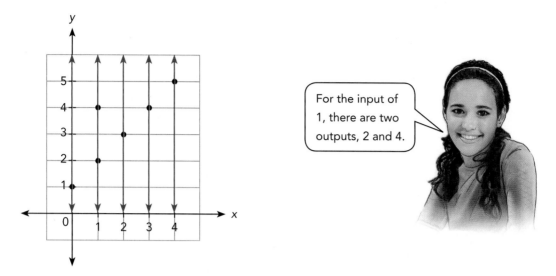

For the input of 1, there are two outputs, 2 and 4.

As you can see, the graph of the relation does not pass the vertical line test. So, this relation is not a function.

Think Math

What does it mean when a vertical line passes through more than one point in the graph of a relation?

Example 3 **Tell whether a relation is a function from a graph.**

The graph shows the relation between the heights eight students can jump into the air, y centimeters, and the students' heights, x centimeters. Tell whether the relation represented by the graph is a function.

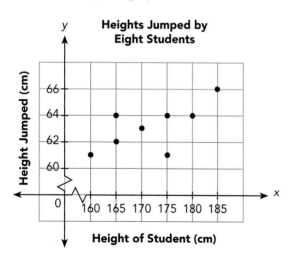

Solution

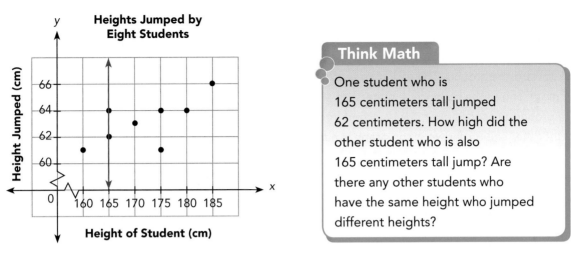

Heights Jumped by Eight Students

Think Math

One student who is 165 centimeters tall jumped 62 centimeters. How high did the other student who is also 165 centimeters tall jump? Are there any other students who have the same height who jumped different heights?

From the graph, there is at least one vertical line that intersects the graph at more than one point. Based on the vertical line test, the relation represented by the graph is not a function.

Guided Practice

Tell whether the relation represented by each graph is a function. Explain.

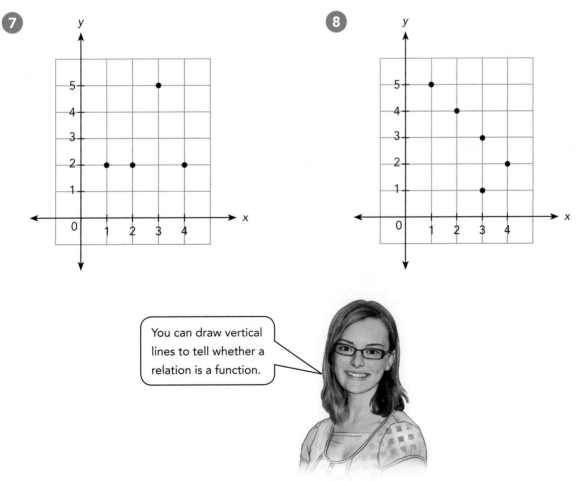

You can draw vertical lines to tell whether a relation is a function.

Example 4 Tell whether a curved graph is a function.

If a rocket is launched straight up in the air, it travels quickly at first and then slows down until it begins to fall back toward the ground. The rocket speeds up as it falls. The graph shows the distance, h meters, of a small rocket from ground t seconds after it is launched into the air. Tell whether the relation shown in the graph is a function.

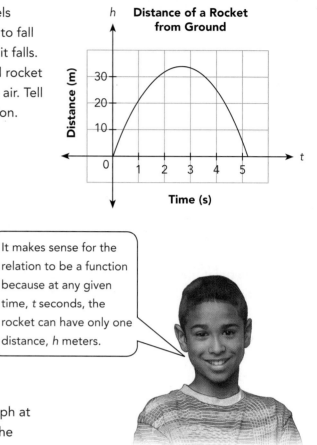

Solution

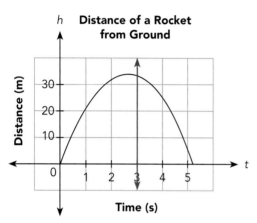

It makes sense for the relation to be a function because at any given time, t seconds, the rocket can have only one distance, h meters.

From the graph, any vertical line intersects the graph at exactly one point. Based on the vertical line test, the relation represented by the graph is a function.

Guided Practice

Tell whether the relation represented by each graph is a function. Explain.

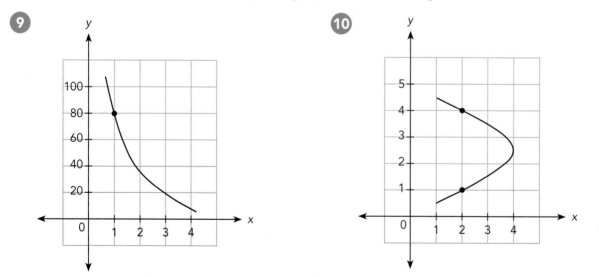

9

10

Practice 6.1

Given the relation described, identify the input and the output.

1 Mrs. Thomas wants to find out the price charged for the same stereo speaker at different stores.

2 Five students, Jessie, Patrick, Wayne, Colin, and Susie, have different heights. Their teacher wants to know their heights.

3 Ginny wants to know what after-school activities each of her friends signed up for so she knows whether she shares the same interests.

Based on the mapping diagram, state the type of relation.

4
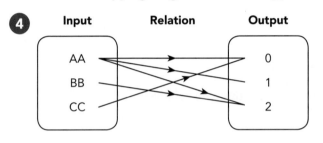

5
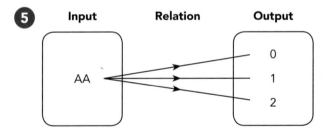

6
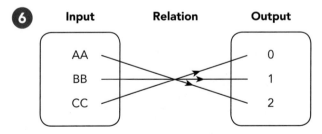

Draw a mapping diagram to represent each relation. Then identify each type of relation.

7 The table shows the numbers of various types of fruit sold in a supermarket. Draw a mapping diagram to represent the relation between each fruit and the number sold by the supermarket. Identify the type of relation between the fruit and the number sold.

Input, Fruit	Apple	Apricot	Lemon	Orange	Papaya
Output, Number Sold	256	187	256	256	93

8 The table shows the scores of a soccer team playing in eight different games. Each game is represented by a number.

Input, Score	3	2	1	0	2	1	3	2
Output, Game	1	2	3	4	5	6	7	8

Draw a mapping diagram to represent the relation between the score for each game and the game number. Identify the type of relation between the score and the game number.

Tell whether each statement is True or False. Explain.

9 A function is a type of relation.

10 All relations are functions.

11 Only a many-to-one relation is a function.

12 A one-to-many relation is a function.

Identify the type of relation in each mapping diagram. Then tell whether the relation is a function. Explain.

13

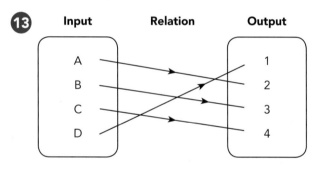

14

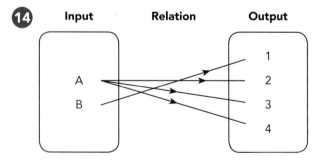

15

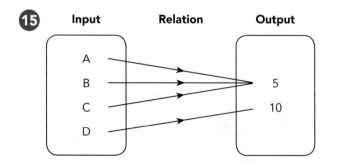

Tell whether the relation represented by each graph is a function. Explain.

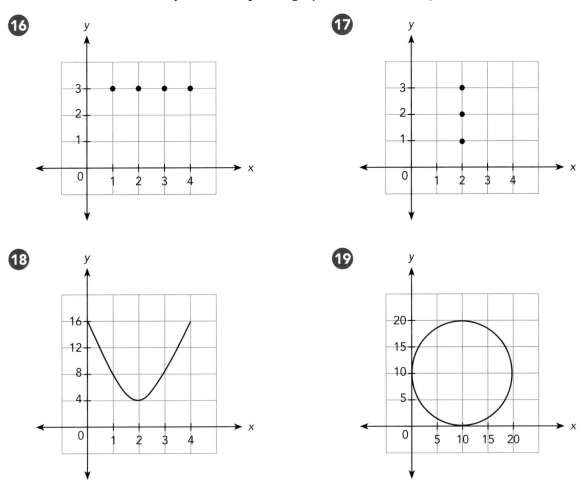

16

17

18

19

Tell whether the relation described is a function. Use a graph to support your answer.

20 The cost, y dollars, of some cheese that costs $3 per pound varies directly with the weight, x pounds, of the cheese. Use 1 unit on the horizontal axis to represent 1 pound for the x interval from 0 to 6, and 1 unit on the vertical axis to represent $3 for the y interval from 0 to 18.

21 A tank contains 3 liters of water. The water in the tank is draining out at a rate of 0.5 liter per hour. Use 1 unit on the horizontal axis to represent 1 hour for the x interval from 0 to 6, and 1 unit on the vertical axis to represent 0.5 liter for the y interval from 0 to 3.0.

22 A veterinarian weighed some puppies to see if weight depends on age. The table shows the ages, x months, and the weights, y pounds, of the puppies. Use 1 unit on the horizontal axis to represent 1 month for the x interval, and 1 unit on the vertical axis to represent 1 pound for the y interval.

Input, Age (x months)	2	3	5	5	6
Output, Weight (y pounds)	1	2	4	5	7

Solve. Show your work.

23 The table shows the number of computers the students have and the number of students in eight schools.

Input, Number of Computers	450	510	563	565	615	615	1,050	1,050
Output, Number of Students	600	680	750	770	820	825	1,400	1,800

a) Draw a mapping diagram to represent the relation between the number of computers and the number of students.

b) From the mapping diagram, identify the relation between the number of computers and the number of students.

c) Tell whether the relation represented by the mapping diagram is a function. Explain.

24 *Math Journal* Is the relationship between the side length of a square and the area of the square an example of a function? Explain.

The table below shows the number of books sold by each of six bookstores and the sales made by each store in a week. Use the table to answer questions 25 to 27.

Bookstore	A	B	C	D	E
Number of Books Sold	523	702	523	982	754
Sales	$2,569	$869	$2,317	$5,032	$869

25 Draw a mapping diagram to represent a relation between the bookstores and the number of books they sold in the week. Identify the type of relation between the bookstores and the number of books sold. Then tell whether the relation represented by the mapping diagram is a function. Explain.

26 Draw a mapping diagram to represent the relation between the sales made by the bookstores and the number of books sold in the week. Identify the type of relation between the sales made by the bookstores and the number of books sold. Then tell whether the relation represented by the mapping diagram is a function. Explain.

27 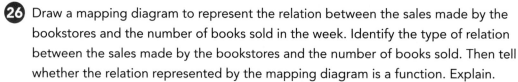 *Math Journal* The store owners want to know if the relation between the number of books sold and the sales made by the bookstores is a function.

a) Draw a mapping diagram, with the number of books sold as the input, and the sales made by each bookstore as the output. Is the relation a function? Explain.

b) Why might one bookstore get more money for selling the same number of books as another bookstore?

6.2 Representing Functions

Lesson Objective

- Represent a function in different forms.

Vocabulary
linear function

Translate Verbal Descriptions of Functions into Algebraic, Numerical, and Graphical Forms.

Janice plans to enroll in a Spanish class at a language school. She has to pay a registration fee of $100 plus $20 for each hour-long lesson she takes. The relation between the total amount she pays and the number of hours of lessons she takes is a function.

Total amount she pays equals
$100 registration fee plus $20 times the **number of hours** she takes lessons.

You can translate this verbal description of a function into an algebraic equation.
Let x be the number of hours.
Let y be the total amount of fees.

$y = 100 + (20 \cdot x)$ Write an equation.
$y = 100 + 20x$ Simplify.

x is the input and y is the output of the function.

You can also use a table of values to represent the function. For example, you can use the values 0, 1, 2, and 3 for x to find the total amount Janice will pay if she takes 0 hours, 1 hour, 2 hours, or 3 hours of lessons.

Substitute 0, 1, 2, and 3 for x into the equation $y = 100 + 20x$:

$y = 100 + 20(0)$ $y = 100 + 20(1)$ $y = 100 + 20(2)$ $y = 100 + 20(3)$
$ = 100$ $= 120$ $= 140$ $= 160$

So, the table of values is:

x	0	1	2	3
y	100	120	140	160

Continue on next page

The table of values can be used to write ordered pairs:
(0, 100), (1, 120), (2, 140), and (3, 160).
When you plot the ordered pairs on a coordinate plane, you can see that they lie on the same line.

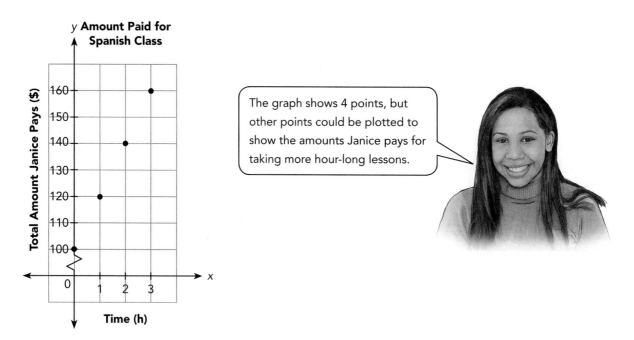

The graph shows 4 points, but other points could be plotted to show the amounts Janice pays for taking more hour-long lessons.

Because the points lie on the same line, the function $y = 20x + 100$ is called a **linear function**.

Notice that the above scenario is a real-world situation where Janice takes hour-long lessons. So, only whole numbers are meaningful for the input and output of the function.

The input values are the number of hour-long lessons Janice takes:
0, 1, 2, 3, …

The output values are the corresponding amounts she pays:
100, 120, 140, 160, …

Think Math

Suppose Janice takes a total of 20 hours of lessons. What are the greatest input and output values for the function?

Example 5 **Represent a function as an algebraic equation, a table, and a graph.**

A tank contains 8 gallons of water. Water is then pumped into the tank at a rate of 2 gallons per minute. The total amount of water in the tank, y gallons, is a function of the number of minutes, x, that water has been pumped into the tank.

a) Write a verbal description of the function. Then write an algebraic equation for the function.

Solution

Total amount of water in the tank equals
amount of water at first plus 2 gallons per minute times the number of minutes.

$y = 8 + (2 \cdot x)$ Write an equation.
$y = 8 + 2x$ Simplify.

> There are 8 gallons of water at first. Then, water flows in at a rate of 2 gallons per minute, so in x minutes, $(2 \cdot x)$ gallons are added to the tank.

b) Construct a table of x- and y-values for the function.

Solution

$y = 8 + 2x$

x	1	2	3
y	10	12	14

> The data values in the table can be written as ordered pairs:
> (1, 10), (2, 12), and (3, 14).

c) Use the table of values to plot a graph to represent the function.

Solution

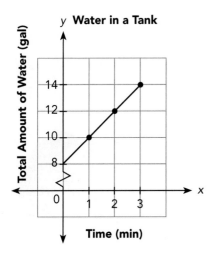

Math Note

The quantities in this situation are "continuous," which means that all the points between the points from the table can also represent inputs and outputs of the function. You can have fractions of minutes and fractions of gallons. So, it makes sense to draw a line through the points.

Guided Practice

Complete.

1 A game shop rents out video games at a rate of $6 per game. The total amount of money the shop collects, y dollars, is a function of the number of games, x, that the shop rents out.

a) Write a verbal description of the function. Then write an algebraic equation for the function.

Total amount of money the shop collects equals product of the rental rate and the __?__.

$\underline{\quad?\quad} = 6 \cdot \underline{\quad?\quad}$ Write an equation.

$\underline{\quad?\quad} = \underline{\quad?\quad}$ Simplify.

b) Construct a table of x- and y-values for the function.

In this situation, only whole numbers make sense for the input and output of the function.

x	1	2	3
y	6	?	?

c) Use the table of values in **b)** to graph the function. Use 1 unit on the horizontal axis to represent 1 game for the x interval, and 1 unit on the vertical axis to represent $6 for the y interval.

2 A fire sprinkler sprays water at a rate of 8 gallons per minute. The total amount of water being sprayed, y gallons, is a function of the number of minutes, x, that the sprinkler sprays water.

a) Write a verbal description of the function. Then write an algebraic equation for the function.

Total amount of water being sprayed equals product of the rate of water flow and the __?__.

$\underline{\quad?\quad} = \underline{\quad?\quad} \cdot \underline{\quad?\quad}$ Write an equation.

$\underline{\quad?\quad} = \underline{\quad?\quad}$ Simplify.

b) Construct a table of x- and y-values for the function.

The quantities in this situation, time and volume, are continuous.

x	1	2	3
y	?	?	?

c) Use the table of values in **b)** to graph the function. Use 1 unit on the horizontal axis to represent 1 minute for the x interval, and 1 unit on the vertical axis to represent 8 gallons for the y interval.

Example 6

Translate a table of values for a function into a graph and an algebraic equation.

Rachel starts cycling a distance away from her house at a constant rate. The table shows her distance from home, *y* meters, as a function of the time she takes to cycle, *x* seconds.

Time Taken (x seconds)	0	1	2	3	4	5
Distance from Home (y meters)	6	10	14	18	22	26

a) Graph the function. Use 1 unit on the horizontal axis to represent 1 second for the *x* interval from 0 to 5, and 1 unit on the vertical axis to represent 4 meters for the *y* interval from 6 to 26.

Solution

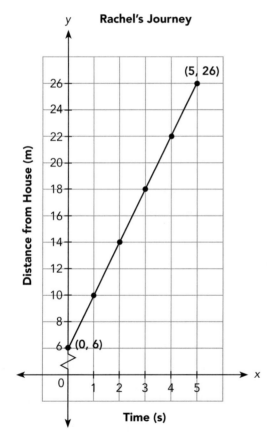

The input is the time taken by Rachel to cycle and the output is her distance from her house.

The data values in the table can be written as ordered pairs:

(0, 6), (1, 10), (2, 14), (3, 18), (4, 22), and (5, 26).

Graph the ordered pairs on a coordinate plane. The quantities in this function are continuous, so it makes sense to connect the points with a line.

Continue on next page

b) Write an algebraic equation for the function.

Solution

The line passes through the points (0, 6) and (5, 26).

Slope $m = \dfrac{y_2 - y_1}{x_2 - x_1}$ Use the slope formula.

$\quad\quad = \dfrac{26 - 6}{5 - 0}$ Substitute values.

$\quad\quad = \dfrac{20}{5}$ Subtract.

$\quad\quad = 4$ Simplify.

> **Caution** ///////
>
> Remember to subtract the coordinates of two points in the correct order when you find a slope.
> Slope is not $\dfrac{x_2 - x_1}{y_2 - y_1}$ or $\dfrac{y_2 - y_1}{x_1 - x_2}$.

The line intersects the y-axis at the point (0, 6).
So, the y-intercept, b, is 6.

Slope-intercept form: $y = 4x + 6$ Substitute the values of m and b.

So, an equation of the line is $y = 4x + 6$.

c) Describe how the slope and the y-intercept of the graph are related to the function.

Solution

The y-intercept, 6, means that Rachel starts cycling when she is 6 meters away from her house. The slope, 4, gives the rate at which Rachel's distance from home is changing. For every second that passes, her distance from her house increases by 4 meters.

Guided Practice

Complete.

3 The table shows the total distance, y miles, indicated on the odometer of Jason's car and the amount of gasoline used, x gallons, on a particular day.

Amount of Gasoline (x gallons)	0	1	2	3	4	5
Total Distance (y miles)	1,000	1,030	1,060	1,090	1,120	1,150

a) Graph the function. Use 1 unit on the horizontal axis to represent 1 gallon for the x interval from 0 to 5, and 1 unit on the vertical axis to represent 30 miles for the y interval from 1,000 to 1,150.

b) Write an algebraic equation for the function.

c) Describe how the slope and the y-intercept of the graph are related to the function.

Practice 6.2

Write a verbal description of each function. Then write an algebraic equation for the function.

1 Gordon is traveling at a constant speed of 80 kilometers per hour. The distance he travels, d kilometers, is a function of the amount of time he takes to travel, t hours.

2 Mr. Henderson pays a monthly charge of $40 for a family cell phone plan. Each additional family member pays $10 every month. The total amount Mr. Henderson and his family members pay each month, y dollars, is a function of the number of the additional family members who use the plan, x.

3 *Math Journal* In questions **1** and **2**, tell whether all values for the input and output are meaningful for the functions. Explain.

Write an algebraic equation for each function. Then construct a table of x- and y-values for the function.

4 The students from the Robotics Club are making model windmills for a workshop. Each windmill has three blades. The total number of blades needed, y, is a function of the number of windmills they make, x.

5 A newly made glass vase has a temperature of 580°C. Its temperature then decreases at an average rate of 56°C per minute. The temperature of the glass vase, y°C, is a function of the number of minutes its temperature has been decreasing, x.

Each of the following graphs represents a function. Write an algebraic equation to represent the function.

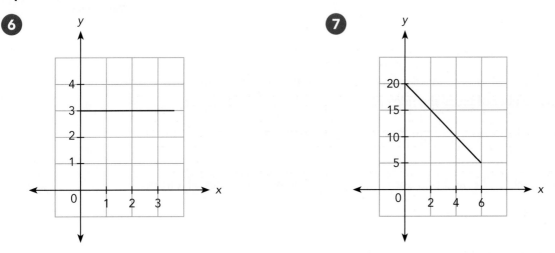

Use the table of values to plot a graph to represent the function.

8 The table shows the number of chairs in a classroom, y, as a function of the number of students in the classroom. Use 1 unit on the horizontal axis to represent 1 student for the x interval, and 1 unit on the vertical axis to represent 4 chairs for the y interval.

Number of Students (x)	0	2	3	10
Number of Chairs in a Classroom (y)	4	8	10	24

Use the table of values to plot a graph to represent the function. Then write an algebraic equation for the function.

9 A motorcyclist rode at a constant speed from City A to City B, which are 240 miles apart. The table shows his distance from City B, y miles, as a function of the number of hours he rode, x hours. Use 1 unit on the horizontal axis to represent 1 hour for the x interval, and 1 unit on the vertical axis to represent 40 miles for the y interval.

Number of Hours (x)	0	1	2	3	4	5	6
Distance from City B (y miles)	240	200	160	120	80	40	0

Solve. Show your work.

10 The graph shows the temperature of a package of food, $y°C$, as a function of the time the food is in the freezer, x minutes.

a) Write an equation in slope-intercept form to represent the function.

b) What information do the values for slope and y-intercept give you about the function?

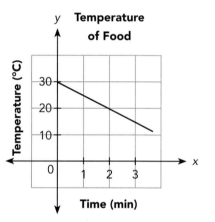

11 Hillary has $60 on her bus card. Every time she rides a bus, $1.50 is deducted from the value on her card. The amount of money she has on her card, y dollars, is a function of the number of times she rides a bus, x.

a) Write a verbal description of the function. Then write an algebraic equation for the function.

b) Construct a table of x- and y-values for the function in **a)**. Use values of x from 0 to 6.

c) Use the table of values in **b)** to plot a graph to represent the function. Use 1 unit on the horizontal axis to represent 1 bus ride for the x interval from 0 to 6, and 2 units on the vertical axis to represent $3 for the y interval from 51 to 60.

d) How many bus rides has Hillary taken if she has $51 left on her card?

Lesson Objectives

- Identify linear functions.
- Identify nonlinear functions from graphs.
- Describe and sketch functions to show their qualitative features.

Identify a Linear Function from a Table.

The ratio of the changes in two quantities, such as the slope of a linear function, is a **rate of change**.

So, the rate of change of a function is:

Slope is the ratio of the change in y-coordinates to the change in x-coordinates.

$$\text{Rate of change} = \frac{\text{Change in output values}}{\text{Change in input values}}$$

You can find tell whether a function is linear by finding the rate of change, as shown below:

a)

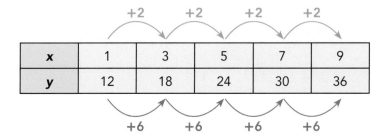

x	1	3	5	7	9
y	12	18	24	30	36

Rate of change: $\frac{6}{2} = 3$ $\frac{6}{2} = 3$ $\frac{6}{2} = 3$ $\frac{6}{2} = 3$

The function has a constant rate of change, 3.
So, the table represents a linear function.

Math Note

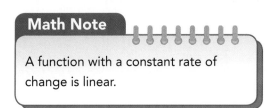

A function with a constant rate of change is linear.

Continue on next page ➡

b)

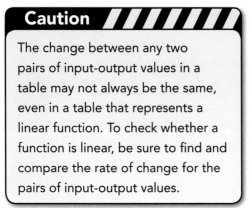

x	1	2	4	7	8
y	18	12	0	−18	−24

Rate of change: $\dfrac{-6}{1} = -6 \quad \dfrac{-12}{2} = -6 \quad \dfrac{-18}{3} = -6 \quad \dfrac{-6}{1} = -6$

The function has a constant rate of change, −6.
So, the table represents a linear function.

Caution

The change between any two pairs of input-output values in a table may not always be the same, even in a table that represents a linear function. To check whether a function is linear, be sure to find and compare the rate of change for the pairs of input-output values.

c)

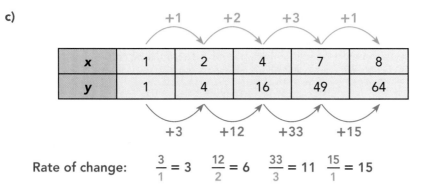

x	1	2	4	7	8
y	1	4	16	49	64

Rate of change: $\dfrac{3}{1} = 3 \quad \dfrac{12}{2} = 6 \quad \dfrac{33}{3} = 11 \quad \dfrac{15}{1} = 15$

The function does not have a constant rate of change.
So, the table represents a **nonlinear function**.

Math Note

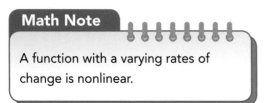

A function with a varying rates of change is nonlinear.

Example 7 **Tell whether a function represented in a table is linear.**

The table shows the cooking times recommended for roasting turkeys of different weights. Tell whether the relation between the weight of a turkey, x pounds, and the time it takes to roast the turkey, t hours, is a linear function.

Weight of Turkey (x pounds)	10	15	20	30
Time Taken (t hours)	3.0	3.5	4.0	5.0

Solution

	+5	+5	+10

Weight of Turkey (x pounds)	10	15	20	30
Time Taken (t hours)	3.0	3.5	4.0	5.0

	+0.5	+0.5	+1.0

Rate of change: $\dfrac{0.5}{5} = 0.1$ $\dfrac{0.5}{5} = 0.1$ $\dfrac{1.0}{10} = 0.1$

The function has a constant rate of change, 0.1.
So, the table represents a linear function.

Guided Practice

Tell whether each table of values represents a linear or nonlinear function. Explain.

1

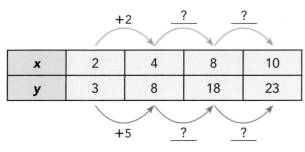

	+2	?	?

x	2	4	8	10
y	3	8	18	23

	+5	?	?

Rate of change: $\dfrac{5}{2} = \underline{\ ?\ }$ $\dfrac{?}{?} = \underline{\ ?\ }$ $\dfrac{?}{?} = \underline{\ ?\ }$

Because the rate of change for the function is __?__,

the table represents a __?__ function.

2

x	−5	−3	−1	1	3
y	28	26	22	14	4

Because the rate of change for the function is __?__,

the table represents a __?__ function.

You have learned that a linear function has a constant rate of change, and has a graph that is a line. You also know that the line can be represented by a linear equation in slope-intercept form, $y = mx + b$, where the constant m is the slope of the line. For the graph of a linear function, the slope is the same as the function's constant rate of change.

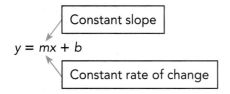

$y = mx + b$

Constant slope

Constant rate of change

> **Math Note**
>
> The equation $y = mx + b$ represents a linear function, whose graph is a straight line.

The graph shows a straight line.

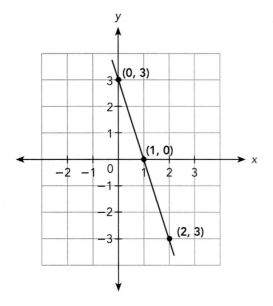

The line passes through (0, 3) and (1, 0).

$$\text{Slope } m = \frac{0 - 3}{1 - 0}$$

$$= \frac{-3}{1}$$

$$= -3$$

The line also passes through (1, 0) and (2, −3).

$$\text{Slope } m = \frac{-3 - 0}{2 - 1}$$

$$= \frac{-3}{1}$$

$$= -3$$

> **Math Note**
>
> You can check to see if a function is linear by finding and comparing rates of change for different pairs of points on its graph.

You can see that the slope of the line is a constant.
So, the straight line graph represents a linear function.

Example 8 **Tell whether a graph is a linear function.**

The graph shows the relation between the area of a square, A square centimeters, and its side length, s centimeters.

a) Explain why the relation between the two variables, A and s, is a function.

Solution

The relation between the two variables, A and s, is a function because from the graph, each input is assigned exactly one output.

b) Explain whether the rate of change of the graph is constant.

Solution

The curve passes through (0, 0) and (3, 9).

$$\text{Rate of change} = \frac{9 - 0}{3 - 0}$$

$$= \frac{9}{3}$$

$$= 3$$

The curve also passes through (3, 9) and (6, 36).

$$\text{Rate of change} = \frac{36 - 9}{6 - 3}$$

$$= \frac{27}{3}$$

$$= 9$$

You can see that the rate of change of the graph is not constant.

c) From the graph, tell whether it is a linear function.

Solution

Because the graph is not a straight line, it represents a nonlinear function.

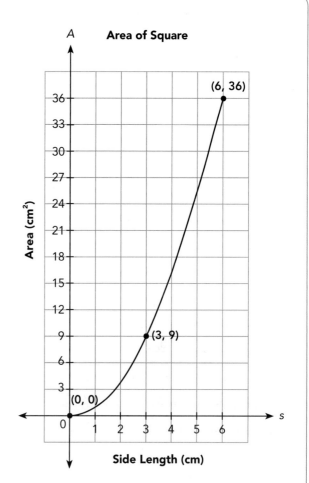

A   **Area of Square**

(6, 36)

(3, 9)

(0, 0)

Area (cm²)

Side Length (cm)

Guided Practice

Tell whether each graph represents a linear function. If so, find the rate of change.

3

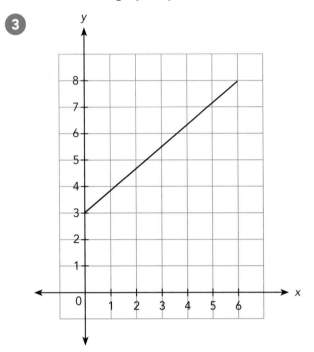

Because the graph is a __?__, it represents a __?__ function.

The line passes through (__?__, __?__) and (__?__, __?__).

Rate of change $= \dfrac{? - ?}{? - ?}$

$\qquad\quad = $ __?__

So, the rate of change of the graph is __?__.

4

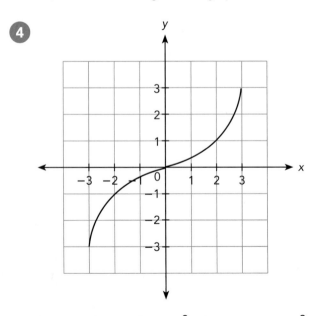

Because the graph is a __?__, it represents a __?__ function.

Use Graphs to Describe Functions Qualitatively.

You have learned to tell whether a graph is linear or nonlinear. Now you will learn to tell whether there is an increasing or a decreasing relationship between the two variables of a function.

Examples of an increasing function

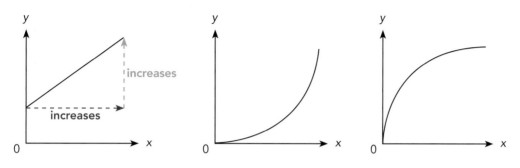

As you move from left to right, the graph rises. As the values of x **increase**, the corresponding values of y also increase.

Examples of a decreasing function

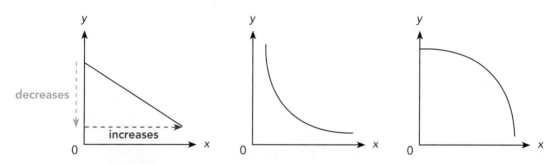

As you move from left to right, the graph falls. As the values of x **increase**, the corresponding values of y decrease.

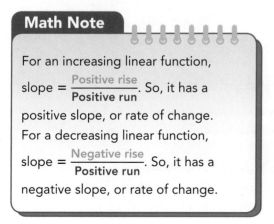

Math Note

For an increasing linear function, slope $= \dfrac{\text{Positive rise}}{\text{Positive run}}$. So, it has a positive slope, or rate of change.

For a decreasing linear function, slope $= \dfrac{\text{Negative rise}}{\text{Positive run}}$. So, it has a negative slope, or rate of change.

Example 9 **Describe a function qualitatively using a graph.**

Kayla wants to buy some grapes from a fruit stand. Each pound of grapes costs the same amount. The amount of money she pays, y dollars, is a function of the weight of grapes she buys, x pounds.

a) Give the least possible input value that makes sense for the function and give the corresponding output value. Tell whether the function is linear or nonlinear. Then tell whether the function is increasing or decreasing. Explain.

Solution

If Kayla buys 0 pounds of grapes, she spends $0. So, the least possible input value is 0 and the corresponding output value is 0. Because each pound of grapes costs the same amount, the rate of change of the function is constant. As the weight of grapes she buys increases, the amount of money she pays also increases. So, the function is a linear and increasing function.

b) Sketch a graph for the function.

Solution

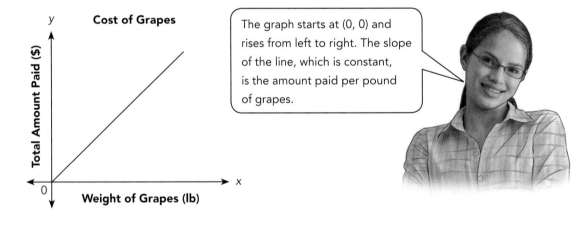

The graph starts at (0, 0) and rises from left to right. The slope of the line, which is constant, is the amount paid per pound of grapes.

Guided Practice

Describe the function. Sketch a graph for the function.

5 A cruise ship traveling at a constant speed consumes 4,000 gallons of gasoline per hour. When fully filled, it has a fuel capacity of 330,000 gallons. The amount of gasoline consumed, y gallons, is a function of the total traveling time, x hours.

a) Give the least possible input value and the corresponding output value. Tell whether the function is linear or nonlinear. Then tell whether the function is increasing or decreasing. Explain.

b) Sketch a graph for the function.

Hands-On Activity

Materials:
- number cards
  (from −5 to 5)

SKETCH LINEAR FUNCTIONS

Work in pairs.

STEP 1 Shuffle the cards and place them face down on the table.

STEP 2 Each player draws two cards. Use your cards to write an equation in slope-intercept form. Use one of the cards for the slope and one for the y-intercept of the equation.

For example:

slope   y-intercept

Slope-intercept form: $y = -2x + 3$

STEP 3 Graph the equation you wrote.

STEP 4 Copy and complete the table. For each equation that you and your partner write, record the slope, the y-intercept, and whether the function is increasing or decreasing.

Slope	y-intercept	Type of Graph
−2	3	Decreasing
?	?	?
?	?	?
?	?	?

STEP 5 Repeat **STEP 2** to **STEP 4** until a player has written two equations that represent increasing functions and two equations that represent decreasing functions. If no player has done this, reshuffle the cards and repeat **STEP 2** to **STEP 4**. The player who reaches this goal first wins the game.

 Math Journal What can you conclude about the slope of the graph of an increasing function and the slope of the graph of a decreasing function? Explain.

Practice 6.3

Tell whether each table of values represents a linear or nonlinear function.

1

x	3	5	7	9
y	6	12	18	24

2

x	−15	−10	−5	20
y	12	8	4	−16

3

x	−8	−3	8	27
y	−2	−1	2	3

4

x	−8	−6	−2	2
y	−1	−4	2	8

Tell whether each graph represents a linear function. If so, find the rate of change.

5 **6**

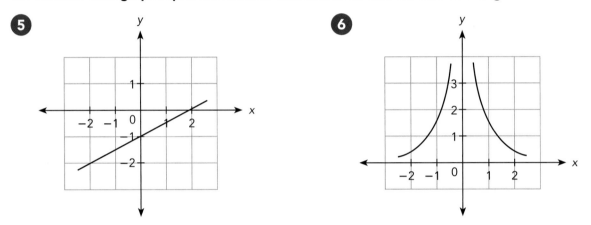

Tell whether each function is linear or nonlinear. Then tell whether the function is increasing or decreasing.

7 **8**

9 **10**

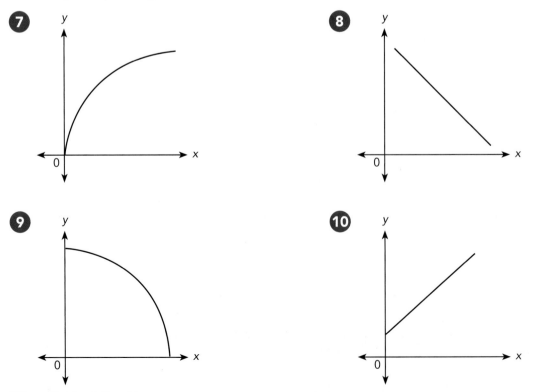

Describe the function. Sketch a graph for the function.

11 A machine at a factory pours juice into bottles at a constant rate of 6 liters per minute. The total amount of juice poured, *y* liters, is a function of the number of minutes that the juice is poured, *x*.

    a) Give the least possible input value and the corresponding output value. Tell whether the function is linear or nonlinear. Then tell whether the function is increasing or decreasing. Explain.

    b) Sketch a graph for the function.

12 Aidan was 100 miles from Town P. He traveled to Town P by car at a constant speed. The distance from Town P, *y* miles, is a function of the traveling time, *x* hours.

    a) Give the least possible input value and the corresponding output value. Tell whether the function is linear or nonlinear. Then tell whether the function is increasing or decreasing. Explain.

    b) Sketch a graph for the function.

Solve. Use graph paper.

13 The table shows the number of students, *y*, as a function of the number of teachers, *x*.

Input, Number of Teachers (x)	4	5	6	10
Output, Number of Students (y)	100	125	150	250

    a) Tell whether the function is linear or nonlinear. Then tell whether the function is increasing or decreasing. Explain.

    b) Graph the table of values and draw a line through the points. Use 1 unit on the horizontal axis to represent 1 teacher for the *x* interval, and 1 unit on the vertical axis to represent 25 students for the *y* interval from 100 to 250. Do the coordinates of every point on the line make sense for the function? Explain.

14 A cyclist starts riding from home to another town. His cycling speed, *y* miles per hour, is a function of the amount of time he takes to cycle, *x* hours.

Input, Time Taken (x hours)	1	2	3	4	6
Output, Cycling Speed (y miles per hour)	12	6	4	3	2

    a) Tell whether the function is linear or nonlinear. Then tell whether the function is increasing or decreasing. Explain.

    b) Graph the table of values and draw a curve through the points. Use 1 unit on the horizontal axis to represent 1 hour for the *x* interval, and 1 unit on the vertical axis to represent 1 mile per hour for the *y* interval. Do the coordinates of every point on the curve make sense for the function? Explain.

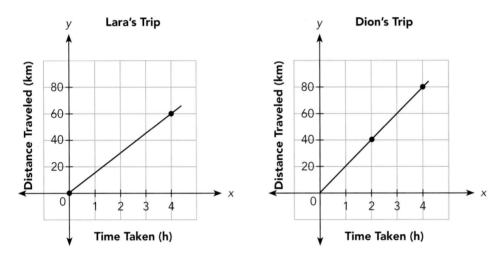

6.4 Comparing Two Functions

Lesson Objective

- Compare linear functions represented in the same and in different forms.

Compare Two Linear Functions Represented in the Same Form.

Lara and Dion went on a cycling trip with the school. The graphs show the distance traveled, y kilometers, and the time taken, x hours, by each of them.

Notice that both graphs show that the functions are linear and increasing functions. The least initial input value for each function is 0, and the corresponding output value is 0. You can say that the function has an initial output value of 0.

You can also use the slopes of the graphs to compare the rates of change for the functions.

Lara's trip
The line passes through the points (0, 0) and (4, 60).

Slope $m = \dfrac{60 - 0}{4 - 0}$

$\quad = \dfrac{60}{4}$

$\quad = 15$

Dion's trip

The line passes through the points (2, 40) and (4, 80).

$$\text{Slope } m = \frac{80 - 40}{4 - 2}$$
$$= \frac{40}{2}$$
$$= 20$$

Because 20 > 15, the graph that represents Dion's trip has a greater rate of change than the function that represents Lara's trip.

You can also represent both trips using tables.

Lara's trip

+1   +1

Time Taken (x hours)	0	1	2
Distance Traveled (y kilometers)	0	15	30

+15   +15

Rate of change: $\frac{15}{1} = 15$ $\frac{15}{1} = 15$

> In each function, the rate of change is constant.
>
> Lara's rate of change: 15 km/h
>
> Dion's rate of change: 20 km/h
>
> In each function, the values of y increase as the values of x increase. So, both functions are increasing.

Dion's trip

+2   +2

Time Taken (x hours)	0	2	4
Distance Traveled (y kilometers)	0	40	80

+40   +40

Rate of change: $\frac{40}{2} = 20$ $\frac{40}{2} = 20$

In addition, you can use equations to compare the two functions. Because the y-intercept for each graph is 0, the equations for the functions are as follows:

Lara's trip: $y = 15x$
Dion's trip: $y = 20x$

Finally, you can use a verbal description to compare the two functions.
Both functions are linear and increasing functions with an initial output value of 0 that corresponds to an input value of 0. Dion travels at a greater speed than Laura, so the function relating his distance traveled to the time taken has a greater rate of change than the function relating Laura's distance traveled to the time taken.

Example 10 **Compare two linear functions with the same initial value.**

The tables show two functions relating the total cost, *y* cents, and the weight of potatoes purchased, *x* pounds, at Shop A and Shop B.

Shop A

Weight of Potatoes (x pounds)	1	2	3	4
Total Cost (y cents)	60	120	180	240

Shop B

Weight of Potatoes (x pounds)	1	2	3	4
Total Cost (y cents)	50	100	150	200

a)   Use a verbal description to compare the two functions.

Solution

Shop A

+1   +1   +1

Weight of Potatoes (x pounds)	1	2	3	4
Total Cost (y cents)	60	120	180	240

+60   +60   +60

Rate of change: $\dfrac{60}{1} = 60$ $\dfrac{60}{1} = 60$ $\dfrac{60}{1} = 60$

Shop B

+1   +1   +1

Weight of Potatoes (x pounds)	1	2	3	4
Total Cost (y cents)	50	100	150	200

+50   +50   +50

Rate of change: $\dfrac{50}{1} = 50$ $\dfrac{50}{1} = 50$ $\dfrac{50}{1} = 50$

In each function, the rate of change is constant, so the function is linear. In each function, the values of *y* increase as the values of *x* increase. So, both functions are increasing.

Both functions are linear and increasing functions. The function for Shop A has a greater rate of change than the function for Shop B.

b) Write an algebraic equation to represent each function.

Solution

Because the two functions are linear, their graphs will be linear. For each graph, you can write an equation in slope-intercept form, $y = mx + b$.

Shop A

Use the ordered pair (1, 60) and the rate of change, 60, to find the value of the y-intercept, b.

Linear function: $\quad y = mx + b$
$\qquad\qquad\qquad 60 = 60(1) + b \qquad$ Substitute the values for m, x and y.
$\qquad\qquad\qquad 60 = 60 + b \qquad$ Simplify.
$\qquad\quad 60 - 60 = 60 + b - 60 \qquad$ Subtract 60 from both sides.
$\qquad\qquad\qquad\;\; 0 = b \qquad$ Simplify.

So, the algebraic equation for Shop A is $y = 60x$.

Shop B

Use the ordered pair (1, 50) and the rate of change, 50, to find the value of the y-intercept, b.

Linear function: $\quad y = mx + b$
$\qquad\qquad\qquad 50 = 50(1) + b \qquad$ Substitute the values for m, x and y.
$\qquad\qquad\qquad 50 = 50 + b \qquad$ Simplify.
$\qquad\quad 50 - 50 = 50 + b - 50 \qquad$ Subtract 50 from both sides.
$\qquad\qquad\qquad\;\; 0 = b \qquad$ Simplify.

Both functions have an initial output value of 0 corresponding to an initial input value of 0. You pay $0 for 0 pounds of potatoes.

So, the algebraic equation for Shop B is $y = 50x$.

c) Which of the two shops, A and B, sells potatoes that cost less?

Solution

Comparing the rates of change for the two shops, Shop B has a lower rate of change. So, the potatoes in Shop B cost less per pound.

Guided Practice

Complete.

1. Water is pumped into two aquariums, P and Q. The tables show two functions relating the total amount of water, y liters, and the time taken, t minutes, to pump the water into each aquarium.

Aquarium P

Time Taken (t minutes)	5	10	20	30
Total Amount of Water (y liters)	70	120	220	320

Aquarium Q

Time Taken (t minutes)	5	10	20	30
Total Amount of Water (y liters)	95	170	320	470

a) Use a verbal description to compare the two functions.

Aquarium P

Time Taken (t minutes)	5	10	20	30
Total Amount of Water (y liters)	70	120	220	320

+5   ?   ?

+50   ?   ?

Rate of change: $\dfrac{50}{5} = \underline{}$ $\dfrac{?}{?} = \underline{}$ $\dfrac{?}{?} = \underline{}$

Aquarium Q

Time Taken (t minutes)	5	10	20	30
Total Amount of Water (y liters)	95	170	320	470

+5   ?   ?

+75   ?   ?

Rate of change: $\dfrac{75}{5} = \underline{}$ $\dfrac{?}{?} = \underline{}$ $\dfrac{?}{?} = \underline{}$

Both functions are __?__ and __?__ functions. The function for Aquarium __?__ has a greater rate of change than the function for Aquarium __?__.

b) Write an algebraic equation to represent each function. Then write the initial input and output values of each function.

Aquarium P

Use the ordered pair (5, 70) and the rate of change, __?__, to find the value of the y-intercept, b.

Linear function:

$y = mt + b$ Let the input be t and output be y.

$\underline{\ ?\ } = \underline{\ ?\ } (\underline{\ ?\ }) + b$ Substitute the values for m, t and y.

$\underline{\ ?\ } = \underline{\ ?\ } + b$ Simplify.

$\underline{\ ?\ } - \underline{\ ?\ } = \underline{\ ?\ } + b - \underline{\ ?\ }$ Subtract __?__ from both sides.

$\underline{\ ?\ } = b$ Simplify.

So, the algebraic equation for Aquarium P is $y = \underline{\ ?\ }$.

Aquarium Q

Use the ordered pair (10, 170) and the rate of change, __?__, to find the value of the y-intercept, b.

Linear function:

$y = mt + b$ Let the input be t and output be y.

$\underline{\ ?\ } = \underline{\ ?\ } (\underline{\ ?\ }) + b$ Substitute the values for m, t and y.

$\underline{\ ?\ } = \underline{\ ?\ } + b$ Simplify.

$\underline{\ ?\ } - \underline{\ ?\ } = \underline{\ ?\ } + b - \underline{\ ?\ }$ Subtract __?__ from both sides.

$\underline{\ ?\ } = b$ Simplify.

So, the algebraic equation for Aquarium Q is $y = \underline{\ ?\ }$.
Both functions have an initial output value of __?__ corresponding to an initial input value of 0.

c) Which of the two aquariums, P and Q, is filled with water more quickly?

Comparing the rates of change for the two shops, Aquarium __?__ has a __?__ rate of change. This means that Aquarium __?__ will be filled with water more quickly.

Compare Two Linear Functions Represented in Different Forms.

Sometimes you may need to compare two linear functions that are represented in different forms. For example, you may want to compare a linear function represented by a table with a linear function represented by a graph. One way to compare the functions is to express them in the same form.

> You can represent two functions in the same form using equations, table, or graphs.

Example 11 **Compare two different linear functions.**

Patrick and Leonard are brothers who each have money saved. The amount of money, y dollars, that each brother has left in savings after x weeks is a linear function. Patrick's function is represented by a table, and Leonard's function is represented by an equation.

Patrick's Savings

Number of Weeks (x)	0	5	15	20
Amount of Money (y dollars)	200	175	125	100

Leonard's Savings

Let x be the number of weeks.

Let y be the amount of savings Leonard has left after x weeks.

Amount of money: $y = 250 - 10x$

To compare the functions, write an equation for Patrick's function. Then compare the equations.

a) Write an algebraic equation to represent Patrick's linear function.

Solution

Patrick's Savings

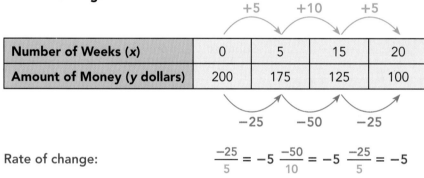

Number of Weeks (x)	0	5	15	20
Amount of Money (y dollars)	200	175	125	100

Rate of change: $\dfrac{-25}{5} = -5 \quad \dfrac{-50}{10} = -5 \quad \dfrac{-25}{5} = -5$

The rate of change is -5.

From the table, when the number of days is 0, Patrick has $200. So he starts with an initial amount of $200, and the algebraic equation is $y = 200 - 5x$.

Think Math

Suppose you are asked to compare a linear function represented by a table with a linear function represented by a graph. What are some steps you could use to compare the two functions?

b) Use a verbal description to compare the two functions.

Solution

Both functions are linear and decreasing functions. Comparing the two equations, because 250 > 200, Leonard has a greater amount of money at first. Comparing the rates of change shows that Leonard's savings decrease by $10 each week, and Patrick's savings decrease by $5 each week. So, Leonard's savings decrease more quickly than Patrick's savings.

Guided Practice

Complete.

2 Two classes, A and B, compare the amount of donations they will raise for a charity by participating in a walkathon. The amount of donations they will raise, y dollars, is a function of the distance the students walk, x miles.

Class A

Distance Walked (x miles)	0	1	2	4
Amount of Donations (y dollars)	100	115	130	160

Class B
Amount of donations: $y = 20x + 50$

a) Write an algebraic equation to represent the table of values representing the amount of donations Class A will raise for the charity.

Class A

Distance Walked (x miles)	0	1	2	4
Amount of Donations (y dollars)	100	115	130	160

+1   ?   ?

+15   ?   ?

Rate of change: $\frac{15}{1} = \underline{\quad?\quad}$ $\frac{?}{?} = \underline{\quad?\quad}$ $\frac{?}{?} = \underline{\quad?\quad}$

The algebraic equation is $y = \underline{\quad?\quad}$.

b) Use a verbal description to compare the two functions.

Both functions are __?__ and __?__ functions. Comparing the two equations, because __?__ > 50, Class __?__ raises a greater amount of money at first. Comparing the rates of change shows that Class A will raise $__?__ for each mile the students walk, and Class B will raise $__?__ for each mile the students walk. So, the amount of donations Class __?__ will raise increases more quickly than the amount of donations Class __?__ will raise.

Tell whether the equation $y = -2x + 3$ can represent each of the following functions.

1

x	2	3	−1
y	−1	−3	5

2

x	1	2	3
y	−1	−3	−5

3

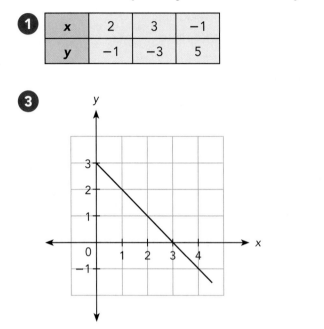

Tell whether each function can represent the table of values.

x	1	2	3
y	−2	1	4

4 $y = 3x - 4$

5 $y = 2x - 5$

6

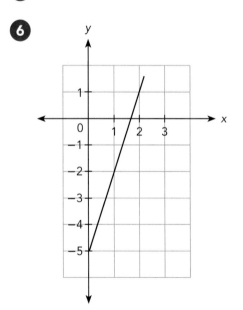

Tell whether each function represents the verbal description.

Bryan has $30 in savings at first. He wants to save $5 per month beginning this month. y represents his total savings, in dollars, and x represents the number of months he saves.

7

Number of Months (x)	4	5	6
Total Savings (y dollars)	60	65	70

8 $y = 30 + 5x$

9 $y = 30 - 5x$

Solve. Show your work.

10 Clara and Elaine have some savings. The functions that relate each girl's total savings, y dollars, to the number of months, x, that each girl saves are as follows:

Clara: $y = 380 + 20x$
Elaine: $y = 400 + 15x$

a) Use a verbal description to compare the two functions.

b) Graph the two functions on the same coordinate plane. Use 1 unit on the horizontal axis to represent 1 month for the x interval from 0 to 8, and 1 unit on the vertical axis to represent $20 for the y interval from 380 to 540. For each function, draw a line through the points.

c) Who will save more over time? Explain.

11 The director of a theater group wants to rent a theater for an upcoming show. The director has two options for paying for the rental. Both options involve paying a deposit and then paying an additional charge for each ticket sold. For each function, the total amount the director would pay, y dollars, is a function of the number of tickets sold, x.

Option A

Number of Tickets Sold (x)	100	150	200
Total Fee (y dollars)	1,400	1,600	1,800

Option B
A deposit of $800 plus $6 per ticket sold.

a) Write an algebraic equation to represent each function.

b) Use a verbal description to compare the two functions.

c) *Math Journal* The theater seats up to 200 people. If the director expects to sell all the tickets, which of the two options, A or B, offers a better deal? Explain.

12 A factory needs to grate at least 8,000 pounds of cheese each day.

The manager of the factory needs to buy a new cheese grating machine. She is trying to decide between Machine A and Machine B. The functions shown describe how many pounds of cheese, y, are left t minutes after each machine starts grating an initial batch of cheese.

Machine A

The function is $y = 2{,}000 - 80t$. The initial value of 2,000 pounds represents the weight of each batch of cheese to be grated. After one batch is grated, another batch can be added to the machine.

Machine B

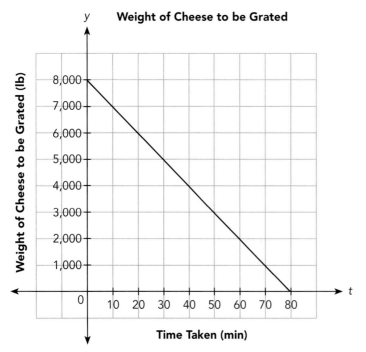

a)   Write an algebraic equation to represent the function for Machine B.

b)   *Math Journal* Assuming that the machines are of the same quality, which machine would you recommend that the manager buy? Explain.

Five teachers at a school brought a group of students to a museum exhibit.

For group tours involving any number of adults and at least 5 students, the museum offers three packages, A, B, and C. The functions shown below represent the total admission fee, y dollars, that five teachers and x students will pay to see the exhibit.

Package A
Each adult ticket costs $30 and each student ticket costs $15.

Package B

Number of Students (x)	0	25	50
Total Admission Fee (y dollars)	250	600	950

Package C
Each adult ticket costs $60 and each student ticket costs $12.

1. Use an algebraic equation to represent each of the three functions.

2. Graph the three functions on the same coordinate plane. Use 1 unit on the horizontal axis to represent 5 students for the x interval from 0 to 50, and 1 unit on the vertical axis to represent $50 for the y interval from 150 to 950. For each function, draw a line though the points.

3. Identify the best deal for the 5 teachers and 40 students. Explain.

4. Identify the best deal for the 5 teachers and 80 students. Explain.

Chapter Wrap Up

Concept Map

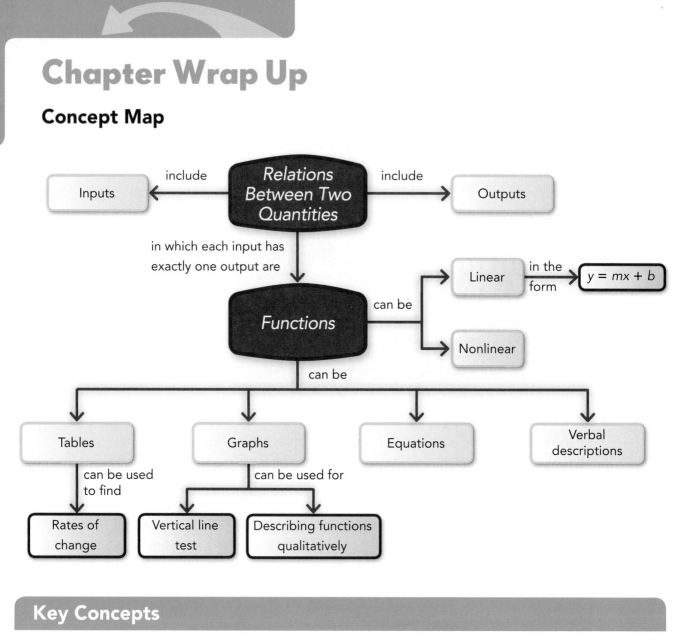

Key Concepts

▶ A relation pairs a set of inputs with a set of outputs. It can also be thought of as a rule that describes the relationship between the inputs and outputs.

▶ The four types of relations are one-to-one, one-to-many, many-to-one, and many-to-many.

▶ A function is a specific type of relation that assigns exactly one output to each input. All functions are either one-to-one relations or many-to-one relations.

▶ Functions can be linear or nonlinear, and can be increasing or decreasing.

▶ A linear function can be represented as an equation in the form $y = mx + b$ and has a constant rate of change.

▶ Functions can be represented in different ways: algebraically, graphically, numerically in tables, or by verbal descriptions.

Chapter Review/Test

Concepts and Skills

Given the relation described, identify the input and the output.

1 Daphne wants to find the area of a circle given its radius.

2 Mr. Reynard wants to find the total cost of the number of items he bought at a store where everything costs one dollar.

3 The head of the English department wants to see how each student in Grade 8 does on an English test.

Based on the mapping diagrams, state the type of relation. Tell whether each relation is a function.

4

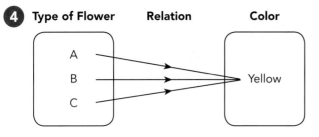

Type of Flower   Relation   Color

5

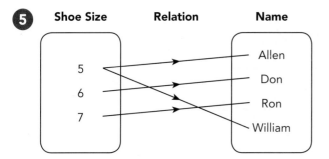

Shoe Size   Relation   Name

Tell whether each relation is a function.

6

Side Length (cm)	4	5	8	9
Perimeter (cm)	16	20	32	36

7

Month	Jan	Feb	May	Jul	Sep	Oct	Nov	Dec
Number of Public Holidays	2	1	1	1	1	1	2	1

8

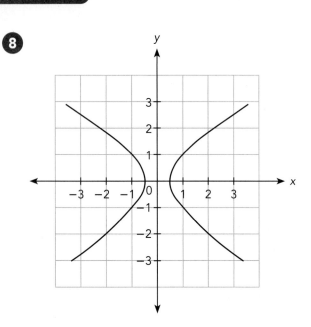

Use graph paper. Show your work.

9 Represent the function $y = -4x + 6$ as a table and as a graph. Use 1 grid square on the horizontal axis to represent 1 unit for the x interval from -3 to 3, and 1 grid square on the vertical axis to represent 2 units for the y interval from -6 to 18.

Tell whether each function is linear or nonlinear. Then tell whether the function is increasing or decreasing.

10

Input, x	2	3	5	6
Output, y	1,500	600	150	60

11 The area of a square, A square centimeters, is a function of its side length, s centimeters, where $A = s^2$.

Problem Solving

Describe the function. Sketch a graph for the function.

12 A large region has experienced heavy rains. Government officials decide to open a floodgate to release water from the reservoir at a constant rate of 1 cubic kilometer per hour. Before they open the gate, there are 29 cubic kilometers of water in the reservoir. The amount of water in the reservoir, y cubic kilometers, is a function of the number of hours the floodgate has been opened, x hours.

a) Give the least possible input value and the corresponding output value. Tell whether the function is linear or nonlinear. Then tell whether the function is increasing or decreasing. Explain.

b) Sketch a graph for the function. Identify the y-intercept of the graph.

Solve. Show your work.

13 The student council orders T-shirts with the school logo from an online company. The cost for each T-shirt is $2, and the shipping charge for all the shirts is $25. The student council wants to find out the total amount of money they pay, y dollars, for the number of T-shirts they order, x.

a) Write an algebraic equation to represent the function.

b) Use graph paper. Graph the relationship between x and y. Use 1 unit on the horizontal axis to represent 1 T-shirt for the x interval from 0 to 10, and 1 unit on the vertical axis to represent $2 for the y interval from 25 to 45.

c) Identify whether the function is linear or nonlinear.

d) Identify whether the function is increasing or decreasing. Explain.

14 A scientist is checking to see whether pollutants are causing a decrease in oxygen levels in a river near a pipe that drains into the river. She notices that the distance downstream from the pipe, in meters, and the concentration of oxygen in the water, in milligrams per liter, can be described by the function $y = 2 + 0.1x$, where y is the concentration of oxygen and x is the distance from the pipe. The scientist also tested oxygen levels upstream from the pipe. The graph shows a function that represents this upstream oxygen level concentration.

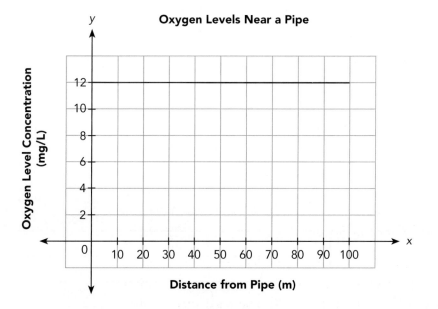

a) Copy the graph shown. Then graph the function $y = 2 + 0.1x$ on the same coordinate plane.

b) Use a verbal description to compare the two functions. Give a possible reason for the difference in oxygen levels upstream and downstream from the pipe.

Cumulative Review Chapters 5–6

Concepts and Skills

Solve each system of linear equations by making tables of values. Each variable x is a positive integer less than 7. (Lesson 5.1)

1 $4x + 3y = 23$
$y - 2x = 1$

2 $4y + 3x = 19$
$x + y = 5$

Solve each system of linear equations by using the elimination or substitution method. Explain your choice of method. (Lesson 5.2)

3 $3a - 2b = 1$

$2a + 3b = 18$

4 $0.7x - 1.2y = -11.5$

$0.5x + 3.5y = 31$

5 $\dfrac{1}{4}h + \dfrac{2}{3}k = 5$

$\dfrac{3}{4}h + k = 6$

Solve each system of linear equations by using the graphical method. Use 1 grid square on both axes to represent 1 unit for the interval from –5 to 10. (Lesson 5.4)

6 $3x + y = 3$
$4x - 2y = 14$

7 $2x - y = 3$
$x + y = 9$

8 $2x + y = 25$
$3x - 4y = -1$

Identify whether each system of linear equations is inconsistent or dependent. Justify your answer. (Lesson 5.5)

9 $3x + 4y = 12$

$\dfrac{3}{4}x + y = 3$

10 $0.2x + 1.2 = y$

$x + 8 = 5y$

11 $3x + 2y = \dfrac{1}{3}$

$9x + 6y = 1$

Tell whether the relation in each mapping diagram, table, or graph is a function. Explain. (Lesson 6.1)

12

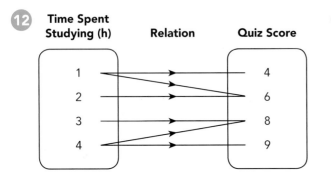

Input, Carnival Stall	Output, Donations Raised ($)
A	80
B	70
C	120
D	80
E	100

13

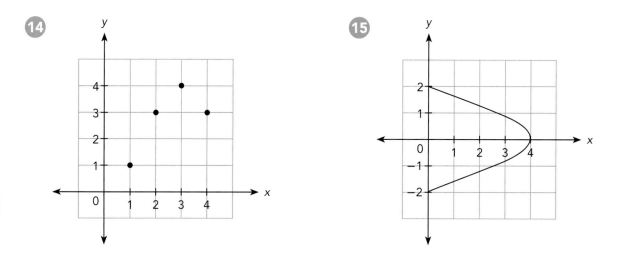

14 (graph showing points at (1,1), (2,3), (3,4), (4,3))

15 (graph showing sideways parabola)

Write an algebraic equation for each function. (Lesson 6.2)

16 A chef makes 100 hot dog buns each morning. In the afternoons, he makes 40 hot dog buns per hour. The total number of hot dog buns he makes each day, y, is a function of the time he takes to make the buns in the afternoons, x hours.

17 Gina walks 2 kilometers from home to a park. She then jogs at an average speed of 7 kilometers per hour. The total distance she traveled, d kilometers, is a function of the time she takes to jog, t hours.

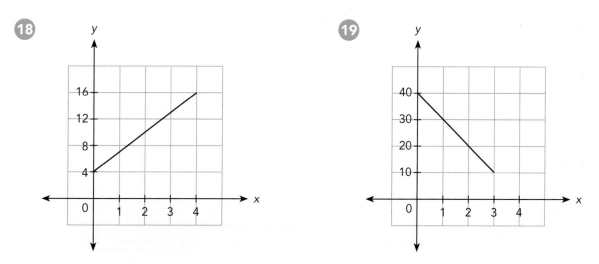

18 (line graph from (0,4) to (4,16))

19 (line graph from (0,40) to (3,10))

Tell whether each table, equation, or graph represents a linear function. If so, find the rate of change. Then tell whether the function is increasing or decreasing.
(Lesson 6.3)

20

x	3	6	9	12
y	−16	−11	−6	−1

21

x	−5	−3	0	4
y	12	6	0	−6

22 $3y + 2x = 10$

23 $V = \ell^3, \ell > 0$

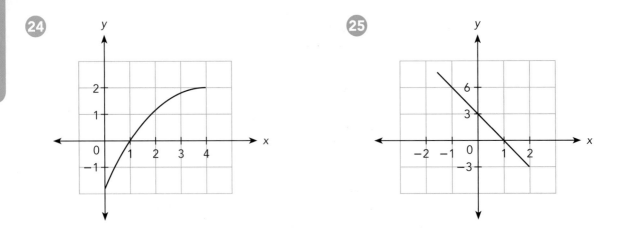

24

25

Problem Solving

Solve. Show your work.

26 A school librarian keeps track of the number of students in the library at any one time, and the number of computers being used. The table shows the data she collected for one day. (Chapter 6)

Number of Students	10	12	5	4	10	14
Number of Computers Used	8	7	2	4	6	9

Draw a mapping diagram to represent the relation between the number of students in the library and the number of computers being used. Is this relation a function? Explain.

27 Find two numbers whose sum is 60, such that twice the lesser number is equal to half of the greater number. (Chapter 5)

28 The diagram shows a parallelogram with side lengths in inches. (Chapter 5)

a) Find the values of a and b.

b) Find the perimeter of the parallelogram.

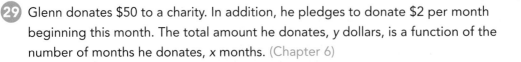

29 Glenn donates $50 to a charity. In addition, he pledges to donate $2 per month beginning this month. The total amount he donates, y dollars, is a function of the number of months he donates, x months. (Chapter 6)

a) Write an algebraic equation for the function.

b) Graph the function and draw a line through the points. Use 1 unit on the horizontal axis to represent 1 month for the x interval from 0 to 6, and 1 unit on the vertical axis to represent $2 for the y interval from 50 to 62. Do the coordinates of every point on the line make sense for the function? Explain.

c) Describe how the slope and y-intercept of the graph are related to the function.

30 In a stationery store, 15 pencils and 20 rulers are sold for $20.50. Jennifer buys 7 pencils and 2 rulers for $5.90. Find the price of each item. (Chapter 5)

31 A group of 70 students and teachers visited a theme park. The teachers were charged a regular price of $50 per ticket. A 30% discount of the regular ticket price was given to each student. The total ticket price for the whole group cost $2,600. Find the number of students and teachers in the group. (Chapter 5)

32 The fuel tank in Tasha's car can hold up to 8 gallons of gasoline. She can drive a distance of 40 miles for each gallon of gasoline. The total amount of gasoline in her fuel tank, y gallons, is a function of the distance she drives, x miles. (Chapter 6)

a) Give the least possible input value and the corresponding output value. Tell whether the function is linear or nonlinear. Then tell whether the function is increasing or decreasing. Explain.

b) Sketch a graph for the function. Identify the y-intercept of the graph.

33 The pressure in two tanks increases at a constant rate of 2 bars per minute. The initial pressure in Tank A is 3 bars. The pressure in Tank B is 14 bars after 3 minutes. (Chapter 5)

a) Write a system of two linear equations for the pressure p in the two tanks in terms of the time t.

b) Graph the two equations on a coordinate plane. Use 1 grid square on both axes to represent 1 unit for the interval from 0 to 5.

c) When will the pressure in both tanks be the same? How do you know?

34 Mr. Johannsen wants to compare how fast water evaporates from two inflatable swimming pools, A and B, placed at different locations. The height of the water level in each pool, h inches, is a function of the time it takes for the water to evaporate, t days. (Chapter 6)

Pool A

Number of Days (t)	0	5	10	15	20
Height of Water Level (h inches)	25.0	22.5	20	17.5	15

Pool B
An initial water level of 24 inches where water evaporates at a rate of 0.4 inch per day

a) Write an algebraic equation to represent each function.

b) Graph the two functions on the same coordinate grid. Use 1 unit on the horizontal axis to represent 5 days for the t interval from 0 to 20, and 1 unit on the vertical axis to represent 1 inch for the h interval from 15 to 25.

c) Use a verbal description to compare the two functions.

Selected Answers

CHAPTER 1

Lesson 1.1, Guided Practice (pp. 6–11)

1. Base = 2; Exponent = 3 **2.** Base = -5; Exponent = 4
3. Correct **4.** Incorrect; The base is 5, not 2, and the exponent is 2, not 5. So, $5 \cdot 5 = 5^2$. **5.** 2^6; 2; 6
6. $(-4)^3$; -4; 3 **7.** $\left(\frac{2}{3}y\right)^4$; $\frac{2}{3}y$; 4 **8.** 3; 3; 3; 3; 3; 81
9. -5; -5; -5; three; -125 **10.** $\frac{3}{4}, \frac{3}{4}, \frac{3}{4}, \frac{3}{4}, \frac{27}{64}$
11. 5; 125; 5;

5; 5; 25; 5; 5; 5; 5; 5; 5^4

5	625
5	125
5	25
5	5
	1

12. 5; 126; 0; 5; 2; 63; even; 5; 2; 7; 9; 63; 7; 5; 2; 7; 3; 3; 9; 3; 2; 3^2; 5; 7

5	630
2	126
7	63
3	9
3	3
	1

13. 3; 3; 3; 3; 3; 3^5; 3^5 or 243 **14.** 65; 25; 40; 2,000; 1; 0.06; 40; 2,000; 40; 0.06; $2,000(1.06)^{40}$; 20,571.44, 20,571.44

Lesson 1.1, Practice (p. 12)

1. 10; 5 **3.** 0.2; 4 **5.** 1; 9 **7.** Incorrect; For the exponential notation, 24^3, the base is 24 and the exponent is 3. So, $24^3 = 24 \cdot 24 \cdot 24$ **9.** $\left(\frac{1}{3}\right)^2$ **11.** $(-2)^3$ **13.** a^3
15. $2 \cdot 2 \cdot 2$; 8 **17.** $10 \cdot 10 \cdot 10 \cdot 10$; 10,000
19. 5^3 **21.** $3^6 \cdot 5^3$ **23.** -3^4; -4^3; $(-3)^4$ **25.** \$2,330.48

Lesson 1.2, Guided Practice (pp. 14–23)

1. 6^{4+3}; product; 6^7 **2.** $(-5)^{1+5}$; product; $(-5)^6$; 5^6
3. $\left(\frac{1}{5}\right)^{3+4}$; product; $\left(\frac{1}{5}\right)^7$ **4.** p^{3+6}; product; p^9
5. c^6 **6.** $(3s)^6$ **7.** p; q^3; p^5; q^2; Rewrite; p; p^5; q^3; q^2; same; p^{1+5}; q^{3+2}; Add; p^6q^5 **8.** 4; s^4; t^3; 5; s^4; t^6; Rewrite; 4; 5; s^4; s^4; t^3; t^6; numbers; same; 20; s^{4+4}; t^{3+6}; Add; $20s^8t^9$ **9.** 10^{8-5}; quotient; 10^3

10. 2.7^{9-6}; quotient; 2.7^3 **11.** $\left(\frac{5}{8}\right)^{6-1}$; quotient; $\left(\frac{5}{8}\right)^5$
12. q^{7-2}; q^5 **13.** p^2 **14.** $\frac{r^8 s^6}{r^5 s^4}$; fraction; $\frac{r^8}{r^5}$; $\frac{s^6}{s^4}$; product; r^3; s^2; quotient; $r^3 s^2$ **15.** $\frac{63 x^9 y^7}{9 x^3 y^4}$; fraction; $\frac{63}{9}$; $\frac{x^9}{x^3}$; $\frac{y^7}{y^4}$; product; 7; x^6; y^3; quotient; $7 x^6 y^3$ **16.** $\frac{6^{7+3+2}}{6^{1+4+5}}$; product; $\frac{6^{12}}{6^{10}}$; 6^{12-10}; quotient; 6^2 **17.** $\frac{7.5^{5+3+1}}{7.5^{2+1+4}}$; product; $\frac{7.5^9}{7.5^7}$; 7.5^{9-7}; quotient; 7.5^2 **18.** $\frac{4 \cdot 9 \cdot a^3 \cdot a^4 \cdot b^5}{2 \cdot 6 \cdot a^2 \cdot a^2 \cdot b^2}$; $\frac{36 \cdot a^{3+4} \cdot b^5}{12 \cdot a^{2+2} \cdot b^2}$; product; $\frac{3 \cdot a^7 \cdot b^5}{a^4 \cdot b^2}$; $3 \cdot a^{7-4} \cdot b^{5-2}$; quotient; $3 a^3 b^3$ **19.** $\frac{10^{10}}{10^8}$; 10^{10-8}; 10^2; 10^2 or 100

Lesson 1.2, Practice (p. 24)

1. 2^8 **3.** 10^9 **5.** p^9 **7.** $x^5 y^5$ **9.** $7.5 x^5 y^{10}$ **11.** 2^5
13. $7 y^3 z^5$ **15.** $16 a^5 b^3$ **17.** $\left(\frac{4}{9}\right)^5$ **19.** b^2
21. $9 b c^5$ **23.** $6 x^3$ units^3; $48 x^3$ units^3; 2^3 or 8

Lesson 1.3, Guided Practice (pp. 28–30)

1. $5^{3 \cdot 4}$; power; 5^{12} **2.** $2.3^{4 \cdot 2}$; power; 2.3^8 **3.** $(3p)^{20}$
4. y^{28} **5.** $[(-3)^{1+6}]^2$; product; $[(-3)^7]^2$; $(-3)^{7 \cdot 2}$; power; $(-3)^{14}$; 3^{14} **6.** $(p^{4+2})^5$; product; $(p^6)^5$; $p^{6 \cdot 5}$; power; p^{30}
7. $(6^{3+3})^7$; 6^{10}; product; $(6^6)^7$; 6^{10}; $(6^{6 \cdot 7})$; 6^{10}; power; 6^{42}; 6^{10}; 6^{42-10}; quotient; 6^{32} **8.** $\frac{(x^{8+4})^2}{x^{3 \cdot 6}}$; product; power; $\frac{(x^{12})^2}{x^{18}}$; power; $\frac{x^{12 \cdot 2}}{x^{18}}$; $\frac{x^{24}}{x^{18}}$; x^{24-18}; quotient; x^6

Lesson 1.3, Practice (p. 31)

1. 2^{12} **3.** 10^{20} **5.** 25^9 **7.** $\left(\frac{1}{8}\right)^{18}$ **9.** $(2y)^{24}$ **11.** 6^{12}
13. Michael is wrong; $(a^3)^2 \overset{?}{=} a^5$; $a^{3 \cdot 2} \overset{?}{=} a^5$; $a^6 \neq a^5$ **15.** p^{36}
17. $\left(\frac{4}{9}\right)^{10}$ **19.** 7^{12} **21.** t^{28} **23.** 3^{14} **25.** h^5
27. $\frac{c^{38}}{6}$ **29.** $\frac{x}{2^5}$

Lesson 1.4, Guided Practice (pp. 33–38)

1. $(6 \cdot 7)^3$; product; 42^3 **2.** $\left[\left(-\frac{5}{6}\right) \cdot \left(-\frac{1}{4}\right)\right]^4$; product; $\left(\frac{5}{24}\right)^4$
3. $[(1.8) \cdot (0.75)]^2$; product; $(1.35)^2$ **4.** $(p \cdot q)^6$; product; $(pq)^6$
5. $(3a \cdot 4b)^4$; product; $(12ab)^4$ **6.** $-\left(\frac{y}{4}\right)^3$ **7.** $\left(\frac{2}{4}\right)^5$; $\left(\frac{1}{2}\right)^5$
8. $\left(\frac{-9}{-3}\right)^3$; 3^3 **9.** $\left(\frac{x}{y}\right)^4$; quotient **10.** $\left(\frac{8p}{3q}\right)^5$

11. $\dfrac{6^{4+3}}{3^{2+5}}$; product; $\dfrac{6^7}{3^7}$; $\left(\dfrac{6}{3}\right)^7$; quotient; 2^7 **12.** $\dfrac{4^{6+2}\cdot 3^8}{12^5}$;

$\dfrac{4^8\cdot 3^8}{12^5}$; $\dfrac{(4\cdot 3)^8}{12^5}$; $\dfrac{12^8}{12^5}$; 12^{8-5}; 12^3 **13.** $\dfrac{9^{4\cdot 2}\cdot 2^8}{3^8}$; $\dfrac{9^8\cdot 2^8}{3^8}$; $\dfrac{(9\cdot 2)^8}{3^8}$; $\dfrac{18^8}{3^8}$;

$\left(\dfrac{18}{3}\right)^8$; 6^8 **14.** 6^5 **15.** 35^6

Lesson 1.4, Practice (p. 39)

1. 30^4 **3.** 20^5 **5.** $(6xy)^5$ **7.** $\left(\dfrac{2}{15}\right)^4$ **9.** 2^6 **11.** $\left(\dfrac{3}{5}\right)^2$

13. $\left(\dfrac{3x}{y}\right)^9$ **15.** $\left(\dfrac{s}{r}\right)^5$ **17.** h^8k^{20} **19.** 3^9 **21.** 3^8 **23.** 6^7

25. Charles is wrong; $a^3\cdot b^3 \stackrel{?}{=} ab^6$; $(ab)^3 \neq ab^6$

Lesson 1.5, Guided Practice (pp. 42–45)

1. 1; 0.4^2; zero; $\dfrac{1}{0.4^2}$; 6.25 **2.** $\dfrac{3^{1+9}}{3^{10}}$; product; $\dfrac{3^{10}}{3^{10}}$; 3^{10-10};

quotient; 3^0; 1 **3.** t^2 **4.** $(2.5)^{-7-(-4)}$; quotient; $(2.5)^{-3}$;

$\dfrac{1}{2.5^3}$; positive; 0.064 **5.** $(-6)^{3-4}$; quotient; $(-6)^{-1}$; $\dfrac{1}{-6}$;

positive; $-\dfrac{1}{6}$ **6.** $\dfrac{14a^{-5}}{7a\cdot 2a^{-4}}$; fraction; $\dfrac{14}{7\cdot 2}\cdot\dfrac{a^{-5}}{a\cdot a^{-4}}$; $\dfrac{14}{14}\cdot\dfrac{a^{-5}}{a^{1+(-4)}}$;

product; $1\cdot a^{-5-(-3)}$; a^{-2}; $\dfrac{1}{a^2}$; positive

Lesson 1.5, Practice (p. 46)

1. 512 **3.** $\dfrac{1}{81}$ **5.** 281 **7.** 25 **9.** 7^{-1} **11.** $\left(\dfrac{3}{4}\right)^{-1}$

13. x^{-5} **15.** $\dfrac{1}{1.8^2}$ **17.** $\dfrac{1}{3^6}$ **19.** $\dfrac{2k^2}{3}$ **21.** $\dfrac{64}{49}$

23. 100 **25.** $-\dfrac{7}{m^3}$

Lesson 1.6, Guided Practice (pp. 48–52)

1. 13; 13; 13; 13; −13; −13; −13; −13 **2.** $\sqrt[3]{\left(\dfrac{1}{9}\right)^3}$; $\dfrac{1}{9}$; $\dfrac{1}{9}$; $\dfrac{1}{9}$;

$\dfrac{1}{9}$; $\dfrac{1}{9}$ **3.** 1.5^2; $(-1.5)^2$; 1.5; 1.5; −1.5; −1.5; 1.5; −1.5;

positive; negative square **4.** $\left(\dfrac{1}{2}\right)^3$; $\sqrt[3]{x^3}$; $\sqrt[3]{\left(\dfrac{1}{2}\right)^3}$; cube; $\dfrac{1}{2}$; cube

5. 98.01; $\sqrt{x^2}$; $\sqrt{98.01}$; square; 9.9; 9.9 **6.** $1,774\dfrac{2}{3}\pi$; $\dfrac{3}{4}$; $\dfrac{4}{3}\pi r^3$;

$\dfrac{3}{4}$; $1,774\dfrac{2}{3}\pi$; $\dfrac{3}{4}$; πr^3; $1,331\pi$; $\dfrac{\pi r^3}{\pi}$; $\dfrac{1,331\pi}{\pi}$; π; r^3; 1,331; $\sqrt[3]{r^3}$; $\sqrt[3]{1,331}$;

cube; r; $\sqrt[3]{1,331}$; 11; 11 **7.** 562.5π; $\dfrac{3}{4}$; $\dfrac{4}{3}\pi r^3$; $\dfrac{3}{4}$; 562.5π; $\dfrac{3}{4}$;

πr^3; 421.875π; $\dfrac{\pi r^3}{\pi}$; $\dfrac{421.875\pi}{\pi}$; π; r^3; 421.875; $\sqrt[3]{r^3}$; $\sqrt[3]{421.875}$;

cube; r; $\sqrt[3]{421.875}$; 7.5; 7.5; 15; 15

Lesson 1.6, Practice (p. 53)

1. 5 and −5 **3.** 8.9 and −8.9 **5.** 8 **7.** 10.0 **9.** 6.8

or −6.8 **11.** 14 or −14 **13.** 4.2 **15.** 12 **17.** 16.8 ft

19. 4%

Lesson 1.6, Brain@Work (p. 54)

1. 25,600 **2.** $x = 2$ or -2; $y =$ Any nonzero number

3. $\dfrac{3^{8-7}\cdot(1+2)^{9-6}}{\sqrt{4+5}} = 3^3$ **4.** 1.5 in.

Chapter Review/Test (pp. 56–57)

1. $-\dfrac{1}{5}$; -3 **3.** Correct **5.** 2^4 **7.** $\left(\dfrac{1}{2}\right)^3$ **9.** $\left(\dfrac{3}{4}k\right)^4$

11. $2^2\cdot 3^3\cdot 5\cdot 7$ **13.** 36 **15.** 100,000 **17.** $-\dfrac{1}{3}$

19. $20m^8n^6$ **21.** $\dfrac{1}{h^6}$ **23.** $\dfrac{5q^5}{9p^2}$ **25.** $\dfrac{4d}{c^4}$

27. 324 **29.** $\dfrac{1}{2}$ **31.** 16 or −16 **33.** 3.2 **35.** 58.19

37. 6.5 ft **39.** $3\cdot 4^6$; 12,228

CHAPTER 2

Lesson 2.1, Guided Practice (pp. 62–65)

1. Yes **2.** Yes **3.** No; The coefficient is less than 1.

4. 8.562; 100; 2; 100; 8.562; 10^2 **5.** $6\cdot 10^{-2}$ **6.** 9; 10,000;

90,000; 10,000 **7.** 2.5; $\dfrac{1}{100}$; 0.025; 100 **8.** 10^1; 10^2;

exponents, $6.5\cdot 10^1$; $4.2\cdot 10^2$; $6.5\cdot 10^1$ **9.** exponents;

3.6; 8.4; coefficients; $3.6\cdot 10^{-3}$; $8.4\cdot 10^{-3}$; $3.6\cdot 10^{-3}$

10. 85,800; 85,800; 75,126; musician; 7.5126; 10^4;

$7.5126\cdot 10^4$; $8.58\cdot 10^4$; exponents; 8.58; 7.5126; musician

11. The spacing between the bacteria **12.** The stadium

Lesson 2.1, Practice (pp. 66–67)

1. Incorrect; Coefficient $\not< 10$ **3.** Incorrect; Coefficient $\not\geq 1$

5. $5.33\cdot 10^5$ **7.** $3.4\cdot 10^{-3}$ **9.** 7,360 **11.** 0.0527

13. $5.9\cdot 10^3$ **15.** $3.1\cdot 10^{-5}$ **17.** Brazil: $1.9\cdot 10^8$;

Singapore: $5.1\cdot 10^6$; Monaco: $3.5\cdot 10^4$; Fiji: $8.61\cdot 10^5$

19a. Caterpillar: $7.6\cdot 10^1$ mm; Mantis: $1.5\cdot 10^2$ mm;

19b. Caterpillar: $7.6\cdot 10^0$ cm; Mantis: $1.5\cdot 10^1$ cm;

Converting one unit into the other allows you to compare like quantities. **21a.** If the positive number in standard form is greater than 1, the exponent is positive when the number is expressed in scientific notation. Conversely, if the positive number in standard form is less than 1, the exponent is negative. **21b.** When the sign of the exponent is positive, the decimal point moves to the right when the number is expressed in scientific notation. Conversely, when the sign of the exponent is negative, the decimal point moves to the left.

Lesson 2.2, Guided Practice (pp. 70–78)

1a. 5.9; 8; 10^5; 10^5; 13.9; 10^5; Add; 1.39; 10^1; 10^5; 13.9; 1.39; 10^{1+5}; 1.39; 10^6; $1.39 \cdot 10^6$ **1b.** 8; 10^5; 5.9; 10^5; 8; 5.9; 10^5; 10^5; 2.1; 10^5; Subtract; $2.1 \cdot 10^5$ **2a.** 1.7; 1.6; 10^{-2}; 10^{-2}; 3.3; 10^{-2}; Add; $3.3 \cdot 10^{-2}$ **2b.** 1.7; 10^{-2}; 1.6; 10^{-2}; 1.7; 1.6; 10^{-2}; 10^{-2}; 0.1; 10^{-2}; Subtract; 1; 10^{-1}; 10^{-2}; 0.1; 1; $10^{-1+(-2)}$; 1; 10^{-3}; $1 \cdot 10^{-3}$ **3a.** 9; 10^6; 13.7; 10^6; 1.37; 10^7; 13.7; 10^6; 9; 13.7; 10^6; 10^6; 22.7; 10^6; Add; 2.27; 10^1; 10^6; 22.7; 2.27; 10^{1+6}; 2.27; 10^7; $2.27 \cdot 10^7$ **3b.** 1.37; 10^7; 9; 10^6; 13.7; 10^6; 9; 10^6; 1.37; 10^7; 13.7; 10^6; 13.7; 9; 10^6; 10^6; 4.7; 10^6; Subtract; $4.7 \cdot 10^6$ **4a.** $2.6 \cdot 10^{-4}$ m
4b. $2.48 \cdot 10^{-4}$ m   **5.** 4,802; 4.802; 10^9; Pluto; Uranus; 4.802; 10^9; 2.992; 10^9; 4.802; 2.992; 10^9; 10^9; 1.81; 10^9; Subtract; Pluto; $1.81 \cdot 10^9$

Lesson 2.2, Practice (pp. 79–80)

1. $1.1 \cdot 10^{-1}$ **3.** $5.6 \cdot 10^4$ **5a.** $2.0 \cdot 10^5$ Cal
5b. $2.5 \cdot 10^4$ Cal   **7.** $1.4 \cdot 10^5$ Cal   **9a.** 15.5 μm
9b. 13.5 μm   **11.** $1.3717 \cdot 10^9$ km   **13.** Greater; $10^9 > 10^8$ **15.** First rewrite the population in scientific notation: $1.1 \cdot 10^8$; $9.7 \cdot 10^6$; $4.6 \cdot 10^6$; $3.1 \cdot 10^8$. Next rewrite numbers to have an exponent of 10^8: $0.097 \cdot 10^8$; $0.046 \cdot 10^8$. Then factor 10^8 from each term: $(1.1 + 0.097 + 0.046 + 3.1) \cdot 10^8$. Finally, add within parentheses: $4.343 \cdot 10^8$.

Lesson 2.3, Guided Practice (pp. 82–84)

1. 1.6; 10^2; 1.5; 10^2; 1.6; 1.5; 10^2; 10^2; 2.4; 10^2; 10^2; Multiply; 2.4; 10^{2+2}; 2.4; 10^4; $2.4 \cdot 10^4$ **2.** 1.02; 10^3; 8.02; 10^2; 1.02; 8.02; 10^3; 10^2; 8.1804; 10^3; 10^2; Multiply; 8.1804; 10^{3+2}; 8.1804; 10^5; $8.1804 \cdot 10^5$ **3.** $\frac{5.6 \cdot 10^6}{3.7 \cdot 10^6}$; $\frac{5.6}{3.7}$; $\frac{10^6}{10^6}$; Divide; divide; 1.5; 10^{6-6}; 1.5; 10^0; 1.5; 1.5   **4.** $\frac{1.5 \cdot 10^6}{6.5 \cdot 10^5}$; $\frac{1.5}{6.5}$; $\frac{10^6}{10^5}$; Divide; divide; 0.23; 10^{6-5}; 0.23; 10^1; 2.3; 10^{-1}; 10^1; 0.23; 2.3; 10^{-1+1}; 2.3; 10^0; 2.3; 2.3

Lesson 2.3, Practice (pp. 85–86)

1. $4.0 \cdot 10^1$ **3.** $8.0 \cdot 10^{-13}$ **5.** 5.9   **7.** 1.2   **9a.** 3.394 MB and 3,394 kB   **9b.** 1.806 MB and 1,806 kB   **9c.** 0.3
9d. 252.6 MB   **11.** $1.6 \cdot 10^8$ ft^3 **13a.** 5.4 μs
13b. 1,636.4

Lesson 2.3, Brain@Work (p. 86)

1. $3 \cdot 10^3$ **2a.** 6,400   **2b.** 15   **3a.** $8.02 \cdot 10^{-5}$ g
3b. $2.3 \cdot 10^9$ B

Chapter Review/Test (pp. 88–89)

1. Incorrect; Coefficient $\not< 10$ **3.** Correct

---

5. $7.14 \cdot 10^5$ **7.** 346   **9.** $7.8 \cdot 10^{-5}$ **11.** $9.3 \cdot 10^{-12}$
13. $1.9 \cdot 10^5$ **15.** $1.2 \cdot 10^{-2}$ **17.** 2.8 km   **19.** 6.4 GB
21. Patiriella parvivipara   **23.** $2.5 \cdot 10^{-4}$ m; $5 \cdot 10^{-3}$ m
25. $9.4 \cdot 10^7$ T   **27a.** 2.3   **27b.** 2.7   **29.** $3.5 \cdot 10^5$ m^3

Cumulative Review Chapters 1–2 (pp. 90–91)

1. 7^5 **3.** $\left(\frac{3}{5}\right)^{12}$ **5.** 90^3 **7.** 12^6 **9.** $\frac{1}{2^5}$ **11.** 24; −24
13. $\frac{1}{2}$ **15.** $6.4 \cdot 10^{11}$; $5.13 \cdot 10^{11}$; Greater number: $6.4 \cdot 10^{11}$
17. $1.68 \cdot 10^{11}$; $6.4 \cdot 10^{-12}$; Greater number: $1.68 \cdot 10^{11}$
19. 20 μm   **21.** 35 MB   **23.** 28 in.   **25.** $1.34 \cdot 10^{-23}$ g
27. $4,793.12

CHAPTER 3

Lesson 3.1, Guided Practice (pp. 97–101)

1. $2x - (2 + x)$; $2x - 2 - x$; $x - 2$; 3; 3; 3; $x - 2$; -12; $x - 2$; 2; -12; 2; 2; -10 **2.** $x = -26$ **3.** $x = \frac{1}{2}$
4. $\frac{1}{11}$ **5.** $\frac{8}{9}$ **6.** $\frac{1}{15}$ **7.** $\frac{1}{2}x + x + 6\frac{1}{4}$; $\frac{3}{2}x + 6\frac{1}{4}$; $\frac{3}{2}x + 6\frac{1}{4} - 6\frac{1}{4}$; $6\frac{1}{4}$; $6\frac{1}{4}$; $\frac{3}{2}x$; $14\frac{1}{4}$; $\frac{3}{2}x$; $\frac{2}{3}$; $14\frac{1}{4}$; $\frac{2}{3}$; $\frac{2}{3}$; $9\frac{1}{2}$; $9\frac{1}{2}$; 21; 6; 15; $\frac{2}{3}$; 15; 10   **8.** $1.60

Lesson 3.1, Practice (pp. 102–103)

1. $x = 3.5$ **3.** $x = 2$ **5.** $x = 1\frac{1}{6}$ **7.** $x = 2$ **9.** $x = -6$
11. $x = -2$ **13.** $\frac{5}{6}$ **15.** $\frac{1}{9}$ **17.** $\frac{1}{18}$ **19.** 30 dimes; 10 quarters   **21a.** $\frac{d}{5}$; $12d$; $\frac{d}{6}$; $10d$ **21b.** 5 km
23. $0.5x + 3 = 0.8x - 1.5$; 15   **25.** 40   **27.** Possible answer: Georgina can recognize that the sum of the widths is 5 in. less than the sum of the lengths. If she rounds the perimeter to 75 in., then she can add 5 in. to this and say that 4 times the length is about 80 in. So, the length should be about 20 in., and the width is about 17.5 in.

Lesson 3.2, Guided Practice (pp. 105–107)

1. $7x$; −; 21; −42; −42; no; inconsistent
2. Inconsistent; Since $1 \neq 3$, the equation has no solution. So the equation is inconsistent.   **3.** Consistent; Since the equation has one solution $x = 0$, it is consistent.
4. $2x$; −; 2; $2x + 1$; $2x + 1 - 2x$; $2x$; $2x$; 1; 1; 1; 1; infinitely many; identity   **5.** $6x$; +; 30; $6x$; −; 9; $6x + 20$; $6x - 9$; $6x + 20 - 6x$; $6x - 9 - 6x$; $6x$; 20; $\neq$; -9; 20; $\neq$; -9; no; inconsistent equation

Lesson 3.2, Practice (p. 108)

1. Infinite solutions; Since the solving of the linear equation ends with a statement that is always true, the equation is true for any value of x. So, the equation has infinitely many solutions and it is an identity. **3.** One solution, $x = -12$; Since the solving of the linear equation ends with a value for x, the equation has one solution and it is consistent. **5.** No solution; Since the solving of the linear equation ends with a false statement, the equation has no solution and it is inconsistent. **7.** One solution, $x = 1.5$; Since the solving of the linear equation ends with a value for x, the equation has one solution and it is consistent. **9.** No solution; Since the solving of the linear equation ends with a false statement, the equation has no solution and it is inconsistent. **11.** Infinite solutions; Since the solving of the linear equation ends with a statement that is always true, the equation is true for any value of x. So, the equation has infinitely many solutions and it is an identity. **13a.** $(x + 5)$ in.; $(x + 3)$ in. **13b.** No; Since the solving of the linear equation ends with a statement that is always true, the equation is true for any value of x. So, the equation has infinitely many solutions and it is an identity. **15.** Grace; Solving the equation $15 + 2x = 3(x - 4)$ gives $x = 27$. So, the equation has one solution.

Lesson 3.3, Guided Practice (pp. 110–115)

1. 7; $d = 7w$, because they are confusing the equivalence relationship 1 week : 7 days with the equation. **2.** 100; 0.10; 0; 0.1; 0; 0.1; 0.1; 1; 0.2; 0.1; 2; 0.3; 0.1; 3; 0.4; 0.1; 4; $C = 100 + 0.1d$ **3.** -5 **4.** -25 **5.** 6.25

6.

x	1	2	3
y	1.1	1.7	2.3

7.

x	1	2	3
y	4.25	7	9.75

8.

x	−1	0	1
y	−1	2	5

9.

x	5	10	15
y	9	$16\frac{1}{2}$	24

Lesson 3.3, Practice (pp. 116–117)

1. $c = 100m$ or $m = \frac{c}{100}$ **3.** $i = 12f$ or $f = \frac{i}{12}$ **5.** -1 **7.** 1.5 **9.** $-8\frac{1}{6}$ **11.** 3.3

13.

x	1	2	3
y	$1\frac{3}{4}$	$1\frac{1}{2}$	$1\frac{1}{4}$

15.

x	1	2	3
y	$-1\frac{3}{4}$	$-2\frac{1}{4}$	$-2\frac{3}{4}$

17.

x	0	1	2
y	15	20	25

19.

x	−3	−2	−1
y	$-2\frac{2}{3}$	$-1\frac{11}{12}$	$-1\frac{1}{6}$

21. $d = 40.5g$ **23a.** $C = 0.05t + 5$

23b.

t	300	400	500
C	20	25	30

23c. 540 min

Lesson 3.4, Guided Practice (pp. 120–121)

1. $2x - 6$; $2x - 6 + 6$; 6; 6; $2x$; $3y + 5$; $2x$; 2; $(3y + 5)$; 2; 2; $\frac{3y + 5}{2}$; $\frac{3y + 5}{2}$; $\frac{3(3) + 5}{2}$; 7 **2.** $x = \frac{2y - 3}{2}$ or $x = y - \frac{3}{2}$; -14.5 **3a.** $\frac{x + x\sqrt{3} + 2}{3}$; $3 \cdot \frac{x + x\sqrt{3} + 2}{3}$; $x + x\sqrt{3} + 2$; 2; $x + x\sqrt{3} + 2 - 2$; 2; $3M - 2$; $x + x\sqrt{3}$; $3M - 2$; $x(1 + \sqrt{3})$; $\frac{3M - 2}{1 + \sqrt{3}}$; $\frac{x(1 + \sqrt{3})}{1 + \sqrt{3}}$; $1 + \sqrt{3}$; $\frac{3M - 2}{1 + \sqrt{3}}$ **3b.** $\frac{3M - 2}{1 + \sqrt{3}}$

M	0	1	2	3
x	−0.73	0.37	1.46	2.56

Lesson 3.4, Practice (pp. 122–123)

1. $y = 5 - 3x$; 8 **3.** $y = x - \frac{19}{6}$; $-4\frac{1}{6}$ **5.** $y = \frac{48 - 2x}{9}$; $5\frac{5}{9}$ **7.** $x = 2y$; 10 **9.** $x = \frac{2}{3} + y$; $5\frac{2}{3}$ **11.** $x = \frac{5y + 6}{2}$; 15.5 **13a.** $d = \frac{2P}{\pi + 2}$ **13b.** 14 in. **15a.** $y = 180 - 2x$ **15b.** 131 **17a.** $x = 2y + 40$

17b.

x	160	200	240	280	320
y	60	80	100	120	140

19. $w = \dfrac{P}{2} - 5$;

P	12	14	16	18
w	1	2	3	4

Lesson 3.4, Brain@Work (p. 124)

1a. $P = 150s - 500$ **1b.** \$5,500 **1c.** 34

2a. $w = \dfrac{16 - 5y}{5}$ or $w = 3.2 - y$ **2b.** $y = \dfrac{16 - 5w}{5}$ or

$y = 3.2 - w$; 2.2 mi **2c.** If y is less than 1.6, the distance Stefanie walks, w, is greater than the total distance, y. If y is greater than 3.2, w is negative. Both cases are not possible.

3.

n	r
3	$2 = 2 \cdot 1 = 2 \cdot (3 - 2)$
4	$4 = 2 \cdot 2 = 2 \cdot (4 - 2)$
5	$6 = 2 \cdot 3 = 2 \cdot (5 - 2)$
6	$8 = 2 \cdot 4 = 2 \cdot (6 - 2)$

The value of r is always 2 times a number that is 2 less than the value of n. The linear equation is $r = 2(n - 2)$.

Chapter Review/Test (pp. 126–127)

1. 19 **3.** 8 **5.** $\dfrac{2}{9}$ **7.** $\dfrac{4}{15}$ **9.** No solution

11. One solution, $x = -6$ **13.** 9 **15.** 10 **17.** 16

19. $x = \dfrac{5}{2}y$; -5 **21.** $x = \dfrac{12 - 5y}{2}$; 11 **23.** $x = 12 - 0.2y$;

12.4 **25.** 25 in. **27a.** $4 \cdot \dfrac{5}{4}p + 5p = 10p$

27b. Identity; Since $0 = 0$ is always true, the linear equation is true for any value of p. So, this equation has infinitely many solutions, and it is an identity.

29a. $M = 25 + 0.04t$ **29b.** $t = 25(M - 25)$ **29c.** 10 h

CHAPTER 4

Lesson 4.1, Guided Practice (pp. 134–144)

1. $\dfrac{100}{1.5}$; $66\dfrac{2}{3}$; $\dfrac{100}{2}$; 50; $66\dfrac{2}{3}$; $66\dfrac{2}{3}$; 50; 50; trucks; cars **2.** -2;

4; 2; -2; $\dfrac{-2 - 4}{2 - (-2)}$; $\dfrac{-6}{4}$; $-\dfrac{3}{2}$; $-\dfrac{3}{2}$ **3.** -2; -1; 4; 3; $\dfrac{3 - (-1)}{4 - (-2)}$;

$\dfrac{4}{6}$; $\dfrac{2}{3}$; $\dfrac{2}{3}$ **4a.** 45 gal/h; The rate at which Pool A is being

filled. **4b.** -37.5 gal/h; The rate at which Pool B is being

drained. **5.** 3; 4; 3; 0; $\dfrac{0 - 4}{3 - 3}$; $\dfrac{-4}{0}$; undefined; undefined

6. $\dfrac{0 - 4}{-2 - 0}$; $\dfrac{-4}{-2}$; 2; $\dfrac{4 - 0}{0 - (-2)}$; $\dfrac{4}{2}$; 2; 2 **7.** $\dfrac{8 - 2}{-5 - (-2)}$; $\dfrac{6}{-3}$; -2;

$\dfrac{2 - 8}{-2 - (-5)}$; $\dfrac{-6}{3}$; -2; -2

Lesson 4.1, Practice (pp. 145–146)

1. $\dfrac{5}{3}$ **3.** 0 **5.** Jason compared the two lines visually. Because the two graphs have different scales for the vertical axes, the slopes cannot be accurately compared by their steepness. **7.** 0 **9.** -4 **11.** The two points have the same x-coordinates but different y-coordinates. A vertical line graph is drawn. Because Slope $= \dfrac{\text{Rise}}{\text{Run}}$ and the run is 0, the slope is undefined. Any number divided by zero is undefined. **13a.** (0, 32); (100, 212)

13b. $\dfrac{9}{5}$ **13c.** By 9°F; The slope of the line is $\dfrac{9}{5}$, so a horizontal change of 5 corresponds to a vertical change of 9.

Lesson 4.2, Guided Practice (p. 151)

1. -4; -2; 6; 3; $\dfrac{3 - (-2)}{6 - (-4)}$ or $\dfrac{-2 - 3}{-4 - 6}$; $\dfrac{5}{10}$ or $\dfrac{-5}{-10}$; $\dfrac{1}{2}$; 0; 0; 0; $y = \dfrac{1}{2}x$

2. -4; 9; 1; -6; $\dfrac{-6 - 9}{1 - (-4)}$ or $\dfrac{9 - (-6)}{-4 - 1}$; $\dfrac{-15}{5}$ or $\dfrac{15}{-5}$; -3; 0;

-3; -3; $y = -3x - 3$ **3.** $y = -2$ **4.** $x = 2$

Lesson 4.2, Practice (pp. 152–153)

1. $b = 0$; $m = 1$ **3.** $b = 3$; $m = -\dfrac{9}{8}$ **5.** $y = \dfrac{3}{4}x$

7. $y = -\dfrac{5}{8}x - 2$

9.

$x = -4$

11. Possible equations: Line A: $y = -3x$; Line B: $y = 5x + 2$; Line C: $y = -2x - 7$. For line A, the value of m in the equation $y = mx + b$ is negative and the value of b is 0. For line B, both m and b have positive values. For line C, both m and b have negative values.

Lesson 4.3, Guided Practice (pp. 155–163)

1. $5x$; $5x$; $4y$; $8 - 5x$; $\dfrac{4y}{4}$; $\dfrac{8 - 5x}{4}$; 4; $-\dfrac{5}{4}x + 2$; $-\dfrac{5}{4}x + 2$; $-\dfrac{5}{4}$; 2

2. $3y$; $3y$; $2x$; $7 + 3y$; $2x - 7$; $7 + 3y - 7$; 7; $2x - 7$; $3y$;

$\dfrac{2x - 7}{3}$; $\dfrac{3y}{3}$; 3; $\dfrac{2}{3}x - \dfrac{7}{3}$; $\dfrac{2}{3}x - \dfrac{7}{3}$; $-\dfrac{7}{3}$ **3.** $m = \dfrac{1}{5}$; $b = 3$

4. $m = \dfrac{3}{2}$; $b = -2$ **5.** $m = -\dfrac{5}{6}$; $b = 4$ **6.** $m = -\dfrac{4}{3}$; $b = 1$

7. $-\frac{2}{3}x + 4$; m **8.** $y = 4x - 7$ **9.** 6; 6; 3y; 10x − 6;

$\frac{10x - 6}{3}$; 3; $\frac{10}{3}x - 2$; $\frac{10}{3}$; −2; $\frac{10}{3}$; 2; $\frac{10}{3}x + 2$; $y = \frac{10}{3}x + 2$

10. $y = -3x - 10$ **11.** $y = \frac{1}{3}x + 1$ **12.** $y = 2x + 3$

13. −3x + 5; −3; −3; −3; 1; −3(−2) + b; 1; 6 + b; 1 − 6;
6 + b − 6; 6; −5; b; −5; $y = -3x - 5$ **14.** $y = x - 3$

Lesson 4.3, Practice (p. 164)

1. −5; 7   **3.** $-\frac{5}{2}$; 3   **5.** $y = \frac{1}{2}x + 3$ **7.** $y = \frac{3}{4}x + 2$

9. No. The slope of the equation $y = -3x + 7$ is −3 and the slope of the equation $y = 3x - 7$ is 3. So, the graphs of the equations are not parallel lines.   **11.** $y = -\frac{1}{2}x - 4$

13. $y = \frac{5}{6}x + 2$ **15.** $y = 3x + 11$

Lesson 4.4, Guided Practice (pp. 166–169)

1.

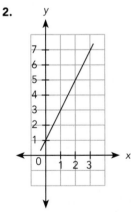

2.

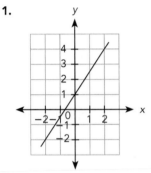

3.

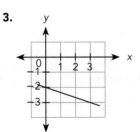

4.

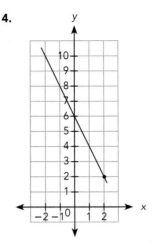

5.

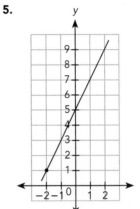

Lesson 4.4, Practice (p. 170)

1.

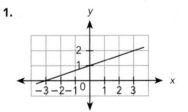

3.

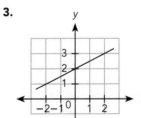

5.

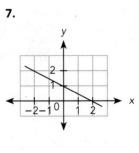

7.

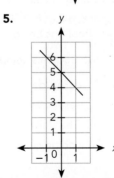

9.

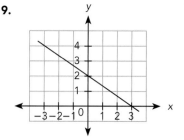

First select a value of the x-coordinate on the x-axis. Then trace it along the vertical grid lines until the grid line intersects with the graph. Then trace horizontally from the graph to the y-axis to obtain the corresponding y-coordinate. This pair of x- and y-coordinates is one solution to the equation.

11.   **13.**

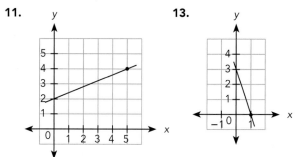

15. Emily made three mistakes. She labeled the coordinates (6, 3) incorrectly, drew the slope of the line incorrectly, and mistook the value for the slope as the y-intercept.

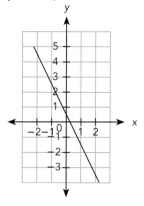

Lesson 4.5, Guided Practice (pp. 174–179)

1. 8; the rental cost of the baby seat; 0; 8; 8; 64; 0; 8; 8; 64; $\dfrac{64 - 8}{8 - 0}$; $\dfrac{56}{8}$; 7; 7; the rental cost of the bike per hour

2a. Zack: $300; Joy: $600   **2b.** Zack   **2c.** Zack: 7.5%; Joy: 5%   **3a.** 240; This is the initial distance George is from his house.   **3b.** −60; The slope represents the rate at which George drives home, 60 mi/h. The slope is negative, because the initial distance from home is decreasing over time.

3c. George; Because 60 > 50, George's distance from home is decreasing more quickly. So, he is driving faster.

Lesson 4.5, Practice (pp. 180–181)

1a. 10; The fixed amount payable for making calls is $0.08 per minute.   **1b.** 0.08; The charge   **3.** Randy's car: 3 gal; Raymond's car: 5 gal; Raymond's car

5a.

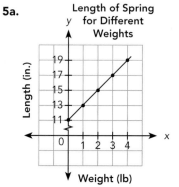

5b. 11; It is the original length of the spring.   **5c.** 2; The slope represents the increase in the spring length for an increase of 1 lb of weight.   **5d.** $y = 2x + 11$

Lesson 4.5, Brain@Work (p. 182)

1a.

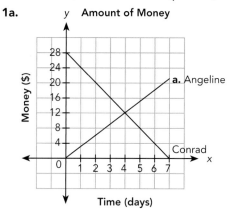

1b. −4; Conrad spends $4 per day

1c. Conrad: $y = 28 - 4x$; Angeline: $y = 3x$

2a.

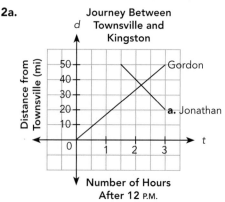

2b. Slope $= \frac{50}{3}$; The slope represents that Gordon biked at a rate of $\frac{50}{3}$ mi/h.   **2c.** Gordon: $d = \frac{50}{3}t$;

Jonathan: $d = -20t + 80$

Chapter Review/Test (pp. 184–185)

1. $\frac{5}{12}$; $y = \frac{5}{12}x$ **3.** 0; $y = 3$ **5.** $\frac{1}{2}$; -3 **7.** $y = -4x - \frac{1}{3}$

9. $y = \frac{3}{5}x + 2$ **11.** $y = \frac{1}{2}x - 2$ **13.** $y = x$

15.

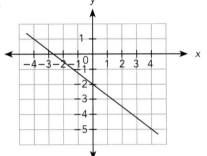

17a. Company A: $400; Company B
17b. Company B

Cumulative Review Chapters 3–4
(pp. 186–189)

1. $x = 10$ **3.** $x = 5$ **5.** $\frac{5}{9}$ **7.** $\frac{5}{18}$ **9.** Infinite solutions

11. Infinite solutions   **13.** No solution   **15.** 6.5

17. $y = -3x + \frac{1}{2}$; $-11\frac{1}{2}$ **19.** $x = \frac{45 + y}{2}$; $21\frac{1}{2}$ **21.** $m = 2$

23. $m = -1$ **25.** $b = 10$; $m = 8$ **27.** 7; 1   **29.** 2; 3

31. $y = 3x + 2$ **33.** $y = 5x - 2$ **35.** $y = 2x + 4$

37. $y = -\frac{2}{3}x + \frac{13}{3}$

39.

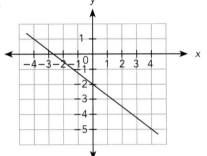

41a. Bobby's savings increased, so he saved money. Chloe's savings decreased, so she withdrew money.
41b. Bobby's changed by $100; Chloe's changed by −$50; Bobby's changed more.   **41c.** After 5 wks, Bobby and Chloe have the same amount of money, which is $75.
43a. $50y + 120y + 30y - 210 = 1,990$ or $200y = 2,200$
43b. $6.70

45a.

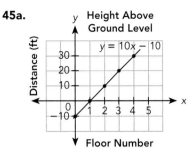

45b. −10; It is the distance of the elevator from ground level, 10 ft below ground level, when it is at the basement level.   **45c.** 10; The slope represents the increase in distance, in ft, of the elevator from ground level for every increase of 1 floor number.   **45d.** $y = 10x - 10$
45e. 160 ft; There is no floor number with distance from ground level of exactly 165 ft.

CHAPTER 5

Lesson 5.1, Guided Practice (pp. 194–195)

1. $3x - y = 1$

x	1	2
y	2	5

$x + y = 3$

x	1	2
y	2	1

1; 2; 1; 2; 1; 2   **2.** $x = 4$, $y = 2$ **3.** $x = 4$, $y = 4$

Lesson 5.1, Practice (p. 196)

1. $x = 1$, $y = 3$ **3.** $x = 2$, $y = 2$ **5.** $x = 2$, $y = 0$
7. $x = 3$, $y = -1$ **9.** $x = 3$, $y = -2$ **11.** $x = 14$, $y = 7$;
Alicia's age: 14 years old; Cousin's age: 7 years old

Lesson 5.2, Guided Practice (pp. 199–208)

1. $2a + 3b - 2a + b$; 12; $4b$; 12; $\frac{4b}{4}$; $\frac{12}{4}$; 4; 3; 3; 3;

$2a - 3 + 3$; $17 + 3$; 3; $2a$; 20; $\frac{2a}{2}$; $\frac{20}{2}$; 2; 10; 10; 3

2. $x = 3$, $y = 4$ **3.** $x = 7$, $y = -1$ **4.** $m = -2$, $n = 3$
5. $x = 4$, $y = -6$ **6.** $x = -2$, $y = -4$ **7.** $2x + 4x - 7$;
5; $6x - 7$; 5; $6x - 7 + 7$; $5 + 7$; 7; $6x$; 12; $6x$; 6; 12; 6; 6; 2;
2; 2; 8; 1; 2; 1   **8.** $5x + y - 5x$; $15 - 5x$; $5x$; y; $15 - 5x$;
$3(15 - 5x)$; $4x + 45 - 15x$; 23; $-11x + 45$; 23;
$-11x + 45 - 45$; $23 - 45$; 45; $-11x$; -22; $-11x$; -11; -22;
-11; -11; 2; 2; $15 - 5(2)$; 5; 2; 5   **9.** $x = 3$, $y = 1$
10. $m = -2$, $n = 3$ **11.** $x = 10$, $y = 3$; Substitution
because y is already expressed in terms of x.
12. $a = -7$, $b = -13$; Elimination to avoid expressions
with fractions in them.

Lesson 5.2, Practice (p. 209)

1. $j = \dfrac{14}{3}$, $k = -\dfrac{10}{3}$ **3.** $m = 10$, $n = 0$ **5.** $s = 3$, $t = 3$

7. $m = \dfrac{1}{3}$, $n = -6$ **9.** $p = -3$, $q = 2$ **11.** $h = 2$, $k = 3$

13. $h = 4$, $k = 2$ **15.** $x = 8$, $y = 4$ **17.** $x = 4$, $y = 0$

19. Elimination; $x = 2$, $y = 4$; Elimination to avoid expressions with fractions in them.   **21.** Elimination; $m = 2$, $n = 3$; Elimination to avoid expressions with fractions in them.   **23.** Elimination; $h = 2$, $k = 4$; Elimination to avoid expressions with fractions in them.
25. Sam should choose the first way. Multiplying by 17 is more difficult and more prone to error than multiplying by 3.

Lesson 5.3, Guided Practice (pp. 212–214)

1. $2b + c$; 800; $b + 2c$; 700; $2b + 2c$; $2b$; 800; $2b$; $2b$; $800 - 2b$; $b + 2(800 - 2b)$; 700; $b + 1,600 - 4b$; 700; $-3b + 1,600 - 1,600$; $700 - 1,600$; 1,600; $-3b$; -900; $-3b$; (-3); -900; (-3); -3; 300; 300; $800 - 2(300)$; 200; 300; 200   **2.** $d - c$; 2; $\dfrac{1}{5}(10c + d) + 1$; $c + d$; $d - c + c$; $2 + c$; $2 + c$; $\dfrac{1}{5}(10c + 2 + c) + 1$; $c + 2 + c$; $\dfrac{1}{5}(11c + 2) + 1 - 1$; $2c + 2 - 1$; $\dfrac{1}{5}(11c + 2)$; $2c + 1$; $\dfrac{1}{5}(11c + 2)$; 5; $2c + 1$; 5; 5; $11c + 2$; 5; $5(2c + 1)$; $11c + 2$; $10c + 5$; $11c + 2 - 10c$; $10c + 5 - 10c$; $c + 2$; 5; $c + 2 - 2$; $5 - 2$; 3; $2 + 3$; 5; 35

3. First integer = 7; Second integer = 20

Lesson 5.3, Practice (pp. 215–217)

1. Male: 20; Female: 16   **3.** Granola bar: $0.60;
Apple: $0.35   **5a.** $a = 4$, $b = 2$ **5b.** 32 in.   **7.** $x = -1$, $y = -5$ **9.** Student's tickets: 25; Adult tickets: 30
11a. $8.70   **11b.** $21.30   **13.** $1,500 and $2,000
15. 30% solution: 7.5 fl oz; 18% solution: 2.5 fl oz

Lesson 5.4, Guided Practice (pp. 221–222)

1. $2x + y = 5$

x	0	1	2
y	5	3	1

$x - y = -2$

x	0	1	2
y	2	3	4

-2; 5; 1; 2; 1; 3; 1; 3

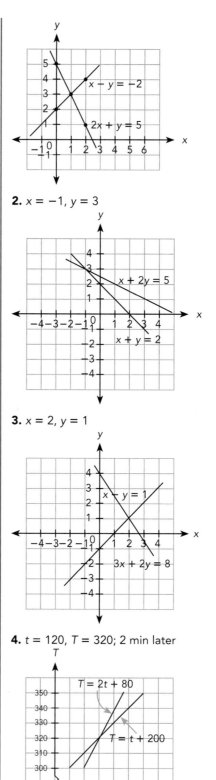

2. $x = -1$, $y = 3$

3. $x = 2$, $y = 1$

4. $t = 120$, $T = 320$; 2 min later

Lesson 5.4, Practice (pp. 223–224)

1a. $x + y = 6$

x	0	1	2
y	6	5	4

$2x + y = 8$

x	0	1	2
y	8	6	4

1b. (2, 4)

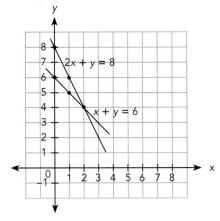

1c. $x = 2$; $y = 4$

3a. (2, 1.5)

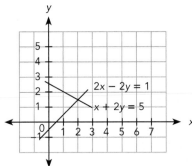

3b. $x = 2$, $y = 1.5$

5. $x = -4$, $y = -2$

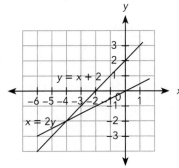

7. $x = 2$, $y = -4$

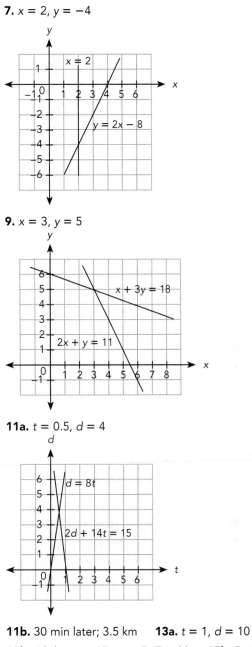

9. $x = 3$, $y = 5$

11a. $t = 0.5$, $d = 4$

11b. 30 min later; 3.5 km   **13a.** $t = 1$, $d = 10$

13b. 1 h later   **15a.** $t = 5$, $T = 80$ **15b.** 5 s later

Lesson 5.5, Guided Practice (pp. 230–233)

1. $11x + y - 11x$; $2 - 11x$; $-11x + 2$; $22x + 2y - 22x$;

$3 - 22x$; $2y$; $-22x + 3$; $\frac{2y}{2}$; $\frac{-22x + 3}{2}$; $-11x + \frac{3}{2}$; -11; 2;

-11; $\frac{3}{2}$; slope; y-intercepts; inconsistent   **2.** Inconsistent;

The coefficients of x and y in Equation 2 are twice the coefficients of x and y in Equation 1. But the constant term in Equation 2 are not twice the constant term in Equation 1.

3. Unique solution; The coefficient of y in Equation 2 is eight times the coefficient of y in Equation 1. But the coefficient of x in Equation 2 is not eight times the coefficient of x in Equation 1.   **4.** Inconsistent; The coefficients of x and y in Equation 2 are three times the coefficients of x and y in Equation 1. But the constant term in Equation 2 is not three times the constant term in Equation 1.   **5.** Inconsistent; The coefficients of x and y in Equation 2 are four times the coefficients of x and y in Equation 1, but the constants are not in this ratio.
6. Unique solution; The coefficient of y in Equation 2 is four times the coefficient of y in Equation 1, but the coefficient of x in Equation 2 is not four times the coefficient of x in Equation 1.   **7.** Dependent; After dividing Equation 1 by 4 and Equation 2 by 3, the equations are $3x + y = 4$. So, Equations 1 and 2 are equivalent.

Lesson 5.5, Practice (p. 234)

1. Inconsistent   **3.** Inconsistent   **5.** Inconsistent;
The coefficients of x and y in Equation 1 are twice the coefficients of x and y in Equation 2. But the constant in Equation 1 is not twice the constant in Equation 2.
7. Inconsistent; The coefficients of x and y in Equation 1 are three times the coefficients of x and y in Equation 2. But the constant in Equation 1 is not three times the constant in Equation 2.   **9.** Dependent; After dividing Equation 2 by 5, the equations are $8x + 7y = 9$. So, Equations 1 and 2 are equivalent.   **11.** Dependent; After dividing Equation 1 by 3 and Equation 2 by 2, the equations are $3x + 7y = 9$. So, Equations 1 and 2 are equivalent.   **13a.** $9x + 6y = 8.5$; $3x + 2y = 7.4$ **13b.** Inconsistent; The coefficients of x and y in Equation 1 are three times the coefficients of x and y in Equation 2. But the constant in Equation 1 is not three times the constant in Equation 2.
13c. The costs changed.   **15.** No; The system of equations $2x + 3.5y = 1,200$ and $4x + 7y = 2,400$ have an infinite number of solutions because they are equivalent equations.

Lesson 5.5, Brain@Work (p. 235)

1a. $C = 110 + 30x$; $C = 600 - 40x$ **1b.** $x = 7$; $C = 320$; $320   **2.** 6 g/cm^3 **3.** Let each minute of local calls cost x dollars, and each minute of overseas calls be y dollars.

Form an equation for the charges for each month, and express them in the form $y = mx + c$.
January: $60x + 30y = 45$ can be written as $y = -2x + 1.5$;
February: $80x + 20y = 46$ can be written as $y = -4x + 2.3$;
March: $40x + 20y = 34$ can be written as $y = -2x + 1.7$;
Equation 1 and Equation 3 have the same slope but different y-intercepts. They are inconsistent. So, the charges are incorrect.

Chapter Review/Test (pp. 238–239)

1. $x = 2$, $y = 6$ **3.** $a = 4$, $b = 5$ **5.** $x = 2$, $y = 1$
7. $x = 3$, $y = 6$

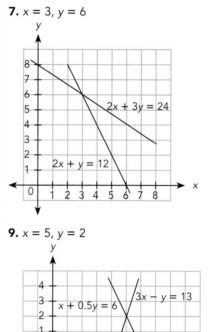

9. $x = 5$, $y = 2$

11. $x = 7$, $y = 5$; Elimination to avoid expressions with fractions in them.   **13.** Dependent; After dividing Equation 2 by 2, the equations are $3x + 2y = 8$. So, Equations 1 and 2 are equivalent.   **15.** Dependent; After dividing Equation 2 by 2, the equations are $\frac{1}{2}x + y = 7$. So, Equations 1 and 2 are equivalent.   **17.** Unique solution; $x = 2$, $y = 5$; The coefficient of x in Equation 2 is twice the coefficient of x in Equation 1. But the coefficient of y in Equation 2 is not twice the coefficient of y in Equation 1.
19. Andy: 40 h; Ben: 48 h   **21.** $x = 4$, $y = 12$ **23.** Bus: 40; Van: 10   **25a.** Tank A: $h = 4t + 3$; Tank B: $h = 4t + 4$

25b.

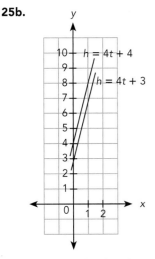

25c. The water level in the two tanks will only be the same when the tanks are full. The graphs of the equations are parallel and do not intersect. So, the equations have no solution and the water level in Tank B will always be higher than the level in Tank A until both tanks are full.

CHAPTER 6

Lesson 6.1, Guided Practice (pp. 245–254)

1. many; one   **2.** many; many   **3.** Height (in.); Weight (lb); 56; 99; one; one   **4.** many; one; is
5. one; many; is not   **6.** one; one; is   **7.** Yes; Because any vertical line intersects the graph at exactly one point, it is a function.   **8.** No; Because there is one vertical line that intersects the graph at two points, it is not a function.   **9.** Yes; Because any vertical line intersects the graph at exactly one point, it is a function.   **10.** No; Because at least one vertical line intersects the graph at more than one point, it is not a function.

Lesson 6.1, Practice (pp. 255–258)

1. Input: Stereo speaker; Output: Prices charged for the same stereo speaker at different stores   **3.** Input: Ginny's friends; Output: After-school activities   **5.** One-to-many relation

7.

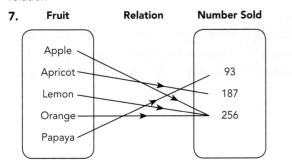

Many-to-one relation

9. True; A function is a type of relation that assigns exactly one output to each input.   **11.** False; Many-to-one and one-to-one relations are functions because there is exactly one output for each input.   **13.** One-to-one relation; Yes; Because each input has exactly one output, it is a function.   **15.** Many-to-one relation; Yes; Because each input has exactly one output, it is a function.   **17.** No; Because a vertical line intersects the graph at more than one point, it is not a function.   **19.** No; Because at least one vertical line intersects the graph at more than one point, it is not a function.   **21.** Yes;

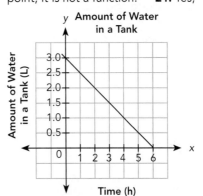

23a.

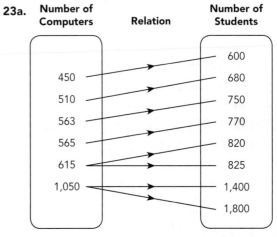

23b. One-to-many relation   **23c.** No; Because two inputs have more than one output each, it is not a function.

25.

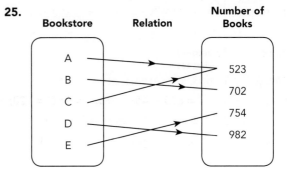

Many-to-one relation; It is a function; Each input has only one output.

27a.

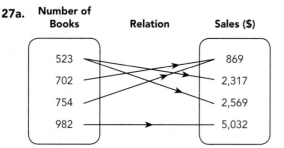

Number of Books — Relation — Sales ($)

No; One input, 523, has more than one output, 2,317 and 2,569.   **27b.** One bookstore could be selling books that are more expensive.

Lesson 6.2, Guided Practice (pp. 262–264)

1a. number of games rented; y; x; y; $6x$

1b.

x	1	2	3
y	6	12	18

1c.

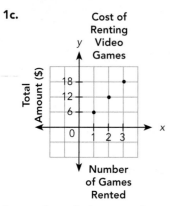

Cost of Renting Video Games

2a. number of minutes; y; 8; x; y; $8x$

2b.

x	1	2	3
y	8	16	24

2c.

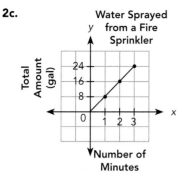

Water Sprayed from a Fire Sprinkler

3a.

Distance Indicated on Jason's Odometer

3b. $y = 30x + 1{,}000$ **3c.** The y-intercept, 1,000, means that the odometer of Jason's car shows 1,000 mi when he starts driving. The slope, 30, gives the rate at which the distance indicated on the odometer is changing. For every gallon of gasoline, the distance indicated on the odometer increases by 30 mi.

Lesson 6.2, Practice (pp. 265–266)

1. The distance Gordon travels equals 80 km/h times the number of hours he takes to travel; $d = 80t$ **3.** In **1.**, all the values for the input and output are meaningful because time and distance are continuous quantities. In **2.**, only whole numbers are meaningful for the input and output. The input values, which are the numbers of additional family members, must be whole numbers. So, the corresponding output values of the function, $y = 10x + 40$, are also whole numbers.

5. $y = 580 - 56x$;

x	1	2	3
y	524	468	412

7. $y = -\dfrac{5}{2}x + 20$

9.

Distance Traveled by a Motorcyclist

$y = -40x + 240$

11a. The amount of money Hillary has on her bus card equals $60 minus $1.50 times the number of times she rides on a bus; $y = 60 - 1.5x$

11b.

Number of Bus Rides (x)	0	1	2	3	4	5	6
Amount of Money on Hillary's Card (y dollars)	60.0	58.5	57.0	55.5	54.0	52.5	51.0

11c.

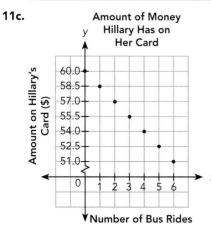

Amount of Money Hillary Has on Her Card

11d. 6

Lesson 6.3, Guided Practice (pp. 269–274)

1. $+4$; $+2$; $+10$; $+5$; $2\frac{1}{2}$; $\frac{10}{4}$; $2\frac{1}{2}$; $\frac{5}{2}$; $2\frac{1}{2}$; constant; linear

2. not constant; nonlinear   **3.** straight line; linear; Answers vary. Sample: 0, 3, 6, 8; Answers vary. Sample: $\frac{8-3}{6-0}$; $\frac{5}{6}$; constant   **4.** curve; nonlinear   **5a.** At the beginning of the trip, the cruise ship has 330,000 gallons of gasoline. So, the least possible input value is 0 and the corresponding output value is 330,000. For every hour of traveling time, the cruise ship consumes 4,000 gallons of gasoline. So, the rate of change of the function is constant. As the total traveling time increases, the amount of gasoline left decreases. So, the function is a linear and decreasing function.

5b.

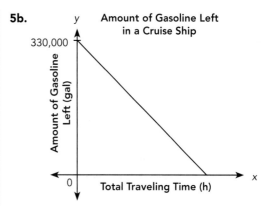

Amount of Gasoline Left in a Cruise Ship

Lesson 6.3, Practice (pp. 276–277)

1. Linear function   **3.** Nonlinear function   **5.** Yes; $\frac{1}{2}$

7. Nonlinear and increasing function   **9.** Nonlinear and decreasing function   **11a.** If the time taken for the machine to pour juice into bottles is 0 min, the amount of juice poured will be 0 L. So, the least possible input value is 0 and the corresponding output value is 0. Because the machine pours juice at 6 L/min, the rate of change of the function is constant. As the time taken for the machine to pour juice into bottles increases, the amount of juice poured also increases. So, the function is a linear and increasing function.

11b.

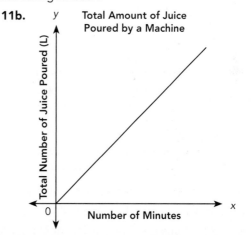

Total Amount of Juice Poured by a Machine

13a. The function has a constant rate of change, 25. So, it is a linear and increasing function. As the number of students increases, the number of teachers also increases.

13b.

Number of Teachers and Students

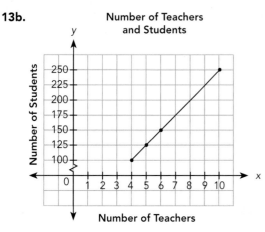

No, because the number of teachers and students must be whole numbers.

Lesson 6.4, Guided Practice (pp. 282–285)

1a. $+10$; $+10$; $+100$; $+100$; 10; $\frac{100}{10}$; 10; $\frac{100}{10}$; 10; $+10$;

$+10$; $+150$; $+150$; 15; $\frac{150}{10}$; 15; $\frac{150}{10}$; 15; linear; increasing

Q; P **1b.** 10; 70; 10; 5; 70; 50; 70; 50; 50; 50; 50; 20;

$10x + 20$; 15; 170; 15; 10; 170; 150; 170; 150; 150; 150;

150; 20; $15x + 20$; 20 **1c.** Q; greater; Q **2a.** $+1$; $+2$;

$+15$; $+30$; 15; $\frac{15}{1}$; 15; $\frac{30}{2}$; 15; $15x + 100$ **2b.** linear;

increasing; 100; A; 15; 20; B; A

Lesson 6.4, Practice (pp. 286–288)

1. Yes **3.** No **5.** No **7.** No **9.** No **11a.** Option A: $y = 1{,}000 + 4x$; Option B: $y = 800 + 6x$

11b. Both functions are linear and increasing functions. Comparing the two equations, because $1{,}000 > 800$, Option A costs more at first. Comparing the rates of change shows that the total fee for Option A increases by \$4 for each ticket sold, and the total fee for Option B increases by \$6 for each ticket sold. So, the total fee the director will pay for Option B will increase more quickly than the total fee for Option A as the number of tickets sold increases. **11c.** Option A; The total fee for Option A is lower than the total fee for Option B when all the tickets are sold.

Lesson 6.4, Brain@Work (p. 289)

1. Package A: $y = 150 + 15x$; Package B: $y = 250 + 14x$; Package C: $y = 300 + 12x$

2.

Museum Admission Fee Packages

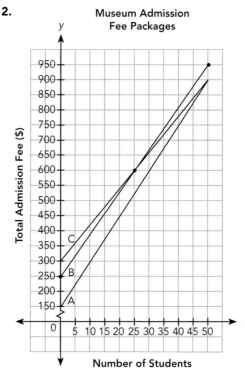

Number of Students

3. Package A; The total admission fee is the least.

4. Package C; The total admission fee is the least.

Chapter Review/Test (pp. 291–293)

1. Input: Radius; Output: Area of circle **3.** Input: Each student's name; Output: Grades for the English test

5. One-to-many relation; No **7.** Yes

9. $y = -4x + 6$

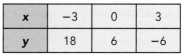

x	−3	0	3
y	18	6	−6

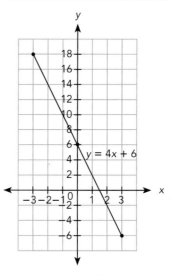

$y = 4x + 6$

11. Nonlinear and increasing function **13a.** $y = 25 + 2x$

13b.

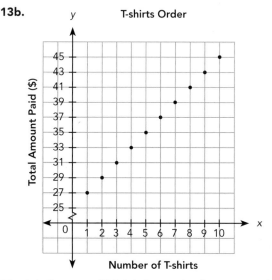

T-shirts Order

Number of T-shirts

13c. It is linear.   **13d.** It is increasing because as the values of x increase, the corresponding values of y also increase.

Cumulative Review Chapters 5–6
(pp. 294–297)

1. $x = 2, y = 5$ **3.** Elimination; $a = 3, b = 4$; Elimination to avoid expressions with fractions in them

5. Substitution; $h = -4, k = 9$; Substitution because you can express k in terms of h conveniently   **7.** $x = 4, y = 5$

$2x - y = 3$

x	−1	0	1
y	−5	−3	−1

$x + y = 9$

x	−1	0	1
y	10	9	8

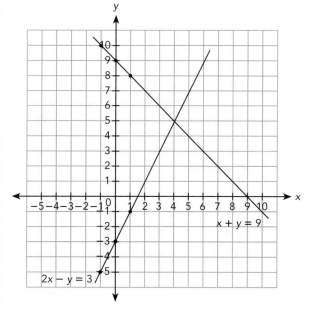

9. Dependent; After multiplying Equation 2 by 4, the equations are $3x + 4y = 12$. So, Equations 1 and 2 are equivalent.   **11.** Dependent; After multiplying Equation 1

by 3, the equations are $9x + 6y = 1$. So, Equations 1 and 2 are equivalent.   **13.** Yes; Because each input has exactly one output, it is a function.   **15.** No; Because at least one vertical line intersects the graph at more than one point, it is not a function.   **17.** $d = 2 + 7t$ **19.** $y = -10x + 40$
21. No; Decreasing   **23.** No; Increasing   **25.** Yes; −3; Decreasing   **27.** 12, 48   **29a.** $y = 50 + 2x$

29b.

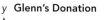

Number of Months (x)	0	1	2	3	4	5	6
Total Amount (y dollars)	50	52	54	56	58	60	62

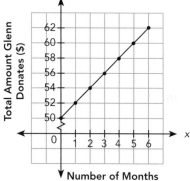

Glenn's Donation

Number of Months

No, only whole numbers are meaningful for the input and output. The input values, which are the number of months, must be whole numbers. Hence, the corresponding output values of the function are also whole numbers.
29c. The y-intercept, 50, means that Glenn donated $50 to the charity at first. The slope, 2, gives the rate that he donates per month. For every month that passes, the total amount he has donated increases by $2.   **31.** 60 students, 10 teachers   **33a.** Tank A: $p = 2t + 3$, Tank B: $p = 2t + 8$

33b.

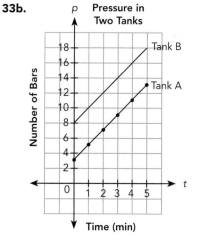

Pressure in Two Tanks

33c. The pressure in both tanks will not be the same; The two lines are parallel.

Glossary

B

base (of an exponent)

In an expression of the form a^n, the base a is used as a factor n times: $a^n = \underbrace{a \cdot a \cdot a \ldots a}_{n \text{ times}}$

Example: In the expression 6^3, 6 is the base.

C

coefficient

A coefficient is a multiplicative factor in scientific notation.

Example: In the scientific notation $5 \cdot 10^{-9}$, 5 is the coefficient.

common term

The same term that appears more than once in a system of equations.

consistent equation

An equation with only one solution.

D

dependent system of equations

A system of equations with an infinite number of solutions.

E

elimination method

A method for solving a system of equations in which equations are added or subtracted to eliminate one variable.

exponent

The number to which a base is raised.

Example: In the expression 5^{10}, 10 is the exponent.

exponential notation

Notation used to write a number as a base raised to an exponent.

Example: 2^3, 3^5, and 6^9 are examples of numbers in exponential notation.

G

graphical method

A method in which equations are graphed to find the point (or points) of intersection.

F

function

A type of relation that assigns exactly one output to each input.

I

identity

An equation that is true for all values of the variable.

inconsistent equation

An equation with no solution.

inconsistent system of equations

A system of equations with no solution.

input

The independent variable of a relation.

L

linear function

A function that can be expressed in the form $y = mx + b$.

linear relationship

A relationship between two quantities in which there is a constant variation between the two quantities.

M

many-to-many

Describes a relation in which one input is mapped onto many outputs and one output is related to many inputs.

many-to-one

Describes a relation in which many inputs are mapped onto one output.

mapping diagram

A diagram that pairs a set of inputs with a set of outputs of a relation.

N

nonlinear function

A function whose points do not lie along a line.

Example:

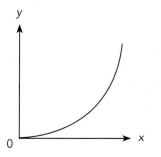

This graph represents a nonlinear function.

O

one-to-many

Describes a relation in which one input is mapped onto many outputs.

one-to-one

Describes a relation in which each input is mapped onto its own, unique output.

output

The dependent variable of a relation.

P

point of intersection

A point where two (or more) graphs meet each other and whose coordinates are the solution to a system of equations.

power

The product of repeated multiplication of the same factor.

Example: 10^2 and a^7 are examples of powers.
The number 10^2 can be read as "10 raised to the second power."

prime factorization

A number written as a product of its prime factors.

Example: $300 = 2^2 \cdot 3 \cdot 5^2$, the prime factorization of 300.

R

rate of change

The ratio of changes in two quantities.

relation

A relation pairs a set of inputs with a set of outputs.

rise

The vertical change from one point to a second point on a coordinate plane.

run

The horizontal change from one point to a second point on a coordinate plane.

S

scientific notation

A way of expressing a large or small number in the form $A \cdot 10^n$, where $1 \leq A < 10$ and n is an integer.

Example: $1.38 \cdot 10^{-2}$ and $5.59 \cdot 10^{12}$ are examples of numbers in scientific notation.

slope

The ratio of the rise, or vertical change, to the run, or horizontal change, between any two points on a nonvertical line on the coordinate plane.

slope-intercept form

A form of a linear equation, $y = mx + b$, where m is the slope and b is the y-intercept of the graph of the equation.

Example: $y = \frac{5}{2}x - 3$ is an example of a linear equation written in slope-intercept form.

standard form (of a linear equation)

A linear equation in the form $ax + by = c$.

Example: $2x + 4y = 3$ is an example of a linear equation written in standard form.

standard form (of numbers)

A way of expressing a number using the ten digits 0 to 9 and place value notation.

Example: -0.005, 9, and 2,158 are numbers in standard form.

substitution method

A method for solving a system of equations in which one variable is expressed in terms of the other to eliminate one variable.

system of linear equations

A set of linear equations that has more than one variable.

U

unique solution

The single set of values that satisfies a system of linear equations.

V

vertical line test

A test to determine whether a graph is a function: If a vertical line intersects a graph at more than one point, then the graph does not represent a function.

X

x-intercept

The x-coordinate of the point where a line intersects the x-axis.

Y

y-intercept

The y-coordinate of the point where a line intersects the y-axis.

Table of Measures, Formulas, and Symbols

METRIC | CUSTOMARY

Length

METRIC	CUSTOMARY
1 kilometer (km) = 1,000 meters (m)	1 mile (mi) = 1,760 yards (yd)
1 meter = 10 decimeters (dm)	1 mile = 5,280 feet (ft)
1 meter = 100 centimeters (cm)	1 yard = 3 feet
1 meter = 1,000 millimeters (mm)	1 yard = 36 inches (in.)
1 centimeter = 10 millimeters	1 foot = 12 inches

Capacity

METRIC	CUSTOMARY
1 liter (L) = 1,000 milliliters (mL)	1 gallon (gal) = 4 quarts (qt)
	1 gallon = 16 cups (c)
	1 gallon = 128 fluid ounces (fl oz)
	1 quart = 2 pints (pt)
	1 quart = 4 cups
	1 pint = 2 cups
	1 cup = 8 fluid ounces

Mass and Weight

METRIC	CUSTOMARY
1 kilogram (kg) = 1,000 grams (g)	1 ton (T) = 2,000 pounds (lb)
1 gram = 1,000 milligrams (mg)	1 pound = 16 ounces (oz)

TIME

1 year (yr) = 365 days	1 week = 7 days
1 year = 12 months (mo)	1 day = 24 hours (h)
1 year = 52 weeks (wk)	1 hour = 60 minutes (min)
leap year = 366 days	1 minute = 60 seconds (s)

CONVERTING MEASUREMENTS

You can use the information below to convert measurements from one unit to another.

To convert from a smaller unit to a larger unit, divide.	To convert from a larger unit to a smaller unit, multiply.
Example: 48 in. = __?__ ft	Example: 0.3 m = __?__ cm

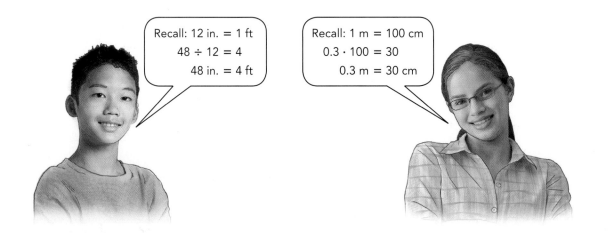

Recall: 12 in. = 1 ft
$48 \div 12 = 4$
48 in. = 4 ft

Recall: 1 m = 100 cm
$0.3 \cdot 100 = 30$
0.3 m = 30 cm

PERIMETER, CIRCUMFERENCE, AND AREA

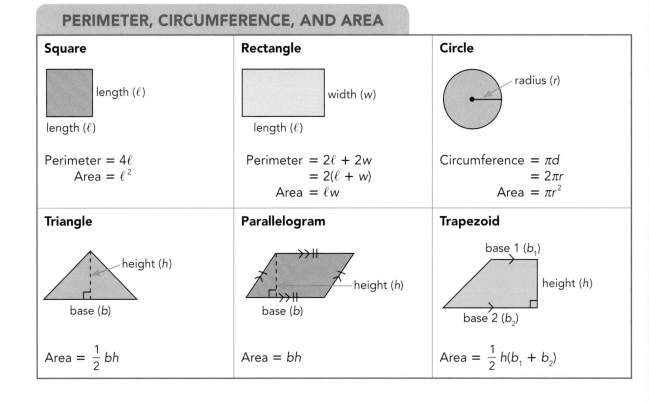

Square

length (ℓ)

length (ℓ)

Perimeter $= 4\ell$
Area $= \ell^2$

Rectangle

width (w)

length (ℓ)

Perimeter $= 2\ell + 2w$
$= 2(\ell + w)$
Area $= \ell w$

Circle

radius (r)

Circumference $= \pi d$
$= 2\pi r$
Area $= \pi r^2$

Triangle

height (h)

base (b)

Area $= \frac{1}{2} bh$

Parallelogram

height (h)

base (b)

Area $= bh$

Trapezoid

base 1 (b_1)

height (h)

base 2 (b_2)

Area $= \frac{1}{2} h(b_1 + b_2)$

SURFACE AREA AND VOLUME

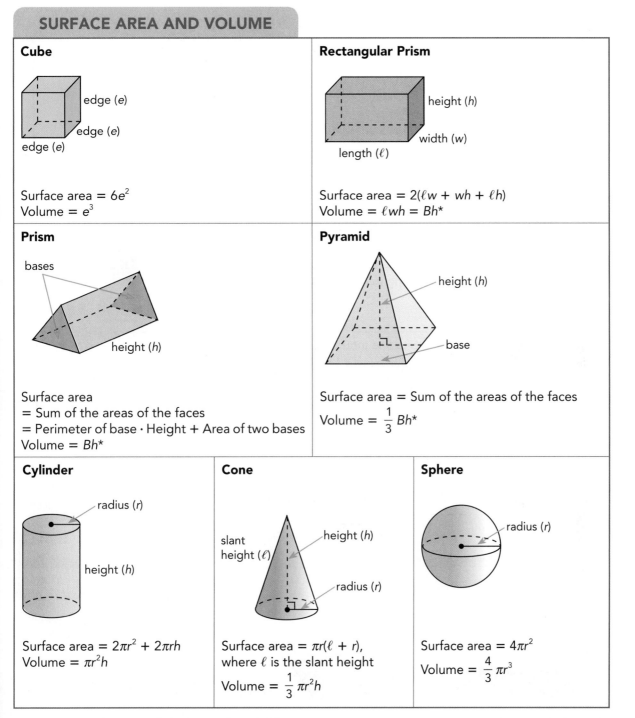

Cube

Surface area = $6e^2$
Volume = e^3

Rectangular Prism

Surface area = $2(\ell w + wh + \ell h)$
Volume = $\ell wh = Bh\star$

Prism

bases

height (h)

Surface area
= Sum of the areas of the faces
= Perimeter of base · Height + Area of two bases
Volume = $Bh\star$

Pyramid

height (h)

base

Surface area = Sum of the areas of the faces
Volume = $\frac{1}{3} Bh\star$

Cylinder

radius (r)

height (h)

Surface area = $2\pi r^2 + 2\pi rh$
Volume = $\pi r^2 h$

Cone

slant height (ℓ)

height (h)

radius (r)

Surface area = $\pi r(\ell + r)$,
where ℓ is the slant height
Volume = $\frac{1}{3} \pi r^2 h$

Sphere

radius (r)

Surface area = $4\pi r^2$
Volume = $\frac{4}{3} \pi r^3$

*B represents the area of the base of a solid figure.

PYTHAGOREAN THEOREM

Right Triangle

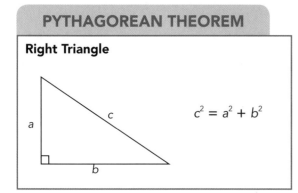

$$c^2 = a^2 + b^2$$

PROBABILITY

Probability of an event A occurring:

$$P(A) = \frac{\text{Number of favorable outcomes}}{\text{Total number of equally likely outcomes}}$$

Probability of an event A not occurring:
$P(A') = 1 - P(A)$

LINEAR GRAPHS

The slope, m, of a line segment joining points $P(x_1, y_1)$ and $Q(x_2, y_2)$ is given by

$$m = \frac{y_2 - y_1}{x_2 - x_1} \text{ or } m = \frac{y_1 - y_2}{x_1 - x_2}.$$

Given the slope, m, the equation of a line intercepting the y-axis at $(0, b)$ is given by $y = mx + b$.

The distance, d, between two points $P(x_1, y_1)$ and $Q(x_2, y_2)$ is given by

$$d = \sqrt{(x_2 - x_1)^2 + (y_2 - y_1)^2} \text{ or } d = \sqrt{(x_1 - x_2)^2 + (y_1 - y_2)^2}.$$

RATE

Distance = Speed · Time

Average speed = $\dfrac{\text{Total distance traveled}}{\text{Total time}}$

Interest = Principal · Rate · Time

TEMPERATURE

Celsius (°C) $C = \dfrac{5}{9} \cdot (F - 32)$

Fahrenheit (°F) $F = \left(\dfrac{5}{9} \cdot C \right) + 32$

$<$	is less than	$\lvert a \rvert$	absolute value of the number a
$>$	is greater than	(x, y)	ordered pair
$\leq$	is less than or equal to	$1 : 2$	ratio of 1 to 2
$\geq$	is greater than or equal to	$/$	per
$\neq$	is not equal to	$\%$	percent
$\approx$	is approximately equal to	$\perp$	is perpendicular to
$\cong$	is congruent to	$\lVert$	is parallel to
$\sim$	is similar to	$\overleftrightarrow{AB}$	line AB
10^2	ten squared	$\overrightarrow{AB}$	ray AB
10^3	ten cubed	$\overline{AB}$	line segment AB
2^6	two to the sixth power	$\angle ABC$	angle ABC
$2.\overline{6}$	repeating decimal 2.66666...	$m\angle A$	measure of angle A
7	positive 7	$\triangle ABC$	triangle ABC
-7	negative 7	$^\circ$	degree
$\sqrt{a}$	positive square root of the number a	π	pi; $\pi \approx 3.14$ or $\pi \approx \dfrac{22}{7}$
$\sqrt[3]{a}$	cube root of the number a	$P(A)$	the probability of the event A happening

Graphing Calculator Guide

A graphing calculator has different sets of function keys you can use for mathematical calculations and graphing. The screen supports both text and graphic displays.

Four Operations

Enter expressions into the Home Screen. Then press **ENTER** to evaluate.

Keys	Example	
Use **.** to enter decimals.	To evaluate $2 + 3.5 \cdot 4$, press **2** **+** **3** **.** **5** **×** **4** **ENTER** Notice that graphing calculators use the order of operations. They do not do evaluation from left to right. If they did, you would get an answer of 22.	$$2+3.5*4$$ $$16$$
Use **(-)** to enter negative numbers. Use **2ND** **^** to enter π.	To evaluate $-10 \div 2 - 7$, press **(-)** **1** **0** **÷** **2** **−** **7** **ENTER** To evaluate $2 \cdot \pi \cdot 7$, press **2** **×** **2ND** **^** **×** **7** **ENTER**	$$-10/2-7$$ $$-12$$ $$2*\pi*7$$ $$43.98229715$$
Use **(** **)** to enclose parts of an expression that must be calculated first.	To evaluate $(3 + 4) \cdot (2 - 9)$, press **(** **3** **+** **4** **)** **×** **(** **2** **−** **9** **)** **ENTER**	$$(3+4)*(2-9)$$ $$-49$$

Fractions

Use **MATH** to enter and convert fractions.

Keys	Example	
Use **MATH** to access Frac to enter fractions.	To enter $\frac{2}{5}$, press **2** **÷** **5** **MATH** then select 1: Frac and press **ENTER** To enter $\frac{5}{2}$, press **5** **÷** **2** **MATH** then select 1: Frac and press **ENTER**	2/5▶Frac $\frac{2}{5}$ 5/2▶Frac $\frac{5}{2}$ ■
Use **MATH** to access Frac and Dec to swap between fractions and decimals.	To convert 0.25 to a fraction, press **.** **2** **5** **MATH** then select 1: Frac and press **ENTER** To convert the fraction back to a decimal, press **MATH** then select 2: Dec and press **ENTER**	.25▶Frac $\frac{1}{4}$ Ans▶Dec .25 ■

Squares and Cubes of Numbers

Use **∧** to enter squares and cubes.

Keys	Example	
Use x^2 to find the square of numbers. Use **∧** to find the cube of numbers.	To evaluate 3^2, press **3** x^2 **ENTER** To evaluate 5^3, press **5** **∧** **3** **ENTER**	3^2 9 5^3 125
Use **2ND** x^2 to find the square root of numbers. Use **MATH** to find the cube root of numbers.	To evaluate $\sqrt{25}$, press **2ND** x^2 **2** **5** **ENTER** To evaluate $\sqrt[3]{27}$, press **MATH** then select 4: $\sqrt[3]{(}$ and press **2** **7** **ENTER**	$\sqrt{25}$ 5 $\sqrt[3]{27}$ 3 ■

Exponents

Use 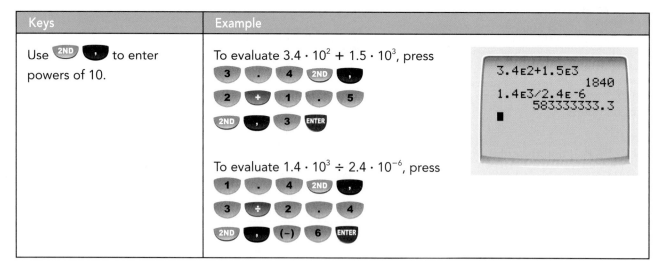 to enter numbers in exponential notation.

Keys	Example
Use $\wedge$ to enter positive exponents.	To evaluate $2^2 \cdot 5^0$, press **2** $\wedge$ **2** **)** **×** **5** $\wedge$ **0** **ENTER** To evaluate $(4^2)^3$, press **(** **4** $\wedge$ **2** **)** **)** $\wedge$ **3** **ENTER**
Use $\wedge$ and **(−)** to enter negative exponents.	To evaluate $2^{-2} \cdot 10$, press **2** $\wedge$ **(−)** **2** **)** **×** **1** **0** **ENTER**

Calculator screens:

2^2*5^0
4

$(4^2)^3$
4096

$2^{-2}*10$
2.5

Scientific Notation

Use **2ND** **,** to enter numbers in scientific notation.

Keys	Example
Use **2ND** **,** to enter powers of 10.	To evaluate $3.4 \cdot 10^2 + 1.5 \cdot 10^3$, press **3** **.** **4** **2ND** **,** **2** **+** **1** **.** **5** **2ND** **,** **3** **ENTER** To evaluate $1.4 \cdot 10^3 \div 2.4 \cdot 10^{-6}$, press **1** **.** **4** **2ND** **,** **3** **÷** **2** **.** **4** **2ND** **,** **(−)** **6** **ENTER**

Calculator screen:

3.4ᴇ2+1.5ᴇ3
1840
1.4ᴇ3/2.4ᴇ⁻6
583333333.3
■

Probability

Use **MATH** to generate random numbers.

Keys	Example
Use **MATH** to access randInt(under PRB to simulate tossing a fair coin multiple times.	To simulate the tossing of a fair coin 20 times and store the outcomes, press **MATH** then select 5: randInt(under PRB and press **0** **,** **1** **,** **2** **0** **)** **ENTER** ```randInt(0,1,20)``` ```{1 0 1 0 0 0 0 ▶``` ```Ans→L1``` ```{1 0 1 0 0 0 0 ▶``` Here 0 indicates a tail, 1 indicates a head, and 20 indicates the number of times the coin is tossed.
Use **STO▸** to store values.	To store the results in a list L1, continue to press **STO▸** **2ND** **1** **ENTER**
Use **STAT** to access Edit to enter data.	To view the list in a table, press **STAT** then select 1: Edit 	L1	L2	L3	1
---	---	---	---
1	------	------	
0			
1			
0			
0			
0			
0				 `L1(1)=1` To get back to the Home Screen, press **2ND** **MODE**
Use **MATH** to access randInt(under PRB to simulate rolling a fair number die multiple times.	To simulate the rolling of a fair number die 10 times and store the outcomes in a list L2, press **MATH** then select 5: randInt(under PRB and press **1** **,** **6** **,** **1** **0** **)** **STO▸** **2ND** **2** **ENTER** ```randInt(1,6,10)▸``` ```{4 4 6 3 2 2 5 ▶``` Here 1 and 6 indicate the least and greatest possible results, 10 indicates the number of times the number die is rolled.
Use **MATH** to access randBin(under PRB to simulate tossing a biased coin multiple times.	To simulate the tossing of a biased coin 20 times and store the outcomes in a list L3, press **MATH** then select 7: randBin(under PRB and press **1** **,** **.** **7** **,** **2** **0** **)** **STO▸** **2ND** **3** **ENTER** ```randBin(1,.7,20▸``` ```{1 0 1 0 1 1 1 ▶``` Here 1 indicates heads, .7 indicates the probability of landing on heads, 20 indicates the number of times the coin is tossed.

Credits

Index

COMMON CORE STATE STANDARDS FOR MATHEMATICAL CONTENT

	STANDARDS	CITATIONS
8.NS THE NUMBER SYSTEM		
Know that there are numbers that are not rational, and approximate them by rational numbers.		
8.NS.1	Understand informally that every number has a decimal expansion; the rational numbers are those with decimal expansions that terminate in 0s or eventually repeat. Know that other numbers are called irrational.	SE Course 3A: 3, 95, 98
8.NS.2	Use rational approximations of irrational numbers to compare the size of irrational numbers, locate them approximately on a number line diagram, and estimate the value of expressions (e.g., π^2).	SE Course 3A: 3, 47−52 SE Course 3B: 5, 31−33, 36−39, 43
8.EE EXPRESSIONS AND EQUATIONS		
Work with radicals and integer exponents.		
8.EE.1	Know and apply the properties of integer exponents to generate equivalent numerical expressions.	SE Course 3A: 5−11, 13−23, 25, 30, 32−38, 40−45, 47−52
8.EE.2	Use square root and cube root symbols to represent solutions to equations of the form $x^2 = p$ and $x^3 = p$, where p is a positive rational number. Evaluate square roots of small perfect squares and cube roots of small perfect cubes. Know that $\sqrt{2}$ is irrational.	SE Course 3A: 3, 47−52 SE Course 3B: 3, 5, 31−33, 36−39
8.EE.3	Use numbers expressed in the form of a single digit times an integer power of 10 to estimate very large or very small quantities, and to express how many times as much one is than the other.	SE Course 3A: 59, 60−65, 81−84
8.EE.4	Perform operations with numbers expressed in scientific notation, including problems where both decimal and scientific notation are used. Use scientific notation and choose units of appropriate size for measurements of very large or very small quantities (e.g., use millimeters per year for seafloor spreading). Interpret scientific notation that has been generated by technology.	SE Course 3A: 68−78, 81−84
Understand the connections between proportional relationships, lines, and linear equations.		
8.EE.5	Graph proportional relationships, interpreting the unit rate as the slope of the graph. Compare two different proportional relationships represented in different ways.	SE Course 3A: 93, 109−115, 118−121, 129, 133−134, 165−169, 171−180, 191 SE Course 3B: 50, 113−114

COMMON CORE STATE STANDARDS FOR MATHEMATICAL CONTENT

	STANDARDS	CITATIONS
8.EE.6	Use similar triangles to explain why the slope m is the same between any two distinct points on a nonvertical line in the coordinate plane; derive the equation $y = mx$ for a line through the origin and the equation $y = mx + b$ for a line intercepting the vertical axis at b.	SE Course 3A: 130–144, 147–151, 154–163, 165–169 SE Course 3B: 190–195
Analyze and solve linear equations and pairs of simultaneous linear equations.		
8.EE.7	Solve linear equations in one variable.	SE Course 3A: 94, 96–101
8.EE.7a	Give examples of linear equations in one variable with one solution, infinitely many solutions, or no solutions. Show which of these possibilities is the case by successively transforming the given equation into simpler forms, until an equivalent equation of the form $x = a$, $a = a$, or $a = b$ results (where a and b are different numbers).	SE Course 3A: 104–107
8.EE.7b	Solve linear equations with rational number coefficients, including equations whose solutions require expanding expressions using the distributive property and collecting like terms.	SE Course 3A: 94, 96–101
8.EE.8	Analyze and solve pairs of simultaneous linear equations.	SE Course 3A: 193–195
8.EE.8a	Understand that solutions to a system of two linear equations in two variables correspond to points of intersection of their graphs, because points of intersection satisfy both equations simultaneously.	SE Course 3A: 218–222
8.EE.8b	Solve systems of two linear equations in two variables algebraically, and estimate solutions by graphing the equations. Solve simple cases by inspection.	SE Course 3A: 197–208
8.EE.8c	Solve real-world and mathematical problems leading to two linear equations in two variables.	SE Course 3A: 210–214
8.F FUNCTIONS		
Define, evaluate, and compare functions.		
8.F.1	Understand that a function is a rule that assigns to each input exactly one output. The graph of a function is the set of ordered pairs consisting of an input and the corresponding output[1].	SE Course 3A: 243–254, 259–264
8.F.2	Compare properties of two functions each represented in a different way (algebraically, graphically, numerically in tables, or by verbal descriptions).	SE Course 3A: 278–285

[1]Function notation is not required in Grade 8.

COMMON CORE STATE STANDARDS FOR MATHEMATICAL CONTENT

	STANDARDS	CITATIONS
8.F.3	Interpret the equation $y = mx + b$ as defining a linear function, whose graph is a straight line; give examples of functions that are not linear.	SE Course 3A: 259–264 SE Course 3B: 190–195

Use functions to model relationships between quantities.

	STANDARDS	CITATIONS
8.F.4	Construct a function to model a linear relationship between two quantities. Determine the rate of change and initial value of the function from a description of a relationship or from two (x, y) values, including reading these from a table or from a graph. Interpret the rate of change and initial value of a linear function in terms of the situation it models, and in terms of its graph or a table of values.	SE Course 3A: 259–264, 266–269, 272–275 SE Course 3B: 190–195
8.F.5	Describe qualitatively the functional relationship between two quantities by analyzing a graph (e.g., where the function is increasing or decreasing, linear or nonlinear). Sketch a graph that exhibits the qualitative features of a function that has been described verbally.	SE Course 3A: 259–264, 266–269, 272–275 SE Course 3B: 190–195

8.G GEOMETRY

Understand congruence and similarity using physical models, transparencies, or geometry software.

	STANDARDS	CITATIONS
8.G.1	Verify experimentally the properties of rotations, reflections, and translations.	SE Course 3B: 51–58, 61–69, 73–79
8.G.1a	Lines are taken to lines, and line segments to line segments of the same length.	SE Course 3B: 54–58, 64–68, 76–77
8.G.1b	Angles are taken to angles of the same measure.	SE Course 3B: 54–58, 64–68, 77–79
8.G.1c	Parallel lines are taken to parallel lines.	SE Course 3B: 55–58, 64–68, 77–79
8.G.2	Understand that a two-dimensional figure is congruent to another if the second can be obtained from the first by a sequence of rotations, reflections, and translations; given two congruent figures, describe a sequence that exhibits the congruence between them.	SE Course 3B: 116–125, 144–145, 150–152
8.G.3	Describe the effect of dilations, translations, rotations, and reflections on two-dimensional figures using coordinates.	SE Course 3B: 55–58, 64–68, 77–79, 88–95, 98–102, 144–153
8.G.4	Understand that a two-dimensional figure is similar to another if the second can be obtained from the first by a sequence of rotations, reflections, translations, and dilations; given two similar two-dimensional figures, describe a sequence that exhibits the similarity between them.	SE Course 3B: 129–139, 146–147, 153

COMMON CORE STATE STANDARDS FOR MATHEMATICAL CONTENT

	STANDARDS	CITATIONS
8.G.5	Use informal arguments to establish facts about the angle sum and exterior angle of triangles, about the angles created when parallel lines are cut by a transversal, and the angle-angle criterion for similarity of triangles.	SE Course 3B: 115, 137–139

Understand and apply the Pythagorean Theorem.

	STANDARDS	CITATIONS
8.G.6	Explain a proof of the Pythagorean Theorem and its converse.	SE Course 3B: 6–15
8.G.7	Apply the Pythagorean Theorem to determine unknown side lengths in right triangles in real-world and mathematical problems in two and three dimensions.	SE Course 3B: 6–10, 13–15, 31–33, 36–39
8.G.8	Apply the Pythagorean Theorem to find the distance between two points in a coordinate system.	SE Course 3B: 20–27

Solve real-world and mathematical problems involving volume of cylinders, cones, and spheres.

	STANDARDS	CITATIONS
8.G.9	Know the formulas for the volumes of cones, cylinders, and spheres and use them to solve real-world and mathematical problems.	SE Course 3B: 5, 31–33, 36–39

8.SP STATISTICS AND PROBABILITY

Investigate patterns of association in bivariate data.

	STANDARDS	CITATIONS
8.SP.1	Construct and interpret scatter plots for bivariate measurement data to investigate patterns of association between two quantities. Describe patterns such as clustering, outliers, positive or negative association, linear association, and nonlinear association.	SE Course 3B: 174–182
8.SP.2	Know that straight lines are widely used to model relationships between two quantitative variables. For scatter plots that suggest a linear association, informally fit a straight line, and informally assess the model fit by judging the closeness of the data points to the line.	SE Course 3A: 165–169, 259–264, 273–274 SE Course 3B: 186–195
8.SP.3	Use the equation of a linear model to solve problems in the context of bivariate measurement data, interpreting the slope and intercept.	SE Course 3A: 171–180, 259–264, 273–274 SE Course 3B: 186–195
8.SP.4	Understand that patterns of association can also be seen in bivariate categorical data by displaying frequencies and relative frequencies in a two-way table. Construct and interpret a two-way table summarizing data on two categorical variables collected from the same subjects. Use relative frequencies calculated for rows or columns to describe possible association between the two variables.	SE Course 3B: 173, 198–206

Math in Focus®, Course 3 aligns to the Common Core State Standards for Mathematical Practice throughout.

	CITATIONS

1. MAKE SENSE OF PROBLEMS AND PERSEVERE IN SOLVING THEM.

How *Math in Focus®* Aligns:

*As seen on the Singapore Mathematics Framework pentagon (see page T8), Problem Solving is at the heart of the **Math in Focus®** curriculum. Students use problem solving to build skills and persevere to solve routine and nonroutine problems that include real-world and mathematical applications in number sense, algebra, functions, geometry, measurement, data analysis, and probability.*

For example:

SE Course 3A: 8, 10–11, 14, 18, 28, 41, 47, 50, 51, 54, 60, 73, 77, 79, 86, 99–101, 109, 119, 120, 124, 138–139, 154, 156, 157, 161, 165, 168, 171–182, 192, 194, 202, 204, 205, 210–217, 235, 246–248, 260, 266, 278–279, 284

SE Course 3B: 9, 13–15, 18–19, 29, 30, 31, 43, 55, 62, 69, 74, 76, 88–90, 92, 94, 99, 118, 128, 129, 131, 144, 149, 185, 189, 204–205, 209, 216, 225, 226, 235, 240, 247, 257

2. REASON ABSTRACTLY AND QUANTITATIVELY.

How *Math in Focus®* Aligns:

*In **Math in Focus®**, concrete to pictorial to abstract progression helps students develop a deep mastery of concepts. Students analyze and solve nonroutine problems, formulate conjectures through explorations, hands-on and technology activities, and observations, identify and explain mathematical situations and relationships, and look for patterns in data and functions.*

For example:

SE Course 3A: 13–23, 25, 28–32, 34, 37–39, 40, 41–45, 50–52, 67, 80, 93, 103, 108–115, 129–131, 132, 145, 147–151, 153, 165–169, 171–174, 178–179, 195, 198, 209, 214–216, 225–230, 234, 243–245, 273–274, 278–285

SE Course 3B: 7–8, 10, 12–14, 55, 63, 77, 90, 98–99, 122, 130, 136, 146–147, 150–151, 153, 175, 177–179, 186–187, 192–195, 201–206, 207–208, 237–243, 246–248

3. CONSTRUCT VIABLE ARGUMENTS AND CRITIQUE THE REASONING OF OTHERS.

How *Math in Focus®* Aligns:

*In **Math in Focus®**, students communicate in Math Journals and Think Maths. They demonstrate and explain mathematical steps using a variety of appropriate materials, models, properties, and skills. They share and critique mathematical ideas with others during class in 5-minute Warm-Up and Hands-On, Technology, and group activities, Guided Practice Exercises, Ticket Out the Door exercises, Projects, and other Differentiated Instruction activities.*

For example:

SE Course 3A: 2B, 5, 12, 13, 24, 25, 26, 31, 32, 40, 43, 47, 60, 68, 81, 96, 104, 109, 111, 118, 130–131, 147, 149, 154, 165, 171, 193, 195, 197, 210, 218, 225, 252, 253, 260, 275, 284, 278–285

SE Course 3B: 2B, 7–8, 11, 16, 28, 34, 40, 44, 55, 59, 63, 70, 77, 83, 90, 96, 98–99, 103, 107, 111, 122, 130, 137, 149, 150, 159, 186–187, 194–195, 194–195, 210, 216, 218, 242–243

	CITATIONS

4. MODEL WITH MATHEMATICS.

How *Math in Focus*® Aligns:

In **Math in Focus**®, *students and teachers represent mathematical ideas, model and record quantities using multiple representations, such as concrete materials, technology, visual models such as number lines, mapping diagrams, bar models, drawings, tables, and coordinate graphs, and symbols such as algebraic expressions, equations, inequalities, and formulas.*

For example:

SE Course 3A: 3, 5–8, 21–23, 26, 28–30, 37–40, 42, 44–46, 49–52, 60–65, 68–76, 81–84, 93, 96–101, 104–107, 109–115, 118–121, 129, 130–134, 136–139, 142–144, 147–151, 154–163, 165–169, 171–174, 191–195, 197–199, 200, 203, 210–214, 218–222, 243–254, 259–264, 266–274

SE Course 3B: 3, 6–11, 12–15, 20–27, 31–36, 36–39, 49, 50, 51–58, 61–69, 73–82, 86–95, 98–102, 113, 115, 116–122, 130–139, 144–153, 174–182, 186–195, 198–206, 217–218, 220–226, 229–232, 252–255

5. USE APPROPRIATE TOOLS STRATEGICALLY.

How *Math in Focus*®Aligns:

Math in Focus® *helps students explore the different mathematical tools that are available to them, such as pencil and paper, estimation, geometry drawing tools, concrete and visual models such as number lines and grids, or technology to model developing skills and interpret everyday situations that involve proportionality, functions, geometric transformations and formulas, variation, data distribution, and probability.*

For example:

SE Course 3A: 3, 11, 12, 26, 40, 42, 47–52, 54, 60–65, 81–84, 93, 96–101, 104–107, 109–115, 118–121, 129, 130–134, 136–144, 147–151, 154–163, 165–169, 171–174, 191–195, 197–199, 200, 203, 207–208, 210–214, 218–222, 243–254, 259–264, 266–275

SE Course 3B: 2C, 3, 5, 7–11, 12–15, 20–27, 31–39, 43, 49, 50, 51–58, 61–69, 73–82, 86–95, 98–102, 113, 115, 116–122, 130–139, 144–153, 174–182, 186–195, 198–206, 217–218, 220–226, 229–232, 252–255

6. ATTEND TO PRECISION.

How *Math in Focus*® Aligns:

In **Math in Focus**®, *students check answers, define, highlight, review, and use mathematical vocabulary, define and interpret symbols, use appropriate forms of numbers and expressions, label bar and geometric models correctly, and compute with appropriate formulas and units in solving problems and explaining reasoning.*

For example:

SE Course 3A: 2, 3, 5–11, 26, 31, 39, 40–45, 55, 58, 60–65, 67, 80, 81–84, 87, 92, 95, 99–101, 103, 108, 112–115, 125, 128, 130–136, 145, 149, 154–158, 165–169, 171–174, 183, 190, 193–195, 207–209, 218–222, 224, 234, 236–237, 240, 246–254, 258, 259–264, 273–274, 278–285, 290

SE Course 3B: 2, 6–15, 19, 20–27, 31–33, 36–39, 42, 44, 49–50, 53, 55, 57, 63, 68–69, 72, 77, 80–82, 86–90, 97, 99, 103, 105, 107, 112, 115, 122–125, 130, 131, 137, 143, 150, 172, 179, 187, 191–195, 198–203, 210, 236, 239, 243, 247, 264

	CITATIONS

7. LOOK FOR AND MAKE USE OF STRUCTURE.

How *Math in Focus*® Aligns:

The inherent pedagogy of **Math in Focus**® allows students to look for and make use of structure. Students recognize patterns and structure and make connections from one mathematical idea to another through, Best Practices, Big Ideas, Math Notes, Think Maths, and Cautions. Also occurs as skills and concepts are interconnected in prior knowledge activities, concept traces, and chapter concept maps.

For example:

SE Course 3A: 2, 5, 14, 18, 28, 41, 47, 51, 52, 55, 58, 60, 62, 64, 69, 73, 74, 75, 79, 82, 83, 87, 92, 96–98, 104, 109, 111, 114, 119, 120, 128, 130, 133, 138, 142, 154, 156, 161, 165, 172, 176, 177, 190, 194, 198, 202, 205, 210, 212, 218, 227, 236–237, 240, 252, 253, 260, 267, 270

SE Course 3B: 2A, 2C, 2–5, 24, 44, 48, 49–50, 51, 65, 73, 93, 107–108, 112–115, 119, 123–125, 131, 159, 172, 173, 187, 191, 193, 210, 217–218, 222, 224, 231, 236, 239, 241, 245, 246, 247, 253, 254, 264

8. LOOK FOR AND EXPRESS REGULARITY IN REPEATED REASONING.

How *Math in Focus*® Aligns:

In **Math in Focus**®, students are given consistent tools for solving problems, such as bar models, algebraic variables, tables, coordinate grids, standard algorithms with rational numbers, numerical and geometric properties, possibility diagrams, and formulas so they see the similarities in how different problems are solved and understand efficient means for solving.

For example:

SE Course 3A: 3–4, 13–23, 25, 28–32, 34, 37–39, 40, 41–45, 50–52, 60–65, 68–78, 81–84, 93, 96–98, 103, 108–115, 129–131, 132, 142–145, 147–151, 154–163, 165–169, 171–174, 178–179, 195, 198, 209, 214–216, 225–230, 234, 243–245, 246–250, 273–274, 278–285

SE Course 3B: 5, 6–15, 20–27, 31–33, 36–39, 50, 55, 63, 77, 88–90, 98–102, 122–125, 130, 132–139, 146–147, 150–153, 175, 177–179, 186–187, 192–195, 201–206, 207–208, 217, 224–226, 229–232, 237–248, 253, 257–258

BLANK

BLANK